NEWSZAK
AND
NEWS MEDIA

BOB FRANKLIN

A member of the Hodder Headline Group
LONDON • NEW YORK • SYDNEY • AUCKLAND

First published in Great Britain in 1997 by
Arnold, a member of the Hodder Headline Group
338 Euston Road, London NW1 3BH
http://arnoldpublishers.com

Distributed exclusively in the USA by
St Martin's Press, Inc.
175 Fifth Avenue, New York, NY 10010

British Library Cataloguing in Publication Data
A catalogue entry for this book is available from the British Library

Library of Congress Cataloging-in-Publication Data
Franklin, Bob, 1949–
  Newszak and news media / Bob Franklin.
    p. 307 cm.
  Includes bibliographical references and index.
  1. Journalism—Great Britain—History—20th century. 2. Broadcast
journalism—Great Britain.   3. Television broadcasting of news–
–Great Britain.   I. Title.
PN5117.F73   1997
072'.09'045—dc 21   97-20880
                     CIP

ISBN 0 340 61416 1 (pb)
ISBN 0 340 69156 5 (hb)

Publisher: Lesley Riddle
Production Editor: Wendy Rooke
Production Controller: Rose James
Cover Designer: Terry Griffiths

Composition by Phoenix Photosetting, Chatham, Kent
Printed and bound in Great Britain by
J.W. Arrowsmith Ltd, Bristol, Avon

Contents

PART IV NEWSZAK: REGULATING EXCESSES

For Annie

Acknowledgements

I owe a debt of thanks to many academic friends and colleagues, journalists and broadcasters, regulators of the press and broadcasting, as well as politicians and officials of the NUJ (National Union of Journalists) and BECTU (Broadcasting, Entertainment, Cinematograph and Theatre Union), for their generosity in finding time in their typically overcommitted schedules to talk to me about the many aspects of change which are currently occurring across all sectors of British media and journalism.

Particular thanks are necessary to Richard Ayre, Antony Bevins, Jay Blumler, Mike Bromley, Vincent Campbell, Robin Corbett, John Corner, Jake Ecclestone, Michael Fay, Kim Fletcher, Ivor Gabor, Brent Garner, David Glencross, Tony Harcup, Martin Harrison, Sylvia Harvey, Simon Heffer, Simon Hoggart, Nicholas Jones, Trevor Kavanagh, Tony Lennon, Steve Ludlam, Brian MacArthur, Lord McGregor of Durris, Brian McNair, Chris Moncrieff, David Morgan, Chris Mullin, David Murphy, Pippa Norris, Tom Nossiter, Robin Oakley, Nicholas O'Shaughnessy, Keith Parker, Matthew Parris, Julian Petley, Rod Pilling, Robert Pinker, Stewart Purvis, Peter Riddell, Maggie Scammell, John Short, Clive Soley, Michael White, Stephen Whittle, Granville Williams and Dominic Wring. Three special thanks are necessary.

First, I am very grateful to Lesley Riddle at Arnold for inviting me to write the book, helping with the structure and development of ideas and her patience in waiting for the manuscript.

Second, many thanks to the students on the MA Political Journalism (1995–6) at Sheffield University who brought such enormous energy, curiosity and commitment to their studies and were greatly helpful in discussing many of the central ideas of the book. Since some of them are now working as local journalists, I regret that the analysis could not prompt more optimistic conclusions about the profession of journalism; their talents and potential deserve so much better encouragement and reward! Many thanks to Michelle Collier, John Gorick (a truly great Prospero), Tim Higgins, Rana Kurian, Nick Lestor and Adam Williams.

Finally, if predictably, the most deserving acknowledgement is to my partner Annie Franklin for her support and help with every aspect of the project. The book was written during an unbelievably stressful period of uncertainty in my professional life, when only the guaranteed affections and certainties of my personal life kept me afloat and made the completion of the book possible. The book is dedicated to Annie with love and thanks for the constant flood of ideas she contributed, her honesty and frank criticism, her warm encouragement and her apparently inexhaustible and inexplicable kindness and help with everything.

List of tables

NEWSZAK AND
NEWS MEDIA

1

Setting the agenda

The argument in outline

This is how ITN (Independent Television News) anchor John Suchet introduced the filmed report of the funeral of James Bulger for the *News at 5.45*: 'Hello. The teddy bears he loved so much sat side by side in church today. The day of the funeral of James Bulger. The toys were propped up on a seat that had been specially made for James by his father. It was placed a few inches from James's coffin.' (The accompanying camera shot moves to the inside of the church and focuses in close-up on the two teddy bears.) It seems unthinkable that this could be the transcript of a *genuine* news bulletin rather than some grotesque parody of the cynical antics of the fictional journalist Damien Day from the satirical television series *Drop the Dead Donkey*. This report of the death of a young child, with its insensitive conjoining of the sentimental and the sensational, the prurient and the populist, bears all the hallmarks of tabloid journalism. The way this news report exploits personal tragedy for public spectacle is increasingly commonplace, but appealing to such morbid curiosity in news coverage would have been unthinkable even a decade ago. Journalism, news and news media have changed. In print journalism too, scandal and sensationalism, too frequently masquerading in perverse guise as 'human interest', have become central ingredients of the news diet.

On 5 January 1997, the *News of the World* carried a 'world exclusive' about Conservative MP Jerry Hayes's alleged relationship with his Commons researcher Paul Stone, under the headline 'Tory MP 2-Timed Wife With Under-Age Gay Lover', despite editor Phil Hall's description of the story as 'a human tragedy' (*Press Gazette,* 10 January 1997). Hall was not the only journalist to report the 'tragedy'. The *Daily Express*, whose editor Richard Addis established the campaign against 'attack journalism' with Andrew Marr, carried a picture of Stone dressed as a pantomime dame under the headline 'Boy Who Dragged [get it?] Down A Tory MP' (*Daily Express,* 6 January 1997, p. 1). But coverage of the Hayes case was only the most recent in a succession of sensational or human-interest stories which showed little regard for the privacy of the individuals concerned. Actor Hugh Grant's meeting with Divine Brown on Sunset Boulevard and later in 1996 Mandy Allwood's pregnancy with octuplets received considerable and invasive press coverage. In October 1996, the *Daily Mirror*'s serialisation of mystic Madame Vasso's book, relating conversations with Sarah Ferguson about her sexual life and attitudes towards the royal family, seemed to mark a particularly unpleasant and ugly downturn in tabloid coverage of 'the royals'. The *Sun* also carried the story on its front page under the headline 'Fergie's Secret Sex Life'. On an inside page under a picture of a goat and the heading 'You The Jury', the paper invited readers to participate in a telephone poll on the question, 'Who would you rather date . . . Fergie or a goat?' (Porter, 1996b, p. 4).

Newszak: entertainment versus news and information

Criticism of these recent trends in journalism and news media, however, has not been limited to the coverage of particular cases nor confined to newspapers. Increasingly it has focused on a more general tendency in contemporary journalism, evident in both print and broadcast media, to retreat from investigative journalism and the reporting of hard news to the preferred territory of 'softer' or 'lighter' stories. Journalism's editorial priorities have changed. Entertainment has superseded the provision of information; human interest has supplanted the public interest; measured judgement has succumbed to sensationalism; the trivial has triumphed over the weighty; the intimate relationships of celebrities from soap operas, the world of sport or the royal family are judged more 'newsworthy' than the reporting of significant issues and events of international consequence. Traditional news values have been undermined by new values; 'infotainment' is rampant.

Since the late 1980s the pressures on news media to win viewers and readers in an increasingly competitive market have generated revised editorial ambitions. News media have increasingly become part of the entertainment industry instead of providing a forum for informed debate of key issues of public concern. Journalists are more concerned to report stories which interest the public than stories which are in the public interest. The phrase which is frequently used to articulate this changing journalistic mood is 'tabloid journalism'. John Pilger regrets this usage since the phrase originally implied a campaigning and crusading tradition of popular journalism which has only recently been perverted into 'cheap, tacky, arcade entertainment' (*Press Gazette*, 7 February 1997); McNair risks falling foul of the tendency he describes, when he offers his preferred designation 'bonk journalism' (McNair, 1994, p. 145). But Malcolm Muggeridge's neologism 'Newszak' captures the phenomenon most closely.

Newszak understands news as a product designed and 'processed' for a particular market and delivered in increasingly homogenous 'snippets' which make only modest demands on the audience. [Newszak is news converted into entertainment.] The institutions of news media and practices of news journalism are more than ever coming to resemble a finely tuned piano which is capable of playing Bach or Beethoven, but too frequently insists on playing chopsticks. In television news bulletins, a commitment to newszak is evident in programme formats in which 'one presenter talks to another' that reduce 'crucial events into a cosy chat show' (Sampson, 1996, pp. 46–7). A senior executive at ITN is unequivocal and unapologetic about the nature of the news business at ITN. He suggests that for the contemporary journalist the processing of newszak involves only a minimal exercise of news judgement and little responsibility for constructing the news agenda. The task of journalism has become merely to deliver and serve up whatever the customer wants; rather like a deep-pan pizza.

> ITN news is on contract. We are an independent supplier to ITV. All programmes on ITV are made by suppliers on a contract to the Network Centre which specifies the nature of the programmes it wants. So all I am to denigrate myself, is the guy who gives the customer what they want. I am not taking a higher, purer judgement – this is what the British people deserve or should have. I am saying this is what the customer is paying me £50 million pounds a year to make and I'm pretty unapologetic about that.
>
> (Interview with author. All other unattributed quotations in the text arise from a series of interviews conducted between 1994 and 1996.)

[The emergence of newszak has not been without its critics; not least journalists and broadcasters themselves.] *Independent* editor, Andrew Marr, criticised the *Guardian* for constantly serving up 'more bite-size McNugget journalism, which is small, tasty, brightly coloured and easy to ingest' (cited in Morgan, 1996, p. 14), while distinguished ex-*Sunday Times* editor, Harold Evans, in a speech to the Guild of Editors warned of the 'drift from substantive news to celebrity hunting, from news to entertainment' and advised editors to guard against 'news mutating into trivia, vigilance into intrusion, public interest into prurient interest'. Evans argues that 'tabloid values appealing to the lowest common denominator have come to prevail' (*Press Gazette*, 1 November 1996, p. 10). This new journalistic environment is not restricted to Britain but approximates closely the phenomenon which McManus has described in America as 'market driven journalism' (McManus, 1992 and 1994). James Fallow believes the changes pose a threat to American democracy, since 'the most influential parts of the media have lost sight of . . . their central values . . . the essence of real journalism which is the search for information of use to the public' (Fallows, 1996, pp. 6–7 and Cronkite, 1997, p. 2). Without an informed citizenry, democracy is impoverished and at risk.

But, in two senses at least, the suggestion of a proliferation of newszak, with all its alleged consequences for public information and democracy, prompts a sense of *déjà vu*. First, critics of contemporary journalism have invariably tended to romanticise and applaud the journalism of an earlier period. As Simon Jenkins observed wryly, 'there is always a golden age of journalism, and it was always when the person discussing the subject came into newspapers' (Engel, 1996a, p. 2). Other observers express weary incredulity and impatience with the succession of visionaries – from T.P. O'Connor, the editor of the *Star* in 1889, to journalist Tom Wolfe in 1973 – who have predicted the emergence of a 'new journalism', only to find their expectations frustrated; 'there is nothing quite so old,' the editor of *British Journalism Review* claims, 'than the periodic bouts of "New Journalism"' (Goodman, 1994, p. 3). The accusation here is that critics have too frequently been guilty of crying wolf.

Second, newspapers, and more recently broadcast media, have always been driven by the potentially conflictual imperatives of providing information that is essential to citizens in a democracy while at the same time entertaining the public: what one historian of the press has described as the 'two major themes' in 'the development of journalism' (Williams, 1957, p. 5). The history of the press is a history of this shifting balance between informing 'public opinion while drumming up the largest number of paying customers' (ibid. p. 10). From their inception, newspapers have tried to entertain and editorial success has always entailed getting the right mix of information, news, truth, story-telling and good old-fashioned gossip. Given this newspaper history, it seems reasonable to question whether the recent changes in journalism constitute a substantive trend or simply a continuation of previous developments. Perhaps this discussion of newszak amounts to little more than a storm in a journalistic teacup? Three unprecedented and significant features of the current changes in journalism and news media seem to suggest otherwise. First, the shifting balance in favour of entertainment in news-media content has rarely, if ever, been so apparent. Second, this shift has been accompanied by a related decline in media attention to news and especially certain kinds of news; foreign and investigative news journalism have virtually disappeared from some news media. Again, the extent of the change is without precedent. Third, this decline in news coverage and the ascendancy of entertainment is evident across all news media, albeit to differing degrees: the broadsheet as well as tabloid newspapers, Radio 4 as much as Talk Radio, television services at BBC (British Broadcasting Corporation), ITN and in the satellite channels. Most significantly, these changes reflect an unprecedented congruence of longer-term changes in the financial, organisational and regulatory structures of news media combined with a deregulatory impulse provided by government media policy which will prove resilient to reversal. Newszak seems set fair to flourish.

Newszak: newspapers, television and radio

The growth of the 'broadloid'

[In British newspapers, the emphasis on newszak and entertainment has long been a defining feature of the tabloid press, but recently concern has been expressed about the increasingly tabloid format and content of broadsheet newspapers (Sampson, 1996, p. 44 and Engel, 1996a, pp. 2–3). Every aspect of the modern broadsheet newspaper has changed since the 1980s. The *Guardian* offers a useful illustrative exemplar of many of these changes. So far as newspaper format is concerned, Engel identifies the emergence of the *Independent* with its 'youthful good looks and verve' as the catalyst for the major redesign of the *Guardian* in 1988 and subsequently of the *Daily Telegraph* (Engel, 1996a, p. 3). The front pages of broadsheets now incorporate many of the characteristic formats of the tabloid genre; *The Times*'s commitment to devote its front page to small ads until May 1966 has become an anachronism with remarkable rapidity (Sampson, 1996, p. 44). Since the 1980s, the broadsheets' derision of the tabloid format has increasingly become mimicry. Tabloid-style banner headlines, alliterative and 'punny' headlines, large print, less text, shorter words, bigger pictures, colour pictures and more of them, have become standard components of the broadsheet front page. But it is the changing content of 'quality' newspapers which is most significant.]

Four aspects of change are noteworthy. First, broadsheet newspapers contain less news, especially foreign news, parliamentary news and investigative stories (Sampson, 1996, Engel, 1996b and this volume, chapters 10 and 11). The decline in all three reflects the increasingly competitive market for readers and advertisers combined with the waning financial resources of newspapers and declining journalistic staffs. Foreign correspondents and foreign news are costly items to sustain with shrinking news budgets: the *Independent*'s once renowned foreign reportage has become lean and narrow, reflecting financial restrictions. Lord Cudlipp, former editor-in-chief of the *Mirror,* regrets the extent to which so much foreign news, especially in the *Mirror*, has become bellicose, opinionated and 'relegated to a three inch yapping editorial insulting foreigners' (*Press Gazette,* 7 February 1997). Antony Sampson attributes the decline in foreign reporting to the increased competition for advertising revenues and the consequently enhanced prominence of advertisers in editorial decision-making. Advertisers determine the allocation of space and prefer subjects such as travel and consumer issues above foreign news which has little product tie-in. Consequently 'the world is disappearing out of sight' (Sampson, 1996, p. 45). Worse, foreign news is increasingly reported only when it can be presented as a human-interest story. Pictures of starving and dying children during a famine, limbless victims of land mines left behind after a recent war and seemingly endless trails of 'helpless refugees' fleeing from a current conflict litter the pages of newspapers. The purpose of such pictures seems less to inform than to elicit sympathy – a collective 'Oh, how dreadful!' – from the readership.

Parliamentary news and reports of debates from the House have virtually disappeared from the broadsheet papers. Gallery journalism is dead, although few obituaries have mourned the passing of this once significant and vigorous tradition (Franklin, 1996, p. 13). The substantial reports of parliamentary debates, considered essential to the contents of serious news-papers until the early 1990s (the *Financial Times* spiked its parliamentary page as recently as 1993) have been replaced by the less weighty, more entertaining, accounts offered by the cheerful and chirpy sketch writers like Simon Hoggart and Matthew Parris. When parliamentary debates are reported in the press, moreover, they are increasingly trivialised, sensation-alist and focused on personal scandals involving individual MPs rather than exploring and constructing a distinctive parliamentary agenda (see chapter 11, below). One senior political journalist explained the collapse of parlia-mentary coverage as part of a broader 'gravitational force of decline in jour-nalism which has taken place in our lifetime'.

Broadsheet newspapers also undertake considerably less investigative journalism. This is not to deny the welcome and excellent exceptions to this general pattern of neglect, such as John Pilger's report on the Liverpool dockers' strike which broke an otherwise extraordinary media silence or the work of journalists Ed Vulliamy and David Leigh in exposing the furtive lobbying activities of Neil Hamilton and Ian Greer (*Guardian*, 16 January 1997, p. 4). But investigative journalism is costly in terms of financial and journalistic resources and unlikely to flourish when both are scarce. It requires a news organisation to commit its most skilled, able and experi-enced journalists for perhaps many months or years without any guaranteed outcome in terms of a publishable story. Newszak is less demanding.

The journalistic ground vacated by foreign and investigative reporting has been eagerly colonised by a growing army of columnists. This is the sec-ond major change: *views* have increasingly replaced *news*. Columnists are not specialist reporters with expertise in a particular area of journalism, but generalists, would-be renaissance figures, and members of the popular literati who routinely appear as guests on late-night chat shows and arts programmes. They seem to possess an endless supply of opinions on every topic and yet the concerns addressed in their columns can be cripplingly banal; columnists may be reduced to telling us 'what happened to them on the way to Sainsburys, what their children did at school, how they enjoyed their holidays' (Sampson, 1996, p. 45). Such routine, if not rather dull and perhaps even private, concerns have become grist to the columnist's mill. But on other occasions, the subject-matter is bizarre. Linda Grant in her *Guardian* column, for example, speculated whether the willingness of nov-elist Jeanette Winterson (in her early days just after Oxford) to offer sexual services to closet, middle-aged lesbians, in return for Le Creuset ovenware, had a more general relevance for family life and for women's sexual relations with their male partners ('Sex For Money Isn't A Flash In The Pan' *Guardian*, 6 January 1997, p. 13). The following day, perhaps predictably, the *Guardian* made Le Creuset the subject of its regular *Pass Notes* feature (no. 948). As if to underscore its newly acquired tabloid credentials, *The Times* 'scooped' the same story two days earlier under the heading, 'Lesbian Novelist Tells Of Sex For Le Creuset' (*The Times,* 4 January 1997, p. 3). How regrettable that the roar of the 'Thunderer' should have become such a trivial and diminutive squeak. Columns typically begin by posing a question to draw the reader in. Charlotte Raven, for example, asked 'Has Vivienne Westwood gone mad? If recent reports are to be believed, the "no knickers" Queen of punk has joined the moral regeneration brigade' (*Guardian*, 14 January 1997, p. 11). The previous day Angela Neustatter's column devoted to cosmetic surgery inquired 'Could you fancy a man who has had his penis surgically enlarged?' (*Guardian,* 13 January 1997, p. 9). At best such journalism is engaging rather than informing; it is newszak but not news.

Third, broadsheet newspapers are allocating a high news priority to stories which until relatively recently would have been dismissed and disdained as merely tabloid stories. Coverage of the royal family offers an obvious example (see below, chapter 10). On the day after Diana's interview for the BBC's *Panorama* special, broadsheet coverage was extensive (21 November 1995). The *Guardian* allocated five full pages (9120 cm^2) to the interview; the *Daily Telegraph* (7008 cm^2) also provided extensive reports. The *Guardian*'s coverage was tabloid in style with remarkable points of contact with reports in the *Sun*. Both papers assembled a panel of 'experts' to offer Diana 'advice'. The motley crew in the *Sun* included Gary Bushell (the paper's television critic) and Max Clifford ('Stars' PR Guru'), while the *Guardian* managed to recruit a slightly more cerebral collection including Lord St John of Fawsley; but in essence, reports in both papers articulated a tabloid agenda expressed in tabloid format. The broadsheets' discovery of sensational and populist news has not been confined to the royal family. The four broadsheet dailies offered an aggregate 1752 column inches to Hugh Grant's meeting with prostitute Divine Brown (Engel, 1996, p. 2).

Fourth and finally, broadsheet newspapers are recently more likely to include many editorial features which previously were the exclusive preserve of the tabloids. The *Guardian*, for example, publishes a 'problem page', although it is loath to admit it, preferring the title *Private Lives*; but the format is unmistakable. The paper publishes a letter outlining a personal problem and invites readers to respond to the letter including details of their personal experience. 'What can you do when other people's children misbehave in your home?' *Private Lives* asked readers (16 January 1997, p. 25). The following week, the newspaper invited readers' responses to a different dilemma: 'Your sister is in love. The problem? He's your cousin and the family have fallen out over it. What can you do?' (*Guardian,* 23 January 1997, p. 25). At weekends, the *Guardian* offers more tabloid distractions including a *What's On* guide and a 'lonely hearts' contacts section entitled *Soul Mates*.

Given these changes, it is little wonder that some observers are concerned that the line separating broadsheet and tabloid newspapers has 'virtually disappeared' (Sampson, 1996, p. 44) or at the very least has become a 'disappearing frontier' (Engel, 1996, p. 2). *Guardian* editor Alan Rusbridger has in part conceded the case; his neologism 'broadloid' signals the extent to which broadsheet newspapers are adopting tabloid stories and styles. Andrew Marr's allegation that *The Times* can be likened to a 'transvestite, full of dinky, *Daily Mail*, values' similarly acknowledges the convergence between broadsheet and tabloid newspapers (cited in *Press Gazette*, 18 October 1996, p. 14).

Television under siege?

Television news is middle aged. ITN was born on 4 May 1955 (Sendall, 1982, p. 87); the BBC is a little older. Both are displaying unmistakable signs of a mid-life crisis. Broadcast news services expanded rapidly after the 1967 watershed when *News at Ten* went on air. *News at Ten* marked the transition of news broadcasting from the short 10-minute news bulletin into the full-blown half-hour programme and triggered an escalation in television news provision. The BBC moved to a longer *Nine O'Clock News* in 1971, launched *Newsnight* in 1980 and added the *Six O'Clock News* in 1984. ITN increased its output to include lunchtime (12.30) and early evening (5.45) slots and won the contract to provide news for the new Channel 4. The dictates of Birtism in 1987 prompted further expansion: lunchtime news, on-the-hour daytime bulletins with regional news opt-outs, news on breakfast television, and the prospect of a 24-hour news channel. Currently there are 6 hours 25 minutes of news or news analysis daily on BBC television, more than 4 hours on channels 3 and 4 (excluding GMTV), plus Sky News and CNN (Cable and Network News) (Dugdale, 1995a, p. 12).

But television news has witnessed other changes. The investigative television journalism of the 1980s evident in programmes such as *World in Action* and *Panorama* has given way to the story-led, tabloid formats of populist programmes such as *3D* and *The Big Story* (see chapters 8 and 9, below). Increased competition, the 'striving for ratings', financial shortages and job cuts offer some explanation, but the government's decision in the Broadcasting Act (1990) to convert ITN from a cost to a profit centre is a major culprit. For the first time in British broadcasting, news had to make a profit. 'We are under siege,' Jon Snow claimed. 'Ratings will be the determinants because the money comes from advertisers.' In America, advertisers know that significant stories like Bosnia make 15 per cent of the audience switch off while 'the stories which got high ratings were ambulance chasing, fires and sadness' even though this coverage generated 'dreadful bulletins. . . . Within a couple of years there could be no serious analytical news programmes on American TV and that is the way we are heading' (cited in *Press Gazette,* 20 September 1996, p. 5 and Snow, 1997, p. 3). David Glencross, chief executive at the ITC (Independent Television Commission) until 1996, expressed similar concerns and regrets that 'factual programming is on a downward path towards the triumph of infotainment over both information and entertainment'. He believes that 'pelvic news' based on the scheduling philosophy of 'if it bleeds it leads' will become increasingly commonplace (Glencross, 1994, pp. 7–8). But despite these shifts in news values, ITV announced further plans in January 1997 to revamp its current-affairs programmes to attract a younger audience and 'avoid being taken on the right flank by Channel 5'. The new channel, which 'will have to be seen to be getting ratings', broadcasts current affairs which are 'non-elitist and bottom up' (Methven, 1997, p. 4). ITV is determined to match these programming ambitions.

The picture, of course, is not wholly bleak. Television, like newspapers, retains a commitment to high-quality news and current affairs which is evident in series such as *Dispatches* and *Cutting Edge,* but such programmes increasingly constitute exceptions in a culture which seems more than ever willing to jettison its public-service commitments. Paul Jackson, director of programming at Carlton, is explicit. 'If *World in Action* were to uncover three more serious miscarriages of justice,' he declared, 'while delivering an audience of . . . five millions, I would cut it. It isn't part of the ITV system to get people out of prison' (quoted in Williams, 1994, p. 16).

At the BBC, audience ratings have similarly assumed a crucial importance if the corporation is to defend the legitimacy of the licence fee, to politicians and the public, in a multi-channel broadcasting environment. Some programme makers concede the significance of audiences in shaping programme contents. Steve Hewlett, editor of *Panorama,* believes the programme needs to be popular and accessible'. 'We live in "zapland" where people are easy to reach,' he concedes, 'so it is absolutely important to turn *Panorama* into something people want to watch' (*Guardian,* 27 September 1996, p. 17). Greg Dyke in his 1994 MacTaggart lecture offers a more pessimistic thesis concerning the future vitality of television current affairs. He suggests that the independence of television journalism has been undermined by a growing 'culture of dependency' in which broadcasters are increasingly obliged to 'seek favours' from government and are reliant on politicians for their financial success or even their very existence. In such circumstances it seems less likely than previously that broadcasters might be unduly critical of government (Dyke, 1994, p. 27). In early 1997, the BBC also announced its intention to revamp all of its news provision. The language of moving 'downmarket' is anathema to the BBC, whereas the 'search for new audiences' seems to trip more readily from the tongue. Consequently, Tony Hall, chief executive of BBC News, announced 'one of the central aims will be to encourage not only a younger audience but also one drawn from further down the socio-economic scale.' If the findings of current audience research are accurate, BBC news will have 'less on political ding dongs at Westminster and more on technology and consumer issues' after the review (Culf, 1997, p. 30).

Few research studies of changing news values exist, but early findings are suggestive. A pilot comparison of ITN news at 5.40 p.m., BBC1 news at 6 p.m., SkyNews at 5 p.m. and Radio 4 news at 6 p.m., conducted on behalf of the Voice of the Viewer and Listener, revealed that BBC programmes devoted approximately twice as much airtime to foreign news as ITN, but only half as much attention to items reporting sport, and entertainment. The study concluded that ITN and SkyNews 'operate to a tabloid agenda while BBC TV and radio operate to a more serious one' (Gabor and Barnett, 1993, p. 8). A second study made a longitudinal comparative analysis of the news content of *News at Ten* programmes broadcast before the Broadcasting Act (1990), with an equivalent sample broadcast in 1995. Findings revealed a 65 per cent decline in international news coverage while the focus on sports and 'show business and entertainment' news doubled (Pilling, 1995, p. 13). Across the same period, suggestions that *News at Ten* is moving downmarket to win larger audiences have grown more common-place. A senior broadcasting trade union official identified neatly the various programme elements in *News at Ten* which constitute almost defining char-acteristics of newszak (see also chapter 12, below):

> The number of items, the duration of each item, the range of subject areas that are reported in terms of domestic, foreign, economic and social news are defining characteristics. But there is a more subjective element which is the packaged and conclusive approach of *News at Ten*. Every item has to be snappy, with a beginning, a middle and a very good end and then move on quickly to the next item to keep peo-ple's attention.

The recently launched Channel 5 seems set to continue the recent trends of more established broadcasters. Channel 5 controller of news, Tim Gardam, announced that his mission was to prevent news from being 'painful' by offering 'less politics and more consumer, sports and entertainment, news'. Gardam's medium-term ambition, he claims, is 'beating *News At Ten*. That's what I want to be measured against' (*Press Gazette*, 17 February 1997, p. 1).

But newszak is evident in recent changes to programme formats as well as in news content. The increasing gimmickry and circus of news presenta-tion too frequently subverts rather than clarifies the presentation of news stories. 'The technology enables us to package, graphicise and meld five minutes of old TV information into 60 seconds of new TV time,' Jon Snow of *Channel 4 News* claims, 'but the content reduction is so acute that nor-mal debate is in danger of being degraded to the absurd' (Snow, 1997, p. 3). But television has become obsessed with pictures above the story: if there are no pictures, there is no news. The emphasis on presentation is now overwhelming. In 1993, the BBC spent £650,000 to create a virtual-reality news studio which seemed to offer a more appropriate setting for a light-entertainment spectacular rather than a news programme; a year previously, ITN had spent considerable sums on a major 'revamp' of *News at Ten*. News programmes now open with a preview of the major headlines accompanied by apocalyptic theme tunes, eye-catching, hi-tech graphics and virtual-reality backdrops. Constant previewing of 'stories still to come' and reviewing of the headline stories already discussed, suggest broadcaster assumptions about viewers' attention span which are insulting.

Newszak has also encouraged the cultivation of star journalists like Michael Brunson and celebrity presenters such as Trevor McDonald and Jeremy Paxman. But while ITN has replaced two presenters with a single newscaster, the BBC prefers the American 'buddy' style where two news anchors offer a double act. When the presenters are a man and a woman, the 'sexual chemistry' between them is believed to be important for the programme's success. Cheerful and chirpy chatting between presenters and the predictable valedictory banter with the weather presenter have become as routine to the contemporary broadcast as the tail-end item about the skateboarding duck. In Channel 5's 'brightly coloured newsroom' reporters 'chat with presenters who move around to discuss stories and issues' (*Press Gazette,* 17 February 1997, p. 1).

Another contemporary obsession is the 'live two-way', where the presenter in the studio gets the latest news from a correspondent live at the scene of the story; they are typically presented side by side on separate screens clearly and patronisingly labelled to avoid viewer confusion. The suggestion implicit in the 'two-way' is clear: this news programme is so up-to-date that the news is happening and unfolding even as the programme is being transmitted. But too frequently the journalist outside the studio has little or no information to add to what the studio presenter has already made clear. If the viewer is confused, it must surely be about the purpose of programme formats which deliver so little news. But the two-way proliferates and journalists spend an increasing amount of airtime talking to each other when their job is surely to elicit information from others. Why not invite an expert, or someone directly involved in the event which the story is relating, to offer genuine insight into what has occurred or to speculate about future developments?

Radio: *the retreat from public-service broadcasting*

Radio news has changed throughout the 1990s; and for the worse! Radio, like newspapers and television, seems to have shifted its focus towards entertainment rather than the provision of information, although to date this tendency is more apparent in the commercial than the public sector of broadcasting. That the BBC is not immune to such trends is evident when the *Today* programme on 14 November 1996 devoted 18 minutes' airtime to an interview with Sarah Ferguson. Radio has a distinguished history as a news broadcaster; but its recent history is that of a medium in retreat from its Reithian public-service origins to a medium in which market forces are increasingly influential in determining the range and quality of services in both the public and private sectors (see below, chapter 6).

In the commercial sector of radio newszak is rampant, in part reflecting government policy changes. The Broadcasting Acts of 1990 and 1996 have triggered a proliferation of Independent Local Radio (ILR) stations, created the first three Independent National Radio (INR) stations, relaxed restrictions on ownership and cross-media ownership and created a new regulatory body for local radio intended to operate with a 'lighter touch' (see chapter 7). The expansion of ILR stations is undeniable: from 120 in 1992 to 218 in 1996. But what is less clear is whether the government's intention, that market forces should generate greater choice and diversity in radio provision, has been achieved. In reality, the policy outcome may have been precisely the opposite. The market penalises those who stray too far from the mainstream; ILR stations offer a dull, homogeneous and predictable output. Most stations describe their output as 'classic gold' or 'easy listening' which is interrupted only on the hour by two minutes' news feed from Independent Radio News (IRN). On some stations this is complemented by locally generated news, although journalistic staffs are very modest and budgets extremely tight. Commercial local radio has little local identity and reports only a scattering of local news. Whether in Blackpool, Bristol or Basingstoke, ILR offers an unrelentingly tedious and uniform output.

National commercial radio fares little better. Any ambitions that Talk Radio might be a serious competitor to Radio 4 as a news provider have long since been dashed. Arriving on air on 14 February 1995 with a mere £8 million in launch capital, the station has always offered cheap radio. Underfunded, understaffed and committed to an unimaginative schedule comprised almost wholly of phone-in programmes, the station initially failed to reach its audience targets. 'Shock jocks' such as Caesar the Geezer routinely abused their callers, denouncing them as 'sad bastards' (Culf, 2 May 1995, p. 6) but, despite this unpromising start, the station had succeeded in attracting an audience in excess of 2 million listeners within one year of going on air and, by early 1997, enjoyed half the weekly audience reach of the award-winning Radio 5 Live (*Press Gazette,* 17 January 1997 p. 7; see chapter 7).

Newszak is less evident in BBC radio programming than at any other point on the news media landscape. But many observers are pessimistic about the prospects for BBC radio and believe that recent trends presage a serious decline. Public-service radio, like its commercial counterpart, has been the subject of close government scrutiny especially in the period immediately prior to the renewal of the BBC's charter. The white paper, *The*

Future of the BBC: Serving the Nation and Competing Worldwide, expressed the government's commitment to retaining BBC local radio, but the number of stations has been reduced from 48 to 38 in 1996 because of budgetary cuts which, across the BBC, have fallen inequitably on radio rather than television and on local radio in particular. In truth the battle for public-service radio is lost. BBC radio had 51 per cent of total radio audience share in the first quarter of 1996 but its own estimates predict this figure declining to approximately 30 per cent in the new millennium with the popular-music output of radios 1 and 2 accounting for more than half of that audience share. The remainder of the radio spectrum will be dominated by the commercial stations with their monotonous diet of pop music, formulaic chit-chat and phone-ins with a smattering of news on the hour provided by the same central, rather than local, news agency. The future for British radio is a bleak prospect; audiences will largely be served a rather unwholesome diet of muzak seasoned with newszak.

Newszak, journalism and news media

These developments in journalism and the major news media of newspapers, radio and television, have been prompted by a number of mutually reinforcing factors; their close interconnectedness makes disentangling their separate effects problematic. The four most significant include: the increasingly competitive environment in which news media are obliged to operate; government media policy; the development of new technologies; and changes from within journalism itself (these are discussed throughout the text but especially in chapters 3, 10, 11 and 12).

The fiercely competitive environment for newspapers is a consequence of the long-term decline in national and local newspapers' circulations since the early 1950s. Sales of all national and Sunday newspapers plummeted from 38 million in 1965 to 29 million in 1993 (see chapter 5). Newspapers' ever more frenzied search for readers and advertisers has led them downmarket. An alternative strategy, initiated by Rupert Murdoch in July 1993, has been dramatically to reduce prices. The subsequent cut-throat price war has witnessed a doubling in sales of *The Times*, but the demise of *Today*. *The Times* has also paid a price. Once widely acknowledged to be a newspaper of record, setting journalistic standards for the industry, *The Times* has effectively become a give-away freesheet with all that implies for editorial quality.

Two lessons emerge from the price war. First, it has prompted the only expansion of overall newspaper sales in the post-war period. The conclusion here, no matter how reluctantly drawn, must be that price is among the most significant factors structuring newspaper sales; by comparison, journalists' and editors' concerns about editorial quality, layout and design appear to count for little. Second, the price war confirms the prominence of proprietors over all aspects of newspapers' operations; Murdoch's invitation to battle was readily accepted by Conrad Black without either proprietor consulting his editor. Proprietors, however, are motivated by considerations of profit and will bring market, rather than journalistic, solutions to problems of sustained circulation decline. For proprietors, reducing a newspaper's price seems a more obvious and readily achieved solution than enhancing its editorial quality (see chapter 5).

In broadcasting, competition has become intense following the burgeoning of media outlets; the growth reflects government policy and technological developments. The four terrestrial channels must now compete for viewers and, apart from the BBC services, for advertisers with Channel 5, BSkyB, 170 satellite and cable television services and the 250 digital satellite services anticipated to be on air in 1998 (see chapter 9). Radio services have witnessed a similar rapid expansion in number with the consequent implications for audiences and advertisers (see chapter 7). In the days of the 'comfortable duopoly', competition between BBC and ITV was judged to be a benign force which fostered improved programme quality; in the new multi-channel broadcasting environment, it has the opposite effect. Intense competition nurtures a 'minimax' programming philosophy in which the broadcasting of low-budget populist programmes such as quiz programmes, US sitcoms and repeats, minimises programme costs while maximising audiences and consequently advertisers. News and current affairs programming is doubly damned since it is expensive to produce and relatively unpopular with viewers.

Increased competition has encouraged the development of newszak in other ways. Competition has buttressed the influence of advertisers (Sampson, 1996, p. 45) but has also prompted considerable job cuts in both print and broadcast media. The *Independent* and the *Independent on Sunday* have shed more than 100 posts between 1994 and 1996 while the *Daily Express* and *Sunday Express* have been obliged to amalgamate their editorial staffs into a seven-day newspaper with considerable job 'savings' – i.e. 72 redundancies (see chapter 5). Losses at the BBC exceed one quarter of total staff (7000 posts) between 1988 and 1994; Central Television has halved its staff and there have been more than 135 redundancies at ITN. Revised working practices have not made good these losses. Opponents of bi-media journalism protest that it prompts a reduction in editorial quality by denying the uniqueness of radio journalism and failing to acknowledge the differences between radio and television cultures (Karpf, 1996, p. 14). Multi-skilling similarly damages editorial quality. Critics object that journalists working at small cable channels who jump into a cab with a portable camera, tripod, lights and recording equipment, writing a script en route to the story and editing the piece on their return to the studio, will not produce work of the same quality as a journalist working with a three-person film and sound crew.

Government policy has been a second factor promoting change. Policy targeted at newspapers has been remarkable for its near complete absence, offering a classic case study of non-decision-making. The white paper, *Privacy and Press Freedom* (Cmnd 2918), published two years after it was originally scheduled, declared the government's opposition to a statutory regime of press regulation despite the widely held view that this would provide the only guaranteed safeguard against increasing tabloid invasions of privacy, factual inaccuracies in press coverage and newspapers' growing obsession with trivia and sensationalism (see chapter 10). Press self-regulation will be a significant factor in ensuring that newszak flourishes. By contrast, legislation relating to broadcasting has transformed almost every aspect of its financial, organisational and regulatory structures (see chapters 7 and 9). The Broadcasting Act (1990) introduced a competitive broadcasting market regulated by a 'lighter touch' intended to make viewers sovereign in programme choices while sustaining programme quality. But the system of 'blind' auction which allocates the franchises to broadcast has diverted funding from programme-making budgets in Channel 3 companies into the treasury; in 1993, this sum amounted to £360 million. Programme-making at network and regional levels is inhibited by these enhanced cost constraints. Market forces, moreover, have proved corrosive of the public-service commitments which previously characterised the system and have reduced the incentive to make quality programming; in a market-driven system why broadcast *World in Action* when *Wheel of Fortune* will suffice? As T.S. Eliot noted in his evidence to the Pilkington Committee in 1962, 'Those who aim to give the public what the public wants begin by underestimating the public taste; they end by debauching it' (cited in Hoggart, 1995a, p. 114).

The Broadcasting Act (1996) has relaxed the existing rules on media concentration and encouraged cross-media ownership. The latter allows a profit centre within a media conglomerate to subsidise an ailing or fledgling enterprise within the larger group. Profits from the *Daily Mirror*, for example, underwrite the loss-making newszak cable channel *Live TV*, in much the same way that News International used revenues from the *Sun* to finance the early days of Sky Television; BSkyB income now finances the give-away *Times* (Seddon, 1996, p. 8). The central point is that cross-media ownership allows the subsidy of newszak.

Perhaps more significant than government policy in their implications for the quality of television and radio services at the BBC have been the successive policy changes emanating from director general John Birt in the period prior to the BBC's charter renewal; these have included the commitment to bi-media journalism and the internal market system known as Producer Choice (see chapters 8 and 9). Birt's proposals for reorganising the BBC, announced on 6 June 1996, were promptly denounced for downgrading domestic radio services, threatening the autonomy and editorial integrity of the World Service, presaging widespread job cuts (the new site at White City will have room for only 60 per cent of current journalists) and triggering an explosion of bureaucracy (Karpf, 1996, p. 12 and Methven and Kelly, 1996, p. 2). John Tusa, ex-managing director of the World Service, claimed that 'tolling like John Donne's bell' this policy would 'sound the death knell of Reith's BBC' (Tusa, 1996, p. 11). Some observers impute a more sinister purpose to the reorganisation: privatisation via the back door. Critics allege that the proposal to separate the commissioning of programmes from their production is a crucial precondition for Birt's plan to privatise parts of the BBC and make the corporation a publisher broadcaster concerned only to commission, but not produce, programmes: a 'virtual corporation' (*Independent,* 31 August 1996, p. 5). Under Birt's stewardship, the BBC has undoubtedly become an increasingly commercial enterprise which is more influenced by market forces, more concerned with audience ratings and less forcefully committed to public-service broadasting than at any point in its distinguished history.

A third factor influencing news media has been developments in print and broadcast technologies. Trade-union opposition to the introduction of the 'new print technology' in the national press eventually prompted Murdoch's move to Wapping and in this sense triggered the demise of Fleet Street. Many thousands of jobs were lost and proprietors and managers were substantially empowered in their relations with printers and journalists. What Gall describes as the 'employers offensive' quickly led to the derecognition of journalists' trades unions and the introduction of individual contracts which offered journalists highly variable salaries and conditions of service (Gall, 1996, p. 2, see also chapter 5). In these revised circumstances, journalists are no longer able to provide a bulwark of probity against those editorial decisions of management which seem less motivated by journalistic concerns than market or advertising considerations. More recently, the development of laptop processors, portable telephones and miniature modems has facilitated a substantial increase in freelance work, an associated decline in staff positions for journalists and the growing casualisation of the profession (see chapter 3).

In broadcasting the development of satellite, cable and digital technologies has created new delivery systems and prompted an explosion in broadcast media services (see chapter 9); in 1996 the ITC licensed 170 satellite and cable television channels while the Broadcasting Act (1996) envisages as many as 300 digital terrestrial and satellite channels (Broadcasting Act (1996) Sect. 6–31). This burgeoning of broadcast outlets has been accompanied by an enhanced competition for audiences, the substitution of 'narrowcasting' for broadcasting, combined with a concern to produce low-cost programming – all factors inimical to public-service broadcasting. The development of ENG (electronic news gathering) and more recently digital cameras has prompted job cuts, destaffing and revised working practices for journalists who are now expected to shoot, record, edit and produce film reports as well as investigate and write them. Again, the editorial quality of such news reports is considerably less than for larger news-gathering organisations.

Finally, developments in the relationship of journalists to news media have been crucial in their consequences for the growing prevalence of newszak. In the period since the end of the second world war, the activity of journalism has come increasingly to be conducted 'outside' the formal institutions of the mass media. There are two concrete manifestations of this trend. First, there has been an explosion in freelance journalism. Freelances have become conscripts rather than volunteers, with redundancy and lack of job opportunities cited as the major reasons for freelance status. The most able and experienced freelances can write copy for any market, in any house style, to any employer-specified objective, and can deploy the most sophisticated electronic technologies to sustain them.

Across the same period, there has been a dramatic increase in the number and range of occupations in which journalism skills are a prerequisite for employment. These include public relations, government, party and interest-group press offices, agency and in-house corporate communications and the press and public-relations staffs which even charities and voluntary organisations now employ. As the editor of *PR Week* observed, 'everyone from the Archbishop of York to the Duchess of York feels the need of a press agent' (*Guardian*, 13 May 1996). The growth in public relations is striking. The 850 press and PR workers in the Government Information Service (GIS), combined with the estimated 2000 PR staff working in local government (Mackey, 1994, p. 26 and Audit Commission, 1995, pp. 10–13) and the 22,500 PR staff in the private sector (Spillius, 1996, p. 10) constitute a total of more than 25,000 public-relations and press officers. Since the membership of the NUJ in 1994 was 26,800, the fourth estate risks being overwhelmed by what Baistow described as the 'fifth estate' if current trends continue (Baistow, 1985, pp. 67–77). The impact of public-relations officers on the editorial and broadcast content of media has always proved contentious and been has hotly contested, especially by journalists. But recent studies by Franklin (1994), Deacon and Golding (1994) and Schlesinger and Tumber (1994) as well as Gandy's pioneering work on agenda building, reveal the significance of news sources in structuring the range and profile of editorial content (Gandy, 1982). The impact of individual PR specialists such as Max Clifford on tabloid newspaper content is considerable; he was central in instigating the extensive coverage of Jerry Hayes MP and Mandy Allwood mentioned at the beginning of this chapter. He understands the PR function to be that of 'filling the role investigative reporters should fill but no longer can because cost cutting has hit journalism heavily' (Armstrong, 1996a, p. 10). Such claims are not merely pompous but misleading. Asked if he ever lied, Clifford answered with alarming honesty, 'frequently. Of course I lie. I'm in PR. I lie all the time. That's what it's all about, lying and corruption' (Clifford in *Hard News*, 19 May 1991). More worryingly, Clifford is not alone. Public-relations staffs have expanded while journalists have been shrinking, creating news media's greater editorial reliance on press officers. The amount of PR-generated material in media is extensive and growing. To cite the editor of *PR Week* again:

> A considered estimate would put this at 50 per cent in a broadsheet newspaper in every section apart from sport. In the local press and the mid-market and tabloid nationals the figure would undoubtedly be higher. Music and fashion journalists and PRs work hand in hand in the editorial process. It is often a game of bluff and brinkmanship, but the relationship is utterly interdependent. PRs provide fodder, but the clever high-powered ones do a lot of journalists' thinking for them.
>
> (*Guardian*, 13 May 1996, p. 10)

These developments have had three consequences for journalists and journalism. First, while journalists working within media remain largely committed, at least in their rhetoric if not always in their news-gathering and reporting practices, to the ideal of disinterested and rational enquiry, observation and reporting, this growing army of journalism-competent public-relations specialists and freelances increasingly subordinate such professional values to the requirements of commercial values or political persuasion. Freelances' independence of media is purely formal: their freelance status guarantees their subservience to the market. They are obliged to produce those stories which editors demand; they must publish or perish. Freelance journalists, moreover, do not enjoy sufficient time or the necessary resources to undertake investigative journalism and this offers some explanation for the evident decline of such stories in print and broadcast media. In much the same way, public-relations and press officers have no desire to explore in-depth issues which may be in the public interest. They are not detached observers and reporters of the world, but hired prize fighters, advocates and defenders of whichever sectional interest employs them. Second, the expansion of freelance journalists and public-relations professionals has reduced significantly the possibilities for effective collective bargaining and resistance to employer pressures both for journalists working within media as well as these 'outsiders' themselves. The consequences, noted above, have been job cuts, understaffing, casualisation of the profession of journalism and an increasing subservience of editorial to managerial and market considerations in news gathering and reporting. Third, these developments have altered dramatically the production processes and working practices necessary for the gathering, validation and distribution of information and news. Freelances are home-based, detached from the professional culture of journalism and the everyday journalistic practice of the newsroom. Public-relations staffs have little interest in contacting a wide range of news sources or developing a news story from a range of different perspectives; their purpose is less to explore issues than to promote them. Similarly, the journalist's concern to see if a story 'stands up' is not in the PR brief; the intention here is to persuade, not to inform.

A related and significant development within journalism has been the growing unwillingness of media organisations to fund the training of the next generation of journalists. Traditionally, new entrants to journalism learned their professional skills during their first job on a local paper or as a BBC trainee; professional quality and standards were maintained by the National Council of Training for Journalism (NCTJ). But training budgets have been trimmed, trainee posts in the local press drastically reduced and the suitability and relevance of NCTJ qualifications increasingly questioned. Young journalists are typically obliged to meet their own training costs by paying fees to enter the burgeoning number of journalism courses in universities and colleges or by subsidising newspapers, radio stations and independent television production companies by working for low wages or even no wages for an initial period. A study for the Guild of Editors reported one trainee journalist's experience: 'it cost me £5,000 to fund my pre entry course and I entered journalism earning £6,500. On this salary I was expected to buy and run a car as well as live and pay off debts incurred while I was training' (Guild of Editors, 1995, p. 6). The report concedes that 'there are horror stories'. These uncertainties and underfunding of training are crucially significant for journalism's future prospects. Amid the current welter of newszak it is still possible to identify the work of distinguished journalists like John Simpson, John Pilger and Roger Bolton, but the system which nurtured them, honed their skill and offered them opportunities for gaining a wide variety of journalistic experience is virtually dead.

The book in outline

Newszak and News Media examines how developments in the organisation, financial and regulatory structures of news media, combined with changes in the composition and news-gathering practices of the profession of journalism, have resulted in shifting editorial standards in newspapers, radio and television which raise important questions about the role of the news media and journalism in a mature democracy. After this introductory chapter, the book is in three sections dealing in turn with journalists, news media and news journalism. In addition to unravelling the argument outlined above, a second purpose has been to provide a detailed, comprehensive and up-to-date account of the history and recent development of the three major news media of newspapers, radio and television. Chapter 2 examines accounts of journalism which represent journalists as fearless and energetic crusaders after truth. This image is countered by reference to journalists' own accounts and different traditions within the sociology of journalism. Chapter 3 offers a profile of the profession of journalism identifying portentous changes and trends and focusing on the rapid expansion of freelance work and the too frequently muted voices of women and black journalists in contemporary journalism. The following section analyses the news media of newspapers, radio and television, both nationally and locally, with detailed consideration of their historical development (chapters 4, 6 and 8) as well as the impact of recent government policy, changing patterns of media ownership, trends in readerships and audiences, the influence of advertisers and the impact of new technologies on news gathering and reporting in the different media (chapters 5, 7 and 9). The final section explores a series of case studies intended to illustrate the revised editorial priorities of journalism as well as the controversies and recent developments surrounding the regulation of newspapers and television. Chapter 10 examines the invasive and sensational newspaper coverage of 'Lady Di', chapter 11 considers the declining and increasingly personalised and trivial media reporting of parliament, while chapter 12 explores the changing news values evident in television news and current-affairs programming and the proliferation and effectiveness of organisations designed to regulate broadcast media.

PART

II

NEWSZAK AND JOURNALISM

| 2 |

The image and reality of journalism

Few people ever meet a journalist. Their knowledge about journalists, much like other professionals such as social workers, lawyers and accountants, is rarely the product of any direct contact with these groups but, for most people, is derived substantively from media sources. The representation of journalism in media is consequently an important factor in public perceptions of journalists as individuals and journalism as a sphere of professional activity. This chapter examines briefly the prominent fictional images of journalism in novels, films and television drama. These representations are then compared with the typically oppositional perceptions of journalists' news-gathering and reporting activities, which emerge from social scientists' analyses and the observations of journalists themselves.

Images of journalism: a brief review

Journalists are popular characters with novelists. Evelyn Waugh's novel *Scoop* is replete with observations on the incompetencies of journalists, the subservience of news editors and the tyranny of proprietors (Waugh, 1964). Michael Frayn's novel *The Tin Men* satirises the formulaic character of much modern journalism by offering a vision of 'automated' newspapers with news stories drafted by programmed computers (randomisers) which carefully invent headlines based on market research of the readership which give 'a newspaper a valuable air of dealing with serious news . . . without alarming or upsetting the customers' (Frayn, 1995, p. 68). Gordon Burns' *fullalove* chronicles tabloid journalist Norman Miller's descent into self-destructive cynicism and portrays journalism as a profession characterised by dishonesty, decadence and decay.

Journalism has also proved a popular focus for British television drama. The BBC's first successful, twice-weekly, soap opera, *Compact* (1962–5), explored the romantic as well as journalistic activities of the staff on a women's magazine. In the later ITV series, *Agony* (1979–80), Maureen Lipmann starred as the editor of the advice page of a women's magazine, while *Lytton's Diary,* written by former *Evening Standard* journalist Ray Connelly, featured Peter Bowles as a Fleet Street gossip columnist. More recently, London Weekend Television produced the series *Hot Metal* in which actor Robert Hardy played Terence Rathbone – proprietor of Rathouse International Corporation – and Russell Spam – a middle-aged cockney, tabloid newspaper editor; a barely concealed parody of Murdoch and Mackenzie.

. Cinema offers an especially rich seam of images of journalism to mine. Ben Hecht and Charles MacArthur's 1928 play, *The Front Page,* which became the 1931 film of the same title, was remade in 1974 with Jack Lemmon as journalist Hildy Johnson and Walter Mathau as his unscrupulous editor, Walter Burns. Mathau manipulates Lemmon into getting a scoop on a condemned man who escapes from jail, even though this involves risking the delay of Lemmon's wedding and honeymoon. Billy Wilder's film *Ace in the Hole* featured Kirk Douglas as the calculating and callous journalist whose determination to get a news story results in the death of a man trapped in a mine. More recently Michael Keaton and Glenn Close, in the film *The Paper,* portrayed journalists working on a New York tabloid who are trying to prove the innocence of two young black people accused of murder. Undoubtedly the most well known film based on journalists, which derives its material from fact, is *All the President's Men* which recalls the work of journalists Woodward and Bernstein in uncovering the Watergate scandal. In short, there are few other professions, perhaps only the police and medicine, which have been such a focus for novels, plays and films. Consequently, the 'eager, bright-eyed reporter, trenchcoated and trilby-hatted, racing into the noisy, bustling newsroom and shouting "Hold the front page"' has become an enduring and widely held image of the journalist (Richards, 1991, p. 23).

But journalism receives a mixed press; images of journalists are diverse (French and Rossell, 1991). Damien Day, the cynical, dishonest and opportunist reporter featured in Channel 4's *Drop the Dead Donkey,* contrasts strongly and unfavourably with the scrupulously fair, independent-minded and investigative journalist and editor of the *Herald Tribune* portrayed by Ed Asner in the American television series *Lou Grant.* An early British television series *Shoestring* featured West Country radio journalist and amateur sleuth Eddie Shoestring who, like Lou Grant, represented the archetypal investigative journalist.

Proprietors, as well as journalists, are popular characters for creative writers, but they are invariably cast in the role of villain. Waugh's character Lord Copper, proprietor of the *Daily Beast,* is unashamedly based on Beaverbrook, while Orson Welles' portrayal in *Citizen Kane* of the founder of a publishing empire who hopes to rule the world is based on American newspaper magnate William Randolph Hearst. Rupert Murdoch alone has provided the inspiration for literally dozens of fictional media moguls, including Lambert La Roux, the interventionist proprietor of the *Victory* in David Hare and Howard Brenton's play *Pravda*; Sir Royston Merchant, absentee owner of Globelink News in the Channel 4 series *Drop the Dead Donkey*; Sir George Fison, the manipulative and highly partisan proprietor of a number of influential newspaper and television stations in Chris Mullin's television drama *A Very British Coup*; media magnate Ben Landless in Michael Dobbs' play *House of Cards*; the ruthless Australian proprietor Keith Tremlett in Jeffrey Archer's *Fourth Estate*; David Siltz, president of Uni-Planet Total Entertainment in Dennis Potter's final play *Cold Lazarus* and, of course, Lord Gnome, the proprietor of *Private Eye* and Gnome TV, Gnome Cable, and Gnome Sky Porno Vision. Lord Gnome is a composite of many Fleet Street proprietors, but his editorial the week after Murdoch's move to Wapping, expressing that he was 'delighted to report that my organ has been successfully transferred . . . to a disused sewage farm on the outskirts of Neasden', confirmed Murdoch's contribution to the fictional proprietorial mix. The last decade has witnessed an extraordinary boom in fiction featuring media moguls, a 'species fast threatening to outnumber randy academics' (Dugdale, 1995a, p. 2). These fictional proprietors, however, may reflect their real-life counterparts more closely than do journalists. Fictional images of journalism can be highly misleading and offer idealised perceptions strongly at variance with journalists' news-gathering and reporting activities. The following section addresses this issue directly by exploring a prominent image of journalists within much creative writing (although it describes a role for journalism which some social scientists would endorse). On this account, the journalist is a crusader, possessed with an almost missionary zeal, who will go to almost any lengths and risk any danger to uncover the truth.

Comforting the afflicted and afflicting the comfortable: the journalist as crusader

Broadly, the image of the journalist as a crusader after truth is highly positive. Journalists underscore basic democratic values; a free press is judged to be a central component of democracy. Journalists have come to symbolise freedom of the individual and they champion freedom of information which, once acquired, is used to expose corruption, oppression and exploitation (Richards, 1991, p. 23). Napoleon allegedly claimed that 'four hostile newspapers are more to be feared than a thousand bayonets' (cited in Randall, 1996, p. 4).

There are six assumptions which inform this understanding of journalists' news-gathering activities. First, journalism is about the quest for truth. Journalists are involved in investigative inquiries – in digging deep and 'getting the facts'. They clarify issues and seek to uncover attempts to manipulate the public. Such activity constitutes the hallmark of good journalism; and it is universal. 'Good journalists', Randall argues, 'will all be attempting the same thing: intelligent fact-based journalism, honest in intent and effect, serving no cause but the discernible truth, and written clearly for its readers whoever they may be' (ibid., p. 2). This leads to a second point. Journalism is an activity conducted independently of government and other powerful individuals and groups. Consequently, the practice of journalism is immune to interference from even the most influential in society. Gray Grantham, the investigative journalist in John Grisham's novel and film *The Pelican Brief,* illustrates this presumed independence of government. According to the book-cover blurb, Grantham, along with law student Darby Shaw (played in the film by Julia Roberts), 'penetrates the highest levels of power in Washington and causes shock waves there'.

Third, newspapers and newsrooms are pluralistic organisations. Journalism is a relatively egalitarian activity in which journalists, because of their professional competencies, enjoy an independence of others with whom they work. There will undoubtedly be differences of opinion, even heated debates, about the value of particular stories, but a good story will always win out; if the story stands up, it will be published. Journalism is an activity conducted within a framework of consensual professional standards. In *All the President's Men* Woodward and Bernstein are criticised at a number of editorial conferences by other journalists who speak against the plausibility of the Watergate story, but ultimately they receive the backing of the editor. Fourth, journalism is an activity conducted independently of economic pressures. Journalists understand, of course, that a newspaper is ultimately a business which must make a profit in order to survive, but a similar market rationale suggests that a newspaper will only survive if it publishes good stories which potential buyers wish to read. Journalists, moreover, tend to rise above the marketplace – the natural habitat of proprietors. The production of news is not driven by market considerations, or by considerations of entertainment value. Stories, significant stories about issues of public concern, are the telos of the journalist's activity. Fifth, journalists act as watchdogs, protecting the public interest: they scrutinise the behaviour of the powerful and the wealthy on the public's behalf. Politicians and governments form an inevitable focus of journalistic activity, and a key role for journalists is to render them accountable for malpractice and corruption. Journalists are 'topplers' of the powerful.

Finally, journalists inform the democratic database. According to this image of journalism, journalists provide members of the public with the factual information and informed opinion which, as citizens, they require to evaluate the issues, especially political issues, they must debate and decide. This perception elevates journalism to a central position in a democratic political system; a free press becomes the sheet anchor for democracy. Randall summarises the essentials of this view.

Good journalists universally agree on their role. This is, above all things, to question; and, by so doing, then to: Discover and publish information that takes the place of rumour and speculation; Resist or evade Government controls; Inform voters; Scrutinise the action and inaction of governments . . . ; Scrutinise businesses, their treatment of workers and customers and quality of products; Comfort the afflicted and afflict the comfortable, providing a voice for those who cannot normally be heard in public; hold up a mirror to society reflecting its virtues and vices . . . ; ensure that justice is done and investigations carried out where it is not; promote the free exchange of ideas, especially by providing a platform for those with philosophies alternative to the prevailing ones.

(Randall, 1996, p. 2).

These are giddy claims which will doubtedless trigger incredulity among many readers of the contemporary British press (Sparks, 1993, pp. 58–75). But can journalists make this perception of their professional activities 'stand up'? On closer examination, each of these assumptions requires qualification.

The claim that journalism is essentially an investigative activity, in which journalists uncover and report previously unknown affairs, contains an element of the truth but does not necessarily tell the whole story. At least four qualifications are necessary. First, while journalists do not actively seek to print lies they may occasionally (whether intentionally or otherwise) publish untruths; this possibility is acknowledged by the presence of libel laws. Second, journalists may, through lack of information, inadequate or insufficient substantiation of a story, or sheer incompetence, publish half-truths or misleading comment. The willingness of the London *Evening Standard* on 17 August 1995 to publish an article by Nick Howard, the son of Conservative Michael Howard, in the belief that it was written by Labour party ex-shadow spokesperson Brian Gould, offers an obvious example. Third, a good deal of the content of newspapers, as well as radio and television bulletins, is concerned with material which requires straightforward exposition rather than investigation. The content may focus, for example, on sport, entertainment, the weather or television programming. Such content does not necessarily lend itself to, nor require, investigative inquiry. Finally, the greater part of journalistic activity is routine rather than investigatory. Schlesinger's study of news production concluded that while journalism may seem to report unpredictable events, most news is 'not spontaneous or unanticipated' (Schlesinger, 1978, p. 69). The great majority of news is routine and is based around 'diary events': coverage of the regular meetings of courts, the monthly council meeting in parishes and local authorities, as well as events in parliament such as question time and PMQs (Franklin, 1991). In truth, the investigative journalist has always been more likely to inhabit the set of a television or film drama, or the covers of a racy novel, than the newsroom. Investigative journalists like John Pilger, Robert Fiske, Paul Foot, James Cameron or the Insider team at the *Sunday Times* have always been a rarer species than fictional accounts of journalism would have their readers and viewers believe. The ever more frenzied search for readers in the tabloid market has prompted a redefinition of 'investigative journalism' for some newspapers: it now involves little more than publishing a few photographs of a member of the royal family snapped in an unguarded moment.

The second claim, that journalists enjoy an independence of government is prima facie an accurate account. Journalists in Britain are not strictly controlled by government in the way that certain governments do seek to censor and restrict what journalists wish to publish. Indeed, it is sobering to recall, when questioning the notion of the journalist as a fearless crusader that, in 1995, no less than 186 journalists around the world were known to be imprisoned and 51 were killed on assignments while trying to report what governments wish to keep secret (Blyth, 1996, p. 9). But in the British setting, journalists' independence of government is not as complete as might be imagined. The British government, for example, does censor journalists: the reporting restrictions in Northern Ireland (lifted in 1994) as well as the Official Secrets Act (1989) offer obvious examples (Newton and Artingstall, 1992). Journalists, moreover, are increasingly reliant on local and central government public-relations specialists and press officers as sources of news about political affairs and government activity. Consequently, some observers believe that the 'popular image of news gathering as investigative journalism is largely a myth, for all papers rely to a great extent on "feeding" from agencies and from official sources. Much of the political news . . . is little more than repetition (sometimes word for word) of government press releases, Whitehall briefings, press conferences and carefully managed "leaks" from Whitehall' (Dearlove and Saunders, 1991, pp. 351–2). Politicians have become increasingly concerned to try to influence newspaper coverage of their party, its policies and its leader – especially during elections. Research findings suggest that politicians may be becoming increasingly successful in their news-management activities (Franklin, 1994). But the overwhelming objection to the view that journalists are independent of politicians, whether in Britain or elsewhere, is that this formulation offers an unduly simplistic understanding of the relationship between these two groups. Media are not simply detached observers of the political game but key players. Their coverage of events has significant consequences for the outcome of the game. The spheres of journalism and government increasingly overlap as journalists and politicians have grown mutually reliant, with each pursuing goals which can only be achieved with some degree of cooperation from the other. *Contra* the image of journalists as independent of government, many observers consider it more accurate to describe their relationship as collusive (Harrison, 1992; Mancini, 1993; Franklin, 1991 and 1994).

The third assumption, that newsrooms are pluralistic organisations, may not conform to many journalists' working experience. In reality newsrooms in television, radio and newspapers constitute finely graded hierarchies (Harris and Spark, 1993, p. 214). When a journalist has written his or her story, a number of gatekeepers, in the guise of news editors, assistant editors and editors lie in waiting to adjudicate on its merits and news value. Even when there is agreement that a story should be published, a sub-editor may change the article radically and adorn it with a headline intended to catch the reader's eye rather than reflect accurately its concerns. Proprietors, as well as senior editorial colleagues, can be highly influential in determining editorial content. Maxwell was legendary for his interference in the editorial content of the *Mirror* and the *European*; Murdoch is similarly decisive in establishing the broad editorial position of his newspapers (Evans, 1984 and Bevins, 1990).

Fourth comes the assumption that journalists are interested in what they call 'good stories'. Again, there is some truth here. Journalists are motivated, of course, by the concern to report good stories; the perennially desirable, if sometimes elusive, exclusive. But there is a growing concern expressed by the public, politicians and some journalists, about changing news values in British journalism arising from commercial pressures, with national and local newspapers increasingly competing for advertisers and readers, and broadcasting media competing for audiences (Barnett, 1994, pp. 5–9 and Glencross, 1994).

It is perhaps the fifth assumption that enjoys the greatest credibility as well as longevity; namely, that journalists are critics, watchdogs and 'topplers of the powerful'. It is certainly on this claim that the identification of the press as central to democracy rests. A moment's reflection conjures images of the corridors of power littered with the bloody victims of press exposure and critique: David Mellor, Norman Lamont, Jonathan Aitken and Neil Hamilton. In all of these cases, of course, press criticism reflected alleged individual shortcomings whether sexual, moral or financial, rather than any principled political objection, ideological dispute or policy debate. Even so, while it is possible to cite cases where the media have toppled the powerful, there is a greater body of evidence to suggest that their role is more typically to serve as a source of support. It is a matter of fact rather than political speculation, for example, that at election times British newspapers, but not radio and television, have overwhelmingly supported the Conservative party (Seymour Ure, 1991). Indeed, after the 1992 general election, many politicians in both the Conservative and Labour parties, as well as journalists and academic observers, believed that the news media were crucially significant in securing victory for the Conservative party after what was the closest-fought election for many years (MacArthur, 1992a). In March 1997, the *Sun* announced its editorial decision to support Tony Blair and the Labour party in the imminent general election. On the day after the election, the newspaper's headline boasted that it was 'The Sun Wot Swung

It', claiming that 'jubilant Tony Blair praised the Sun last night for helping to clinch his stunning electoral victory' (*Sun*, 2 May 1997, p. 2). But in 1997, few observers shared the *Sun*'s belief in the electoral importance of its advocacy of the Labour cause.

Finally, the assumption that journalists provide the information necessary for informed public debate of political and policy issues is difficult to sustain, especially in the case of tabloid newspapers but increasingly for many sectors of broadcast journalism. Peter Golding underscores the point with welcome good humour and enviable wit:

> To what extent do the media keep us informed parading before us the great issues of the day, analysed, debated and provided in full? How much do we learn of the complex relationship between the intelligence services and the state in a story about 'MI5 Wife in Secret Love Split' (*Sun* 18 December 1991)? For informed insights into Britain's role in the world and the variety of international affairs, exploring the subtle nuances of cross national relations, we can turn to the complexities unveiled in 'Up Yours Jacques' (*Daily Star* 24 November 1992). Equally significant for our understanding of the changing structure of family life in contemporary society would be such front page features as 'Sex Op Sister Stole My Man' (*Daily Star* 7 December 1992).
>
> (Golding, 1994, p. 464)

The study of newspapers' parliamentary reporting across the period 1990–5 (see chapter 11) which divided the parliamentary stories into 40 subject areas, discovered that 'scandal and personal misconduct' was the third most frequently reported topic, far ahead of significant policy issues such as race (thirty-eighth), health (eighth), education (tenth) and social services (thirty-fifth) (Franklin, 1995, see also chapter 11). This caricatured, highly personalised and often misleading presentation of political issues has a particular significance for a democracy where it may influence the decision-making process.

To sum up, the obstacles to independent journalism are more considerable than some creative writers imagine. A different and oppositional perception of journalism has recently gained increasing public credibility. On this account, it is a distorting mirror which journalists hold up to reality. According to Bernard Ingham, journalists are prone to exaggeration, speculation, oversimplification and trivialisation. 'The Media', he claims, 'have a rare gift of bringing the tablets of invention down from the mountain of ignorance and cementing them into the wall as fact.' A central law of journalism seems to be, ' "don't let the facts get in the way of the story" ' (Ingham, 1990).

Bernard Ingham: a poacher turned gamekeeper

Bernard Ingham offers a classic example of the poacher turned gamekeeper. He began his working life as a journalist on a local weekly newspaper, the *Hebden Bridge Times*, when he left school at 16. His autobiography, *Kill the Messenger*, and Robert Harris's 'unofficial' biography, *Good and Faithful Servant*, attest to Ingham's diligence as a journalist. He moved quickly to the Leeds-based *Yorkshire Post* and later to the *Guardian* before becoming press secretary to Mrs Thatcher in 1979. Ingham's recollections of the profession of journalism, based on his experiences of working at the *Hebden Bridge Times*, are visions gleaned through rose-tinted spectacles; his account bears more than a passing resemblance to the crusader image. Consider the following quotation. 'The dominating obligation for the journalist', Ingham claimed, 'was to inform the reader accurately, objectively and comprehensively of matters affecting the public interest; to keep him abreast of developments and responsibly to cultivate an informed public opinion. And don't miss anything lad!' Ingham's romantic evocation of the bygone days of journalism might well be set to the background music from a Hovis advert. Ah, but how things have changed.

In Ingham's view, four factors underlie the changes in journalistic standards which he believes constitute a noticeable decline. First, the fact that a substantial increase in commercial pressures on both print and broadcast journalism has obliged journalists to seek to capture and retain audiences. To that end, journalists have abandoned factual reporting for exaggeration, sensationalism and speculation. 'The stock in trade of most papers,' he claims, is now 'speculation; the government may be on the verge of . . . or the government might soon . . .' (Ingham, 1990). A second factor has been the rapid and extensive growth in media: new cable and television services, breakfast news and 24-hour television and radio channels devoted to news reporting. This growth in news media has created an incessant demand for instant comment to suit media deadlines. In the rush of this process, facts get lost. As an ex-government spokesperson, Ingham has been on the sharp end of such demands for comment and statements, which lead him to describe journalists as 'an insatiable, fractious horde'. Third, journalists have become damagingly conceited and arrogant. They have their own conception of news which, he believes, is preferred to reporting the real world. Finally, media have become obsessed with attacking authority. Ingham cites what he claims is a second law of journalism: 'if you can catch somebody out and make them look foolish, do it!' He regrets the development among broadcasters amd journalists of a 'confrontational approach to interviews and the determination to take the mickey out of authority' which 'seems to require that any self respecting reporter should knock seven bells out of symbols of authority, especially government' (ibid.).

These changes have reduced the profession of journalism to a 'debilitated state' which stands only shabby comparison with the standards at the

Hebden Bridge Times. Ingham diagnoses a number of specific ailments which are plaguing journalism (Harris, 1990, pp. 126–9). First, what he calls the Le Carré syndrome or the conspiracy theory of government: the rampant 'belief among journalists that government is chronically up to no good'. It is this malaise which has led certain newspapers to oppose the system of lobby briefings, albeit temporarily. In severe cases, Ingham argues, this can lead to the delusion that governments try to manage the news; surely a calumny against the mere 850 press officers and public-relations specialists of the Government Information Service! The Conan Doyle 'complication' is a nasty affliction which Ingham suggests leads journalists to become obsessed with deduction which too often leads to the wrong conclusion. Journalists afflicted with this complication carry deduction to such excesses, Ingham suggests, 'that 2+2 become 22 because there must be a catch in the simple answer of 4' (Ingham, 1990). Next, there is Columnar Pox, a social disease to which the chattering classes, but especially journalists and diarists, seem particularly vulnerable and which manifests itself 'as a wilful refusal to check any fact for fear that a paragraph is lost to truth' (ibid.). Fourth, there is the Coleman/Carpenter phenomenon, which seems to remove reporters' capacity just to report the facts concerning what is going on; no story, they believe, is complete without their interpretation and comment. Ingham claims the BBC is highly prone to this phenomenon, which manifests itself in statements such as 'the government climbed down last night' (ibid.).

How is Ingham's view of journalists and journalism, with its evident lack of measure, to be assessed? From his reversed perspective as press secretary rather than journalist, he seems unable to accept that the press should do precisely what he criticises them for doing: namely scrutinising government, expressing reasonable scepticism about government and refusing to accept the word of a government spokesperson as the infallible and absolute truth of the matter. The criticism which many observers level against the British press is precisely that it does not engage in such activities sufficiently frequently. What Ingham conveys unequivocally is his intense dislike of journalists. Senior conservative politician and ex-leader of the House, John Biffen, observed that Ingham 'hated journalists. He really treated them like shit. They were all up to no good as far as he was concerned. There wasn't one he wouldn't have suspected of being a child molester or of selling his grandmother into white slavery' (Harris, 1990, p. 145). Underlying Biffen's hyperbole is a fairly accurate observation, but much of Ingham's critique of journalism none the less strikes a chord. Newspaper reporting is increasingly sensational, trivial, speculative and exaggerated, concerned less to inform than entertain. A challenging and assertive interview style is to be applauded, but undue lack of respect for the person being interviewed, leading questions and misrepresentation are less worthy.

The sociology of journalism

It is not only ex-journalists and press officers who are critical of journalism. The distinctive analyses of the processes of news gathering and news reporting elaborated by different traditions within the sociology of journalism also contest popular images. What follows is a brief overview of three broad traditions in the sociology of journalism: the organisational approach; the marxist or what has come to be designated the political economy approach and, finally, what James Curran has described as the culturalist approach.

The organisational approach: time, space and 'fallible human beings'

The organisational approach argues that it is the various ways in which journalism is organised as an activity, combined with the professional practices and values of journalists, which are central to understanding the forces that shape the eventual character of media content. In his study, *Creating Reality*, David Altheide analyses the 'complex of . . . organisational and personal factors that determine the biases and slants built into news reporting' (Altheide, 1976, p. 1). Shortages of time and space are typically identified as the two major organisational constraints on the journalistic enterprise, but Murphy's study of a local newspaper office reveals four constraints on local journalism which often pull in contradictory directions: time, space, money and competition (Murphy, 1974, p. 16).

According to the organisational account, it is the perennial problem of limited space which explains the exclusion of particular news stories or their prioritising on different pages within the newspaper. Similarly, it is likely to be restrictions of time which explain the exclusion of a particular story – or its ranking in the running order of a television or radio news programme. Broadcasters' obsession with time is reflected in all facets of the construction of news bulletins. Schlesinger's study of a BBC newsroom, for example, observed journalists' professional concern to inject 'pace' into news bulletins – the need to 'keep the interest moving' (Schlesinger, 1978, p. 103). This may, in turn, influence running order as stories using film are scattered throughout the bulletin to create variety and sustain viewer interest. Such editorial judgements signal journalistic assessments of news priority less than professional strategies for ameliorating the organisational limitations of space/time.

In their classic study of news values, Galtung and Ruge argued for the significance of time in the selection and reporting of news. 'Events' are likely to be reported and become 'news' to the extent that they 'fit' into the time-span and work schedule of the news organisation concerned. 'The more similar the frequency of the event is to the frequency of the news medium', they claim, 'the more probable that it will be recorded as news by that medium' (Galtung and Ruge, 1973, p. 53). Most national newspapers and radio and television news organisations operate on a 24-hour news day and this cycle influences the daily selection of news. Consequently, a fire at Kings Cross underground station can be reported comprehensively – as an event – in a daily newspaper or a television news bulletin, but the analysis and discussion of the various factors leading to the fire will be reported by news organisations with a longer news cycle: a weekly newspaper or current-affairs programme. Conversely, events which take place over a longer time-span will not be reported by news organisations running on a daily cycle, unless they reach 'some kind of dramatic climax'. In Galtung and Ruge's example, the building of a dam will be ignored but its opening will be reported. This congruence between the time-span of events and the length of the organisational news cycle explains the focus of bulletins on 'events' rather than the contextualising 'processes' or trends which explain them (ibid.).

Gaye Tuchman's influential article, 'Objectivity as strategic ritual', identifies different organisational constraints on news production – this time in the guise of journalists' professional values and practices (Tuchman, 1972). Writing news stories under the pressure of deadlines poses professional risks for the news journalist which can be reduced and managed by adopting certain editorial protocols. These procedures or 'rituals' give the journalist's work credibility by suggesting a degree of objectivity in news reporting, but in reality they are simply routine ways of coping with the risks inherent in producing news under the severe constraints of time. On this account, journalism's central professional value of objectivity is reduced to an organisational constraint – little more than a safety net against possible censure. In Tuchman's words, 'Objectivity refers to routine procedures . . . which protect the professional from mistakes and his critics' (ibid. p. 678).

Tuchman identifies a number of such protective and strategic rituals. The first involves the 'presentation of conflicting possibilities' (ibid., p. 665) on occasions when a journalist is unable, or lacks sufficient time, to establish the veracity of a particular statement; for example, Politician A's claim that X is good. But if the journalist is able to find a second politician (Politician B) who offers an alternative view (that X is bad), the reporter can simply publish both statements without establishing which politician is right. The deadline is met, objectivity is achieved (or at least both sides of the case have been presented), but the accuracy of both statements remains unsubstantiated. The second ritual, 'presentation of supporting evidence', involves the provision of additional information in support of claims made by the journalist (ibid., p. 667). Tuchman offers the example of an obituary which described the deceased person as a 'master musician'. Challenged by the editor, the journalist offered the additional information that the musician had once played with a distinguished composer. The supporting evidence was sufficient to persuade the editor of the journalist's original claim but, in reality, the statement falls far short of objectivity. On such occasions, journalistic objectivity does not require confirmation, only that all assertions are substantiated with supporting evidence. A third ritual employs 'the judicious use of quotation marks' to create an impression of distance between the reporter and the report of events and thereby to avoid accusations of bias. Tuchman's example is of a journalist reporting a demonstration against the Vietnamese war. The reporter supports the demonstration's objectives but cannot draft an approving story without being censured by the editor and readers for partisanship. But the skilful use of quotes allows the reporter to write a favourable account while appearing to maintain a distant, objective and impartial stance; in this way, 'hard news' appears to be separated from 'comment'. Tuchman suggests the text might read: 'thousands of persons swarmed to a sunny city park yesterday to an "incredibly successful" anti-draft, anti-war rally' (ibid., p. 669). In aggregate these strategies, designed to permit the production of high-quality editorial work within conditions of time constraint, create an impression of objectivity.

These rather prosaic, if not commonsensical, organisational accounts of media content make the explanations offered by other sociologists seem unduly sophisticated. Shortages of time and space, the availability of information and the errors committed by journalists working to deadlines provide a sufficient account of the constraints on journalism. Organisational theorists are content to explain ideological skew or bias in media content by reference to 'cock up' rather than 'conspiracy'; in this sense they let journalism off the hook. Randall captures the essence of the organisational approach with the humorous prescription that,

> Every daily newspaper ought to print a disclaimer in each issue. It would read something like this:

> This paper and the hundreds of thousands of words it contains has been produced in about 15 hours by a group of fallible human beings, working out of cramped offices while trying to find out what happened in the world from people who are sometimes reluctant to tell us and, at others, positively obstructive.

> (Randall, 1996, p. 5)

Marxism, political economy and journalism: 'there is a mass of such rabble'

The marxist or political economy approach to journalism suggests that the production of news and other journalistic products is structurally constrained by economic and political factors, especially the private and increasingly concentrated ownership of media industries (Golding and Murdock, 1973; Miliband, 1970). The suggestion reflects a fundamental belief that the economic structure of society, based on a division between owners and non-owners of the means of production, has significant implications for the social, political, legal and cultural spheres. The study of media must examine 'the social contexts of production and reception (of media messages) and their relations to the central institutions and processes of class society' (Murdock and Golding, 1978, p. 345). While their products may be cultural, the mass media are 'first and foremost industrial and commercial organisations which produce and distribute commodities' (Golding and Murdock, 1973, p. 227). Consequently, the analysis of media and journalism should adopt as its starting point the economic organisation of media and very high degree to which media industries are characterised by concentration of ownership (Murdock, 1980 and Williams, 1994).

This analysis has a number of implications which run counter to the perception of the journalist as crusader. First, journalists lack autonomy. They do not enjoy any genuine journalistic independence because media are largely owned and controlled by private capital. Journalists are subject to the control of proprietors in one of two possible ways. Ralph Miliband, an 'instrumentalist' within the political-economy school, suggests that because individual proprietors own particular newspapers and possess the power of 'hire and fire', journalists must acquiesce in proprietorial incursions into editorial matters (Miliband, 1970, p. 205); this is a lesson which even distinguished journalists such as Harold Evans have found they must learn if they wish to retain their jobs (Evans, 1984). But 'structuralist' marxists believe that this type of argument, with its emphasis on personal decision-making by media moguls, smacks of conspiracy theory. Murdock argues that proprietorial intervention may not always be necessary since the 'logic of the prevailing market structure ensures that by and large the [journalistic] output endorses, rather than opposes, their [proprietors] interests' (Murdock, 1980, p. 57). In brief the structure of the market usually guarantees a congruence between proprietorial and journalistic perceptions. But whatever the process, both approaches within the political-economy school concur on the outcome: journalists lack independence and editorial autonomy. Second, journalists are not critical watchdogs of government but more akin to lapdogs: the poodles of government and the powerful. Instead of criticising government and corporate interests, they endorse and support them. This leads to a third and related claim. Media content is necessarily ideologically biased in favour of certain social groups. In Marx's celebrated phrase, 'the class which has the means of production at its disposal has control at the same time over the means of mental production' and is able to 'regulate the production and distribution of the ideas of their age' (Marx and Engels, [1845] 1965, p. 61). Journalists are 'interested' parties and media articulate sectional interests. Finally, media fulfil a legitimation function by obscuring the economic, social and political inequalities which characterise capitalist society; media help to create and sustain a 'false consciousness' about social and political reality. Journalists, so the argument runs, are blinded *by* their interests while their product, the various forms of media content and output, serves to blind others *to* their interests (ibid., pp. 62–3). In this way, media become an important weapon of deception, legitimation and social control in a perpetual class war (Miliband, 1970, ch. 8; Althusser, 1971, p. 146).

Marx had worked as a reporter on the German newspaper *Rheinische Zeitung*, but he remained implacably hostile towards journalists. He believed they should be classified along with civil servants, lawyers, judges, doctors, schoolmasters, poets, professors, priests and musicians, as members of what he described very disparagingly as the ideological professions. He rounded forcefully on such 'professionals', believing them to be worthless parasites. 'From whore to Pope', he denounced, 'there is a mass of such rabble' (Marx, [1887] 1973, p. 272; see also *Capital* vol. 1, p. 446). Since their trade was in 'ideological products', their survival required them to adopt a wholly uncritical attitude towards the prevailing ideology. Their function was to help formulate and disseminate the ideas and values of the dominant social group.

The political-economy approach derived from Marx's initial thinking has prompted substantial debate and attracted as much criticism. Pluralists express three perennial objections to this analysis. First, it is alleged that political economy confuses the matter of the ownership of media industries with their control. Proprietors, claim pluralists, own newspapers but do not control them; this is the prerogative of the editor, senior colleagues and journalists. Second, it is no longer wealthy and powerful individual capitalists who own media enterprises but much greater numbers of smaller investors and shareholders. Ownership has become diffused, plural and democratised since Thatcher's revolution announced the arrival of popular capitalism. Third, while the political-economy approach may possess some explanatory value for the production of news and news content in the privately owned media sector, it provides an inadequate theoretical framework for broadcast media which operate on public-service principles, including an explicit commitment to disinterested broadcasting, and subject to statutory regulation designed to exclude any editorial influence arising from political and economic interests. Let us consider each criticism in turn.

First, pluralists argue that the days when powerful press barons dominated newspapers have given way to a 'journalistic troika' in which the owner's search for profit is constrained and balanced by the editor's professional journalistic commitments as well as the demands of the readers. In this newly achieved balance of power, editorial priorities prevail over economic concerns. Consequently the power of the proprietor, 'where it survives at all . . . must still defer to the influence of readers' (Whale, 1977, p. 84). What is on offer here is a specific variant of the more general thesis concerning the development of managerialism; namely that decision-making within companies has increasingly become the preserve of a new elite of managers. Armed with professional expertise and day-to-day knowledge of the company, the managers control the company and require owners merely to rubberstamp their decisions. But editors are simply workers – albeit at a high grade – and, as such, remain subject to the discipline of proprietors. Marx understood as much. He acknowledged that joint-stock companies tended 'to separate this . . . managerial work more and more from the possession of capital' but managers were 'mere managers' whose salary was 'simply the wage for a certain kind of skilled labour' (Marx, from *Capital* vol. 3, cited in Glover, 1984, p. 52). It would certainly be difficult to persuade an editor that proprietors were no longer in control of their newspapers. A succession of editors from Harold Evans to Andrew Neil acknowledge the power of proprietors in autobiographies which invariably detail their prompt removal from the editorial chair following a disagreement with the owner (Evans, 1984 and Neil, 1996). Proprietors' power to 'hire and fire' makes them formidable figures, but they also control all aspects of a newspaper's financial and staffing resources (Bevins, 1990; see also chapter 5).

Second, pluralists suggest that political economy's analysis has been undermined by changes in the nature of the capitalist enterprise following the development of the joint-stock company in the 1860s. The capitalist entrepreneurs who controlled all aspects of companies' operations have been replaced by smaller shareholders and institutional shareholders such as pension companies, leaving no individual or small elite group of shareholders with a sufficient holding to be dominant. But again, this argument has been contested. In UK media industries the stake of the small shareholder is extremely modest compared to the substantial holdings of moguls such as Murdoch; their power over policy-making is similarly diminutive (Williams, 1994). The 1980s, moreover, witnessed a remarkable increase in the concentration of media ownership which has accelerated during the 1990s and received statutory endorsement in the Broadcasting Act (1996) which relaxed rules governing media ownership (see chapter 9). The boardroom battle for proprietorial supremacy between Lord Stevens and Lord Hollick, following the merger of United News and Media and MAI in February 1996, which has been won so decisively by Hollick, refutes the pluralist claim in two ways. First, it confirms the continuing power of proprietors. Hollick has revamped every aspect of the new company including the merger of editorial staffs of the *Daily Express* and the *Sunday Express* to create a seven-day newspaper; the editor of the latter has been sacked. Hollick has also shifted the newspaper's partisanship in the direction of the Labour party (Williams, 1997, p. 13). Second, the example illustrates well the inconsequence of small shareholders. In the battle between powerful players for control of a £3 billion media empire, small shareholders will at best be marginalised or, at worst, be crushed between the two contenders. Even Lord Stevens, who is a substantial shareholder, seems to have little influence in the affairs of the newly merged conglomerate.

The third argument put forward by pluralists is that the political-economy tradition, which imputes a relationship between the ownership, control and editorial content of media, has relevance only to print journalism since *all* broadcast media, whether privately (the ITC) or publicly owned (the BBC board of governors), are regulated by statutory bodies with an explicit brief to protect broadcasters from sectional economic or political interests seeking to influence programming, especially news and current-affairs journalism. The Broadcasting Act (1990), moreover, included a specific requirement for broadcasters to guarantee impartiality in programming. But political economy insists that, in much the same way as the press, radio and television 'whether commercially or publicly owned . . . perform a highly "functional" role; they are . . . the expression of a system of domination and a means of enforcing it' (Miliband, 1970, p. 221). To this end programmes are broadcast which promote the interests of the dominant class. In support of this claim, political-economy scholars allege the existence of an elite within the senior echelons of the BBC and other broadcasting organisations. The board of governors of the BBC, for example:

> tends to be drawn from the ranks of the 'great and the good' and to mirror the predominance of the upper middle classes in the ranks of political life in elected and non-elected positions of power. Of the eighty-five governors who have served in the first fifty years of the BBC's history, fifty-six had a university education (forty at Oxford or Cambridge) and twenty were products of Eton, Harrow or Winchester. The political experience of Board members has come mainly from the House of Lords although there have been nineteen former MPs.
>
> (Dearlove and Saunders, 1984, p. 353; see also Scott, 1991, p. 113)

But the ability to illustrate the existence of an elite using such sociodemographic data does not confirm the claim that this elite uses its privileged access to media institutions to produce programming which is partial and supportive of a particular class interest. The series of *Bad News* studies by Glasgow University Media Group (GUMG) (1976, 1980, 1982, 1985), however, offers ample, if not uncontested (Harrison, 1985), evidence of a systematic skew in the reporting of certain kinds of news. After a detailed content analysis of the reporting of industrial-relations stories in British television news, the Glasgow scholars concluded in their first study that 'television news is a cultural artifact; a sequence of socially manufactured messages which carry many of the culturally dominant assumptions of our society' (GUMG, 1976, p. 1). The group's later study, *More Bad News*, confirmed that despite journalists' stress on balance and impartiality, television news reporting 'consistently maintains and supports a cultural framework within which viewpoints favourable to the *status quo* are given *preferred* and *privileged* readings' (GUMG, 1980, p. 122).

Pluralists rejoin the debate by challenging the political-economy school to explain the fact that both the BBC and ITV have broadcast a creditable number of programmes which have been highly critical of both Labour and Conservative governments as well as vested political and economic interests, if programming is ideologically encoded with messages which support social elites. The BBC's coverage of the Gulf War, the Falklands and Northern Ireland combined with Thames Television's *Death on the Rock* and the BBC's *Secret Society* have proved a considerable irritant to politicians. But broadcasters' ability to challenge orthodoxy, annoy politicians and impact on policy and popular opinion has not been restricted to news and current affairs coverage. A succession of radical plays like *Cathy Come Home, The Price of Coal, The Nation's Health, Days of Hope* and *The Monocled Mutineer* have also shattered political complacency and orthodoxies. Political economy has responded with two arguments. First, Miliband claims that the independence and impartiality of broadcast media is 'rather superficial and misleading' (Miliband, 1970, p. 220) but none the less invests broadcasts with considerable public credibility. The BBC and ITV have confused 'impartiality' with 'mainstream' opinion and strived for balance in the middle ground of consensus politics. But the collapse of the post-war consensus prompts a debate about whether a single, mainstream political culture exists and, if not, there is an obvious danger that in expressing 'mainstream culture, the media are actually expressing establishment values'. In a polity which is divided on major issues an attempt to seek balance in the middle ground is a recipe for bias. Views which 'fall outside this consensus' are subject to 'a steady stream of propaganda' (ibid., p. 224). Second, the provision of programmes which challenge mainstream views is very modest compared to the overwhelming majority of programmes which endorse them. The broadcasting of 'dissident' programmes, moreover, is ideologically functional since it buttresses audiences' belief in the balance, independence and impartiality of broadcast media; media in capitalist states operate according to the principles which Marcuse designated as 'repressive tolerance' (Marcuse, 1969). Miliband summarises the political economy case by arguing that:

> radio and television in all capitalist countries have been consistently and predominantly agencies of conservative indoctrination . . . that have done what they could to inoculate their listeners and viewers against dissident thought. This does not require that all dissident thought should be prevented from getting an airing. It only requires the overwhelming bias of the media should be on the other side. And that requirement has been amply met.

> (Miliband, 1970, p. 224)

'FILTERING THE NEWS': HERMAN AND CHOMSKY

Edward Herman and Noam Chomsky propose a significant variant of the political-economy approach but share many of its fundamental assumptions. American mass media, they argue, are propaganda agencies of the state which are used systematically to mobilise ideological support for state policies; dissenting news is rare (Herman and Chomsky, 1988).

While media function to 'amuse, entertain and inform', Herman and Chomsky argue that their essential function is 'to inculcate individuals with the values, beliefs and codes of behaviour that will integrate them into the institutional structures of the larger society. In a world of concentrated wealth and major conflicts of class interest, to fulfil this role requires systematic propaganda' (ibid., p. 1). Private ownership of the media and the absence of censorship make this system of propaganda less evident but no less effective than in single-party politics where the mass media are under the direct control of the state. All potentially newsworthy events must pass through five filters which leave only a 'residue', which has been 'cleansed' of dissenting opinions, available for broadcast and publication in the media. By filtering the news in this way, the media 'marginalise dissent and allow the government and dominant private interests to get their messages across to the public' (ibid., p. 2).

The first filter is a consequence of the ownership and control of media by a very narrow group of individuals, families and corporations. In much the same way that Miliband identifies elite control of broadcasting in the UK, Herman and Chomsky suggest the owners of the media industries share common interests with other major corporations, banks and governments and are interlocked through board membership with those corporations; their control of media is used to protect and prosecute those interests. The second filter reflects media reliance on advertising as their prime source of income and operates in two ways. Advertising revenues reduce the price of media for readers/viewers and give a competitive edge to advertising-based media above media which are wholly reliant on sales revenue. Consequently the media market is influenced by advertisers' choices as much as by consumers' preferences. Advertisers, moreover, wage war on their ideological enemies, refusing to sponsor or place advertisements in television programmes critical of their interests. Consequently, broadcast discussions of issues such as environmental degradation or the operation of the American military-industrial complex are rare in, if not totally absent from, US television (ibid., p. 17). A third filter operates because of American media reliance on government, business and other semi-official sources of news: the White House, the Pentagon and the State Department in Washington DC are crucial. The media rely on these sources for reasons of economic necessity (they provide ready and cheap access to news stories) but also because of the claims to objectivity and authority which are uniquely invested in official government sources. The Pentagon alone employs thousands of public-relations staff and a budget of 'hundreds of millions of dollars a year . . . dwarfing not only the public information resources of any dissenting individual or group, but the aggregate of such groups' (ibid., p. 19). The fourth filter involves the use of 'flak' – negative responses to media output – to discipline and control media. Flak takes the form of letters, law suits and politicians' speeches; it is the prerogative of the wealthy and powerful and may be organised directly – a letter from the White House to a particular programme or network – or indirectly by generating institutional advertising which is critical of media or by funding oppositional think tanks. The Center for Media and Public Affairs, for example, endorsed by Ronald Reagan and Pat Buchanan, conducts research and monitors the alleged liberal bias and anti-business tendencies of American mass media (ibid., p. 27). The final filter is the ideology of anticommunism, reflecting the deep fear and suspicion which communism invokes among 'property owners' in America. Communism, loosely defined to embrace effectively any ideas and opinions which 'threaten property interests' or espouse radicalism, is used by media to 'mobilise the populace against an enemy' (ibid., p. 29). This ideology may be used to launch propagandist attacks on domestic 'liberals' who are presented as being 'too soft on communists' or to justify the support of fascist regimes abroad since these offer a preferable alternative to communism.

In aggregate these five filters select and structure news in ways which mobilise ideological support among the public for the 'national interest' – a euphemism for the interests of the powerful among corporate, military and political elites. Such support is articulated through the radically different presentation of similar international events in news coverage, reflecting whether the country concerned is broadly friendly or hostile to American interests; a process which Herman and Chomsky describe as 'dichotemization' (ibid., p. 31). This dichotomous presentation of news is routine, reflecting the systemic biases of American media. Herman and Chomsky conclude: 'The mass media never explain *why* Andrei Sakharov is worthy and Jose Luis Massera in Uruguay is unworthy – the attention and general dichotomization occur "naturally" as a result of the working of the filters, but the result is the same as if a commissar had instructed the media' (ibid., p. 32). This last sentence is uncompromising. In a society without formal censorship or state ownership of media, the central function of journalism and the media is to manufacture consent in ways which exclude dissenting and oppositional viewpoints as effectively as any dictatorship.

Culturalist perspectives: 'relative' or 'licensed' autonomy for journalists?

For their part, Culturalists suggest that the production of news cannot be understood as merely a function of media ownership, nor as a consequence of journalists' professional routines, but reflects the impact of cultural and ideological influences on 'relatively autonomous' journalists working in media organisations whose 'reporting is structured by cultural and ideological influences . . . rather than by hierarchical supervision and control' (Curran, 1990, p. 120). This approach is reflected in the work of widely contrasting media theorists, articulating distinctive models of society from pluralist (Tunstall, 1971 and Hetherington, 1985) to political economy (Murdock, 1982 and Golding and Middleton, 1982), but what unifies this diversity is a 'paradox': namely the 'claim that control of the media lies primarily outside the media' (Curran, 1990, p. 114). Belief in the 'independence of journalists' is another 'foundation stone of the culturalist faith in all its denominational forms' (ibid., p. 118).

Two variants of the 'neo-liberal culturalist' approach are summarily dismissed by Curran. First, there is the view of the news process to which most journalists subscribe, which understands the media as a mirror reflecting events in society. On this account, news is the product of journalists who serve as the neutral reporters of events occurring in the real world. But theorists such as Altheide and Tuchman have illustrated convincingly the extent to which journalists' professional values and routines of news gathering and reporting fundamentally influence their journalistic output. Second, and also popular with journalists, is the belief that media content is driven by sovereign consumer choices exercised in a free and competitive market. To cite a popular adage which broadly captures this view, 'We get the press we deserve.' Popular or not, Curran is unhappy with this adage since it takes little account of the ways in which advertising distorts consumer preferences and likewise ignores the imperfections in the 'free' market which oligopoly and the concentration of media ownership present.

Curran is more impressed by the 'structuralist culturalist' tradition exemplified in Stuart Hall et al.'s analysis of media-generated moral panics about 'mugging' in their study, *Policing the Crisis* (1978). Hall argued that news content is influenced by journalists' reliance on primary definers – those accredited spokespeople for elite interests (police, lawyers, politicians, judges), who enjoy routine and ready access to media and whose opinions journalists endow with credibility and authority and use to inform their reports. The significance of these primary definers is thus twofold. They provide journalists with factual information about particular events (the raw material of news) but, more importantly, they provide them with ideological frameworks to incorporate in the construction of their reports. Consequently a journalist reporting the poll-tax riots is more likely to seek out a senior police officer or the home secretary (both primary definers) to provide information and offer a perspective on the cause and consequences of the riots, than to try to elicit the equivalent information and ideological position from a participant in the riot; these routine news-gathering procedures guarantee that the ideological definitions of the less powerful in society will be largely ignored. Thus, for the culturalist, 'the news media are shaped more by the patterns of thought and power relationships outside the media to which journalists respond, than by direct controls exerted within media organisations' (Curran, 1990, p. 116). On this account, media and the processes of news production become the focus of a perpetual ideological 'battle between a multitude of differentially powerful parties over the definition of reality' (Turow, 1989, p. 206 cited in Deacon, 1996, p. 174). But this is a struggle between unequal contestants with the dominant societal interests most likely to be heard since 'access to the media is structured by the hierarchy of power in society' (Curran, 1990, p. 117). Culturalists assert that journalists are not obliged to endorse the dominant ideological accounts of reality because of direct pressure from proprietors or others, but because they have internalised the dominant societal values. In Hall's words:

> The media then do not simply 'create' the news; nor do they simply transmit the ideology of the ruling class in a conspiratorial fashion. Indeed we have suggested that, in a critical sense, the media are frequently not the 'primary definers' of news events at all; but their structured relation to power has the effect of making them play a crucial secondary role in reproducing the definitions of those who have privileged access, as of right, to the media as accredited sources.

> (Hall et al., 1978, p. 59)

The 'more sophisticated versions' of the culturalist perspective have been critical of this early notion of primary definition on six grounds (Curran, 1990, p. 121–33 and Schlesinger, 1990, p. 66–7). First, the model exaggerates the degree of ideological congruence between primary definers; the meaning of an event is rarely uncontested. If, for example, two members of the same government are trying to influence the news agenda in distinctive directions, who is to be identified as the primary definer? This prompts a second difficulty. Even among politicians, access to the media is inequitable. The prime minister and other senior ministers enjoy the support of a number of press officers and other substantial information resources (Seymour Ure, 1987). In reality politicians form a ranked hierarchy of primary definers, although this problem is not discussed by Hall, and the notion of a 'hierarchy of primary definition' may be inherently contradictory (Franklin, 1994, pp. 19–22). Third, primary definition must confront the difficulties inherent in the lobby and other systems of official briefing which have anonymity built into their protocols. In a clandestine system of unattributable briefings, identifying primary definers is all but impossible. Fourth, structures of access to the media shift over time, prompting considerable fluctuations in the relative significance of groups as primary definers. Schlesinger notes, for example, the declining importance of the TUC (Trades Unions Congress) and the CBI (Confederation of British Industry) as 'major voices' since the post-Thatcherite collapse of corporatism. Fifth,

Hall's model of ideological reproduction is 'uni-directional' – i.e. the process of definition is exclusively from power centre to media. There is no discussion of those many occasions when the media seize the initiative, challenge the primary definers and force them to defend their ideological definitions (Schlesinger, 1990, pp. 66–7). Finally, this model of primary definition understates the significance of hierarchies within media organisations. Curran's case study of media reporting of the Greater London Council (GLC) between 1982 and 1985 confounded aspects of the culturalist analysis by findings which suggested that different media brought distinctive perspectives to their GLC coverage, reflecting differences of ownership and control; in certain media, journalists' autonomy was routinely subordinated to managerial and proprietorial pressures. Television and radio reports of the GLC were relatively even-handed, but national tabloid press coverage was highly critical, alleging the council was 'incompetent, authoritarian and morally subversive'. Broadsheet coverage was positioned midway between tabloid and broadcast reports. But if, as culturalists suggest, journalists' reporting is structured by factors external to the media, by the cultural and ideological processes of primary definition, how are these substantial differences in media coverage to be explained? Curran argues persuasively that the distinctive reports in different newspapers and the differences between print and broadcast media are explained by the partisan and adversarial attitudes of press owners and chief executives. The relative autonomy of the journalists, so loudly trumpeted by the culturalist perspective, was in reality merely a 'licensed autonomy' which allows journalists a degree of editorial independence so long as it is exercised in ways which do not conflict with the interests of employing organisations (Curran, 1990, p. 120).

Conclusion

This chapter has discussed a number of conflicting images of journalists and their role in the processes of news gathering and news reporting. The most positive account presents journalists as independently minded investigators after truth and critics of the powerful: to cite a journalistic adage attributed to William Randolph Hearst, 'News is what someone wants to stop you printing; all the rest is ads'. At its most valuable, journalism plays a central role in democratic systems. Freedom of the press is the essential freedom; some suggest the press has earned and deserves the title 'fourth estate'. But this account of journalism has been criticised, not least by journalists themselves. The public seems increasingly critical of frequently invasive news-gathering activities and the sensational, uncritical and partial character of a growing proportion of journalistic endeavours. The game is up; people have recognised that newszak is on the increase. Journalists' public image is poor and getting worse. In 1993, MORI asked 1800 adults whether or not they trusted particular categories of professionals to tell the truth; findings for selected professions were clergymen 80 per cent, judges 68 per cent, police 63 per cent, civil servants 37 per cent, politicians 14 per cent and government ministers 11 per cent. At the very bottom of this hierarchy of distrust, the public placed journalists: only 10 per cent trusted them to be truthful. Worse, this figure represented a decline of almost 50 per cent from the previous decade (Worcester, 1994). The public image of journalism seems to have little point of contact with those fearless crusading journalists who appear with such regularity on cinema and television screens. Rightly or wrongly, public perceptions of journalism share a greater affinity with the view expressed by Bernard Ingham and others that crusading and investigative journalism is a trust which journalists have betrayed.

|3|

The upstairs downstairs profession of journalism

Myths about journalism abound; the reality is more prosaic. The muck-raking, crusading, investigative journalist, who so routinely inhabits Hollywood film sets, is an increasingly rare species in the newsroom. Woodward and Bernstein investigated and confronted 'all the president's men'; the modern journalist must tackle the more intractable problems of redundancy and repetitive strain injury (RSI). Journalism is a radically different profession now from the one it was even a decade ago. The investigative crusader has become more akin to a glorified clerk: 'rewriting a press release forms an integral part of the journalists' professional exams' but 'digging the dirt does not' (Head, 1995, p. 66). Change has been endemic. New directions in government media policy, developments in new technology, changes to the regulation of media industries, combined with the increasingly competitive market in which journalism is conducted, have altered the social and demographic character of the profession, the news-gathering and news-reporting practices of journalism and any prospect that journalism might fulfil its traditional role of informing public debate, holding governments and the powerful to public account and uncovering inconvenient truths. Serious news journalism has been replaced by newszak. While it is important not to manufacture romantic images of a previous golden age of journalism which never existed, there can be little doubt that journalism has changed radically in recent years (Sampson, 1996, pp. 42–52, Sparks, 1993, pp. 58–75).

Young journalists entering the profession face an uncertain future characterised by falling wages and deteriorating conditions of service (Guild of Editors, 1995, p. 5 and Bromley, 1994, p. 170). Increasing job insecurity reflects the growing trends towards casualisation of the profession by substituting freelances and journalists employed on short-term contracts for established staff posts; many staff journalists have become 'permanent part-timers' (Keeble, 1994, p. 3). But journalism has become a thoroughly middle-class profession with a clear majority of journalists having A, B and C1 social class backgrounds; a radically changed social profile from the late 1960s (Boyd-Barrett, 1970, pp. 181–201 and Guild of Editors, 1995, p. 2); two thirds of new entrants describe themselves as middle class (Delano and Hennington, 1995, p. 10). This 'gentrification' of journalism has been accompanied by an increasingly high educational profile within the profession. Twenty per cent of journalists are public-school educated and 48 per cent are graduates; 15 per cent have Oxbridge degrees. In the late 1960s only 30 per cent of specialist reporters and a mere 12 per cent of journalists working in the provincial press had degrees (ibid., p. 14 and Tunstall, 1971, p. 59). But while factors such as social class and educational attainment tend to support claims for an increasing professionalism within journalism, they seem wholly incongruent with the comparatively poor pay for journalists compared to other professionals, the deterioration in their conditions of service and the derecognition of their trades union. Some even distinguished practitioners eschew any notion of journalism as a profession. 'Journalists,' Peter Preston claims, 'like to think of themselves as professionals – doctors, lawyers, that sort of thing. Wrong. They're tradesmen and sometimes the trade is rough' (*Guardian*, 5 April 1996, p. 5).

Greater numbers of women are entering journalism but, much like their counterparts in other media-related industries such as public relations, they are excluded from senior positions within the industry; especially in print journalism (Dougary, 1994, p. 115). Some things never change. The prospects for black and Asian journalists securing a job in mainstream white media remain as rare as hens' teeth (Ainley, 1994a). The implications of this social profile of journalism, for the range and quality of news services, is increasingly prompting critical comment. In the 1995 McTaggart Lecture, Janet Street Porter offered her 'Dreaded four Ms' assessment which derided British television as 'male, middle class, middle aged and mediocre' (twentieth MacTaggart Lecture to the Edinburgh Television Festival, text in *Guardian*, 26 August 1995, p. 2).

But in reality journalism has become a complex and diverse profession. Journalism on a local weekly newspaper is very different from a journalistic career in television or radio broadcasting or again from the journalistic enterprise on a national tabloid. Apparently similar journalists may enjoy radically different opportunities and possibilities. A woman freelance typically earns a low income and enjoys few prospects, but as a woman journalist reminded, 'Germaine Greer and Lynda Lee Potter are among the best paid people in journalism and can ask whatever they like for a short feature'; freelance life is 'a famine or a feast' (*Journalist* Supplement, March 1995, p. 2). In truth the profession of journalism is fissured by a series of overlapping divisions between freelance and staff journalists, black and white journalists, men and women journalists, journalists working in different sectors of the industry, tabloid and broadsheet journalists and between editors and other editorial workers. On occasion, the effect of these divisions is mutually reinforcing but, on others, the positive influence of one offsets the potentially negative impact of another. Each division signals differential prospects for each group of journalists' access to senior positions, job security, conditions of service, higher salaries and social celebrity; in the post-fordist world of core and peripheral workers, journalism has become an 'upstairs downstairs' profession. Editors increasingly acknowledge a 'two tier system of journalists' in which 'top quality reporters engaged on complex and important news gatherings' compare favourably with a 'lower tier of editorial assistants who can deal with rewrites, obits, wedding reports'; a 'structured salary differential to reflect the value of the employee' is inevitable (Guild of Editors, 1995, p. 8 and Tunstall, 1995, p. 54). But substantial salary differentials are already evident. Two per cent of journalists earn in excess of £50,000, while one in ten earns less than £10,000 and one quarter of journalists earn below £15,000 a year (National Union of Journalists, 1994, p. 6).

This chapter offers a largely statistical profile of the contemporary profession of journalism, identifying changes and trends which are portentous in their implications for established journalistic practices of news gathering and news reporting. But there is a significant and prior question: How many journalists are there in Britain?

British journalism: the numbers game

With honourable exceptions, the question of how many journalists work in Britain has rarely been posed (Tunstall, 1971 and 1983). On those occasions when it has, precise answers have proved elusive. Reliable data have not been available because 'journalist' has never been an official professional category for the purposes of census data. Problems arising from lack of information have been compounded by increasing uncertainties about how journalism and journalists might be defined. It is perhaps unsurprising therefore to discover disagreements between research findings concerning the profession.

In his pioneering study, Tunstall suggests Britain's journalist population grew from less than 2000 in 1861, to 10,000 in the late 1930s and 20,000 in the late 1960s; a doubling of the profession within 30 years (Tunstall, 1971, p. 12 and 1983, p. 188). By 1969, there were 20,375 journalists in Britain, working: on national daily and Sunday newspapers (3550); on daily, Sunday and weekly provincial newspapers (9700); on periodicals and magazines (4000); in broadcasting nationally and regionally (675) and in news agencies (450); while a further 2000 worked as full-time freelances (Tunstall, 1971, p. 13). Twenty-five years later, one 'guesstimate' of the number of journalists was 35,000 (Bromley, 1994, p. 1). Two new sources of data about journalism became available in the mid-1990s. The Trades Union Research Unit at Ruskin College, Oxford, commissioned by the National Union of Journalists, conducted a questionnaire-based survey of *journalists who were members of the union.* The 5008 responses provided a significant social and demographic profile of journalists (National Union of Journalists, 1994). A second study conducted jointly by researchers at the London College of Printing and the Department of Journalism at the University of Queensland, interviewed 726 news journalists (4.8 per cent of the estimated population) to establish the social characteristics of *news journalists* and their attitudes towards aspects of their professional practice (Delano and Hennington, 1995).

The NUJ calculated its membership for the UK at 26,769 (see Table 3.1) for the year ending April 1995, with a further 2805 members in the Republic of Ireland (National Union of Journalists, 1994, p. 2). The NUJ's rival union, the Institute of Journalists (IOJ), claims a membership of 2000 while the Broadcasting, Entertainment, Cinematograph and Theatre Union (BECTU) has approximately 1000 journalists all working in broadcasting. If Bromley is correct to estimate that approximately 75 per cent of journalists are members of a trades union, this suggests an overall journalist population of 39,692 (Bromley, 1994, p. 1). The NUJ's full members are distributed throughout the different media sectors of the industry reflecting their particular skills (see Table 3.2). Delano and Hennington estimated the total population of UK news journalists to be 15,175. These journalists are distributed very unevenly between national daily newspapers (2462 – 16.2 per cent), national weekly newspapers (820 – 5.4 per cent), regional

Table 3.1 NUJ Membership (UK) by member type, 1994–5

Type of member	Number	Percentage
Full	19,661	73.6
Temporary	469	1.8
Student	2006	7.5
Non-payment grade	4633	17.3
TOTAL	26,769	100

Table 3.2 NUJ full members by industrial sector, 1994–5

Media sector	Number	Percentage
Books	839	4.3
Broadcasting	3839	19.5
Freelance	4471	22.7
Magazines	2210	11.2
National newspapers	2666	13.6
News agencies	501	2.5
Public relations	1259	6.4
Provincial newspapers	3819	19.4
Not known	57	0.3
TOTAL	19,661	100

daily/evening newspapers (6105 – 40.2 per cent), regional weekly newspapers (2035 – 13.4 per cent), national and regional independent television and radio (1015 – 6.7 per cent), Reuters, the Press Association and other wire services (1000 – 6.6 per cent), national and regional BBC television and radio (1038 – 6.8 per cent) and news agencies (600 – 4 per cent).

The lack of agreement between certain findings of these two studies suggests the need for caution concerning the accuracy of both data sets. The surveys, of course, measure different constituencies, but some of the sector totals derived from the NUJ survey substantially underestimate numbers of journalists when compared with Delano and Hennington's figures. Even allowing for the fact that not all journalists are members of the NUJ, disagreement between the findings of the two studies is greater than might be imagined. Delano and Hennington conclude, for example, that the total figure for news journalists in the provincial press is 8140; a figure which would be supplemented substantially by other non-news journalists to construct the overall total. But the NUJ survey suggests only 3819 journalists (a total of news and non-news journalists) working in the provincial press; this is a considerable mismatch of findings. But while the surveys' data must be judged indicative rather than substantive, in tandem the studies offer useful insights into the profession of journalism.

Scribes for hire: the explosion of freelance journalism

The last decade has witnessed a remarkable change in the contractual status of journalists with greater numbers working as freelances, prompting a growing casualisation of the profession. In 1969, one in ten journalists freelanced (2000 among 12,000, Tunstall, 1971, p. 21); by 1994 the figures ranged between one quarter and one third of all journalists (11,000 among 33,000, National Union of Journalists, 1994). Another significant change is evident. In the past many journalists preferred to freelance because it offered the prospect of working from home, an escape from the daily routine, the avoidance of 'office politics' and a degree of freedom not available to staff writers, but increasingly freelance work has become geared to the needs of employers rather than reflecting the lifestyle choices of individual journalists (Keeble, 1994, p. 313, Van den Bergh, 1995a, p. 40). There are fewer volunteers and considerably more conscripts in the growing army of freelances. Some of the most highly paid, skilful and busy journalists have always chosen to freelance but the sustained recession, job cuts and the intensifying competition for staff posts have increased pressures on freelance work while at the same time obliging many more journalists to work as freelances.

Less than two thirds of working journalists are currently employed in full-time staff positions, with the remainder working as full-time freelances (23.5 per cent), employed on a contractual basis (5.9 per cent), combining freelance work with a part-time contract post (5.3 per cent) or having some other non-staff employment arrangement (3.8 per cent) (National Union of Journalists, 1994, p. 7). Freelance journalists are self employed and enjoy little job security. They must negotiate jobs with a range of employers; more than half (57.2 per cent) of freelances did less than 25 per cent of their work for a single employer. Journalists employed on contracts fare little better since the duration of contracts is typically very short. Almost three quarters (72 per cent) of journalists are employed on contracts of less than 12 months, with 43.4 per cent holding contracts of 7–12 months, a further 21 per cent are working contracts of between 3 and 6 months' duration while 8 per cent of journalists are employed on contracts of less than 3 months' duration. Just over half (56 per cent) of journalists would prefer a permanent staff position to contract-based working (ibid., p. 11). Given this expressed preference for staff jobs and the obvious uncertainties which accompany the more casual contract and freelance status, why is freelance work expanding?

The first explanation can be expressed in a single word: redundancy! Three quarters of freelances previously held staff posts. One in four free-lances cite compulsory redundancy (sacking) as the reason for leaving their last job; a further 8 per cent left because of voluntary redundancy. In tandem this suggests that redundancy is the motive behind one in three journalists becoming freelance (ibid., p. 12). Second, freelance working offers considerable advantages to employers. It is much cheaper. There are no office or equipment costs and none of the usual costs such as superannuation which are associated with employing staff. Freelancing is also a euphemism for 'piece work'. Unlike staff journalists, freelances are paid only when they deliver copy. Third, freelance work has been encouraged by broader changes within media. Commercial television, for example, operates increasingly as a publisher rather than a producer, commissioning programmes from independent producers who require fewer staff journalists. In the age of newszak, there is less news space in newspapers and television programming as news and current affairs journalism has lost ground to entertainment. News coverage is, moreover, increasingly provided by news agencies with consequent reductions in staff posts. Fourth, access to digital superhighways and multi-media workstations equipped with modems, connects the freelance journalist in Wigan with Wapping. Working from home presents no technical difficulties and offers management considerable savings. Fifth, the derecognition of the NUJ means that the union is less able to protect members against the company's desire for the 'flexibility' of freelance, part-time or fixed-term contract employment located outside the workplace. Finally, government policy changes to pension and health-care schemes, which oblige individuals to make greater provision for their own arrangements, is gearing the welfare system towards self employment.

The advantages of freelance work to employers and managers seem clear; the disadvantages for journalists are equally evident. First, for most freelances the rewards are extremely poor; the phrase 'Dickensian wages' would not be inappropriate. There are exceptions. Anne Robinson reputedly earned 'at least £200,000 a year for writing a column in *Today* newspaper and a further £200,000 for television and other related work' (Bromley, 1994, p. 15). These sums are in striking contrast to the earning expectations of the typical freelance. Journalists are paid by the line. The NUJ recommended pay guideline, which is above the rate which is usually paid, advises freelances to charge weekly papers £1.52 for up to 10 lines and 15.2p for each additional line; equivalent rates for provincial daily, evening and Sunday papers are £2.66 and 24p. A news story in a provincial paper will typically generate £4; a journalist will be paid no more than £10 even for a lead story. But even these miserly rates are often undercut. A freelance journalist working in an agency claimed that for 'a front-page lead story which continued into the inside pages with pictures, we were sent £7.50p' (quoted in Van den Bergh, 1995a, p. 18). It is perhaps unsurprising that the NUJ national survey discovered that freelances constituted two thirds (65.6 per cent) of those journalists who are earning less than £10,000 a year (National Union of Journalists, 1994, p. 15). Freelance pay has always been poor but rates cited in 1923 are closer to current levels than might be anticipated. The *Daily Express* paid between 15 and 21 shillings (75p to £1.05) for 300 words, the *Daily Mail* between ten shillings and six pence and twenty-five shillings (52.5p to £1.25) for 200 words; provincial papers offered between ten shillings and six pence and twenty-one shillings for 250–500 words (Meggy, 1923). But agreeing a rate is only the start of the freelance's difficulties. Employers are slow to make payment and freelances must set aside time to chase bad debts. Occasionally, freelances are obliged to issue writs against editors to secure payments (*UK Press Gazette*, 4 March 1994, p. 4).

The second major disadvantage of freelance journalism is that some newspapers breach copyright and behave unethically in their dealings with freelances. One freelance alleges that newspapers 'frequently rewrite exclusive items of copy sent in by us, to subsequently appear as one of their own stories, for which we don't receive any payment' (Van de Bergh, 1995a, p. 18). Occasionally freelances are doubly damned when provincial staff journalists 'sell on' freelance stories to national newspapers but deny the freelance a fee for either publication.

Third, freelance work is accompanied by considerable job insecurity; this in turn favours compliance with managerial requirements with the obvious consequences for editorial independence. In the competitive news market, the freelance's copy is simply a product for sale; it will sell most readily, if at all, when it conforms to the buyer's requirements. Freelance journalists may wish to escape the ideological and professional conformity which working in a large media organisation may impose, but in truth the market obliges them to produce certain kinds of material. The independence of the freelance is a myth.

Fourth, freelance work transfers the burden of capital costs necessary for journalistic production from management to the individual journalist. Keeble lists what he describes as the 'basic requirements' for travelling the 'daunting freelance road': an office with a working desk, filing cabinet and key reference texts; a personal computer and printer; telephone, answering machine and fax; a tape recorder and television; an accountant for tax and pension purposes; an invoice book, headed notepaper, camera and transport (Keeble, 1994, pp. 315–16).

Finally, the freelance life is solitary, lacking the companionship of colleagues and semi-detached from the professional culture of journalism. The benefits of home working can be much overrated. But the factors which have generated the recent explosion in freelance work seem unlikely to be reversed in the short term. Journalism will be characterised by a continued expansion of freelancing; contracts will become the norm and staff jobs a rarity.

Apartheid in journalism: black journalists, white journalism

British journalism represents an almost perfect system of apartheid. Black and Asian journalists are employed almost exclusively on black newspapers and periodicals, while white journalists work within mainstream white media. There is a rich and flourishing tradition of black journalism in Britain with more than 100 newspapers and periodicals owned, controlled and published by black and Asian people in 1990; the majority of these publications are sited in London. By the year 2000, a rapid expansion is estimated to result in more than 400 black publications in the UK. It is unlikely that any white journalists will be employed on these newspapers.

For their part, black and Asian journalists are absent at all levels and within all spheres of mainstream British media. Despite the fact that almost one third of national newspapers' column inches are filled by regular columnists who are increasingly defining what is newsworthy, none of them at the time of writing are black. The black journalistic voice reaches few white ears. Statistics for the provincial press are especially striking; only an estimated 15 of the 8000 journalists working on provincial newspapers are black or Asian (Ainley, 1994, p. 57). There are no black people occupying any of the 138 editorial positions in the broadsheet and tabloid national press (Benjamin, 1995, p. 58). Only 350 of the 27,000 members of the NUJ are black (Ainley, 1994, p. 291). Academic research has been uncharacteristically silent about the position of black journalists. Those studies which have been conducted (Hartmann and Husband 1974, Critcher et al. 1975, Gordon and Rosenberg 1989, Searle 1989 and Van Dijk 1991) have tended to focus on the allegedly racist character of much reporting, rather than examining the racial profile of journalists. Troyna's suggestion that the National Council for the Training of Journalists (NCTJ) should actively encourage black school-leavers and graduates to enter journalism in the hope of providing equality of opportunity as well as contributing 'to the more informed and sensitive reporting of race issues', remains exceptional (Troyna, 1981, p. 86). Studies of journalism by Tunstall and Boyd-Barrett focused exclusively on white journalists (Tunstall, 1971 and Boyd-Barrett, 1970). But despite widespread agreement among academics about the racist character of some media reporting, especially in the tabloid press, the Press Complaints Commission (PCC) has not upheld any of the 112 complaints about alleged newspaper racism which it has received during the last two years (*Free Press*, Jan./Feb. 1996, p. 2). There is no black member of the PCC.

Table 3.3 reveals that the 205 black journalists working in mainstream white media are numerically overwhelmed by their 28,644 white colleagues; a ratio of white to black journalists of 140:1. The absence of black journalists is especially noticeable in the press, with only 35 of the 12,000 journalists in the national and provincial press being from ethnic minorities. In 1995, the liberal *Guardian* newspaper employed four black journalists and two sub-editors. But senior positions have proved elusive. Black journalist Angella Johnson claimed that 'on a scale of one to three in terms of seniority all of the black journalists are at scale three. There are no women or blacks at the top' (Benjamin, 1995, p. 57). This under-representation of black journalists and black opinion persists despite substantial black readership of the mainstream press. News International's marketing department, for example, claims a combined black and Asian readership for its three daily (*Sun*, *Times* and *Today* – study before closure in November 1995) and two Sunday (*News of the World* and the *Sunday Times*) titles of 884,000 with 330,000 *Sun* readers (ibid., p. 8).

Black journalists enjoy a stronger presence in broadcast media. In 1994, 2.7 per cent of journalists employed by the BBC and ITV were black or Asian, which represented a considerable advance over 1983 when the equivalent figure was 0.8 per cent (Ainley, 1994, p. 63). BSkyB and ITN still

Table 3.3 Black journalists employed in different media sectors

Media sector	Total journalists	Number of black journalists	Percentage of black journalists
National newspapers	4012	20	0.5
Provincial newspapers	8000	15	0.2
Broadcasting BBC and commercial	3700	100	2.7
Magazines	7000	20	0.3
Public relations	1432	30	2.1
Black newspapers and magazines	500	500	
Freelance	4500	20	0.4

Source: NUJ/IOJ 1990/91 cited in Ainley, 1994, p. 57

employ only a few black journalists, but Channel 4 and the BBC have adopted quotas to expand numbers of journalists recruited from ethnic minorities. But even these modest figures require some qualification since they risk overstating the black presence. First, not all black employees in broadcasting are employed as journalists; at the BBC, only 2.6 per cent of ethnic minority staff are employed as journalists. The BBC's equal opportunities statement specified an overall target for ethnic minority workers of 8 per cent but there is currently no target figure for black *journalists* (BBC, 1993c, pp. 2–3). Second, despite the BBC's best efforts, the number of black and Asian journalists declined from 6.8 per cent in 1988 to 5.9 per cent in March 1993, reflecting the differential impact of overall staff reductions on employees from ethnic minorities (Ainley, 1994, p. 59). Third, a considerable number of black journalists work on black-only programming; in Ainley's study the figure was 40 per cent of black journalists (ibid., p. 104). *Race Today* reported a leaked memo (October 1984) from the then executive producer to Barry Cox at LWT suggesting that the staff of *Eastern Eye* and *Black on Black* 'want out of the television ghetto' (quoted in Benjamin, 1995, p. 108). Fourth, few black people hold senior positions in broadcasting. Finally, there has been a decline in the output of black programming on mainstream media during the 1990s. Since the Broadcasting Act 1990 the search for large audiences has been relentless. Television programmes such as *Black on Black*, *Eastern Eye*, *Bandung File* and *Ebony* have been scrapped and replaced only in 1996 with BBC2's new series *Black Britain*. The BBC's Afro-Caribbean Unit at Pebble Mill in Birmingham has been closed and incorporated within the Asian Unit.

How are these very modest numbers of black journalists working in British media to be explained? One possible explanation identifies inadequate or insufficient education, but the educational attainments of respondents in Ainley's study were considerably higher than the journalistic average. The 100 journalists in the study shared 870 'O' levels, 302 'A' levels, 71 BA degrees, 15 MAs and 6 doctorates (Ainley, 1994, p. 35). But despite these academic achievements, only 47 of the 100 journalists were successful in winning a place on a recognised course of training for journalists. Course directors and trainers argue that black people do not apply for courses; black journalists cite discrimination. When the BBC announced an Afro-Caribbean and Asian Reporters Training Trust, however, the organisation received 900 applicants from black people for 6 places. The BBC's black trainee post production course attracted 1000 applicants for 12 places (Ainley, 1995, p. 100). Black journalists argue that racial discrimination explains their long-term and continuing under-representation in mainstream white media. There is certainly evidence to support such a view. In October 1996 a tribunal in Leeds heard the case of an Afro-Caribbean woman who was told by the manager in the advertising department at the Bradford *Telegraph and Argus* that she should expect to hear black staff occasionally called 'black bastards'; fortunately the tribunal believed such racism was unacceptable (Harcup, 1996, p. 13). It seems improbable that news media are able to offer any comprehensive appraisal of issues which articulates a genuine public interest when black voices are so silenced, absent from the debate and ghettoised in an alternative black media.

Hard women and soft stories: women, news and journalism

Male journalists' attitudes towards their women colleagues have too frequently been ambiguous and, at worst, downright unacceptable. Cecil King, for example, believed that 'an influx of women journalists, photographers and executives would give the national press a new look and a new lease of life', but he was also concerned that 'news reporting is a hard life for anyone and perhaps too hard for women' (quoted in Sebba, 1994, p. 236). Brian Hitchen offers a less reflective view about women journalists. 'Having more women reporters is not a good thing. They should stick to fashion and women's magazines. I am probably old fashioned but there are some things a woman shouldn't see, I don't like hard women and you certainly get hard in this job' (Pollard, 1995, p. 16). But in certain respects Fleet Street has taken him at his word; women journalists are less evident in national newspapers than in any other media sector, while the proportion of women 'working in news as opposed to periodical and other "soft" journalism is only 25 per cent'; less than their female colleagues in the USA (33.8 per cent) and Australia (33 per cent) (Delano and Hennington, 1995, p. 3). Hitchen's 'old-fashioned' world of news journalism is collapsing as the number of women journalists approaches 37 per cent of the profession and promises to outnumber male journalists within a decade (National Union of Journalists, 1994, p. 3).

But despite women's growing involvement in all sectors of journalism, their exclusion from three arenas is significant. First, women journalists are excluded from senior posts. A survey by the NUJ in 1984 revealed that the *Guardian* staff of 35 general news reporters contained only 9 women; there were 3 women news reporters at the *Mirror* out of a staff of 32; the *Sunday Times* contained a single woman journalist in the team of 9 general news reporters and 2 women journalists among 8 foreign news reporters. At the *Sun*, 3 of the 40 general news reporters were women; the newspapers' 55 sports staff were all male. The *Financial Times* employed 37 women from a total staff of 300 but only one woman held a managerial position above other journalists (NUJ Survey cited in Sebba, 1994, pp. 237–8). In the 1990s, women fare little better. A survey inquiring about the gender of those holding the posts of editor, deputy editor, foreign editor, political editor, business editor, news editor and sports editor on national broadsheet and tabloid newspapers revealed that the *Independent*, the *Independent on Sunday*, the *Guardian*, the *Sunday Telegraph*, *The Times*, the *Sunday Times* and the

Financial Times, employed women in none of these senior posts. The *Observer* employed a woman foreign editor and the *Telegraph* a news editor who interestingly was described as the 'home editor'. Of these 63 senior editorial jobs, 61 were held by men. In the tabloids the position of women is marginally better although the *Mirror*, *Mail On Sunday*, *Express* and *Daily Star* have men in all of these senior editorial positions; women hold 11 of the 75 editorial posts in the tabloid press (Dougary, 1994, pp. 115–20). Consequently, few women attend the crucial news and leader conferences which determine the structure and content of the news stories for the day. Of the 265 journalists attending news conferences in national newspapers, only 46 (21 per cent) are women. Only 9 of the 45 regular leader writers are women; 13 of the 68 national newspaper columnists are women (Women in Journalism, 1995). In broadcasting, too, men dominate the higher echelons of journalism and management; by 1994 only 16 per cent of those on the senior executive grade at the BBC were women (Bromley 1994, pp. 37–8). 'Women are so woefully under-represented in TV management' claimed Janet Street Porter, 'it makes me want to weep' (Street Porter, 1995, p. 2). The BBC aims to raise the number of women in senior management from 10 per cent to 30 per cent and in middle management from 18 per cent to 40 per cent; by 1996, 66 of the top 200 jobs should have been filled by women but the BBC's 1996 annual report reveals a considerable shortfall from these targets. After John Birt's 1996 restructuring of the BBC only two women (Margaret Salmon – Personnel – and Patricia Hodgson – Policy and Planning) held executive posts in the new structure, but neither is responsible for any oversight of broadcasting or journalism as Liz Forgan had been.

Women are allegedly reluctant to apply for senior positions. Some areas of journalism involve long working hours which are incompatible with family life and, on occasion, the need to drop everything and rush to cover events abroad. Such work regimes and anti-social hours perhaps explain the frequency of single women in journalism; more than half (53.5 per cent) remain single compared with 31 per cent of their male colleagues and 21 per cent of women in the general population (Delano and Hennington, 1995, p. 11). It might also explain why women, who account for 37 per cent of journalists overall, constitute more than 60 per cent of part-time journalists (National Union of Journalists, 1994, p. 27).

The second significant exclusion of women is from highly paid positions in journalism. Exceptions must always be noted. Pollard herself was an editor first at the *Sunday Mirror* and later the *Sunday Express*; editors can anticipate a salary in excess of £50,000 a year. But most women journalists can only aspire to, not achieve, such incomes. Inequalities between gender groups are evident. For men the median salary is £32,500, for women £22,500; men earn 44.4 per cent more than women. The NUJ report identifies a 'disproportionately high number of women in the lower earnings bands'; only 56 per cent of male journalists earn less than £25,000 a year compared to 72 per cent of women. The report also anticipates, 'a smaller number of women in the higher earnings band than would have been expected based on women comprising 37 per cent of the total sample' (National Union of Journalists, 1994, p. 6); 29 per cent of male journalists, but only 15 per cent of women journalists, earn in excess of £30,000 a year. Less than a fifth of journalists in the highest income band of more than £50,000 a year are women (ibid., p. 27).

Third, women are excluded from certain areas of journalism, especially the national press, and are disproportionately located in broadcasting. Women comprise 9 per cent of journalists working on national dailies, but 44 per cent of journalists in independent television, 38 per cent in independent radio and 37 per cent at the BBC. This 'ghettoising' of women in certain media sectors has consequences for their career prospects as well as their salaries. The median salary for journalists on national newspapers is £37,500 compared with only £27,500 in commercial television and radio and £17,500 in the provincial press (Delano and Hennington, 1995, p. 16). But material rewards seem incapable of offsetting what seem to women to be the substantial disincentives against working on national newspapers. Liz Forgan reminisces about her working life at the *Guardian*. 'Newspapers took women seriously more promptly than other media,' she claims, 'but the macho heavy-drinking, show-off, male culture is also very strong in newspapers. The daily banter was much more openly and crudely sexist than it was in television.' Even the *Guardian*'s women's page was not exempt. 'Guardian Women was a formidable force – a daily reminder – against all that, but it didn't stop some of the men . . . deliberately uttering sexist jokes in our hearing and expecting us to fall off our chairs' (Forgan, 1994, p. 69).

Perceptions of sexism are widespread and correspond closely to gender. Two thirds of women believe it is harder for capable women journalists to move ahead in their careers, with 60 per cent of women journalists claiming personal experience or knowledge of women being victims of prejudice in the newsroom; corresponding figures for men are 36 per cent and 31 per cent (Marks, 1995, p. 15). Interestingly, while newspapers give widespread coverage to stories and features about the various ways in which women are prevented from reaching the top of career ladders in other industries, there has been little consideration of unequal opportunities in their own backyards.

Newspaper editors: power without security

The recent turnover of editors on national newspapers has been quite remarkable. Eleven editors were appointed between 1993 and 1995; a further six took up their posts in 1992. Since 1991, 20 of the 21 editorial chairs in national newspapers have had new occupants. At some titles the changes have been rapid. The *Mirror,* for example, has had three editors (David Banks,

Colin Myler and currently Piers Morgan) since 1994. Some proprietors and chief executives display an evident enthusiasm for changing editors. Since David Montgomery's arrival at MGN (Mirror Group Newspapers) in 1992, there have been four editors at the *Daily Mirror*, three at the *People* and four at the *Sunday Mirror*. Montgomery has also overseen three changes of editor at the *Independent* and three at the *Independent on Sunday*; Peter Wilby was sacked on 8 October 1996. Lord Stevens has appointed four editors at the *Star*, five at the *Sunday Express* and three at the *Daily Express*. Mobility or, more accurately, insecurity has become a defining characteristic of the editor's job. It never used to be like this. It is sobering to recall that Peter Preston, who resigned as *Guardian* editor in 1995, had been in that post since 1975. His predecessor, Alastair Hetherington, was editor from 1956; two editors across 40 years. The consequences of the new rapid turnover in senior editorial posts for contemporary journalism is all too obvious. Short tenancy of the editorial chair and the constant change of occupants means that editors have no time to stamp any authority and style on their newspapers; continuity and development of editorial style is subverted.

But while life has become precarious for editors, there are perks. Editors constitute a journalistic elite. They form the 'above stairs' crowd in the increasingly upstairs downstairs world of journalism, separated from other journalists by their power, celebrity, salaries, education and other social indicators. These editors are often highly individualistic and flamboyant characters. In Tunstall's words:

> this journalistic elite work long hours each week. They wake with the BBC Today radio show; they return home to BBC's Newsnight at 10.30 pm, when some of them are still phoning back to the office to check late developments. They have a strong personal sense of successful achievement in a highly competitive occupation. Self confident and extrovert demeanours are not in short supply.
>
> (Tunstall, 1995, p. 59)

There is little similarity between those who occupy the editorial chair in national and provincial newspapers except their common title of 'editor'. An early ethnographic account of provincial newspaper editors makes the point:

> The most striking thing about these men [they always were men] was their homogeneity – they were local men, locally educated and locally recruited, trained and promoted . . . None had a stint on a national paper behind him and none had any formal higher education. War service apart, their working lives had been spent on Merseyside.
>
> (Cox and Morgan, 1973, p. 110)

This profile of the local editor has now been rendered anachronistic by graduate entry to journalism and the incorporation of the local press into conglomerate ownership, but even so the contemporary provincial editor is not necessarily a member of the editorial elite.

Editors in the national press are set apart from their journalistic colleagues by education, age, salary and editorial power. Of the 20 editors of national newspapers in 1995, 11 had attended public schools; for the broadsheet press the figure was 6 out of 9. Eleven editors were graduates; seven had attended Oxbridge colleges. Again the figures are distinctive for the broadsheets; all nine editors were graduates and six of the nine went to Oxbridge (Bromley, 1994, p. 17). Editors' educational attainments, moreover, have increased dramatically over the last decade. In 1985 only three broadsheet editors boasted a public-school education, with seven public-school boys overall. Similarly, only six editors were graduates and a mere three graduated from Oxbridge. A university education, ideally at Oxbridge, seems increasingly to be a precondition for editing in the national press.

Editors are, perhaps predictably, older than other journalists. In 1995, the average age of editors was 45 (44 for broadsheets); an average undoubtedly reduced by such precocious editorial talents as Piers Morgan and Alan Rusbridger. But there are fewer signs of greying editorial temples than used to be evident. The average age of editors has fallen sharply. In 1985, three editors were over 60 and the average editorial age was 50 (52 for broadsheets).

Most editors of national papers, rather like university professors, negotiate a personal salary package; the rewards for the modern editor go beyond any agreed national pay scale. The NUJ survey offers the only guide to editorial salaries. Earnings of above £50,000 a year are given for 3 per cent of editors, while a further 3 per cent earn between £45,000 and £49,000. These data clearly relate to national editors. Other survey data for editorial salaries more probably relate to editors within the provincial press; these findings reveal that one in three editors earns £30,000 and above while just less than half earn between £15,000 and £25,000 a year. More than one in ten earn less than £15,000 a year (National Union of Journalists, 1994, p. 24). These figures suggest a broad range of incomes but serve to underscore the divisions within contemporary journalism between national and local editors and between editors and other journalists in both local and national contexts. But they also highlight the complexities of salary and status structures. With one in ten editors earning less than £15,000 a year, it is clear that being a reporter on a national paper might offer considerably greater salary, if not status prospects, than occupancy of an editorial chair on a 'local rag'.

It is the power of editors which sets them apart from other journalists. At a time when they are increasingly held accountable by proprietors for the fortunes of their papers, editors are demanding greater editorial control. They are properly judged to be influential figures. Hetherington, for example, considered his leaders to be dialogues with decision-makers: they were placed on Harold Wilson's desk and on J.F. Kennedy's, as Scott's had been on Lloyd George's' (Taylor, 1993, p. x). Editors are courted by politicians. At a time when politics and politicians are increasingly packaged for public consumption and when research has shown that the support of the newspapers is crucial to electoral outcomes, such overtures to editors seem inevitable (Linton, 1995). Editors have become powerful players in political life; some assert their influence in vulgar headlines such as 'It's The Sun Wot Won It'. The comparison with ordinary journalists is striking: *their* influence has never been more modest. But there is another irony here. Editors have perhaps never been so vulnerable to proprietorial influence and power.

The new recruits

The new entrants to journalism are better educated, increasingly drawn from middle-class backgrounds and are more likely to be women than a decade ago. One constant feature in this changing scene is the continuing significance of the local and regional press as the provider of 'on the job' training for new journalists: 65 per cent of new entrants will begin their careers in the provincial press (Delano and Hennington, 1995, p. 16). But new recruits confront unprecedented difficulties concerning pay and initial training. The pay for journalism has traditionally been poor but is becoming increasingly impoverished. In 1900 the pay for a provincial journalist was around £1 for a 60- to 70-hour week, but by 1921 price inflation meant that the wages of £4.7 shillings and 6 pence for weeklies and £5.15 shillings for dailies, represented a considerable pay cut; salaries should have been 16 guineas by 1900 levels. Salaries fell sharply again after the second world war (Strick, 1957, pp. 473–4). But during the 1980s and 1990s, increasing competition for jobs in a dwindling market, the reduction of newsroom staffs, combined with the derecognition of the NUJ, have undermined any agreed scale of pay and conditions for those entering journalism. Four out of five trainee journalists earn less than £10,000 a year – and occasionally pay is considerably below this level. Low pay, long hours and high educational entry conditions prompt feelings of being exploited. Disenchantment sets in early, with trainees contemplating leaving newspaper journalism, even at this very early stage in their careers, seduced by the better salaries and conditions of service available in public relations and journalism in other sectors of the industry. 'Young journalists will continue to leave in droves for PR, broadcasting etc,' a trainee claimed, 'rather than work in understaffed sweatshops for little pay' (Guild of Editors, 1995, p. 5).

Other problems new entrants must confront arise from the industry's growing uncertainties about what constitutes an appropriate training for journalists. Two thirds of journalists receive some kind of in-house training with a media organisation or undertake the National Council of Training for Journalism (NCTJ) course, but surprisingly few (40 per cent) held the NCTJ qualification. Virtually no journalist is interested in the National Vocational Qualification, with only 3 per cent holding or studying for one (Delano and Hennington, 1995, p. 15). Many new journalists believe they receive inadequate training prior to entry to the profession. Insufficient training in newsroom operations and feature writing as well as inadequate preparation for tribunal and court reporting are mentioned in a recent survey of training needs. Many journalists, moreover, had little understanding of matters such as newspaper circulation, advertising sales and marketing. In all, only two thirds of journalists believed their training had been unsatisfactory; a quarter believed it had not (Guild of Editors, 1995, p. 4).

Editors disagree with trainees concerning the crucial elements in a journalistic training programme, with less than 2 per cent believing that an understanding of journalism history was essential; two thirds of trainees disagreed. Editors split almost evenly about whether shorthand remains an essential tool for journalists. It is undoubtedly a telling indictment of the pedestrian and uncritical grind which much of the new journalism has become, that editors listed the ability to rewrite handouts as the most essential competence required of trainees after six months (Guild of Editors, 1995, p. 7). Many editors seem hostile to the middle-class graduates entering journalism, preferring the 'streetwise council-estate youngsters': 'working class recruits with local knowledge' (Sands, 1996, p. 16). Some editors still display the anti-intellectualism noted by an early study of journalism published in 1923.

> There is always with newspaper editors a quite understandable prejudice against engaging a man – no matter how brilliant his mental attainments – who is more or less matured . . . It is difficult to train a man who looks at everything from the academic standpoint . . . In the majority of cases therefore, it would seem that a university education is not only *not* an advantage; more often than not it is a positive drawback.
>
> (Warren, 1923, p. 22; emphasis in the original)

A major complaint of trainees is that editors do not seem to attach too great a significance to any form of training. Journalists are born, not made. Alastair Hetherington recalls the comment of an old friend who was a deputy editor of BBC news: 'it's like riding a bike; if you stop to think about it you'll fall off' (Hetherington, 1985, p. viii). A trainee claimed:

> Training is no longer valued by editors across the country in the belt-tightening 90s. We fear it will become obsolete as the NCTJ is dismantled and inadequate replacements put forward. A junior with five years experience on £6K makes more sense to newspaper owners than an employee who completes the NCE test in two years and expects £10K.
>
> (Quoted in Guild of Editors, 1995, p. 4)

The final concern about training relates to funding. Most young journalists finance their training by drawing on personal resources or borrowing from family; both methods guarantee that most start their working life repaying a substantial debt.

Entertainers as well as adversaries: journalists' attitudes to their work

Changes in the profession of journalism as well as the media in which it is conducted have been considerable across the last decade. But the impact of many of these changes on journalists' perceptions of their work has not been as substantial as might have been anticipated. Journalists continue to be motivated by the highest professional commitment despite the rather routine nature of much of the daily practice of journalism. There is still a whiff of idealism and romanticism about their perceptions: journalism continues to be seen as a central mechanism of accountability in a modern democracy.

Two significant changes in journalistic attitudes are noteworthy. First, by 1995, journalists were placing a much greater emphasis on journalism as a provider of entertainment with the great majority accepting that the provision of entertainment and relaxation is a very (47 per cent) or fairly (44 per cent) important function of media. Second, only about half of journalists consider it to be appropriate for the media to adopt the role of public adversary, constantly sceptical of officials (51 per cent) or businesses (45 per cent). These are important shifts in journalists' perceptions of their work which find clear expression in the editorial content of more recent journalism.

There is a final aspect of journalists' perceptions of their task which warrants examination: their many concerns about the way their occupation is organised and practised. Most journalists believe the degree of media freedom in the UK is high (42 per cent) or medium (39 per cent), but nearly half (49 per cent) believe that media freedom is decreasing. The same proportion believe that standards of journalism have declined during their working life. Many journalists disparage the tabloid press; only 1 per cent believe that the *Mirror* serves its readers well. Journalists are strongly opposed to increased concentration of media ownership. More than three quarters (77 per cent) wish the government to prevent further concentration within newspapers, with figures for radio and television (including cable and satellite) rising to 80 per cent; 51 per cent support controls on cross-media ownership. The July 1995 white paper on privacy which rejected the need for privacy legislation did not find universal favour with journalists. One in four (26 per cent) believe that a privacy law would be justified and 36 per cent believe that certain circumstances would warrant a privacy law. The high principles surviving among journalists leave room for optimism. Many entrants to the profession are highly motivated and are inspired by the ideals of their predecessors, although they understand the market imperative to entertain as well as inform. The expectations of their seniors may be that they will perform as clerks, but in their hearts they are often still crusaders. There remains some hope that newszak may be ousted by a more vital and investigative journalism.

PART

III

NEWS MEDIA

4

Read all about it

A history of the British press

A debee concer⬛⬛⬛⬛⬛⬛⬛⬛⬛⬛⬛⬛⬛⬛d the quality of print journalism has rage⬛⬛⬛⬛⬛⬛⬛⬛⬛⬛ntensity of the debate has increased with ⬛⬛⬛⬛⬛⬛⬛⬛gy and the prospect of the electronic news⬛⬛⬛⬛⬛⬛⬛⬛⬛⬛nal newspapers have been foundering since the end of the second ⬛⬛⬛ar. Newspapers' readers are ageing, their advertising revenues are declining, their circulations are dwindling and the number of published titles is diminishing; and at a rate! Television, especially since the arrival of teletext, has subverted newspapers' mission to provide a readily accessible news service; it has also stolen some of their best journalists, many of their younger readers as well as readers from lower social class groups. Local cable television and radio services are even stealing local newspapers' most valuable and enduring asset: their unashamed parochialism. Twenty-four-hour news services like CNN, SkyNews and BBC Radio 5, as well as on-line computer news services, deliver news with such speed and regularity that much of the content of newspapers is effectively redundant even before it is printed. Virtually everything that newspapers provide, information and entertainment, is now offered more readily, cheaply, efficiently and interestingly by some other news medium. The demise of newspapers seems inevitable.

Optimists counter that newspapers continue to be a constant feature of the rapidly changing media landscape, despite the fact that their demise has been predicted for almost as long as they have been in existence. Newspapers enjoy obvious advantages above other media. They are silent, highly portable and require neither batteries nor arcane commands for readers to enjoy their contents; newspapers don't catch viruses, crash, flicker or stray off station! They can be stored and readily retrieved to be consumed over a period of time, in small easily digestible bites; they are the only news medium to allow consumers autonomy and control over the rate of consumption. In this respect at least, newspapers are about personal freedom and choice. At their best newspapers are informative, stimulating and entertaining; on occasion investigative and even fearless in their reporting of events and their advocacy of causes.

But newspapers fail to satisfy the whimsical, media fads of the 1990s. Their qualities are not encapsulated by the currently voguish and computer-derived buzzwords; they are relentlessly one-way, passive and non-interactive – apart from letters to the editor! Much of the pessimists' argument can be sustained, but a good case is spoiled by exaggeration. Pundits wax eloquent, for example, about the imminent prospect of people programming computers at bedtime (much like they currently set their alarm) to construct a personalised 'mix and match' newspaper incorporating their favoured elements of editorial – perhaps the letters page from *The Times*, Matthew Parris's parliamentary sketch, Steve Bell's cartoon and the sports pages from the *Sun* – to be printed off while they sleep ready for them to read in the morning. But life without newspapers seems unthinkable; the brave new world of the electronic newspaper, such a clear vision for the precocious trend spotter, seems both undesirable and incredible. Technological feasibility is only part of the story and the pundits' enthusiasm too frequently ignores the ability of culture, politics, history and institutions to deflect, modify or obstruct the course of technological change. A MORI (Marketing and Organisational Research Institute) survey in 1996, for example, revealed that a mere 9 per cent of respondents used the internet regularly (Millar, 1996, p. 10). A host of additional cultural factors mitigate against the prospect of an electronic press. Newspaper boys and girls will be consigned to history. Breakfast times will be transformed: the clutter of marmalade pots, muesli, toast and tea cups on the kitchen table will need to make way for the family computer(s?) so that everyone can read their personalised selection of news. The cries of newspaper sellers will disappear from city streets, while university researchers will begin 'looking at the possibility of setting up multimedia kiosks in newsagents' (*Press Gazette,* 29 March 1996, p. 9).

The electronic newspaper must resolve fundamental problems, moreover, before it can become a reality. An obvious difficulty is what to call such a publication; there would be no reason to describe it as a newspaper since there would be no paper involved. How would such a publication generate revenues? How would people buy it? How would it earn crucial advertising revenues and at what levels? Why should advertisers pay for space in such publications without knowledge about the size, socio-economic status and demography of readerships? These 'newspapers' would certainly require clicking traps with delays so that advertisers could be guaranteed that readers would consult the advertisements rather than only flitting between news stories. Other problems concern distribution as well as issues arising from copyright and author royalties in the context of a 'mix and match' electronic newspaper.

The arrival of the electronic newspaper has undoubtedly been over-hyped; real newspapers will survive for a number of reasons. First, consumer loyalty and inertia is central to newspaper sales. It is precisely the organisational and informational predictability of newspapers which is their great marketing strength. Readers like to know that they can always find the TV listings, the weather or their horoscope by turning to a particular page; they like to know the day on which their favourite journalist's column will appear on a certain page. Second, the explosion of new media may create a greater need for what the best newspapers have always offered: quality journalism which helps form public opinion and sets an agenda for discussions of public policy. Third, newspapers retain their traditional advantage over electronic media: space. This provides the scope to discuss in much greater detail issues addressed more superficially in television and radio news. Finally, the personalised selection of news and entertainment offered by mix and match publications might be characterised more negatively as merely self-indulgent, allowing individuals to nurture their own narrow interests and viewpoints. To offer an increasingly unfashionable public-service viewpoint, there may be truths about the world which we need to know no matter how distasteful and unpalatable; informing us of these has always been one of the roles assumed by serious journalists and quality newspapers.

British newspapers are not confronting any imminent demise, but they undoubtedly face an uncertain future which, like their recent past, will be characterised by significant change. This chapter briefly outlines the history and development of the British national and local press and considers the extent to which it is characterised by diversity.

Yesterday's news: a brief history of British newspapers

Three persistent features characterise the development of British newspapers. First, from their inception, newspapers have been involved in a struggle for press freedom; the struggle has assumed different forms and been more or less intense at different stages in press history. The significant milestones on the road to press freedom, according to conventional wisdom, are the abolition of the Court of Star Chamber in 1641; Fox's Libel Act, 1792; and the repeal of the notorious 'taxes on knowledge' – a series of government-imposed fiscal measures designed to restrict the ownership, control and readership of newspapers. The political struggle has been accompanied by the press's economic struggle to secure the financial independence necessary to guarantee editorial autonomy. The outcome of this struggle is hotly disputed. Press historians like Asquith (1978) and Koss (1984) argue that newspapers owe their economic independence, and hence their achievement of editorial freedom, to the expansion of advertising revenues since the middle of the eighteenth century. On this view, advertising has been the 'midwife of press independence' (Curran and Seaton, 1988, p. 10) and a capitalist free market the indispensable prerequisite for a free press. But Curran wishes to stand this analysis 'on its head' (ibid., p. 9) by suggesting that the expanding market system was antipathetic to press freedom. Curran argues that 'market forces succeeded where legal repression had failed in conscripting the press to the social order' (ibid., p. 9). The need to produce newspapers in compliance with the demands of a competitive market means merely that the tyranny of the market in the twentieth century has replaced the state controls and the patronage of political parties which dominated press content in the nineteenth century; in this way, 'the swords of one generation become the fetters of the next' (Lee, 1976, p. 105).

Second, newspapers have always suffered a certain schizophrenia concerning their primary purposes and objectives (ibid., p. 76). Macaulay, for example, believed the press to be a fourth estate. Proprietorship of a newspaper was a form of public service and journalism had a distinctive role to inform public opinion and debate on the key issues of the day. In the rather euphuistic phrase of one observer, the press is 'a weapon of freedom, a sword in the hands of those fighting old and new tyrannies' (Williams, 1957, pp. 5–6). A different, more prosaic conception has understood the press as an industry in which proprietors are business people and journalism is seen as a trade or a craft (Lee, 1978, p. 118). This perception of the press as an industry has typically stressed the need for newspapers to entertain as well as inform. On this view, the press has always provided a 'medium for satisfying the human appetite for gossip', while the journalist has 'traditionally been an entertainer; he must entertain or find another trade' (Williams, 1957, p10). The history of the British press, since the emergence of popular journalism and the establishment of newspapers like Harmsworth's *Daily Mail* (1896) and the *News of the World* (1843), has been a history of newspapers increasingly shifting its editorial emphasis towards entertainment.

Third, as Engel notes, the history of newspapers reflects a broader history: nothing less than the 'history of the last hundred years in Britain' (Engel, 1996b, p. 17). This is not only because the press is a significant chronicler of events. Engel's claim is based on the fact that newspapers' popularity reflects their attraction for certain sections and social groupings in society and their ability to capture and articulate the interests and aspirations of those groups. The shifting popularity of particular newspapers is a barometer of the changing fortunes of specific social groups. *The Times* was the best seller from the Napoleonic era until 1855, when it was supplanted by the *Daily Telegraph* which appealed to the middle classes. In 1896, the *Telegraph* was overtaken by the popular *Daily Mail* which, in turn, was superseded by the *Daily Express*, then the *Daily Mirror* and finally the *Sun* (ibid., p. 17). Each stage of succession, moreover, signals journalistic as well as social change, with newspapers increasingly likely to 'undercut' the standards of their best-selling predecessor and conform to the spirit of the nineteenth-century anonymous verse:

Tickle the public, make 'em grin
The more you tickle the more you'll win;
Teach the public, you'll never get rich
You'll live like a beggar and live in a ditch.

(quoted in ibid.)

The early precursors

Identifying the origins of newspapers has always prompted controversy.
The earliest ancestor of the modern newspaper can be traced to the daily
reports of events published by the Romans which Seneca described as the
Acta Diurna. They were issued on the authority of the government and
posted in central locations so their news content was readily accessible to
citizens. They were sufficiently widely read and popular to have their style
parodied by Petronius in his *Satyrica*. The writers (*actuarii*) seem to have
developed and been skilled in some form of shorthand since their reports
occasionally included accounts of proceedings in the Senate and the courts
of law. Dr Johnson recorded some examples of these daily news sheets in the
Gentleman's Magazine for 1740, which reveal what might be considered
untypically Roman activities but useful grist to the journalistic mill.

> Thus we have reports of an assault case before the Magistrates – of a
> brawl at the Hog-in-Armour Tavern, in Banker's Street – of a thun-
> derstorm – of a fire on Mount Coelius – of the funeral of Marcia –
> and other everyday occurrences, which curiously remind us that the
> Romans were but men; Marcus Fuscus and Lucius Albus were brought
> up to the police court for being drunk and disorderly and Titus Lanius
> was fined for giving short weight.

(Andrews, 1859, vol. 1, p. 9)

The *Acta Diurna* ceased publication with the death of Caesar. Because they
were produced in manuscript rather than printed (the Romans of course did
not possess printing presses), the *Acta Diurna* have not been universally
accepted as the earliest newspapers, but their concern with news and its
periodic publication seems sufficient to establish Rome as the birthplace of
journalism (Frank, 1961, p. 1).

Another precursor of the modern newspaper, 'the first modern sheet of
news', which made its appearance in Venice in 1536, was intended initially
to inform the Venetians about the progress of the war with Turkey. It was
again in manuscript, appeared monthly and was read aloud in central parts
of the city. Later editions of this *Gazzetta* were printed and extended their
news content beyond the narrow concerns of war reporting. Although relatively insignificant in terms of size, influence and informational content, the
Gazzetta or *Gazette* has become a commonplace name for newspapers.

Originally the name *Gazzetta* was thought to have derived from the Italian word *gazza* or *gazzara*, meaning a magpie or chatterer, but it is more likely a derivative of the word *gazzetta* meaning a coin, worth somewhere between a farthing and an old halfpenny, which was the price of the paper or the fee paid for reading the sheet of manuscript (Williams, 1908, p. 3). The *Shorter Oxford English Dictionary* entry claims 'Venetian *Gazeta* de la novita, quasi "a ha'porth of news" so called because sold for a gazetta, Venetian coin of small value; a news sheet; a periodic publication giving an account of current events' (*Shorter Oxford English Dictionary*, 1978, vol. 1, p. 837).

There were other forerunners to the modern press. From the beginning of the sixteenth century, printed pamphlets giving news of particular events of interest to readers were distributed. In 1513, for example, an early news book giving 'The Trewe Encounter' of the battle of Flodden Field was published. Approximately 450 of these books were published between 1590 and 1610 (Carter, 1971, p. 28). By the early 1620s, the first small, single-sheet weekly newspapers, illustrated occasionally with woodcuts, were published. The access of the majority of poor people to these emergent publications was restricted by government censorship and their inability to pay. They relied on the ballads and broadsheets which were sung and sold very cheaply in the streets. Ballads were a major source of news for the emergent working classes and 'were the precursors of a later era's sensational newspapers: never was a celebrated highwayman executed or a catastrophe visited upon a hapless town but the event was described in crude language and cruder woodcuts' (Altick, 1957, p. 28). Governments made every effort to kill the new medium at birth. Restrictions on the press throughout the seventeenth century prompted Milton's classic defence of press freedom in *Areopagitica* (1644), in which he argued that censorship discredited governments and demoralised the people. Motivated more by political expediency than rational discussion, the government enacted the Licensing Act in 1662 to prevent the publication of 'seditious, treasonable and unlicensed books and pamphlets'. The Act remained in force until 1695 when parliament refused to renew it (Carter, 1971, p. 29).

The development of the daily, Sunday, provincial and radical press

In the new mood of press freedom, the first daily newspaper was published at Ludgate Hill on 11 March 1702. The *Daily Courant* offered readers a digest of news extracts culled from various continental newspapers. The 'news' was hardly new; some items in the first issue were 17 days old. It cost a penny (Black, 1991, p. 12). The *Courant's* editorial philosophy was unambitious. The paper made 'no pretence of private intelligence' and expressed its determination to offer factual news without any editorial spin. In an

'Advertisement' in its launch issue, the editor announced that he would not 'take it upon himself to give any comments or conjectures of his own', preferring to 'relate only matters of fact; supposing other people to have sense enough to make reflections for themselves' (Williams, 1957, p. 14). The commitment to distinguish news and opinion was undoubtedly laudable but made the newspaper a rather dull read. The *Daily Courant* traded in second-hand news and eschewed opinion; the paper 'took no risks with this new liberty'. Others were less reticent. The literary, social and political periodicals like Daniel Defoe's *Review* (1704), the *Tatler* (1709) and *Spectator* (1711), both established by Joseph Addison and Richard Steele, heralded a 'golden dawn' for the press and journalism; the press now 'had giants to write for it' (ibid.). There were also significant issues to report. Defoe's *Review*, which he drafted in its entirety by himself, was published initially as a weekly, then twice weekly and eventually three times weekly. It contained articles on political, commercial and social matters. His essays were detailed in content and moderate in style, seeking to persuade rather than convert. He established a 'tradition of responsible popular reporting'. 'If any man was to ask me', he said, 'what I would suppose to be a perfect style of language, I would answer, that in which a man speaking to five hundred people of all common and various capacities, idiots or lunatics excepted, should be understood by them all' (ibid., p. 18). Publication of the *Review* ceased when Defoe was imprisoned in 1712 for publishing a satirical pamphlet. Similar journals, including the *Gentleman's Magazine* (1731) which contained parliamentary 'reports' reconstructed from Dr Johnson's recollections and minimal evidence, began to appear throughout the eighteenth century.

Four other significant developments in press history occurred during the eighteenth century. First, daily newspapers such as the *Morning Chronicle* (1769) and the *Morning Post* (1772) were beginning to win considerable middle-class readerships. Undoubtedly the most significant development was the establishment of *The Times* in 1788. In 1784, John Walter bought the King's Printing House and began publishing the *Daily Universal Register* which changed its name to *The Times* in January 1788. Throughout its history *The Times* pioneered new print technologies, employing the first steam printing press in 1814 and a new rotary press in 1848. The newspaper's emphasis on foreign news, its nationwide reporting of domestic news combined with the strong editorial views expressed by fiery editors such as Thomas Barnes and John Delane attracted high readerships and earned the paper the nickname 'The Thunderer' (ibid., p. 7). *The Times*'s circulation figures were substantially higher than any metropolitan competitor, rising from 3000 in 1801 to almost 60,000 in 1855 (Carter, 1971, p. 32). It dominated metropolitan journalism and 'more than any other paper . . . captured the voice of respectable reform opposing the government on Peterloo' (Golding, 1974, p. 25).

Second, the first Sunday newspapers made their appearance towards the end of the seventeenth century. The *Observer* (1791), *Bell's Weekly Messenger* (1796) and the *Weekly Dispatch* (1801) were followed by the *Sunday Times* (1822) and the *News of the World* (1843) (Williams, 1957, p. 13). From the outset, there was evidence of the diet of crime stories, sexual gossip and lightweight news which has subsequently become the Sunday newspapers' trademark (Hall, 1967, pp. 68–9). As Raymond Williams observed, 'No lion of the new journalism would have had anything to teach eighteenth century journalists in the matter of crudeness and vulgarity' (Williams, 1965, p. 219). The papers carried so little news that many were exempted from stamp duties, making them relatively cheap. They sold widely in coffee-houses, pubs and clubs and their circulations quickly overtook those of the daily newspapers and have subsequently remained ahead. By 1850 the aggregate Sunday circulation was in excess of a quarter of a million with the *News of the World* and *Lloyds Weekly News* selling almost 100,000 copies weekly (Golding, 1974, pp. 25–6, Carter, 1971, p. 33, Cranfield, 1978, p. 204).

Third, the provincial press began to emerge at the beginning of the eighteenth century; its history has been largely neglected and where investigated, largely misunderstood (Cranfield, 1962, p. v). In 1700 no provincial newspapers were published but by 1760 the local newspaper was firmly established as part of provincial life: 130 newspapers were published, together with a number of literary magazines and periodicals. Small, badly printed and primitive in design and content, these newspapers survived the various attempts of a hostile government to undermine them. Paradoxically, the provincial press contained little local news and was unashamedly derivative of the London newspapers. The local paper was local only in the sense that it was published locally. As a weekly press, its purpose was to amuse as much as to inform. Contemporary assessments of provincial journalism were harsh. The *New Monthly* claimed

> there was scarcely a single provincial journalist who could have hazarded an original article on public affairs. Their comments were confined to events in their own towns and districts so sparingly administered, with such obvious distrust of their own ability, and with such cautious timidity, that they were absolutely of no account. The London papers, a pot of paste and a pair of scissors supplied all the materials for the miscellaneous articles . . . the provincial journalist of that day was in fact not much above a mechanic . . . and intellect had as little as possible to do with it.
>
> (quoted in Cranfield, 1978, p. 179)

Despite these judgements, circulations rose steadily. In July 1739 the first issue of the *Newcastle Journal* sold 2000 copies while the *York Chronicle* enjoyed a circulation of between 1900 and 2500. But readerships were substantially higher; Cranfield estimates as many as 20 readers for each copy sold (Cranfield, 1962, p. v). The provincial press really came of age in the nineteenth century. The growth in published titles was considerable. In 1832 there were 23 local weekly papers in Lancashire and 20 in Yorkshire; by 1854 there were 33 and 31 respectively. By 1854 there were 290 provincial newspapers with 5 in Manchester and 12 in Liverpool alone. The *Manchester Guardian*, founded as a weekly in 1821 by a group of Manchester radicals, enjoyed the highest circulation of the provincial newspapers, selling 8000 copies in 1842 (Asquith, 1978, pp. 117–30).

Fourth, in the late stages of the eighteenth century, in the wake of the French revolution, a radical press began to emerge which targeted the urban-based working labourers and articulated the concerns of this new social class for social reform and justice. William Cobbett's *Political Register*, Thomas Wooler's *Black Dwarf* and Henry Hetherington's *Poor Man's Guardian* exemplified the style of these radical new papers. Government alarm at the content of these papers was evident in the mood of anti-jacobinism it sponsored and the enactment of the notorious Six Acts of 1819, described as the 'high water mark of legislation restricting the freedom of the press' (Aspinall, 1973, p. 59). Passed from hand to hand, read in public houses and even to crowds in the open air, these radical papers with their hard-hitting political rhetoric reached an enormous public. Reading the papers aloud in public houses guaranteed that the political message reached many who were unable to read. Cobbett suggests the newspapers were more popular than the beer. 'Ask any landlord why he takes the newspapers,' Cobbett claimed, 'and he will tell you that it attracts people to his house; and in many ways its attractions are much stronger than those of the liquor there drunk. Thousands upon thousands of men have become sots through the attractions [of these papers]' (quoted in Cranfield, 1978, p. 89). Cobbett established an ingenious and extensive system of nationwide distribution to ensure the widest possible access to the *Political Register* (Aspinall, 1973, pp. 28–9). The sales of 40–50,000 were quite remarkable given the efforts of government – including the fining, flogging and imprisonment of some of those who sold the paper – to restrict circulation (Williams, 1957, pp. 67–70, Aspinall, 1973, p. 46).

Taxes on knowledge and the birth of popular journalism

Throughout the eighteenth century, expansion of advertising revenues and developments in postal services which aided the distribution of newspapers and the collection of up-to-date news, prompted a fair growth in the number and range of British newspapers. But the extent of expansion should not be overstated. In the early part of the nineteenth century few newspapers enjoyed circulations in excess of 5000 copies, most were still produced on a barely post-Caxton technology which made larger print runs impossible, while the price of newspapers, inflated by government-imposed stamp duties, placed them beyond the reach of the greater part of the public.

Developments during the nineteenth century were crucial to the emergence of the modern mass-readership newspapers. Undoubtedly the most necessary change was the removal of what opponents dubbed the 'taxes on knowledge'. The advertising duties which taxed all newspaper advertisements were abolished in 1853, the newspaper stamp duty which imposed a fixed levy on each copy of all newspapers sold was withdrawn in 1855, while the paper duties which taxed the paper on which the news was printed, were repealed in 1861 (Weiner, 1969, p. xi). The rigorous policing of the stamp duty had proved especially effective in constraining the growth of the radical press. The government increased the duty by 266 per cent between 1789 and 1815 and prosecuted 1130 cases of selling unstamped newspapers in London alone between 1830 and 1836 (Curran and Seaton, 1988, p. 11). The significance of the ending of these fiscal restrictions on press expansion was both political and economic. Their removal opened the door 'not only to the establishment of a 'free' press, but also to that of a cheap one' (Lee, 1978, p. 117). The prospect of cheap newspapers triggered predictable opposition from the established newspapers. The manager of *The Times* claimed it was desirable 'to confine the newspaper press as much as possible in the hands of a few persons with large capitals' (quoted in ibid.) – a view reflecting Lord Castlereagh's earlier observation that 'persons exercising the power of the press should be men of some respectability and property' (Hansard, vol. 91, col. 1177). The Provincial Newspaper Society, motivated by similar commercial concerns, argued that cheap newspapers would reduce standards and undermine the 'gentlemanly' status of the proprietors (Lee, 1978, p. 117). But the repeal of the taxes on knowledge provided only the necessary but not sufficient conditions for the development of mass-circulation newspapers. They created the possibility, however, to exploit the 'awesome potential of both technological change and expanding markets' (ibid., p. 118).

Technological changes were substantial. The new printing presses, compositing machines and 'linotype' machines, in combination with the reduced costs of paper and unrestricted advertising, prompted expansive circulations, which generated ever larger advertising revenues, lower unit production costs and incentives towards even larger circulations (Nevett, 1986, p. 149). A benign spiral of expansion was quickly established. Other technological changes supported such growth. The expansion of the railways assisted distribution while the development of the electric telegraph in the 1840s reduced the reliance of the provincial newspapers on the metropolitan press for national and foreign news and 'virtually created the evening press of the provinces' (Lee, 1978, p. 119). The establishment of a press agency by Julius Reuter in 1851, followed by the Press Association in 1868, confirmed the provincial press's ready access to national and international news stories.

These changes were complemented and reinforced by an expanding market. Rapid growth in population and the process of urbanisation, increasing material prosperity and the increase and spread of literacy, combined to provide fertile terrain for the British press. Golding believes the development of British newspapers owes more to these broader economic factors than 'the romantic deeds of individual journalists and owners'. He cites Cecil King with approval:

> The form which the popular press has taken, of popular national newspapers dominating the market, was created largely by circumstances over which newspaper owners had little or no control; by the shape of the country and its railway system; by the existence of huge concentrated populations in a handful of linked towns; by the dominance of London over the provinces; and by the advanced structure of British business, which sought a national market for branded goods and needed a national press for its sales campaigns.
>
> (Golding, 1974, pp. 23–4).

The success of the *Daily Telegraph*, established by Joseph Levy on the day that stamp duty ended in 1855, was portentous of these changes. Marketed as the 'paper of the man on the knifeboard of the omnibus' and initially priced at 2d, the newspaper made a conscious appeal to the ambitions of the new but ascendant Victorian lower middle class (ibid., p. 26). The *Daily Telegraph* was an immediate success. It cut its cover price to 1d, and adopted a lighter style of journalism than *The Times*. 'What we want is a human note,' Levy told his staff. While the paper did report foreign and domestic news, politics was not assumed to be the sole interest of the readers. The news was reported in a dramatic, lively and colloquial style and the paper adopted the typographical and photographic techniques of the American press which Matthew Arnold characterised as the 'new journalism': the use of headlines and interviews, sports news and less politics (Lee, 1976, p. 125, Cranfield, 1978, p. 207). The paper ran 'spirited crusades' which made lively reading. The description of the members of the Tractarian Movement as 'the little finicking man milliners who duck and bob before crucifixes' was typical. Politicians remained predictable targets. The House of Lords was caricatured as 'the chartered lords of misrule ogling in the ancient face of bigotry', while Disraeli was denounced as a 'windbag of surfeited acrimony and undigested sophisms' (Cranfield, 1978, p. 208). Within six years, sales of the newspaper were twice those achieved by *The Times*. Circulation grew from 27,000 in January 1856 to 141,700 in 1860 and 191,000 by 1871; it reached a quarter of a million by 1880. The *Daily Telegraph* dominated the British press for the next 30 years and Levy claimed 'the largest circulation in the world' (ibid., p. 207). Expansion was not confined to the *Daily Telegraph*. In 1850, 60,000 morning papers were published in London each day; by 1860 that figure had trebled. Between 1866 and 1914, more than 500 periodicals for children alone were published (Dixon, 1986, p. 133).

The progenitor of truly popular journalism and mass-circulation newspapers is generally recognised to be Alfred Harmsworth (later Lord Northcliffe), assisted by his brother Harold (later Lord Rothermere). In 1986 he launched a new morning newspaper, the *Daily Mail*, priced at 1d. The paper styled itself 'The Busy Man's Daily Journal' and offered readers coverage of the day's events in articles which were well focused and succinct. Editorial coverage was wide-ranging, embracing sport, gossip, a serialised story, features for women, politics and even stock exchange prices. The paper's success was unprecedented. The first edition sold more than a third of a million copies; by 1900 the circulation was almost a million. In 1903 Harmsworth launched the *Daily Mirror,* a paper for women selling at 1d. It became the first paper to achieve a circulation of 1 million copies. When he visited America in 1900, Harmsworth accepted a challenge by Joseph Pulitzer, the proprietor of *The World*, to take editorial control of the paper for one day, 'remodelling it in the light of his ideas of newspaper development in the twentieth century' (Pound and Harmsworth, 1959, p. 266). Harmsworth reduced the size of the newspaper, cut back on illustrations and insisted on 'no story of more than two hundred and fifty words'. On 1 January 1901, the New York edition of *The World* proclaimed itself 'The Busy Man's Paper'. In his editorial, Harmsworth claimed: '*The World* enters today upon the twentieth or Time-saving century. I claim that by my system of condensed or tabloid journalism hundreds of working hours can be saved each year. By glancing down the subjoined list of contents and following the arrangement of the pages the outline of today's news can be gathered in sixty seconds' (ibid., p. 267).

It was not only the editorial content of Harmsworth's papers and their revolutionary presentation which made them successful. He welcomed new print technologies into the production process, developed innovatory systems for distributing newspapers and, perhaps most significantly, exploited the possibilities for earning revenues from advertising in an age of expansive mass consumption (Smith, 1979, p. 157). Harmsworth's editorial, managerial and business qualities were thus complemented by broader conditions such as the availability of certain technologies and the prevailing social and economic circumstances. As Golding observed: 'mass consumption entailed mass selling and the buoyant daily press was the ideal advertising medium. The alliance of this development to American journalistic techniques, the possibilities of the new linotype process, and the recognition of an expanding public, are normally designated "the Northcliffe revolution"' (Golding, 1974, p. 27).

Newspapers in the modern age

The twentieth-century development of the press up to the second world war has been characterised by three features: expanding circulations, declining numbers of titles and an increasing concentration of ownership. The first half of the twentieth century witnessed the emergence of a mass-circulation popular press based in London; the growth was explosive and dramatic. National daily newspaper circulations grew from 3.1 million in 1918, to 4.7 million in 1926, 10.6 million in 1939, reaching 15.5 million in 1947 (Murdock and Golding, 1978, p. 130). Competition was fierce, with newspapers using a range of promotional gimmicks such as free gifts, door-to-door canvassers (who accounted for 40 per cent of newspaper staffs) and free accident insurance for readers, to win further circulation. Competition led to a decline in the number of national daily, Sunday and provincial newspapers, although Murdock and Golding claim 'the major victims of this expansion in the national popular press were the provincial papers' (ibid., p. 132). Between 1921 and 1937, 3 national morning, 4 national Sunday, but 13 provincial morning newspapers (from 41 to 28) had ceased publication. The contraction of titles prompted local monopoly. In 1921, 33 of the 65 towns outside London with a daily newspaper had more than one, but by 1947 this was reduced to 20 and in 12 of these towns the competing newspapers were owned by the same proprietor. Concentration of ownership increased. Between 1921 and 1937 no less than 30 daily and Sunday newspapers ceased publication. By 1948, the newspaper market was dominated by three newspapers groups which had established their circulation supremacy across the previous decade by 'swapping and reorganising their holdings in a gigantic game of newspaper *Monopoly*' (Carter, 1971, p. 38). Beaverbrook was market leader with 16 per cent of overall circulation, followed by Rothermere's Associated Press (14 per cent) and finally Lord Kelmsley's newspapers which accounted for 13 per cent of circulation; the largest three controlled 43 per cent of national press circulation. These trends towards concentration have continued in the post-war period.

In the period immediately after the second world war newsprint was rationed, making data for numbers of titles and circulations of newspapers unreliable since pagination decreased radically and many people bought more than one paper. The development of the newspaper industry during this period is discussed in detail in chapter 5.

| 5 |

Read all about it

The changing political economy of national and local newspapers

The political economy of the British press has changed radically since 1945, with the launch of new titles and the closure of existing newspapers, declining circulations, the emergence of free newspapers, the demise of Fleet Street, the introduction of new printing technologies in newspaper production, a dramatic reduction of both printers and journalists, the emergence of multi-skilling, the increasing concentration of ownership of national and local newspapers and their incorporation into cross-media, multinational empires, a growing job insecurity for editors and journalists and an increasing role for proprietors in all aspects of newspaper production. The consequences of these changes for journalists' news-gathering and reporting practices and standards have been considerable, and have created the conditions in which the new tabloid journalism can flourish.

Bad news: the stagnant newspaper market

The British national press is comprised of 10 national newspapers published daily (if the Scottish *Daily Record* is included with its sister paper the *Daily Mirror*), complemented by 11 Sunday papers. These daily and Sunday papers are usually designated as tabloid or broadsheet – the latter also being known as the qualities, or 'heavies' as Alastair Hetherington preferred to call them (Hetherington, 1985, p. 299). The distinction rested initially on little more than the size of the paper on which the newspaper was printed. Subsequently, the different labels have come to signal variety in the sheer amount and journalistic style of editorial content, the size of circulation, the social background, occupation and level of educational achievement of readers and the sources and levels of advertising revenues. But the intense competition between newspapers for readers and advertisers is blurring these once clear boundaries, with broadsheets increasingly supplanting their traditional editorial with reporting of 'showbiz' stories and royal gossip (see chapters 1 and 10). Since 1994, the Audit Bureau of Circulations (ABC) have subdivided the tabloid category into 'national morning popular' (the *Daily Mirror*, the *Daily Star* and the *Sun*) and 'national morning mid-market' (the *Daily Express* and the *Daily Mail*). 'National morning quality' papers include the *Daily Telegraph*, the *Financial Times*, the *Guardian*, the *Independent* and *The Times*. Sunday newspapers are similarly classified as 'national Sunday popular' (*News of the World*, *Sunday Mirror*, *Sunday Sport* and *The People*), 'national Sunday mid-market' (*Mail on Sunday* and the *Sunday Express*) and 'national Sunday quality' (*Independent on Sunday*, the *Observer*, *Sunday Telegraph*, *Sunday Times* and, since 21 April 1996, *Sunday Business*).

A number of other newspapers should be mentioned to give the complete picture of the national daily press. The (London) *Evening Standard* might best be described as a 'London provincial paper' but its circulation of 475,000 and its readership reach beyond the metropolis suggest it may be more than this. The soft pornography *Daily Sport*, stablemate of the *Sunday Sport*, has suffered rapidly declining circulation and is currently published three times weekly. The specialist papers *Racing Post* and *Sporting Life* serve exclusive and modest readerships. The *Jewish Chronicle*, as well as the *Morning Star* (the daily paper of the Democratic Centre – ex British Communist Party) and *News Line* (the left-wing tabloid published by the Workers Revolutionary Party), reach similar readerships. Eight daily papers targeted at Arab, Asian, Chinese, Turkish and Urdu-speaking communities are also published (Peak and Fisher, 1996, pp. 69–72). But despite this evident plurality of publications, the number of newspaper titles has been virtually static during the post-war period as closures and mergers of existing newspapers cancel out the arrival of new titles. The merger of the *News Chronicle* (October 1960) and the *Daily Sketch* (May 1971) with the *Daily Mail*, combined with the closure of *Today* (November 1995), more than compensate for the launch of the *Daily Star* in April 1979 and the *Independent* in 1986.

The five years between 1986 and 1990 represented something of a 'Golden Age' for British newspapers, with 10 new national paper launches: *Today* (1986), the *Independent* (1986), the *Sport* (1986), the *Sunday Sport* (1986), the *London Daily News* (1987), the *News on Sunday* (1987), the *Post* (1988), the *Correspondent* (1989), the *Independent On Sunday* (1990) and the *European* (1990). New print technology, lower production costs, disenfranchised print and journalistic trades unions, the belief that newspapers could now survive with smaller circulations combined with the prospect of healthy advertising revenues and a booming economy, created a mood of optimism which tempted a number of entrepreneurs and working journalists to establish these new papers. Some of them were sickly from birth and died remarkably quickly. Maxwell's *London Daily News*, launched in February 1987 as Britain's first 24-hour newspaper, triggered Associated Newspapers into a fierce defence of its *Evening Standard*;

Rothermere relaunched the *London Evening News* to drive Maxwell's new paper into the ground. The *London Daily News* closed within 5 months, having publishing only 126 issues. Circulation topped 90,000, largely as a result of reducing the cover price to 10p within a month of launch, but estimates suggest the venture cost Maxwell £50 million. Rothermere claimed that 'squashing' the paper gave him 'great pleasure . . . the product was aimed at the wrong market, it was badly thought out and poorly constructed' (quoted in Snoddy, 1988, p. 8). The *News on Sunday* survived only the eight months from its April 1987 launch to its humiliating November closure, but was in financial difficulties within the first week of publication. Conceived by journalist John Pilger, the paper was financed by the labour and trades union movement and organised on cooperative principles. Eventually edited by Keith Sutton, the newspaper's mission became populist; in Sutton's words, it was to be a 'leftwing *Sun*'. The newspaper was undercapitalised from the outset and never achieved anticipated readership figures or advertising revenues. Eddie Shah's new paper *The Post*, edited by Lloyd Turner, ceased publication in December 1988 after a mere 33 issues. The paper was published at Shah's Warrington Messenger works and required a break-even circulation of 370,000, but failed to find a market, never achieved more than 100,000 circulation and cost shareholders £6 million (Lewis, 1989, p. 17). The innovative Sunday newspaper the *Correspondent*, launched in October 1989 with £18 million capital, needed to achieve 400,000 sales weekly to break even. By February 1990, the paper required a rescue package of £10 million as circulation figures stuck at 200,000 copies while losses rose above £250,000 weekly. The paper relaunched in tabloid format, but closed in November 1990 in the wake of fierce competition from Newspaper Publishing's launch of the *Independent on Sunday* (Mullin, 1995, p. 3).

But while death came quickly for some newspapers, others have suffered a more lingering malaise. Both of David Sullivan's '*Sport*' titles are haemorrhaging readers and losing advertising revenues following restrictions on advertisements for certain kinds of telephone 'talk lines'. The *European* was launched in 1990 amid a bluster of optimistic and inflated claims which were typical of its proprietor Robert Maxwell; within a short while the newspaper was being given away free. Following Maxwell's death in November 1991, the paper became part of the growing media empire of the Barclay brothers. It is now published on Thursdays and finally achieves its target circulation of 225,000 copies.

The *Independent* has also survived, but cost-cutting measures, a series of staff redundancies and a number of refinancing deals to offset crises, have undermined staff morale and much of the newspaper's early idealism and considerable success. *The Independent* was launched in October 1986 by three journalists from the *Daily Telegraph*: Andreas Whittam Smith, Matthew Symonds and Stephen Glover. Whittam Smith's mission was to establish a truly independent newspaper of the highest editorial quality. The paper's title enshrined that mission; the newspaper's launch slogan was 'It is. Are you?' It was an enormous initial success. The economy was buoyant, advertising revenues were high and the new paper was successful in attracting a number of distinguished journalists who were disaffected with News International and unhappy at the prospect of working in Wapping. By 1990, the sustained recession, combined with the undoubtedly ambitious launch of the *Independent on Sunday*, created financial difficulties. Already weak with circulation falling, the newspaper suffered heavily during the price war initiated by Murdoch in July 1993 (see below, pp. 90–2). In March 1995, having lost £25 million in the preceding 12 months, Mirror Group Newspapers (MGN) and Tony O'Reilly's Independent Newspapers each increased their stake in Newspaper Publishing to 43 per cent. The repeal of the company's rule that no shareholder could own more than 15 per cent of the newspaper led the Advertising Standards Authority on 7 March 1995 to ask the newspaper to withdraw its claim that shareholders could not influence editorial. On 10 June 1995 the paper changed its name from *The Independent* to *Independent*. 1996 witnessed further cuts in journalistic staff and, on 26 April 1996, the appointment of Andrew Marr as editor – the third editor in the five months since Ian Hargreaves resigned in November 1995 after refusing to implement staff and other cuts proposed by David Montgomery of MGN.

The closure of *Today*, a mid-market tabloid, on 17 November 1995 and the launch of the quality *Sunday Business* on 21 April 1996 highlight the uncertainties of the national newspaper business and the radically divergent appraisals of the state of the newspaper market which currently are being made. *Today* was launched by provincial newspaper entrepreneur Eddie Shah on 4 March 1986. With £18 million start-up capital the newspaper aimed for a circulation of 800,000. A number of factors seemed favourable to the new paper's success. First, *Today* pioneered the use of the new direct-input technology which included the possibility of colour printing. Second, the newspaper was produced with non-union labour; costs were low and working practices were flexible. Third, Eddie Shah had become something of a celebrity, as well as a favourite of Mrs Thatcher, as a consequence of the media attention devoted to the protracted industrial dispute outside his Warrington plant. Newspaper proprietors were broadly backing his enterprise and Shah and his paper enjoyed enormous launch publicity. Fourth, the newspaper appeared to fill a genuine gap in the middle of the newspaper market. The launch of the new paper was judged to be portentous, heralding nothing less than the dawn of a new age for British journalism. The editorial in *UK Press Gazette* announced that 'the significance of this launch can scarcely be underestimated . . . the way is clear for many other publishers to follow in Shah's footsteps' (*UK Press Gazette*, 3 March 1986, p. 2).

But from the outset there were difficulties (Snoddy, 1987, p. 7, Willis, 1986, p. 7). The launch was disrupted by technical difficulties and distribution problems. The newspaper's colour printing, one of its principal selling features, was invariably blurred and was quickly dubbed 'Shahvision' by competitors. Brian MacArthur, the first editor, identified some of the difficulties. 'We were trying to stage a revolution overnight,' he claims. 'We only had a quarter of the staff of other Fleet Street papers – around 150 – who were working with state of the art technology. In retrospect, £18 million was not enough to start a paper' (quoted in Donegan, 1995, p. 2). Shah sold his controlling stake in the paper to Lonhro for £20 million within four months of the launch. MacArthur resigned in December 1986 with the paper's circulation achieving approximately half its target. Lonhro ceased publication of *Sunday Today,* produced by a staff of 13 journalists, in May 1987. In July 1987 Robert Maxwell announced he was planning to buy *Today* for £40 million; the next day the paper was bought by Murdoch's News International (Slattery, 1987, pp. 4–5). David Montgomery was appointed editor and took the newspaper down market; sales began to rise. Montgomery was replaced by Martin Dunn in 1991 and Dunn by Richard Stott in 1993. Stott is credited with making *Today* into a high-quality newspaper and, in February 1994, received the 'What the Papers Say' award as Editor of the Year. But despite its editorial merits, *Today* never achieved a circulation much in excess of 550,000.

There were other reasons for the closure. First, *Today* was costing Murdoch substantial sums of money estimated at £14 million a year and approximately £140 million in aggregate across the period of his ownership of the newspaper; this considerable expenditure had little beneficial impact on circulation. The resulting losses were exacerbated by the stupendous rises in the price of newsprint during 1995. Second, the newspaper was utilising valuable print capacity at Wapping which was needed to print the enhanced runs of *The Times* and the *Sun* during the price war. Third, the newspaper price war meant Murdoch was suffering enormous losses to increase the circulation of *The Times* in order to squeeze the *Independent* and the *Daily Telegraph*; the losses at *The Times* required savings elsewhere. Fourth, *Today* never found a market niche. The paper never seriously challenged the *Daily Mail* and was only a modest rival to the more substantial *Mirror*.

The death of *Today* witnessed a rather sordid rush by its competitor papers to grab its readers. The final edition of *Today*, which carried the headline 'Goodbye. It's Been Great To Know You', also included a four-page supplement inviting readers to buy the *Sun* and offering two weeks' supply of cut-price coupons; Tony Blair endorsed the supplement's *Sun* editorial which claimed 'there is another daily paper you can turn to: one where you can feel at home, one you can trust, one that will welcome you and brighten your day' (*Today* supplement, 17 November 1995, p. 1). The *Daily Mirror* countered by offering its readers £5 for signing up *Today* readers. The *Daily Mail* and the *Daily Express* both carried front-page banners welcoming '*Today* readers'.

The first issue of *Sunday Business* was published on 21 April 1996.

Proprietor Tom Rubython established the paper with only £15 million capital and just over 40 journalists. The new paper was designed to challenge the dominance of the *Sunday Times* among business readers and projected a first-issue circulation around 150,000. The first issue was certainly substantive in volume although its editorial qualities seemed less clear (Greenslade, 1996, p. 13). The newspaper has five sections, in both broadsheet and tabloid formats, devoted to news, personal finance, global finance, computing and a colour magazine. In the week prior to launch, journalists and other industry observers seemed sceptical about the prospects for a new paper with such limited resources. The leading article in the first issue of *Sunday Business* attacked its detractors and tempted fate with a rather pompous and perhaps unduly confident boast. 'Some sectors of the media industry,' the article claimed, 'have done everything in their power to disrupt the birth of an independent newspaper . . . [*Sunday Business*] is living proof that in a capitalist society, entrepreneurs can turn concepts into products and create a market no matter what the odds.' The newspaper was beset by difficulties from the outset; 48 hours before the launch, the original advertising agency withdrew, claiming there was insufficient funding to complete a television commercial, while printers refused to print the first run without the cost of the newsprint being met in advance. The paper confronted more general problems. It was launched at a historic low-point in the Sunday newspaper market which reflected, at least in part, the expansive Saturday editions and supplements. The market niche identified by the paper, moreover, was uncertain: it seems unlikely that a newcomer, even if better resourced, could challenge the authority, prestige and reader loyalty enjoyed by the field-leading competitor, the *Financial Times*. Five days after the launch issue, *UK Press Gazette* published a leaked financial statement revealing that the new paper was already in severe crisis. Journalists had not been paid for a month, the paper was losing a projected £150,000 per issue and had accumulated £900,000 total liabilities. Within a week of his boast, proprietor and editor Tom Rubython was offering to step down if this would help to construct a financial rescue package (Smallman and Morgan, 1996, p. 1). Stephen Glover, one of the founding editors of the *Independent,* described the new Sunday paper as 'one of the biggest journalistic cock-ups of all time' (Glover in *Press Gazette,* 10 May 1996, p. 28). But despite such appraisals, the *Sunday Business* is still in business.

A number of general lessons for success in launching a newspaper emerge from the preceding case histories. Substantial capital sums are necessary to establish a new paper and finance any initial problems. The newspaper must identify and target a clearly defined readership; there must be space for the new title in the market. The paper should also recruit high-quality journalists and, perhaps crucially, anticipate recessionary trends in the economy which immediately undercut newspapers' crucial revenue source: advertising income.

More bad news: war, competition and decline

Newspaper circulations have shown a relentless downward trend during the post-war years, and in virtually all newspaper sectors. Aggregate circulation figures for all national daily and Sunday titles fell from 38,420,000 in 1965 to 34,924,000 in 1975, slipping to 32,619,000 in 1985 and declining still further to 29,251,000 in 1997; a reduction of more than 9 million or 24 per cent of circulation (ABC figures published quarterly). The price war waged by the major newspaper groups since July 1993 has artificially inflated the circulation of some titles. Consequently, more recent newspaper circulation figures have become unreliable indicators which tend to obscure rather than illustrate underlying and long-term trends.

Despite the price war, circulation decline has been apparent in most sectors, but most dramatic among Sunday tabloid newspapers (Table 5.1). The arrival of the *Mail on Sunday* has done little to stem the loss of almost 8 million sales (38 per cent of the market) across 3 decades. In 1997, circulation of the *People* was down to 2 million.

Circulation figures for Sunday quality newspapers (Table 5.2) have also declined since 1965 although the reduction is not as striking as in the tabloid market. Even the addition of the new *Independent on Sunday* has failed to halt the long-term downturn, with aggregate circulation figures in 1993 lower than for 30 years. Some individual titles have enjoyed success against this broader trend. The *Sunday Telegraph,* for example, increased sales by 25 per cent across 1996–7.

Table 5.1   Circulation of the Sunday tabloids

	1965	1975	1985	July 1993
News of the World	6175	5646	4787	4601
Sunday Mirror	5022	4284	3211	2644
People	5509	4218	3090	2006
Sunday Express	4187	3786	2405	1711
Mail on Sunday			1605	1968
TOTALS	20,893	17,934	15,098	12,930

Table 5.2 Circulation of Sunday broadsheets

	1965	1975	1985	July 1993
Sunday Times	1275	1396	1258	1217
Observer	829	761	746	497
Sunday Telegraph	662	757	690	581
Independent on Sunday				373*
TOTALS	2766	2914	2694	2668

* IoS circulation at December 1992 was 406,978

Table 5.3 illustrates the mixed fortunes of the various tabloid titles although the overall trend in circulations is downward. The remarkable circulation success story, sustained throughout the 1970s and much of the 1980s, has been the growth of *Sun* readers. The paper was purchased by Rupert Murdoch in 1969 and edited with considerable skill, but perhaps greater controversy, by Larry Lamb and Kelvin MacKenzie. But by 1993, the *Sun* was suffering the same circulation decline which had plagued all tabloid titles since the mid-1960s.

The discernible irony in editors' move downmarket to attract more readers, is that the broadsheet daily sector has offered the only sign of growth in newspaper circulations (Table 5.4). Again, the record has been mixed with the *Daily Telegraph* suffering a steady decline while the *Financial Times* has recorded persistent growth. A plateau of circulation seems to have been reached in the mid-1980s while the overall increase in circulation seems to reflect little more than the addition of the *Independent* in 1987. The phenomenal growth in the circulation of *The Times* to 767,000 copies reflects very clearly the impact of the price war; Murdoch has reduced the cover price of the newspaper to 10p on Mondays.

Table 5.3 Circulation of tabloid newspapers

	1965	1975	1985	July 1993
Daily Mirror	4957	3943	3253	3419*
Daily Express	3981	2798	1875	1481
Daily Mail	2425	1725	1828	1761
Sun	1361	3477	4065	3573
Daily Star			1435**	774
Today				548***
TOTALS	12,724	11,943	12,456	11,556

*   Includes the *Daily Record* 749,606
** Launched April 1979
*** Launched 1986; closed 1995

Table 5.4 Circulation of broadsheet dailies

	1965	1975	1985	July 1993
The Times	258	315	480	361
Guardian	276	315	487	407
Daily Telegraph	1351	1323	1221	1020
Financial Times	152	180	229	287
Independent				339*
TOTALS	2037	2133	2417	2414

* Launched 1987

The reasons underlying this sustained post-war decline in circulations are well understood. Undoubtedly the most significant factor has been the degree to which expanding television and radio news services have supplanted national and to a lesser extent local newspapers as the primary source of many people's news; in 1990, 80 per cent of people cited television as their major news source (Goodman, 1993, p. 4). Television has proliferated, with 38 million receivers in 22 million homes; 40 per cent of homes have access to Teletext, moreover, which offers news digests at the press of a button (MacArthur, 1992b, p. 65). Unemployment has reduced sales further with many people preferring to buy only their local newspapers which, in response to this trend, increasingly feature national news stories. The successive increases in newspapers' cover prices since the 1970s and the increasingly visual, rather than literary, character of popular cultural forms consolidates the decline.

Newspapers have responded by developing new, often tabloid, supplements, publishing colour photographs and substantially increasing the size of newspapers. In autumn 1993 alone, 13 new sections were launched by national newspapers at an estimated cost of £100 million (MacArthur, 1993, p. 25). Pagination has increased substantially across the last decade (Table 5.5). In 1994, for example, the *Sunday Express* published almost six times the 1984 number of pages. But circulations looked set to continue to decline despite these efforts. In July 1993, Rupert Murdoch decided that the

Table 5.5 Changing newspaper pagination, 1984–94

Newspaper	Pages in 1984	Pages in 1994
Sun	32	52
Daily Mirror	32	48
Daily Record	40	48
Daily Star	28	36
Daily Mail	36	64
Daily Express	36	64
Today	—	52
Daily Telegraph	36	38
Guardian	28	72
The Times	32	72
Independent	—	48
Financial Times	48	78
News of the World	92	106
Sunday Mirror	48	120
People	48	124
Mail on Sunday	64	220
Sunday Express	32	184
Sunday Times	178	362
Sunday Telegraph	100	100
Observer	96	196
Independent on Sunday	—	160

only way to reverse these long-term trends was to cut the cover price. On 12 July the price of the *Sun* was reduced by 5p; the 20p *Sun* undercut the *Mirror* by 7p and triggered a price war. In September, the price of *The Times* was reduced from 45p to 30p. Murdoch hoped that the reductions would hurt competitors and possibly squeeze the ailing *Independent* from the market. The *Mirror* and *Telegraph* responded with major television advertising campaigns and other promotional offers. In June 1994, the *Telegraph* reluctantly lowered its price from 48p to 30p; Murdoch reduced *The Times* to 20p (Greenslade, 1995, p. 16). Under pressure the *Independent* dropped its price by 20p to 30p, having suffered a 19 per cent decline in sales across the previous year. These low prices were sustained across a two-year period until the 45 per cent increase in newsprint costs between January and July 1995 forced Murdoch to lift the price of *The Times* to 25p; it currently sells for 10p on Monday.

The price war has had a number of significant consequences. First, after three years of price cutting, aggregate circulations of daily newspapers had increased only marginally from 13,970,000 in July 1993 (see Tables 5.3 and 5.4) to 14,021,380 in February 1997; an increase of 51,380 copies or 0.4 per cent of total sales. These figures for total sales obscure the mixed fortunes of particular titles. In early 1997 *The Times* was selling a record 767,809 copies daily – more than twice the daily sales in 1993. The *Sun* also achieved sales beyond the 4 million mark daily. But for the *Express*, the *Telegraph* (which seemed as if it might descend below 1 million sales), the *Mirror* and the *Star* sales continued to decline or, at best, held steady.

Second, the war has resulted in fatalities. *Today* closed in November 1995 and the *Independent*, the *Independent on Sunday* and the *Star* face severe financial and circulation difficulties. Third, the price war with its inevitable 'squeeze on costs' has resulted in 'a decline in the quality of journalism' (Glover, 1995, p. 59). Fourth, the price war has established what may be an unpalatable truth to many journalists. While the best efforts of journalists, photo journalists, sub-editors and designers and their elaborate schemes to relaunch and redesign newspapers have failed to improve circulation, cheapness seems to have done the trick. Price, not editorial quality, has proved itself the magnet which attracts readers. Fifth, the *Guardian* did not lower its cover price but by September 1994 was selling more copies than a year previously. The paper could claim that its readers were loyal in a way that other newspapers' readers were not. The significance of this claim in winning advertising revenues is clear. Sixth, the war illustrated the significance of cross-media ownership. In the early days of BSkyB, the fledgling satellite channel was heavily subsidised by News International's group profits deriving from the *Sun* and Murdoch's other newspaper holdings. But in 1994, it was BSkyB's half-yearly profits of £70 million which sponsored Murdoch's £1 million a week losses resulting from the price war (Donovan and Atkinson, 1994, p. 2). Competitors without such group resources risk financial ruin. Seventh, the price war undermined all group profits. After one year, MGN shares dived by one fifth to 134p, United Newspapers' shares dropped 83p to 510p and, less dramatically, News International slipped by 9p to 235p (Cowe, 1994, p. 2).

Yet more bad news: advertising and influence

A significant feature of advertising revenues is often neglected: they make newspapers and other media much cheaper and hence more accessible to larger audiences. Advertising revenues are important to the financial well-being of all newspapers but to some they are critical. Local newspapers which are distributed for free, for example, derive all their income from advertising revenues. The reliance of other newspapers on advertising is variable. Provincial dailies and local weeklies derive approximately 60 per cent and 80 per cent respectively of their total income from advertising; these figures have remained fairly constant between 1970 and 1990 (Seymour Ure, 1991, p. 119). For tabloids and broadsheets the figures are 30 per cent and 70 per cent (Baistow, 1985, p. 33). In 1994, advertising revenues for the national press amounted to £1.2 billion (Advertising Association, 1994).

The answers to two questions signal the attractiveness of a particular newspaper to advertisers: 'How many people read the paper?' and 'What kind of people read the paper?' Size of readership is obviously important since it dictates the number of potential buyers which advertisers can reach with their message. But advertisers are more concerned to reach particular groups of readers distinguished by their social class, gender or age. Consequently, 'If you sell frozen foods or consumer durables, from cameras to washing machines you put your ads in the *Sun* or *Mirror* for blanket coverage of the household market . . . if you sell Rolls Royces, capital goods like computer systems or share flotations, you advertise in the *Financial Times* or the *Sunday Times*' (Baistow, 1985, p. 37). Newspapers undertake extensive market research to offer potential advertisers a very precise profile of their readership. Readers aged between 25 and 44 in AB social groups are particularly prized for their high spending potential. Advertisers' desire for high readerships combined with certain kinds of readers, means that the apparent simplicity of newspapers' advertising rates can hide an underlying complexity (see Table 5.6). The *Independent* is a broadsheet newspaper which is read by many people who are influential in business, the City, Whitehall and Westminster. Consequently, although advertising space in the *Independent* is only half the cost of each page in the *Sun* (£14k compared to £28k) reflecting the newspaper's much smaller readership, the cost of reaching each reader in the *Independent* is considerably higher than in the *Sun*. The amount that advertisers are prepared to pay to reach the highly influential and affluent *Financial Times* reader would buy access to no less than 14 *Sun* readers.

Competition for advertising revenues is fierce, both within and between

Table 5.6 Advertising ratecard costs of selected national newspapers

Newspaper	£/page	£/000 adult readers
Sun	28,000	2.84
Daily Mail	22,680	4.80
Independent	14,000	12.20
Daily Telgraph	34,500	12.71
Sunday Times	47,000	13.28
Financial Times	29,568	39.69

Source: British Rate and Advertising Data, 1994

media – between different newspapers and between newspapers and, for example, television. The long-term picture is mixed, but the broad trend has been for newspapers to lose revenues to television and more recently to commercial radio. Advertising revenues for television rose from 6 per cent of overall share in 1956 to 29 per cent in 1995. National newspapers' share of aggregate revenues has been remarkably stable at 16 per cent, but revenues for regional daily papers (16.4 per cent to 10.3 per cent), paid weekly papers (8.2 per cent to 4.7 per cent) and magazines and periodicals (7.8 per cent to 5.4 per cent) declined between 1978 and 1988. Among the press, only free newspapers have enjoyed a growth (1.9 per cent to 7.7 per cent) in advertising revenues across the period (Franklin, 1994, p. 42). Table 5.7 illustrates the long-term trends in advertising revenues.

Newspapers' reliance on advertising has a predictable and significant impact on all aspects of their production and distribution. Some categories of newspapers would simply not exist without advertising. Local free newspapers, which are less concerned to sell news to readers than consumers to advertisers, offer an obvious example. But the expansion of Sunday newspaper colour supplements in the 1970s, the development of supplements in

Table 5.7 Advertising expenditure by medium at constant 1990 prices

	Total	Press	Television	Radio	Other*
1985	6736	3960	1533	109	833
1986	7280	4322	2158	117	883
1987	8130	4782	2318	137	893
1988	8986	5376	2510	164	936
1989	9460	5616	2504	174	1346
1990	8925	5137	2325	163	1300
1991	8060	4614	2168	141	1054
1992	8068	4514	2251	143	1160
1993	8195	4560	2334	174	1127
1994	8869	4858	2527	212	1272
1995	9273	5059	2626	250	1338
1995 at current prices	10,959	5978	3103	296	1582

* Includes cinema, direct mail, billboard and transport
Source: *Advertising Statistics Yearbook 1996*

the Saturday broadsheets during the 1990s, as well as the publication of specialist colour magazines devoted to everything from computing (*Computer Weekly*) to drumming (*Rhythm* and *Modern Drummer*) owe their birth and existence to advertising revenues. Other newspapers trace their deaths to the same source. The *News Chronicle* and the *Daily Herald* attracted millions of readers but failed to win advertising revenues and closed.

The pagination of newspapers, which can rise and fall across the news week, often reflects the extent of advertising rather than the amount of news which may warrant publishing on any particular day. Similarly, particular sections within newspapers reflect advertising as much as, if not more than, reader interest. The expanding financial sections in the dailies during the 1990s illustrate how advertising revenues structure editorial content; the *Guardian* supplements devoted to media (Monday), education (Tuesday) and social and welfare issues (Wednesday) again reflect advertising revenue as much as reader interest.

Undoubtedly the most controversial aspect of the relationship between advertisers and newspapers is the suggestion that advertisers might influence editorial content; it seems clear that such influence exists and might be exercised in one of three ways. First, significant advertisers may threaten to remove their advertising if a newspaper plans to publish a story which threatens their commercial or other interests. There are few well-documented cases but many observers believe that all newspapers are subject to this kind of pressure from advertisers (Morley and Whitaker, 1986, p. 11). Distillers, the manufacturer of Thalidomide and the largest single advertiser with the *Sunday Times*, withdrew their advertising from the paper when it began a campaign for improved compensation for the drug's victims (Evans, 1984, p. 93). Similarly, in the mid-1980s a number of Labour-controlled local authorities imposed an advertising boycott on Murdoch newspapers in the wake of the lockout at *The Times* and the highly adverse reporting of Labour's 'loony left'. What both these examples reveal is that some editors will ignore threats of withdrawn advertising; others collapse when confronted by them. In 1986, Lord Stevens appointed a new editor at the *Star* who promptly took the paper 'downmarket' in the hope of winning new readers and reversing declining sales. Advertisers became increasingly unhappy about their products appearing alongside 'kiss-and-tell' journalism until eventually Tesco withdrew its account; within days, the editor was sacked. Local papers are typically more vulnerable to such threats than national papers because of their generally weaker financial position, their greater reliance on advertising revenues and the narrower range of advertisers from which they derive revenues. A free newspaper with a modest circulation and which is largely dependent on advertising from house sales seems unlikely to run an investigative piece on freemasonry and corruption in the estate-agent trade. In 1986, the *Sheffield Telegraph* temporarily ceased publication when estate agents distributed their own free paper carrying housing advertising (Franklin, 1994, p. 43).

There is a second, less obvious, way in which advertisers may influence editorial. Advertiser pressure can trigger self-censorship. Journalists are aware of their newspaper's most significant advertisers and understand that their career prospects will not be enhanced by causing offence. But, as a second line of defence, a hierarchy of news editors and sub-editors will sift any offensive material which threatens the revenue base of the newspaper. The injunction 'Don't bite the hand that feeds you' is metaphorically written on every newsroom wall.

Finally, newspapers are increasingly collusive with their advertisers and have developed new journalistic formats for the presentation of advertising material: 'advertorials' (see below, pp. 114). In brief, advertorials are advertising features masquerading as editorial and reflect 'rising pressure to find new ways of getting cash from advertisers'. One observer claimed that 'the once sacred split between editorial and advertising is now being sewn together' (Smallman, 1996, p. 11). As newspaper circulations, especially local newspaper readerships, decline the reliance on advertisers will become greater while their numbers grow fewer. In these circumstances, any influence which advertisers currently possess over editorial seems bound to increase.

Really bad news: concentration and cross-media ownership of the national press

The history of the British national press during the twentieth century has been a story of ever increasing concentration of ownership of newspapers. This trend towards monopoly, with ownership of the press vested in a handful of powerful individuals, has frequently occasioned concern among politicians, the public and pressure groups. In October 1994, Liberty and the Campaign for Press and Broadcasting Freedom (CPBF) published a report claiming that limited ownership of British newspapers reduced the range and diversity of expressed editorial opinion and had serious consequences for the quality of democracy (Liberty and CPBF, 1994 and Williams, 1994).

The extent of monopoly in the newspaper market is very evident. The various media organisations' market share is typically calculated on the basis of sales reflected in circulation figures. ABC figures for March 1996 signal total weekly sales of 84,487,134 for daily tabloid and broadsheet newspapers which, when added to the 15,378,366 Sunday tabloid and broadsheet sales, give an aggregate weekly circulation figure of 99,865,500. Within this overall picture, News International titles predominate. Murdoch captured 51 per cent of the popular market with the *Sun*, 25 per cent of the broadsheet market with *The Times*, 48 per cent of the quality Sunday market with the *Sunday Times* and 49 per cent of the popular Sunday market with the *News of the World*. News International's overall sales of 34,491,023 represent 35 per cent of the national newspaper market (ABC figures from *UK Press Gazette*, 26 April 1996). MGN claim a further 26 per cent of the market (25,732,561 weekly), Associated Newspapers enjoy an additional 15 per cent share (14,446,666 discounting the *Evening Standard*), United Newspapers/MAI control 13 per cent of the market (13,304,963) and Conrad Black's *Telegraph* and *Sunday Telegraph* account for a further 7 per cent (6,914,774) of weekly sales. These five organisations jointly publish 96 per cent of all national newspapers sold in Britain.

The measuring of concentration and monopoly in the newspaper industry by reference to circulations proved uncontentious until early in 1995 when the British Media Industry Group (BMIG) suggested an alternative. The BMIG, a lobbying group comprising the Guardian Media Group, Associated Newspapers, Pearson and the *Telegraph*, published a report entitled *A New Approach to Cross Media Ownership* which argued for the relaxation of government restrictions on newspapers' ownership of terrestrial television companies. BMIG suggested that calculations of market share based on circulation alone should be replaced by a system which measured each group's 'share of voice' across the media industry as a whole whether articulated via newspapers, television or radio. In assessing 'share of voice', radio audience figures would be weighted 50 per cent less than newspaper and television values, because radio – especially music radio – allegedly impacts less on people's views. According to BMIG, it is consumers' overall usage of media which should be established and possibly regulated in order to maintain diversity of viewpoint. When share of voice is calculated (Table 5.8), the relative significance of the various media organisations is radically reordered; interestingly three of BMIG's four members now assume the least influential positions among the leading sectors of the media industry (BMIG 1995 data, cited in Buckingham, 1995a).

The concentration of the newspaper market is a consequence of a series of takeovers and mergers between newspaper titles. Takeovers have been a constant feature of the newspaper landscape. In the early 1980s Murdoch acquired *The Times* and *Sunday Times*; his purchase of *Today* in 1987

Table 5.8 Share of national voice (%)

BBC	19.7
News International	10.6
Daily Mail	7.8
MGN	7.6
United Newspapers	5.7
Carlton	3.1
Thomson Regional	2.9
Channel 4	2.9
Granada Group	2.5
Pearson	2.3
Guardian Media Group	2.0
Daily Telegraph	9

incorporated an independently owned newspaper into multinational ownership. More recently, this 'editorial cannibalism' has continued apace with the *Guardian* purchasing the *Observer* in 1993, while MGN acquired the *Independent* and its sister Sunday paper in February 1994. The economic imperatives fuelling takeovers and the consequent concentration of ownership are clear. In an increasingly global market for media industries and their products, owners believe that 'big' not 'small' is beautiful and that media businesses must achieve a certain critical mass to survive. But mergers and large-scale operation also generate opportunities for economies of scale. Government policy, embodied most recently in the Broadcasting Act 1996, has relaxed restraints on cross-media ownership and seems persuaded by industry arguments that British media industries can only compete in global markets if they achieve a certain scale.

An evident consequence of these economic and policy developments has been the growth of cross-media ownership. Newspapers are increasingly owned by large corporations with interests in newspapers, radio, television and multi-media, as well as other non-media interests. Cross-media ownership is now so extensive that it makes little sense to talk of a newspaper industry; it has become a media industry, of which newspapers simply form one part. Two examples illustrate the point neatly. On 8 February 1996, United Newspapers headed by Conservative peer Lord Stevens announced a £3 billion merger with socialist Lord Hollick's MAI group. United Newspapers' ownership of the *Daily Express*, *Sunday Express*, *Daily Star* and approximately 100 regional and local newspapers including the prestigious *Yorkshire Post* and *Lancashire Evening Post* will now combine with MAI's interests in Channel 3 companies Meridien and Anglia and Channel 5. Additionally the new group owns business magazines, advertising periodicals like *Exchange and Mart*, the opinion polling organisation NOP (National Opinion Polls) and a range of financial and brokering information services. The merger makes United Newspapers and MAI substantial media players (Williams, 1997, p. 13). A month later, Associated Newspapers, which owns the *Daily Mail*, the *Evening Standard* and the *Mail on Sunday*, purchased a 20 per cent stake in ITN for £20.2 million. Associated is also the third largest publisher of provincial papers, owns a 20 per cent stake in Westcountry TV, a large holding in Independent radio GWR and Classic FM, as well as a 45 per cent holding in Teletext, 14 per cent in SelecTV and a range of magazines and television production companies including London's Channel One.

Dire news: proprietorialism, profits and power

Critics suggest that the incorporation of newspapers into these large, multinational, cross-media corporations reduces editorial autonomy and journalistic standards. Financial considerations and the drive for profit predominate over editorial concerns. A central factor informing these allegations has been the empowerment of proprietors. A widely circulating myth obscures this empowerment by suggesting that the age of the great press barons is over and that contemporary media moguls are less powerful figures who own newspapers to make profits rather than exercise power. But the last two decades have witnessed a remarkable growth in the scale of media empires and a substantial reduction in the number of proprietors who control them.

> The great myth about modern proprietors is that their power is less than it used to be. The fiefdoms of Beaverbrook, Northcliffe and Hearst, often invoked as the zenith of proprietorial omnipotence, were in fact smaller by every criteria than the enormous, geographically diffuse, multi-lingual empires of the latest newspaper tycoons. The profits and total circulations of the old-school proprietors were invariably lower, their papers thinner, the scope of their influence and newsgathering machines more local; none dominated so many world markets simultaneously as does Murdoch in Britain, the Far East and Australia . . . In terms of the circulation they collectively control the two dozen leading proprietors are unprecedentedly powerful and becoming more so. Every week their newspapers sell 200 million copies . . . As they have become more influential so have they dwindled in number. As recently as 1970 there were 125 significant newspaper owning families around the world . . . now they have diminished to fewer than 30. The last two decades have seen newspapers concentrated in fewer and fewer hands.
>
> (Coleridge, 1994, p. 2)

Proprietors influence their newspapers in at least two ways, reflecting their concerns with both economic and political matters. First, in a general but very clear way, proprietors' economic and financial requirements create the broad context in which a particular newspaper operates. Proprietors and their managers impose budgetary constraints which in turn signal staffing levels and, where necessary, cuts. In March 1996, for example, 44 staff were cut from the *Independent*, 30 jobs went at the *Financial Times*; a month later, on Will Hutton's first day in the *Observer's* editorial chair, he sacked 8 journalistic colleagues in an effort to balance the financial books. Proprietors and their resources set clear parameters within which the creative activity of journalism must be conducted; they are evident restraints. The single exception to this rule is the *Guardian* which is owned and controlled by the Scott Trust. Under the conditions of the trust established in 1936, financial and editorial matters are kept strictly separate, the former being the concern of the 10 trustees and the latter the remit of the editor (Taylor, 1993, pp. 3–7).

Second, and more specifically, proprietors may intervene directly to influence the editorial content of their newspapers – especially when a particular story threatens a proprietor's broader business or political interests. The exploits of Northcliffe, Rothermere and Beaverbrook offer textbook examples of the interventionist proprietor. During the general election campaign of 1918, for example, Northcliffe's newspapers tried to dictate government policy towards a defeated Germany. Northcliffe 'appealed to the men in uniform to vote against the government, flooding the silent battlefields with hundreds of thousands of free copies of the Daily Mail . . . his message was the advocacy of vindictive and punitive measures, revenge against Germany and malice against Lloyd George' (Cudlipp, 1980, p. 131). Stanley Baldwin's riposte to the hostile treatment meted out to him by the *Daily Mail* and *Daily Express* has become a classic statement of the dangers of proprietorial power:

> The newspapers attacking me are not newspapers in the ordinary sense. They are engines of propaganda for the constantly changing policies, personal wishes, personal likes and dislikes of the two men [Rothermere and Beaverbrook] . . . their methods are direct falsehood, misrepresentation, half truths, the alteration of the speaker's meaning by publishing a sentence apart form the context . . . suppression and editorial criticism of speeches which are not reported in the paper . . . What the proprietorship of these papers is aiming at is power, and power without responsibility – the prerogative of the harlot throughout the ages.
>
> (ibid., p. 274).

Proprietorial intervention resulted in anti-democratic consequences. The publication of the Zinoviev letter in the *Daily Mail* in 1924, just four days before the election, was evidently calculated to damage the Labour party's prospects, while Rothermere's enthusiastic acclamation of the Nazis in Germany led him to publish an article under his own name entitled 'Hurrah For The Black Shirts' (Cudlipp, 1980, p. 169). Editors have never proved effective in subduing their proprietors' journalistic ambitions. Forty years ago, an observer regretted 'the diminution of the status of the editor to no more than a paid servant of proprietorial interest that has proceeded at so fast a pace during the commercialisation of the press'. This subordination of the editor to the proprietor is 'manifestly contrary to the public interest' (Williams, 1956, p. 21).

Press barons have been redesignated media moguls but little else has changed; the desire to control the editorial content of their newspapers remains as strong as ever (Bevins, 1990, p. 13). Harry Evans, for example, offers a fulsome account of the various ways in which Murdoch interfered in every aspect of the production and content of the *Sunday Times* (Evans, 1984 and Hollingsworth, 1986, pp. 16–17). This was Murdoch's perennial style. When he acquired the *News of the World* in 1969 he told incumbent editor Stafford Somerfield, 'I didn't come all this way not to interfere.' According to Somerfield, the new proprietor 'wanted to read proofs, write a leader if he felt like it, change the paper about and give instructions to the staff' (quoted in ibid., p. 18). But relationships between editors and proprietors are typically more congenial. Proprietors appoint editors who share, rather than oppose, their political views. Murdoch's appointment of Andrew Neil to the editor's chair at the *Sunday Times* is illustrative. As Hollingsworth notes, 'with such an editor at the helm, Murdoch could relax and look forward to every Sunday morning when his view of the world would be read in millions of households throughout the country' (ibid., p. 18). But in his autobiography, *Full Disclosure*, Neil speaks of a stormier relationship while conceding the point concerning proprietorial intevention. 'Rupert expects his papers to stand broadly for what he believes,' Neil acknowledged: 'a combination of right wing Republicanism from America mixed with undiluted Thatcherism from Britain' (Neil, 1996, p. 127). Murdoch's removal of Kelvin MacKenzie, his most successful editor, in January 1994 is testament to proprietorial control over all aspects of newspaper production.

Some proprietors are judged to possess influence beyond their media empires; not least by their peers. David Montgomery, chief executive of MGN, for example, claims that Murdoch's influence extends to government; albeit on this occasion a weak government, with waning support, in a pre-election period. 'There is no doubt that Murdoch is setting the agenda,' Montgomery claimed in 1995. 'His broadcast and print media companies dominate the market and his satellite TV operation is vertically integrated with programme makers and hardware suppliers. The Government is frightened of Murdoch and is unwilling to regulate the media' (Montgomery, quoted in *UK Press Gazette*, 27 November 1995, p. 10).

The Wapping revolution and the demise of Fleet Street

On 23 January 1986 Rupert Murdoch implemented the plan he had hatched two years previously, to move production of his newspapers from Fleet Street to a new non-union plant at Wapping within sight of Tower Bridge. Over a single weekend and without any discernible disruption of production, he moved the *Sun*, the *News of the World*, *The Times* and the *Sunday Times* from Bouverie Street and Grays Inn Road into his new Wapping plant. The planning, building and equipping of the new plant with its computer-based printing technology was undoubtedly one of the most well-kept secrets in newspaper history. Wapping, with its barbed-wire perimeter fencing, security guards and dogs, floodlights and many hundreds of angry pickets, undoubtedly lacked the congeniality of Fleet Street, with its older traditions of news gathering and reporting and its nearby pubs well known to Street hacks, but the move gave Murdoch massive advantages above his rivals. He had introduced new technology into Fleet Street at a stroke, disposed of more than 5000 print workers, cut his costs and substantially enhanced his profits. The move marked a decisive watershed for British newspapers. In the words of one observer, 'two hundred years of Fleet Street history were over' (Melvern, 1988, p. 155). Murdoch's move to Wapping was nothing less than a revolution; no aspect of newspapers' production was untouched by the changes it set in train. As Rothermere noted, 'There was before Wapping and there was after Wapping' (quoted in MacArthur, 1988, p. 106). Murdoch had obliged his rivals to follow him or to see their newspaper businesses collapse.

The introduction of the new print technology into the national press seemed inevitable after the National Graphical Association's (NGA) protracted, but ultimately unsuccessful, battle with Shah and his Messenger group of provincial papers in 1983. The computerised printing technology had begun to displace many thousands of craft printing jobs across the previous decade and was beginning to hurt the NGA very seriously. The trade unions had been fairly successful in resisting the new technology because of their financial and organisational strength. Printers' high rates of pay, their ability to secure closed-shop agreements and their control over entry into the printing trade, reflected their indispensable position in the newspaper production process. The highly skilled printers operated the 'linotype' machines used in the 'hot-metal' process which had been used to produce newspapers since the nineteenth century. Linotype machines used molten lead to form the letters and text of articles into literal 'lines of type' to be used in printing. The new computer-based print technology allowed journalists to 'direct input' their copy, making many printing jobs unnecessary and dramatically reducing costs. The new technology allowed greater opportunities to update editions with late stories but, more significantly, also offered managements much greater control over the production process (Noon, 1994, p. 27). Facsimile transmission allowed the physical separation of the editorial and production processes so that newspapers could be printed simultaneously at different sites. This was a particularly significant development in the empowerment of owners, in tandem with trades-union legislation outlawing secondary picketing. Given the advantages and availability of new technology and managements' hostility to the print unions' power over newspaper production, it seemed clear that the unions would only be able to delay rather than resist its introduction. Even voices within the unions came to concede the inevitability of change and the damaging consequences of resisting innovation. Joe Wade, general secretary of the NGA, told the union conference in 1982 that 'if we are not prepared to embrace new technology . . . then competition from alternative sources in the country, or from abroad, will spell the death knell of the newspaper industry as we have known it' (cited in Goodhart and Wintour, 1986, p. 16). By the end of 1986 the unions had conceded defeat.

More recent developments in the computer technology, increasingly used in news gathering and reporting, have radical implications for journalism.

The availability of high-powered laptop computers/word processors, equipped with modems no bigger than a credit card, portable telephones and digital cameras, mean that pictures and reports of events can be filed within seconds. The popular image of the journalist with a telephone between shoulder and ear, a notepad in one hand, a cigarette in the other and a copy typist at the end of the line has been replaced by the less romantic but more accurate image of the journalist plugging a laptop into a phone socket and filing copy electronically. Speed, accuracy and efficiency are the obvious benefits of such technology as a 1000-word story can be submitted in two seconds using email and without the need for rekeying. Journalists, moreover, can use their mobile computers to keep in touch with news agencies and world events via the Internet. The drawbacks of such technology are perhaps more evident to copy typists than managers within the newspaper industry. New technology also isolates journalists by removing them from the newsroom, encourages and facilitates freelance work, nurtures multi-skilling practices and empowers managers against journalists and other production workers.

Murdoch's move to Wapping combined with these constant developments in new technology created a heady climate of optimism about the future prospects for the newspaper industry. Advocates believed that new technology would lower the production costs of newspapers by reducing staffing levels and promoting multi-skilling. There would be an explosion of new titles and an unprecedented pluralism as different cultural and political groups, empowered by the new technology, established their own newspapers and challenged the dominance of established publishers in the local newspaper market. Eddie Shah and Rupert Murdoch were cast as the unlikely heroes of 'the Fleet Street Revolution'. Some observers undoubtedly allowed their enthusiasms to overwhelm their judgement. Goodhart and Wintour, in their biography of Shah, shared the rosy vision of the future of the press held by so many.

> 1986 has been billed as year zero of the Fleet Street revolution. It opened momentously. In the course of just one week at the end of January, Eddie Shah successfully concluded the first dummy run of his new colour daily, *Today*; Robert Maxwell, having reduced the work force at Mirror Group Newspapers by 2000, told advertisers they could expect cuts up to half in his paper's advertising rates; United Newspapers formally confirmed that it wanted a one third reduction in manning at the Express Group; and most dramatic of all, Rupert Murdoch's News International produced its four titles . . . from behind barbed wire at a new printing plant in Wapping while in effect locking out 5000 members of the traditional print unions.
>
> (Goodhart and Wintour, 1986, p. xi)

The vision that gleamed so bright in 1986 looks hopelessly tarnished with the hindsight of a decade. But even in the mid-1980s, critics argued that the new technology would simply strengthen the market prominence of the already powerful newspaper monopolies. The 10 new papers launched in the aftermath of Wapping have either closed or face financial difficulties with falling circulations. So why did the dream become a nightmare?

The answer is that the introduction of new technology has done little, if anything, to alter the essential economic conditions of the national newspaper market. There are three specific points here. First, labour has never constituted the main element in newspaper production costs. Even before the arrival of new technology, the wages bill accounted for only 21 per cent of Fleet Street costs (McNair, 1994, p. 139). Subsequently, it is the ever mushrooming costs of newsprint which have been critical to newspaper economics. Second, new technology has done little to reduce the launch costs of a new paper although it has made matters slightly better for established companies and proprietors. In this sense, technological change has simply reinforced the hand of existing players. Finally, but perhaps most significantly, any opportunities for cost cutting which have derived from new technology have been undermined by the competitive newspaper market and the tactics of existing newspaper proprietors designed to exclude new entrants. Two strategies have been significant here. Companies engaged in the national newspaper price war chose to disobey the economic laws of the market by selling their newspapers below cost price, with the political intention of permanently restructuring the market to exclude competitors. A second strategy has involved the major newspaper groups deliberately increasing production costs to deter the launch of new papers. The explosion of pagination evident in the ever growing Saturday supplements is testament to proprietors' eagerness to retain their market share. New technology has not challenged the hegemony of the few powerful individuals who control the national newspaper market, nor prompted a new pluralism in which diversity and new titles are evident. On the contrary, it has buttressed those with an interest in opposing such developments.

Local newspapers

Local and regional newspapers, to a greater extent than their sister national newspapers, are suffering decline. Fewer newspapers are published, bought and read; the survivors publish less news, especially local news. The factors which have triggered the decline are evident: the intensified competition in worsening markets for readers and advertisers; the reduction of local editorial autonomy which accompanies the incorporation of local papers into multinational conglomerates; the rapid expansion of free newspapers which rely on non-journalistic sources of news and derive their income wholly from advertising revenues; paid weekly papers' need to compete with free newspapers and, where possible, to adopt similar cost-cutting strategies; local newspapers' adoption of new technology which has empowered proprietors against both production and editorial staffs; the imposition of individual contracts for journalists with implications for their working conditions, the expansion of multi-skilling and the content of newspapers; and the recent growth of alternative sources of local news provided by ever greater numbers of local radio and regional television services. Some of these factors are discussed briefly below.

Collapsing markets for readers and advertisers

The number of local newspapers has decreased dramatically since the second world war. The 108 daily newspapers published in 1948 had reduced to 98 by 1961 and slumped to 89 by 1995 (McGregor, 1977, and ABC figures, December 1995). Paid weekly papers have suffered a similar decline from 1306 titles published in 1948, to 1228 in 1961, with a further reduction to 797 by 1988; a 32 per cent decline across the period (McGregor, 1977, and Peak and Fisher, 1995, pp. 38–43). Free local newspapers have expanded against this trend. Published titles have grown from 185 in 1975 to 325 in 1980. By 1987 there were 822 free newspapers but by 1990 figures had reached 1156 titles (Franklin and Murphy, 1991, p. 85). Circulation figures mirror the reduction in published titles. The reasons underlying the ever diminishing readership are similar to those prompting a similar decline in national circulations: increases in the supply of television news, unemployment and the price of newspapers. Since 1993, two other factors have been significant, although their impact has typically been discussed only in the context of the national press. The price war, which reduced the price of national newspapers and thus made them increasingly attractive to local newspaper readerships, combined with sharp rises in the price of newsprint, have taken a heavy toll. Increasing costs of newsprint were cited as one of the major causes for the closure of the editorially excellent *Yorkshire on Sunday* in July 1995.

Whatever the reasons, the evidence of long-term post-war circulation decline is clear. The Royal Commission on the Press (McGregor, 1977) reported a sustained decline in daily newspaper sales from 11.1 million in 1961, to 9.1 million in 1976 and 6.8 million in 1987 – a decline of 39 per cent across the period. By December 1995, the aggregate circulation of daily regional papers in England, Northern Ireland, Scotland and Wales was down to 5,310,323; a 53 per cent reduction in circulation in less than two decades (ABC figures, October 1995). Only 14 of the 87 regional morning/evening newspapers listed by ABC (excluding Northern Ireland) showed any circulation increases between January and June 1996 when compared with the same period in 1995 (ABC figures, October 1996). Moreover, where increases were registered, these were typically slight. The *Birmingham Post*, for example, improved its 1995 circulation of 28,054 by a mere 19 (0.1 per cent) copies. Decreases in sales, however, were usually more substantial. The

Yorkshire Evening Press, for example, lost 7.5 per cent of its sales from the previous year, while *Kent Today* reduced circulation by 12.9 per cent. Major regional newspapers confront a very bleak future as annual circulation losses accumulate to alarming figures. The *Manchester Evening News,* which was selling 237,772 in 1992, saw daily sales reduce to 183,543 in 1996; a reduction of 54,229 copies (23 per cent) across three years (ABC figures, October 1996). This compares with a total daily sale of nearly 700,000 evening papers in Manchester in 1964. Circulations of paid weekly papers have suffered an equivalent post war decline but remain tolerably high at 7.7 million copies with an additional 2.45 million copies for regional Sunday newspapers. Against this trend for paid newspapers, free newspaper distribution has been spectacular, achieving more than 43.5 million newspapers per week by 1991 (Franklin, 1994, p. 34).

The declining sales of daily and weekly paid newspapers has led to the virtual elimination of competition and the creation of monopolies in many local press markets. The decline in titles and circulations has also affected local press advertising revenues – and adversely. The press share of total advertising fell from 90 per cent in 1956 to 65 per cent by the mid-1960s. By the late 1980s, paid weekly newspapers' share had almost halved to 4.7 per cent while regional daily share had diminished from 16.4 per cent to 10.3 per cent. Certain types of advertising, such as the jobs adverts which account for approximately one third of regional advertising revenues, have fallen by as much as 50 per cent (MacArthur, 1991, p. 6). By contrast, free newspapers had expanded their share of total advertising revenues to 7.7 per cent (Association of Free Newspapers, 1990, p. 14). By 1989, the total regional press share of 22.8 per cent of all advertising revenues was worth £1.7 billion although it was predicted to fall to 18 per cent by 1999. Advertising is a crucial source of revenue for all newspapers but as circulations continue to decline, newspapers will find it increasingly difficult to attract advertisers for their dwindling readerships. A vicious circle is very apparent in the affairs of many regional and local newspapers.

New technology, individual contracts and multi-skilling

The arrival of new printing technology in the local press preceded the much publicised battles surrounding its later introduction into the national press with the establishment of printing facilities at Wapping. The birth pangs of the new technology in the local-press setting, however, were similarly painful. The battles outside Eddie Shah's Warrington plant between the crowds of 200 to 2000 pickets, demonstrators and local police, on Tuesday and Wednesday nights when he printed and distributed his local free newspaper, *The Messenger*, were dramatic and often violent.

The dispute had been triggered by Shah introducing new print technology into his plant, rejecting the print industry's traditional right to exercise a closed-shop system of trades-union membership and asserting his right to manage. Shah argued that trades unions were abusing the existing closed-shop agreements and enforcing anachronistic, if not bizarre, working practices, which militated against the efficient production and distribution of newspapers. The National Graphical Association (NGA) began to organise mass pickets outside the plant in late October 1983. The dispute quickly spread into the national arena. The NGA called a strike of its members in Fleet Street, halting production of Saturday and Sunday national newspapers; seven national newspapers were granted injunctions prohibiting the NGA from repeating the action in subsequent weeks. In parliament, Prime Minister Thatcher spoke in support of management's right to manage. Eddie Shah and what the national press described as his 'stand for freedom' became a symbol of newspaper managements' desire, both in Fleet Street and the provinces, to introduce the new technology which they believed would allow them to be more flexible in staffing, cut costs, produce technically better newspapers and encourage a general expansion in the newspaper industry. The NGA and the other newspaper unions understood that if Shah was successful in Warrington, the implications for Fleet Street and other provincial papers would be severe; the consequences for printers and the NGA even more so. A national demonstration of support for the NGA was organised for 29 November 1983. The Tactical Aid Group in full riot gear were sent in and 'cut through the crowd with their batons flailing'. The events of that night were an 'uncomfortable reminder that even in a mature democracy the struggle for industrial power can still involve a literal battle' (Goodhart and Wintour, 1986, pp. 12–13). The battle marked the end of the Messenger dispute. Shah's Warrington plant became the 'symbolic birthplace of a project which two and a half years later was to help transform the national newspaper industry and directly inspire Rupert Murdoch's Wapping escapade' (ibid., p. 13).

With the benefit of hindsight, the hope that new technology would generate benefits for the industry is hotly contested. There is certainly little evidence that it has prompted any expansion in the number of local newspapers published; quite the contrary is clear from the statistical data presented above. But the real losers have been the many printers and journalists whose jobs have disappeared as a consequence of this new technology. Initially, the shedding of labour was limited to production workers and was achieved by signing 'new technology agreements' with the printing trades unions. Proprietors and managers then turned to the journalists and imposed individual contracts of employment on the members of local newspaper chapels; this two-stage process of undermining the power of both printers and journalists within the production process has been described as an 'employers' offensive' (Gall, 1996, p. 2). The objectives of the offensive have been clear. First, newspaper groups wished to end the system of collective bargaining and impose wage settlements determined by market

forces – essentially an economic goal. Second, companies wished to eradicate any basis for effective trade-union practice by 'individualising' the
employment relationship. Finally, newspaper groups wished to prevent the
NUJ using the new direct-input technology, as a lever to increase its bargaining power in relationship to management. From the company's perspective, there was little point in simply replacing the NGA with the NUJ
(ibid., p. 108). The introduction of the new contracts was achieved very
rapidly; by 1989 more than half the NUJ's provincial members no longer
enjoyed collective bargaining agreements (ibid., p. 93).

Journalists' new contracts typically dissolve existing agreements between
the NUJ and the newspaper company and replace them with a contract
between the individual employee and the company (Franklin and Murphy,
1991, p. 51). Journalists retain their entitlement to be a member of a trades
union but their union no longer enjoys collective bargaining rights concerning pay and other conditions. Journalists on local newspapers across the
country have been obliged to sign these contracts. Individual journalists
must now negotiate with the management of multinational corporations for
their pay rises – a classic case of David versus Goliath. The consequences for
levels of pay, staffing and conditions of service in the local press seem obvious; the knock-on effects of these latter changes for the range and quality of
editorial content are similarly clear.

One notable consequence of new technology and the changed bargaining
position of journalists in the local press has been the emergence of 'multi-
skilling': the erosion of the division of labour which traditionally demar-
cated the various processes and jobs involved in newspaper production.
Expressed broadly, journalists wrote stories, editors and sub-editors revised
them and added headlines, photographers and graphic designers added
visual materials to make the text more attractive, while typesetters and
printers produced the overall package which was the newspaper.
Technological development has gradually eliminated production skills.
Multi-skilling, although it was not described by this term, emerged with the
introduction of the new direct-input technology which allowed journalists
to input their reports directly into a computer typesetting and print system.
Recently, multi-skilling has become so commonplace that it is barely commented upon. Cuts in jobs and the inability of trades unions to resist the
blurring of job boundaries has increasingly resulted in journalists being
expected by newspaper managements to take photographs to accompany
their stories and also to become involved in the editing and subbing of their
own and colleagues' work (Gall, 1996, p. 302). The job of a local journalist
has been broadened to include tasks previously performed by specialist colleagues. Managements laud multi-skilling as one aspect of a more flexible
approach to newspaper production; journalists refer to the job losses
involved and the decline in quality of newspapers which are the inevitable
consequence. The extension of multi-skilling to the national press has
resulted in the growth of temporary contracts for journalists, the

burgeoning of freelance work and the casualisation of the once well organised and unionised profession of journalism.

Owning the parish pump: monopoly and the local press

It is fast becoming a cliché to observe that local newspapers are local in name only, since large sections of the local press are owned and controlled by a handful of large companies. 'Behind the parish pump', as one study expressed the matter, 'lies corporate power' (Franklin and Murphy, 1991, p. 54). By the mid-1990s, over 60 per cent of the British local press was owned by the largest 10 companies with more than 80 per cent owned by the top 15 companies. This concentration of ownership is a consequence of mergers and takeovers rather than the effect of the larger groups launching new titles. The process of concentration, moreover, has been remarkably rapid. For more than a hundred years, the typical British local newspaper was a modest operation, owned by a local company or a local family, which reported the local court and local council. But these individual enterprises have rapidly been incorporated into large multinational corporations. There is a second point to note. The increasing tendency towards concentration of ownership of the local press has been accompanied by an ever greater overlapping of ownership of the national and local press. Associated Newspapers, which publishes the *Daily Mail*, controls a substantial regional newspaper empire, while United Newspapers/MAI owns the Express group as well as more than 80 provincial titles including the large-circulation regional newspapers such as the *Yorkshire Post* and the *Sheffield Star*.

This tendency towards concentration of ownership achieved by merger received renewed impetus late in 1995 when the Thomson group (TRN) sold its regional newspaper holdings. The Barclay twins paid £90m for *The Scotsman*, *Scotland on Sunday* and the *Edinburgh Evening News* and Northcliffe's Associated Newspapers £82m for the *Aberdeen Press and Journal* and *Evening Express*. Trinity Holdings acquired TRN's 50 local titles in England, Wales and Northern Ireland for a further £327.5 million (May and Clouston, 1995, p. 3). The sale confirms the market position of Associated Newspapers and continues the development of Trinity as one of the largest regional newspaper groups in the country. There were other substantial sales of local newspapers in 1995 and 1996. In January 1996, for example, the management group Newsquest bought 123 regional newspapers from Reed Elsevier, the Anglo-Dutch publishing company; the £205 million necessary for the Newsquest buyout was financed by Kohlberg Kravis Roberts, the Wall Street finance house. In June 1996, Johnston Press brought EMAP's 65 titles including 4 evening papers, 30 paid weekly papers and 31 free newspapers (Sharpe, 1996, p. 1). In September 1996 UPN offered 40 of its local newspapers for sale and in November 1996 Newsquest bought Westminster Press titles for £305 million (*Press Gazette*, 13 December 1996, p. 16). The Trinity International group now controls the publication of more than 9 million local newspapers each week, which represents 13 per cent of the total market; the group owns 10 daily titles, 52 weekly paid titles and 61 weekly free newspapers. Johnstone Press owns more newspaper titles but enjoys a slightly smaller circulation. The Monopolies and Mergers Commission (MMC) did not believe this concentration of ownership to be 'unduly high' (Morgan, 1995, p. 7). Home Counties Newspapers moved into the top 20 for the first time as a result of buying Herald Newspaper group in 1995 (*Press Gazette*, 5 February 1996, p. 6). Just 20 publishers produce more than 61 million of the 71 million local newspapers published each week; 86 per cent of the market. The remaining 14 per cent of the local newspaper market is divided between 150 smaller newspaper groups (Newspaper Society Intelligence Unit, 1 January 1996).

In February 1996, the merger between MAI, Lord Hollick's company which holds the Channel 3 franchises Meridian, Anglia and HTV as well as Channel 5, and United Newspapers which owns Express newspapers and a large chain of local and regional newspapers, marked a significant development in the ownership of Britain's local press. This was the first merger of a major newspaper group with a terrestrial commercial television company and established a systemic change in the form of corporate ownership of local papers. Newspapers now constitute only a single medium in a corporate package rather than the central focus of business activity within the group. Newspaper companies are eager to diversify into the new technologies. Associated Newspapers are expanding their £30m cable TV company, Channel One, to provide a 24-hour local news service in the West Country. The *Birmingham Post and Mail* is similarly broadcasting one hour of local news daily on local cable television.

No *news is bad news: the collapse of the alternative local press*

The closure of the *Northern Star*, an alternative newspaper which had been published and circulated in Leeds and West Yorkshire for 20 years, marked the end of an important era for the local press. It was the last alternative newspaper; its closure highlighted many of the recent changes in the local press. Most significantly, it illustrated how the free market – far from encouraging choice and diversity in local newspapers – serves to undermine them (Harcup, 1994, p. 1).

The death of the alternative press was sudden and dramatic. In the late 1980s there were an estimated 120 alternative newspapers, selling up to 4000 copies weekly with readerships probably much greater than the three per copy calculated for traditional newspapers (Murphy, 1988, p. 5). According to one definition, alternative newspapers were 'local, anti-racist, anti-sexist, politically on the left, overtly rather than covertly political, not produced for profit, editorially free from the influence of advertisers, run on broadly collective principles . . . the voice of the alternative newspaper is an important counterweight. Small need not mean insignificant' (Harcup, 1994, p. 14). By 1994 the tradition of alternative local newspapers was at an end. The demise was regrettable. At a time when independently owned weekly local newspapers are being supplanted by corporately owned free newspapers with little news content, the absence of the alternative press with its tradition of investigative local journalism represents a considerable loss. Regrettable too, because the alternative press always provided a training ground for some of the best and most radical journalists such as Duncan Campbell.

The alternative local press was born in the late 1960s, flourished during the 1970s and 1980s, but died in the 1990s. Alternative newspapers typically combined news with a 'What's On' guide to events within their circulation area. Typographically they adopted a magazine format with glossy covers and a self consciously 'arty' layout. Staffing levels were usually very low – often little more than a single journalist supported by an enthusiastic group of amateur stringers and others who helped with all aspects of production and distribution. Everything about alternative newspapers was alternative. They espoused an alternative political agenda which was usually left wing, supported sexual and racial minorities and increasingly focused on green and ecological concerns. The alternative values explicitly and implicitly expressed in content and form were reflected in the way the newspapers were organised – typically as workers' cooperatives informed by democratic decision-making procedures. The alternative press eschewed the hierarchical structures of the traditional local press, preferring open editorial meetings which anyone involved in the newspapers' production could attend.

The alternative press was bought by an alternative readership which was alienated from mainstream media. It followed an alternative news agenda informed by alternative news values. An internal discussion paper circulated at *Northern Star* entitled 'Views On The News' was explicit: 'Politically, a good news story is one that reinforces the ability of the mass of people to do things for themselves' (Harcup, 1994, p. 5). Given this news agenda, it is perhaps unsurprising that the *Northern Star* published different kinds of stories to its local sister paper, the *Yorkshire Evening Post*. While *YEP* coverage of the Chapeltown area of Leeds, where many of the city's Afro-Caribbean community is centred, focused on prostitution, drugs and rioting, the alternative newspaper was reporting stories about a new multicultural centre, a Police Community Forum and a proposed dance centre. The *Northern Star*'s coverage of the coal dispute in 1984–5 stood in stark contrast to the hostility expressed by many orthodox newspapers; 'whereas most journalists stayed behind the police line, *Northern Star* journalists and photographers stood with the strikers' (ibid., p. 5). The paper was less interested in stories about personalities, whether union or coal board leaders, than in trying to record events as they impacted on the lives of ordinary people. Hardly surprising that Radio 4's *Wilko's Weekly*, a series about the local press, described the newspaper as 'the parish magazine of Leeds' dispossessed'.

Although small compared to its sister local papers, the alternative press was far from journalistically insignificant. The *Northern Star* enjoyed many journalistic successes. The paper's coverage of the Helen Smith case, the early reporting of the dangers to public health arising from asbestos production in West Leeds and the leaking of the government pamphlet 'Protect and Survive' show that a poorly resourced paper can nonetheless beat a prestigious rival such as the *Yorkshire Post* to a good story. But after 20 years struggling to survive on the iron rations of Thatcherism, the *Northern Star* eventually closed after 820 issues on 20 January 1994 (Wainwright, 1994, p. 9).

The total collapse of the alternative local press across a very short period of two to three years is an intriguing journalistic phenomenon which warrants detailed examination. The failure of the alternative press is too frequently attributed to the alleged incompatibility of its democratic structures and the need for economic efficiency (Landry et al., 1985, and Fountain, 1988). Although this was certainly a factor in the demise of the cooperatively organised *News on Sunday*, more probable factors for the alternative press as a whole include the ruthlessly competitive character of the local-press market in the early 1990s along with lack of capital and new technology resources.

Newszak and the rise of the 'freesheet'

The relentless decline in the circulations of the daily and weekly local press and the complete collapse of the alternative press stands in striking contrast to the expansion of free local newspapers during the last two decades. The growth in the number of published titles, their achieved levels of weekly distribution and their share of advertising revenues has been quite remarkable.

Free newspapers were first published in the early 1960s. They boasted little news and editorial content, were mainly devoted to advertising and displayed little affinity for the communities they allegedly reported; they were what the Americans had called 'shoppers'. As they grew in editorial quality, their numbers spiralled from less than 200 in the mid-seventies, to over 800 a decade later and over 1200 by the mid-1990s; the aggregate distribution of these free newspapers is in excess of 40 million copies weekly. The free-newspaper phenomenon has occurred in America, Canada and throughout Europe as well as in the UK. Germany, France, Belgium and Great Britain publish more than 4000 free newspapers with a distribution approaching 200 million each week. They employ 150,000 people, plus a further

500,000 people on a part-time basis to distribute the newspapers (Porter, 1987, p. 7). Growth in advertising revenues for the free press mirrors the expansion in titles and distribution. In 1980 advertising revenues were approximately £84 million but had mushroomed seven times by 1989 to £600 million (Fletcher, 1988, p. 8). In 1984, free newspapers' 24.7 per cent share of the advertising market placed them ahead of paid weekly newspapers and, following sustained growth in 1986, free newspapers overtook regional daily newspapers' advertising market share (Barnes, 1987, p. 6). In a short period of less than three decades, free newspapers have come to dominate the local newspaper market.

But these new papers were initially disparaged by journalists working in the traditional local press as 'freesheets'. Journalists were reluctant to acknowledge that these publications were newspapers for two reasons: first, they were free and relied wholly on advertising for their income, and second, they contained very little news. These two features were of course connected. An executive for a major free newspaper publisher, conceded that the papers, 'varied enormously in quality. Some justifiably were called freesheets, keeping the ads apart with PR puffery and plugs for their advertisers. Some made circulation claims that were at best wishful thinking and at worst downright "porkies"' (quoted in Franklin and Murphy, 1991, p. 77). What distinguished free newspapers from the traditional paid papers was, of course, their total reliance on advertising as their sole source of income. A number of significant consequences for free newspapers' staffing levels, news-gathering routines and other matters stem from this fundamental difference in their revenue base. First, a considerably greater proportion of space is devoted to advertising compared to editorial content. Second, their reliance on advertising makes them vulnerable to advertising interests when these potentially conflict with editorial concerns. Certain sections within a paper – whether local politics, business or travel – might be dropped not because readers do not find the material interesting but because it is failing to attract advertising. Third, free newspapers typically employ fewer journalists because they have less need to gather news than paid papers. There is also a lesser emphasis on training in free newspapers. Fourth, free newspapers are less accountable to their readers because they do not have to win a readership; they are distributed free to selected audiences targeted to meet advertisers' requirements. Fifth, to keep advertising rates to a minimum and achieve a competitive edge over their paid counterparts, free newspapers have tried to minimise their news-gathering costs in ways which journalists working in the traditional press have usually considered undesirable.

The growth of free newspapers, with their particular news-gathering routines, has had a crucial impact on local newspapers – both on the number of titles and especially on their news content. Because free newspapers employ fewer journalists they have become increasingly reliant on non-journalistic sources of news for their stories. Free newspapers also feature a smaller proportion of news in their editorial columns. But because paid newspapers compete in the same local market for readers and advertisers, they have been obliged to follow free newspapers' editorial lead. In both free and paid papers the formula for success increasingly requires a combination of minimum production costs and maximum readerships and revenues. But there is a significant difference between free and paid newspapers. The news content of free newspapers, even when it is poor, is incidental to their distribution; loved or loathed, they are delivered just the same. But paid newspapers have to win a circulation. Competition forces paid papers into the same cost-cutting strategies as their free rivals but they must maintain sufficient editorial quality for readers to wish to buy them. The strain involved in meeting these contradictory demands has led to the demise of many paid newspapers. Consequently the growth and expansion of free newspapers is a dual-edged sword. On the one hand it has buttressed the local press by sustaining circulation and advertising revenues against a long-term downward trend. On the other, it has resulted in a reduction in the numbers of journalists employed by local papers, a decline in the number of paid newspapers, changes to the news content of the local press and the development of a new kind of local journalism.

By the 1990s, these trends have resulted in the emergence of a 'tabloid' local press; newszak abounds and many local papers have literally changed size from broadsheet to tabloid format. But in order to capture more readers, newspapers have followed similar strategies to national papers and exhibit similar editorial changes. The story count is higher, editorial is 'livelier' and increasingly focused on consumer and human-interest stories. Newspapers seek to entertain and divert rather than inform and engage readers with the affairs of their communities. Analysis of weekly newspapers, but especially of the free newspapers, reveal that news content may be less than 20 per cent of total newspaper content, while figures of around 30 per cent are common. But the constitution of even this impoverished news content is changing in significant ways.

First, public-relations handouts are increasingly a major source of news and are published with little, if any, editorial revision. These 'information subsidies', as Gandy describes them, are essential to newspapers because the substantially reduced number of journalists must nonetheless continue to fill the editorial columns that remain. Simply reprocessing PR handouts is the most efficient way to minimise production costs. Such revised newsgathering protocols mean that even major news stories such as the general election may be very inadequately reported in the local press (Franklin, 1994, p. 177). Local newspapers' coverage of local political news is similarly driven by the information subsidies emanating from town-hall public-relations departments and other communications-conscious political interest groups; again the editorial integrity of the coverage is compromised by the partisanship of the source (Williams, 1996, p. 11 and Franklin, 1986, p. 28).

A second change which is compromising editorial and by that process redefining what constitutes news, is the growth of what journalists denounce as 'advertorial', a mix of advert and editorial. These 'features' are designed specifically to attract advertising but also facilitate the general move from traditional 'news' articles to items with a consumer focus. Their formats are highly stylised. Typically they feature a local company which is moving premises, celebrating a centenary or expanding its business in some way. A rather tedious formulaic article celebrates the history of the company in euphuistic tones while, on the strength of the article, the paper solicits adverts – usually in the form of best wishes messages – from the firm's suppliers and major customers (Gall, 1993, p. 20 and Smallman, 1996, p. 11).

Local newspapers should articulate the history and concerns of a local community and be central to local democracy by providing a forum for public debate. But the increasingly competitive market in which they are obliged to operate has triggered the demise of the alternative press, the decline of the traditional paid press and the prominence of free newspapers with a spartan editorial content, deriving from external news sources, and more concerned about reporting consumer oriented stories than issues of substantive public concern. The pursuit of income through advertising and expansive readerships results in the perennial search for news which is judged according to its low-cost, high-earning, potential. Entertainment, trivia sensationalism and newszak are increasingly the products of local journalism; choice, diversity and alternative voices have been lost from the local newspaper market.

|6|

Changing radio times
A history of British radio

Radio news has changed rapidly and for the worse during the 1990s. This is how a radio journalist reported an early morning transatlantic exchange on Radio Heart FM.

> Heart FM London 106.2: 8.30am. Marsha (in the USA) is being two-wayed by our intrepid Brit Presenter. She tells him that Pamela Anderson is rumoured to be pregnant. 'How can she have a baby?' she wonders. 'She's so slim she must have an 18 inch waist.'

> Presenter: 'She could have a baby in her breasts. One in each breast, twins.'

The journalist states the obvious: this 'joke' 'wouldn't be funny at a club after 12 lagers, let alone at half-past eight in the morning' (Kaye, 1995, p. 28). Whatever else it may purport to be, this is *not* news. At best it is conversational wallpaper, at worst it offers offence. But radio, like newspapers and television, seems increasingly to find news value in the personal, even intimate, details of the lives of celebrities as much as stories concerning economic, political or international events of public significance. Radio has a distinguished history as a news and current affairs broadcaster and consequently these recent changes to the style and content of its journalism are striking. 'Shock jocks' on *Talk Radio UK* vilified listeners who dared to disagree with them, calling them 'twats' and 'sad bastards' and inviting them to 'piss off' (Culf, 2 May 1995, p. 6). The BBC is not immune to 'chat-show' journalism. Flagship programmes like *Today* and *World at One* routinely invite rent-a-quote MPs to inject controversy into the presentation of issues at the expense of analysis. On occasion the programming is little more than tabloid. On 14 November 1996, for example, *Today* devoted 18 minutes' airtime to Sue McGregor's interview with Sarah Ferguson – an interview which constituted little more than a PR puff for the duchess's newly published and poorly reviewed autobiography. Cuts are biting into Radio 4's core programming. *Woman's Hour*, currently celebrating its fiftieth birthday, has been obliged to replace one programme each fortnight with a low-budget phone-in. More recently, in a reorganisation of the BBC announced in June 1996, Birt relegated radio in the organisational structures of the BBC and proposed that the World Service news should lose its independent news-gathering services and become an adjunct of the BBC domestic news unit (Tusa, 1996, p. 11). Such trends are guaranteed to ring alarm bells among those nurtured on the quietude of public-service broadcasting.

The argument informing this chapter is that from its beginnings as a Reithian public-service broadcaster, radio has gradually metamorphosed into a medium where market forces are considerably more evident in determining the range and quality of services – and not only in the commercial sector. Regrettably, market forces are corrosive of public-service traditions. Some observers have implied a 'logic' to a market-driven radio system which leads it to 'swallow up new markets and extend its frontiers to compete with, even undermine the public service domain' (Lewis and Booth, 1989, p. 10). In this changed environment, characterised by a relentless search for audiences, the concern must be that journalistic standards have been revised. Radio, like newspapers, has changed in ways which allow newszak to flourish. This argument is unravelled by exploring the historical development of radio in Britain. In the next chapter recent changes in radio policy are considered, current provision of radio services is assessed, and patterns of ownership and audiences for radio are analysed. But this chapter begins by addressing a different, more general, question: What is distinctive and important about the medium of radio?

Radio: a unique medium in decline?

In 1896, the year that Alfred Harmsworth launched Britain's first mass-circulation daily newspaper, the *Daily Mail*, Italian inventor Guglielmo Marconi arrived in Britain to demonstrate to Post Office engineers how he could send wireless signals over distances up to 100 yards; Marconi died a quarter of a century later in 1922, the year in which the British Broadcasting Company (BBC) was founded. Asa Briggs, author of the authoritative five-volume history of the BBC, describes these significant events in the life of broadcasting – not to mention Marconi – in a rather dismissive phrase as an 'interesting coincidence' in the 'history of the mass media' (Briggs, 1961, p. 21; see also Briggs, 1965, 1970, 1979, 1995). But the events were enormously significant and portentous for news media. Marconi's early and rather primitive experiments with the transmission of radio signals, using an aerial hanging from a kite, created both the possibility and the prospect of radio broadcasting in Britain. The system developed with remarkable rapidity. The audience for wireless programmes grew faster during the early 1920s (from 35,744 licences in 1922 to 2,178,259 in 1926) than the growth of television audiences during an equivalent initial period (from 14,560 licences in 1947 to 763, 941 in 1951) (Briggs, 1961, p. 18); after four years of broadcasting, the audience for BBC programming had also outstripped the readership of Britain's most popular newspaper, the *Daily Mail*. From its inception, radio had significant implications for other news media. It proved a keen rival for newspapers' diet of printed news but, perhaps more importantly, its organisational structures, financial arrangements and journalistic principles and philosophy provided a model which television could later adopt. Other milestones in broadcasting followed promptly. The British Broadcasting Corporation was established in 1927, the 1930s heralded the 'golden age of radio' characterised by expanding audiences and broadcasting staffs, the second world war triggered a remarkable growth in the public popularity, acclaim and authority of radio's news reports, the 1970s saw the establishment of BBC and commercial local radio stations, while the 1990s witnessed the substantial proliferation of radio services in line with the intentions of the 1990 Broadcasting Act. Less than a century after Marconi was flying his kite in Cornwall, attempting to transmit a radio signal to Newfoundland, the reach of radio has become global, with individual countries being served by a broad range of indigenous and international radio services delivered by satellite and cable.

But in recent times, radio seems more typically to be dubbed the 'Cinderella' or 'poor relation' of mass media, reflecting its smaller audiences, revenues and budgets than its sister medium of television (McNair, 1994, p. 112 and Wilby and Conroy, 1994, p. 15). Other commentators allege that radio 'has been displaced by television from its former command of the domestic hearth' (Lewis and Booth, 1989, p. xii). Alternative descriptions of radio are rarely more flattering. A recent study designated radio 'the invisible medium' since it is allegedly marginalised in policy debates, which typically focus on television and new technologies, and similarly neglected in academic studies of mass media (ibid., p. 2). When radio is the subject of academic study, the focus is usually historical or the concern is with the practice and techniques of radio journalism (for example, Boyd 1993, Herbert 1976, Horstmann 1993, Wilby and Conroy 1994).

Radio, however, remains significant for at least three reasons. First, as Crisell and others insist, radio is a unique medium with a distinctive mode of communication. Most significantly, radio is *blind* (Crisell, 1986, p. 2, Horstmann, 1993, p. 2). Audiences cannot see radio's messages, which consist only of sounds and silence; unlike on television, there is no image. This distinctive characteristic allegedly provides radio with its greatest advantage over other media: its capacity to appeal to the imagination (Crisell, 1986, p. 7, *Radio: Choices and Opportunities*, Cmnd 92, p. 5). On this account radio is not 'television without pictures' but a commentary which allows listeners to provide their own pictures from the relatively limitless resources of their imaginations. Little wonder, perhaps, that cricket enthusiasts assert the supremacy of radio commentary above television coverage of test matches. Radio is also an intimate medium. Radio audiences are measured in millions but the cheapness, mobility and hence ubiquity of receivers means that listeners are millions of individuals, perhaps solitary individuals, sitting in their kitchens or in their cars. Consequently, the style of radio address has grown increasingly intimate, with the broadcaster 'only as far from his audience as his mouth is from the microphone and his listener's chair is from the loudspeaker at the other end' (Horstmann, 1993, p. 3). Radio offers personal companionship, with the broadcaster able 'to whisper into the ear of the isolated listener' (Crisell, 1986, p. 13). Radio is also flexible, offering listeners the freedom to engage in other activities. Television and newspapers require the listener's complete attention; not so radio. The listener can hear a news report about the divorce of an English princess, or the election of a labour government, while snoozing in bed, climbing a mountain or driving a car. Television and newspapers cannot 'match radio in terms of this immediacy as a purveyor of news and information' (ibid., p. 15).

Second, *contra* Lewis and Booth, radio has always been and remains a considerable and central arena for media policy debates, as well as a focus of government policy. Radio is undoubtedly a less significant policy focus than television, but to suggest on this basis that it is marginal, overstates the case. A few examples will illustrate the point. The green paper *Radio: Choices and Opportunities* (Cmnd 92, 1987), for example, proposed deregulation of radio services ahead of similar proposals for television embodied in the 1988 white paper *Broadcasting in the '90s: Competition, Choice and Quality*. The green paper triggered a wide-ranging and controversial debate concerning the prospect of retaining quality radio programming within a commercial system policed by a regulatory regime with a 'lighter touch' (Jenkins, 1989, pp. 4–6). More recently in June 1996, when the director general, John Birt, proposed changes to the organisational structures of the BBC, with particular measures targeted at World Service programming (see below, pp. 136–9), there was a substantial public outcry, an all-party early day motion signed by 274 MPs, a request from the foreign secretary for the chair of the board of governors to attend a foreign office meeting to explain the changes, a campaign organised by the *Guardian* newspaper with daily articles on the newspaper's front page displaying a coloured logo, 'Save The World Service', and a 'grilling' of John Birt by the all-party Foreign Affairs Select Committee (Kettle, 1996, p. 1). Such *furor* undoubtedly expresses the concerns of few beyond the confines of the chattering classes, but it is difficult to imagine such a wave of protest about a reorganisation of television services.

Third, radio remains ubiquitous. Technology has long since liberated radio, making it literally wire-less. Radios are mobile, cheap and accessible. Public demand for a range of radio programming remains high. By the end of the 1970s there were 2.5 radios per household or one for every person in the UK (Paulu, 1981, p. 351). Worldwide there are 37 radios per 100 people while in Western Europe there are approximately 310 million radio receivers or approximately 750 per thousand households (Newton, 1996, p. 3).

The gripes of Reith: the history of radio from public-service to market-driven medium

The history of radio across the twentieth century reveals that four factors have proved persistently influential in the development and growth of the medium. First, it is striking how frequently and significantly technological developments have shaped the fortunes of radio. The development and use of the transistor in the early 1960s, which made radios cheaper, more reliable and portable at a time when their popularity was waning, is an obvious example (Crisell, 1986, p. 31). Second, the impact of government policy has been crucial to the initial establishment of radio as well as its later development. The influence of the public enquiries conducted by Sykes (1923), Crawford (1926), Ullswater (1935), Beveridge (1949) and Pilkington (1962) on government radio policy cannot easily be overstressed. Third, the interests of newspapers and subsequently television have been powerful determinants, typically curtailing radio's development. Newspaper organisations, for example, conscious of the potential competitive threat of radio, lobbied to guarantee that in its early years the BBC was forbidden to broadcast news bulletins before 7 p.m. and that all news must be provided by, and purchased from, one of the major news agencies (Lewis and Booth, 1989, p. 57). Similarly, the growing popularity of television services during the 1950s had undoubted implications for the provision of radio services. The introduction of breakfast television on BBC and ITV in 1983 coincided with a 10 per cent reduction in the amount of time the average listener devoted to radio each week. Finally, but most significantly, the history of radio has been a history of the tension between Reith's original public-service mission to educate and inform audiences and the need to entertain and provide audiences with popular programming. This latter component of the Reithian trilogy has become increasingly significant as the BBC has been obliged to compete with other radio services and other media for audiences. But for Reith, writing in 1925, the purposes of broadcasting seemed uncontentious and obvious. 'I think it will be admitted by all,' he claimed, 'that to have exploited so great a scientific invention for the purpose and pursuit of entertainment alone would have been a prostitution of its powers and an insult to the character and intelligence of the people' (Reith, 1925, p. 17).

From company to corporation: the early history of the BBC

The British Broadcasting Company was formed in October 1922 and broadcast its first programme on 14 November 1922, although the company was not formally registered until 15 December of that year (Briggs, 1961, p. 21). The Company was a consortium of the leading manufacturers of radio receivers, who for some time had been broadcasting programmes to stimulate demand for their radio sets. Licensed by the Post Office, the Company derived its revenues from royalties on the receivers which its member companies sold and from a share of the revenues generated by the receivers' licences (Crisell, 1986, p. 20).

The early American experience of broadcasting had been influential in the establishment of the BBC. The world's first regular radio service was the American Station KDKA, established in Pittsburgh in 1920. The service was popular and other stations quickly followed on air; within four years 670 radio stations were transmitting. The airwaves promptly became congested and chaotic, with little room for newcomers (Briggs, 1961, p. 20, Lewis and Booth, 1989, pp. 35–6). The Post Office was unwilling to replicate this American experience. But similar experimental transmissions had been occurring in the UK. In February 1922, for example, the Marconi company began broadcasting regular programmes from a base in Writtle near Chelmsford and in May of that year from the London Station 2LO (Briggs, 1961, p. 20). The Post Office was also subject to increasing pressures from the armed services about the security risks allegedly associated with broadcasting. Against this background, the Post Office decided that access to the airwaves needed to be regulated. Britain needed a more ordered system of broadcasting and the BBC was the instrument to achieve this (Crisell, 1986, p. 20).

John Reith was appointed to be the first general manager of the BBC on 14 December 1922 for an agreed salary of £1750 a year. Reith, a Scottish engineer and son of a prominent Presbyterian minister, was enormously influential in shaping the institutional structures of the BBC and nurturing its philosophy of public-service broadcasting. Reith's domination of the BBC was described as 'massive, totalitarian and idiosyncratic, and for many decades the traditions of the BBC seemed to flow directly from his personality' (Curran and Seaton, 1988, p. 118). The central role which he assumed would perhaps have surprised no one more than Reith himself. When he saw the job advertised in the *Morning Post*, he had to ask a friend the meaning of the word 'broadcasting' (McIntyre, 1993, p. 114). But progress in the early years was rapid, with landmarks such as the publication of the *Radio Times* (1923), the first schools broadcasts (1924) and an outside broadcast speech by King George V from Wembley (1925). The public response was as enthusiastic in Britain as it had been in America. In 1923 the Post Office issued 80,000 licences and a further million in 1924, but probably four or five times as many sets were in use (Crisell, 1986, p. 20).

However, financial and constitutional problems plagued the fledgeling BBC; the Sykes Committee addressed the former, the Crawford Committee the latter.The Sykes Committee which reported in October 1923 advocated a single licence fee as the source of income for the BBC. Sykes explicitly rejected advertising as the financial basis for the BBC because of the belief that 'advertising would lower standards' (Cmnd 1951, 1923, para. 41). So far as constitutional issues were concerned Crawford recommended that the commercial company (the BBC) should be replaced by a public corporation 'acting as a trustee for the national interest', licensed for a period of 'not less than ten years', and governed by a board of governors appointed by the crown for a five-year period. The governors were, in turn, to work through a permanent director general, the Corporation's chief executive (Crawford, Cmnd 2599, 1926, pp. 14–15). Public funding, combined with the buffer which the governors provided between broadcasters and politicians, would guarantee the political and editorial independence of the Corporation. Despite these formal constitutional arrangements, the BBC has always been subject to 'informal' state pressures since the state renews the BBC's charter, increases the licence fee and appoints governors to its board (Franklin, 1994, pp. 77–82, Scannell and Cardiff, 1982, p. 162). Crawford also specified that the new Corporation should be encouraged to broadcast 'a moderate amount of controversial matter' so long as the material 'is of high quality and distributed with scrupulous fairness' (ibid.). From the outset, impartiality has been a constitutional requirement for the BBC.

The greater part of Crawford's recommendations were accepted by the government and the BBC was given a royal charter on 1 January 1927; John Reith was appointed its first director general. The transition from company to corporation was accomplished with little disruption of the principles of public-service broadcasting which were already well established; the move seemed 'logical and inevitable' (Briggs, 1965, p. 3). In truth the Corporation's political and editorial independence owed less to Crawford than the performance of the BBC's news services during the general strike of May 1926. The standing of the BBC and John Reith in both politicians' and the public's perceptions was greatly enhanced by the events of the general strike, increasing the likelihood that the postmaster general would accept Crawford's recommendations (Briggs, 1961, p. 360 and Gabor, 1995, p. 13). The strike split the cabinet into two factions characterised by distinctive views about the strike itself and the possible role of the BBC. The first, typified by Winston Churchill, wished to crush the strike and was willing to commandeer the BBC and use its broadcasting services for propagandist purposes. Such a takeover would have permanently destroyed the BBC's credibility. A second group believed it would be better to leave the BBC a measure of independence (Briggs, 1961, p. 362). Reith's diplomacy as well as his broadcasting skills prevented an outright takeover of the BBC.

Throughout the nine days of the strike no newspapers were published
except the government's *British Gazette* which Churchill managed and
edited from 11 Downing Street. Before the strike, the BBC was not allowed
to gather its own news, broadcast any news before 7 p.m. or broadcast on
matters of controversy (Gabor, 1995, p. 13). News bulletins were provided
by the leading news agencies and were literally nothing more than 'newspapers read over the air' (Herbert, 1976, p. 11). But the absence of other, independent, sources of news changed this restrictive pattern of broadcasting.
For the first time, the BBC broadcast news bulletins during the day which
were listened to by millions who came to rely on them for information.
News bulletins were broadcast at 10 a.m., 1 p.m., 4 p.m., 7 p.m. and 9 p.m.
daily – what would today be called a 'rolling news format'. The 10 a.m. bulletin on the second day of the strike set out the BBC's determination to
maintain its editorial independence and impartiality. The text was designed
to win public confidence and deter political intervention.

> The BBC fully realizes the gravity of its responsibility to all sections of
> the public and will do its best to discharge it in the most impartial
> spirit . . . we would ask the public to take as serious a view as we do
> ourselves of the necessity of plain objective news being audible to
> everyone. Nothing is more likely to create panic than the complete
> interruption of authentic news. This would only leave the field open to
> wild rumour and the consequences would be very serious. We shall do
> our best to maintain our tradition of fairness and we shall ask for fair
> play in return.
>
> (cited in Briggs, 1961, p. 368)

It is often suggested that Reith supported the government in the strike and
his well-known conservative syllogism is cited to make this point. 'Since the
BBC was a national institution,' Reith claimed, 'and since in this crisis the
government were acting for the people . . . the BBC was for the government
in this crisis too' (Scannell and Cardiff, 1991, p. 33). But Reith was concerned to defend the independence of the BBC. The latter had to be 'for the
government' but he insisted that the BBC 'be allowed to define its position
to the country' (cited in Briggs, 1961, p. 363). The Labour opposition were
highly critical of the BBC output during the strike and every news bulletin
had to secure the censor's approval, but for many millions they provided a
lifeline of information and stood in stark contrast to the evident propaganda
of the *British Gazette*.

The BBC emerged from the strike with greatly enhanced credibility as a
news provider and this was reflected in the increased news provision. More
generally, programme schedules revealed a remarkable variety for an organisation in its infancy with limited, if expanding, staff and resources. In one
week in 1927, for example, there were '16 hours of dance music, 16 of classical music, 5 and a half of music-hall entertainment. In the same week there
were nearly 15 hours of talks and readings of various kinds, including

almost 5 hours of news. There were outside broadcasts, as well as "Children's Hour" and broadcasts for schools. On average transmissions continued for about eleven hours a day but started late. Even in 1939 programmes did not start until 10.15 a.m.' (Carter, 1971, p. 41).

The 1930s were known as the 'Golden Age' of broadcasting because of the substantial expansion of both audiences and broadcasting staffs. On 1 January 1927 there were just over 2 million license holders but by 1939 this figure had risen to more than 9 million. The potentially large number of listeners to each licensed radio prompted one observer to calculate that even in 1928, radio audiences were possibly as high as 15 million (Black, 1972, p. 26). The staff of 773 employed in early 1927 was a remarkable and rapid expansion on the four initial employees of the original BBC in 1922, but by September 1939 the BBC staff had grown to almost 5000. The 'Golden Age' witnessed the transformation of the BBC. 'To put the matter simply,' Briggs reminds, 'in 1927 the BBC was still a small organisation, catering for a minority, if a large and growing minority of the British public. In 1939, the BBC was a large organisation and it was catering for a majority of the British public' (Briggs, 1965, p. 6). This expansion in staffs and services prompted the BBC to move in 1932 from the cramped quarters at Savoy Hill to Broadcasting House (BH) in London.

Preventing 'incalculable harm': Reith and public-service broadcasting

Reith was convinced that broadcasting should be organised as a public service and not according to free-market principles, where finance was derived from advertising or sponsorship and the ultimate goal was to make a profit (Lewis and Booth, 1989, p. 5). 'I wonder if many have paused to consider the incalculable harm which might have been done,' he speculated, 'had different principles guided the conduct of the service in the early days' (Reith, 1925, p. 31). His commitment to public-service principles was encapsulated in the often quoted belief that broadcasting should seek to 'inform, educate and entertain'. That ordering of priorities had clear implications for broadcasting practice and programming schedules (Seymour Ure, 1991, p. 65). The emphasis on information signalled the need for strong news services, documentaries and international news. Education implied quality schools programming but also a more general mission to improve the audience. In Reith's words, 'our responsibility is to carry into the greatest possible number of homes everything that is best in every department of human knowledge, endeavour and achievement' (Reith, 1925, p. 34). This implied that broadcasting should not merely give the audience what it wanted or strive to satisfy the lowest common denominator of taste. Reith was conscious of the allegations of paternalism which his commitments evoked, but dismissed them; although not always convincingly. 'It is occasionally indicated to us,' he claimed, 'that we are apparently setting out to give the public what we think they need – and not what they want, but few know what they want, and very few what they need. There is often no difference' (ibid.).

Reith believe that four principles were central to public-service broadcasting. First, broadcasting should be protected from commercial pressures and should not be sullied by the profit motive. Second, broadcasting should extend its services to the whole community and reach the entire nation. Third, there should be 'unified control', that is, broadcasting should be characterised in Reith's phrase by the 'brute force of monopoly' rather than any sectional or regional interest. Finally, broadcasting must maintain high standards and produce quality programming (Briggs, 1961, pp. 235–9, Golding, 1974, p. 33, Lewis and Booth, 1986, p. 58). Given Reith's role as the first general manager and then director general of the BBC, the philosophy of public-service broadcasting was not only a set of principles which might inform an ideal-type system of broadcasting (see Lewis and Booth, 1989, pp. 6–8), but also came to offer an account of the particular organisational form which broadcasting has assumed in the British setting. A series of government white papers, broadcasting legislation and committee reports published across the last 70 years have supplemented Reith's initial ideas and helped to shape the changing character of the public-service tradition.

In 1985, when the Peacock Committee was established to explore the funding of the BBC, the Broadcasting Research Unit (BRU) surveyed the opinions of key broadcasters in an effort to establish a contemporary definition of public-service broadcasting which might inform Peacock's investigations (Broadcasting Research Unit, 1985). Eight principles emerged. First, geographic universality. Programmes should be available to the whole population regardless of remoteness or inaccessibility. Second, universality of appeal. Programmes should appeal to all tastes. Third, universality of payment. At least one major broadcaster should be financed by everyone who receives and uses broadcasting services. Fourth, broadcasters should be distanced from vested interests, whether commercial or political, but especially the interests of the government of the day. Fifth, broadcasters should reflect national concerns, interests and cultures. Sixth, minority groups, especially disadvantaged minorities, should enjoy particular provision. Seventh, broadcasting should encourage competition to produce quality programming rather than competition for audiences. Finally, the public guidelines for broadcasting should be designed to liberate not restrict programme makers (ibid., pp. 25–32). A senior journalist and later head of BBC radio summarised: 'Public-service broadcasting must stand for quality but more importantly for range of programming. It must be universal, national and independent of government. It must take risks, nurture ideas until they blossom, take the long view about what will come good or what the audience will come to love' (Forgan, 1991, p. 21). What Blumler describes as these 'vulnerable values' of public-service broadcasting have been severely challenged since the mid-1980s by the growing emphasis on market forces as the key determinants of programming in the broadcasting system (Blumler, 1992).

The development of radio news journalism

The provision of authoritative, impartial and independent news programming has always been a central ambition of the public-service tradition, but opposition from established press interests, especially the Newspaper Proprietors' Association, inhibited the development of BBC radio newsrooms. Initially, the BBC was allowed to transmit only a single news bulletin each day. The bulletin was composed by the news agencies and delivered by special messenger to the BBC for an announcer to read after 7 p.m. when all the daily and evening newspapers had been sold. In 1923, the Sykes Committee confirmed that 'the British Broadcasting Company's licence provides that they shall not broadcast news except such as they obtain from certain approved News Agencies' (Sykes, Cmnd 1951, 1923, para 69). Sykes identified the financial interests of print journalism as the source of such restrictions. 'The Newspaper Proprietors' Association, the Newspaper Society and the principle News Agencies . . . spend very large sums in the collection and distribution of news, and they urge with some justice that it would not be in the public interest that the broadcasting system . . . should be allowed to publish news otherwise than from authoritative and responsible sources of information' (ibid.). But Sykes argued in favour of relaxing restrictions and hoped the press 'might well agree to more latitude being given for the broadcasting of news' (ibid.).

The general strike obliged Reith and his staff to improvise a rudimentary newsroom which, as noted above, revealed the potential and public popularity of radio news. By 1930, more than half of British homes had a radio set and the majority listened to radio news. The bulletins were authoritative but dull. They were still drafted by print-based news agencies and written in the style of print journalism. Even in the 1930s, BBC news readers had to preface each bulletin with: 'Here is the news, copyright by Reuters, Press Association, Exchange Telegraph and Central News' (Herbert, 1976, p. 12). But it was becoming increasingly clear that broadcast journalism required radically different techniques, skills and approaches from print journalism; radio needed to achieve autonomy from the press. In 1936, a young journalist drafted proposals for a revised BBC news style and sent them to the chief news editor; the letter is worth quoting at some length.

It is my impression . . . that it would be possible to enliven the news to some extent without spoiling the authoritative tone for which it is famed . . . I suggest that a member or members of your staff – they could be called BBC reporters, or BBC correspondents – should be held in readiness, just as are the evening paper men, to cover unexpected news for the day . . . In the event of a big fire, strikes, civil commotion, railway accidents, pit accidents or any other of the major catastrophes in which the public, I fear, is deeply interested, a reporter could be sent out from Broadcasting House to cover the event for the bulletin. At the scene it would be his job, in addition to writing his own account of the event, to secure an eye witness . . . to give a short eye witness account of the part he or she played that day. In this way, I really believe that news could be presented in a gripping manner and, at the same time, remain authentic . . . It should be possible to record his or her [the eye witness's] brief description . . . Such a news bulletin would itself be a type of actuality programme.

(cited ibid., pp. 12–14)

Signed by Richard Dimbleby, the letter outlined the essential elements of a modern news report. Radio news was to be authoritative and independent, but also immediate, possibly even live, with the inclusion of recorded interviews and actuality. In 1936 the Crystal Palace fire offered Dimbleby an opportunity to implement his ideas for news presentation. The fire began just after the final editions of the evening papers hit the streets. The BBC had an exclusive on the story for the rest of the night. At the scene of the fire, Dimbleby and his colleague were cut off from their broadcast van by the huge crowds and were unable to transmit their eye-witness interviews. Dimbleby used a telephone from a nearby cafe to broadcast live coverage of the event with the roar of the flames, the din of the sirens and the shouting of the crowd as background noise. In that moment news journalism changed. Dimbleby's point was dramatically proven. Newspapers could never match the immediacy of such reporting or so accurately convey the 'feel' of an event (Black, 1972, p. 73, Crisell, 1986, p. 22 and Herbert, 1976, p. 22).

The second world war further enhanced the legitimacy and public credibility of radio news while also encouraging the development of innovatory news techniques. It triggered a surge in the demand for news which could not be met by newspapers with their depleted staffs and restrictions on news print. Newspapers, moreover, could not match the speed and immediacy of radio. Listening to the nine o'clock news for information about the prosecution of the war became a national and collective ritual generating 'huge and avid audiences' (Crisell, 1986, p. 25, Herbert, 1976, p. 15, Briggs, 1970). News techniques and programme formats developed rapidly. Information was collected by specialist war reporters, recorded interviews and other materials were inserted into news programmes, special news programmes were established, comment was associated with fact and news bulletins moved into peak listening times (Briggs, 1970, p. 327, Crisell, 1986, p. 25). In 1942, a special News Division was established and a corps of BBC foreign correspondents was beginning to develop. Unlike reporters, correspondents did not merely report the news but probed the facts to explain and offer comment on the news. The BBC was no longer reliant on official handouts or press agencies. BBC news was coming of age; Dimbleby's dream was becoming reality. Addressing a national conference of journalists in 1943, H.G. Wells announced with a certainty matched only by its inaccuracy that 'the day of the newspaper was done' (cited in Briggs, 1970, p. 48).

Populism, pirates and programming: the transition from 'mixed' to 'streamed' networks

The war was to prove influential on a broader range of BBC programming than just the news services. From 1932, the BBC organised programming on two networks. The National Programme originated largely from London while the Regional Programme derived materials from six regional services. Both were 'mixed-programme' networks which, according to Reithian principles, offered a diverse range of programming in the paternalistic hope of introducing listeners to new and 'uplifting' material. Typically the range included: 'news, drama, sport, religion, music (light to classical), variety or light entertainment. Not only did it cater for different social needs (education, information, entertainment), but for different sectional interests within the listening public (children, women, businessmen, farmers and fishermen)' (Scannell and Cardiff, 1982, pp. 167–8).

The advent of war triggered a change in programme philosophy. In 1940, the BBC introduced the Forces Network, an entertainment station of dance music, sport and variety which was intended to boost the morale of troops, especially those stationed abroad. A second station, the Home Service, combined the national and regional programmes, was more 'serious' and carried 'all really minority material' including the main news bulletins (Briggs, 1970, p. 46 and Seymour Ure, 1991, p. 71). The Forces Service was intended as a temporary expedient but, in the austere circumstances of war, the emphasis on entertainment proved popular; within two years it attracted more civilian than military listeners and outstripped the audience for the Home Service by 50 per cent (Briggs, 1970, p. 47 and 1979, p. 51). The popularity of the forces network meant the BBC was unlikely to return to the pre-war structure of two broadly similar 'mixed-programme' networks (Crisell, 1986, p. 27).

In 1945, William Haley, the director general, announced a new tripartite structure for broadcasting. The London-based Home Service was to remain intact and supply materials to a range of regional services. The Forces Service was replaced by the virtually identical Light Programme on 29 July 1945 (Briggs, 1979, p. 55). A new network, the Third Programme, which targeted an elite 'whose tastes, education and mental habits enable them to take pleasure in . . . broadcasts of artistic and intellectual distinction', was launched in 1946 (Annan, 1977, p. 12); its audience was approximately the same as for the *Sunday Times* (Briggs, 1979, p. 66). Haley viewed society hierarchically as a 'pyramid of taste'. Each new service targeted an appropriate audience; the Third Programme marked the high point. Listeners would, he hoped, slowly aspire upwards, 'being induced through the years increasingly to discriminate in favour of the things that are more worthwhile' (Haley, 1948, quoted in Smith, 1974, p. 83). In combination, the three networks 'represented an ingenious reconciliation of popular demand and the old Reithian seriousness of purpose, a compromise of streamed and mixed programming which was to work fairly well for the next ten or fifteen years' (Crisell, 1986, pp. 26–7).

The post-war decade represented the 'heyday' of radio broadcasting; the quality and range of programming broadcast on the three new networks won acclaim.

> It was the period of *Children's Hour* and *Radio Newsreel*, of discussions and debates such as *The Brains Trust* and *Any Questions*, of drama – not only classical plays but popular serials like *Dick Barton* and *The Archers* – of light entertainment such as *ITMA* and *Workers' Playtime*, and of a vast output of classical and popular music both on record and performed by innumerable orchestras including the BBC's own.
>
> (ibid., p. 28)

But three factors undermined radio's popularity. First, the availability of television programming, especially the arrival of the commercial television network in 1955, was corrosive of radio audiences. The advent of BBC2 in 1963 and the introduction of colour transmissions in 1967 exacerbated radio's declining popularity. Second, the problems of overlap between the three radio networks were reinforced by the unpopularity of the Third Programme whose audience fell to 2 per cent of the total audience (Seymour Ure, 1991, p. 72). Third, a number of pirate radio stations broadcasting pop music proved considerably more popular than the BBC networks. From its inception in 1932, Radio Luxembourg nurtured a growing audience which, by 1955, was larger than the number of listeners for the Home Service. But it was the arrival of Radio Caroline, a former Danish ferry anchored four miles off Harwich, which came on air on Easter Sunday, 29 March 1964, which offered the more significant challenge to BBC radio. Within a year the station was attracting audiences of 15 million daily by playing non-stop 'best-selling pop music with disc-jockey chat' (Barnard, 1989, p. 40, Hind and Mosco, 1985, p. 12). The economic success of the pirates rested on advertising revenues and their failure to make royalty payments. The pirates were finally forced off air by the Marine Broadcasting Offences Act on 14 August 1967, but within six weeks (30 September 1967) the BBC launched Radio 1, a copy-cat station which employed many of the pirate DJs. The Light, Third and Home continued as mixed-programme networks but were renamed Radios 2, 3 and 4 respectively (Seymour Ure, 1991, p. 73).

Technological advances shored up radio's flagging popularity. Broadcasts in stereo, VHF transmissions which improved quality and reduced interference, combined with the development of transistors which made radios portable, did much to offset radio's decline but the indicators of BBC radio's dwindling popularity were evident. The number of radio licences fell from just over 10 million in 1955 to 2.7 million in 1965; the separate radio licence was abolished in 1971. Across the same period, television licences rocketed from 4 to more than 13 million (ibid., p. 76). In 1955, radio consumed 61 per cent of expenditure on broadcasting compared to television's 39 per cent, but by 1965 the figure was 31 per cent for radio and 69 per cent for television (ibid., p. 78). The BBC's policy response to this decline was *Broadcasting in the '70s* which signalled a retreat from mixed into streamed programming. The BBC would no longer offer a comprehensive public service in each network but only across all networks. In April 1970, Radio 2 became a station devoted to light or middle-of-the-road music, Radio 3 provided serious or 'classical' music, while Radio 4 was for talk, news and current affairs and drama. *Broadcasting in the '70s* marked the BBC's acceptance that the 'Reith/Haley commitment to "mixed" programming on each station simply did not correspond to listening preferences' (ibid., p. 73 and Barnard, 1989, p. 47).

Local radio: 'set up in idealism and run on enthusiasm'

There was another legacy of the pirates: the establishment of local radio. The Pilkington Committee (1962) recommended that a system of local radio broadcasting should be established by the BBC; Pilkington expressly declared its belief that a system financed by advertising revenues was wholly incompatible with the needs of the local audience (Lewis and Booth, 1989, p. 94). The subsequent development of local radio in Britain has mirrored the fortunes of the different political parties. In 1966, the Labour government authorised an experiment in local radio. The first station was established in Leicester on 8 November 1967; by 1970, 20 BBC local stations were on air reaching 70 per cent of the population. In that same year, the newly returned Conservative government favoured a commercially financed local radio system. Following a substantial and public debate, the government published the white paper *An Alternative Service of Broadcasting* in March 1971 which seemed to concede much to the BBC. There were to be no national stations in the commercial radio sector and the broadcasting practice of the Independent Local Radio (ILR) stations was to be inspired by public-service principles (Barnard, 1989, p. 70, Johnson, 1985, p. 10). The white paper stated for example that ILR programmes had to 'combine the usual elements of entertaining radio programming with programmes of a strong local flavour, in order to provide a service which can develop into a true alternative to the BBC services particularly in news, news commentary and information' (cited in Barnard, 1989, p. 75). Fifty years after the creation of the BBC and 20 years after commercial television, ILR stations were to be established in the wake of the Sound Broadcasting Act 1972.

The Independent Broadcasting Authority (IBA) was allowed to license 60 ILR stations, with Capital Radio and LBC going on air in October 1973. Another 17 ILR stations followed quickly before a change of government in February 1974 halted further expansion until after the Annan report. A second and rapid phase of expansion began in April 1980 with seven new stations that year, six in 1981, six in 1982, five in 1983 and six in 1984 when the IBA decided on a pause for consolidation (Johnson, 1985, p. 11). The election in 1979 of the Thatcher government with its commitment to deregulation triggered a further and considerable expansion in local radio.

From the outset, BBC local radio was a 'shoestring operation' to be funded from existing licence revenues. One managing director of radio admitted it was 'set up in idealism and run on enthusiasm' (cited in Lewis and Booth, 1989, p. 90). More sombre appraisals suggest that BBC local radio was 'at best forgotten, at worst cut and diluted' (ibid., p. 70). From 1967 to 1973, the programme content of BBC local radio was a mixture of BBC-owned library music, local news and chat and programmes on local themes, with music and speech programmes generally being distinct. The output might broadly be described as 'a worthy local answer to Radios 2 and 4' (Barnard, 1989, p. 66). The competition provided by the arrival of ILR stations from 1973 onwards influenced programming at the BBC in the direction of playing records interspersed with dedications, local information and the quickly established as well as cheap format developed by ILR stations, the 'phone-in' (Lewis and Booth, 1989, p. 102). There is a discernible irony in the fact that while the ILR stations were intended to be public-service driven, yet distinctive from the BBC, they quickly influenced the BBC stations. Both BBC and ILR stations have been criticised for the sexist nature of much of their programming. Until recently, presenters were almost exclusively male with daytime listeners presumed to be women. Male presenters invariably 'flirt' with listeners and are somewhat akin to 'romantic visitors' who offer verbal palliatives for the lonely tasks of housework or childcare, but always support the extant division of sexual labour. In the words of one critic, radio is like 'valium taken aurally' (Karpf, 1987, p. 173).

But the achievements of local radio have never matched the aspirations of its advocates. A number of factors prevented the development of BBC local radio into a more dynamic and desirable service. The most obvious has been financial constraints. Radio as a whole receives lower budgets than television and local radio has always suffered disproportionately from budget cuts within radio services. Local radio, moreover, lacked autonomy, with even decisions about significant matters such as the location of stations and their budgets being decided by London management. The significance attributed to news journalism by centralised BBC managers has also militated against developing the principle of 'access' local radio, while national agreements have restricted 'needle time' and the availability of music for programmes (Lewis and Booth, 1989, pp. 95–6). For ILR stations financial restrictions have also been considerable. The early difficulties of stations such as Capital and LBC reflected their miscalculation of overheads and running costs, while more recently it has been the increasing competition within commercial radio combined with the long-term effects of recession which have created difficulties (Barnard, 1989, p. 75, Franklin, 1994, p. 56).

Despite these constraints, recent government policy articulated in the Broadcasting Act 1990 has favoured a rapid and unprecedented expansion in commercial local radio. The following chapter examines and assesses recent radio policy and the prospects for programming in the new deregulated radio marketplace.

|7|

Changing radio times
Public service and markets

The last decade has witnessed radio's growing estrangement from the pub-lic-service tradition. Since the late 1980s, the range and quality of program-ming, in both the commercial and public sectors of radio broadcasting, has become increasingly susceptible to the influence of market forces. This chap-ter analyses these changes in local and national radio by: (1) evaluating recent government radio policy as well as analysing the intentions and pol-icy statements of broadcasting organisations such as the BBC; (2) detailing the current provision of radio services in both public and private sectors, nationally and locally, with a particular focus on selected new commercial stations like Jazz FM and Viva, the station for women listeners, as well as the unique provision of the World Service; (3) outlining patterns of radio ownership and cross-media ownership and assessing the prospects for viable and sustained growth in the commercial sector of radio; (4) analysing audi-ences for public and commercial radio services; and (5) comparing the early experiences of two new radio stations, Radio Five Live and Talk Radio, which articulate divergent broadcasting philosophies, emerge from distinc-tive broadcasting traditions, reside on different sides of the commercial divide, seek different audiences and enjoy differential access to resources.

Recent developments in radio policy: deregulation, choice and charters

The broad thrust of governments' radio policy since the mid-1980s has been to encourage deregulation (*Radio: Choices and Opportunities*, Cmnd 92, 1987, p. 11). More specifically, the intention has been to deliver greater choice for listeners combined with a proliferation of new stations, operating in an increasingly competitive market and policed by a new regulatory body working with a 'lighter touch' (ibid., p. 31, para. 7.2 and p. 39, para. 8.5). Government policy has, in turn, prompted a policy response from broadcasters. The concern of BBC policy statements has been to respond to government initiatives but also to propose revisions to its organisational structures and working practices in the run-up period to charter renewal in 1997. Whether government policy or the BBC's own policy shifts have done more to create a climate in which tabloid journalism can flourish, is a contentious matter.

Green and white but read all over? Government radio policy

These policy ambitions were initially articulated in a systematic way in the February 1987 green paper *Radio: Choices and Opportunities* (Cmnd 92). The proposals triggered a substantial public debate with opponents arguing that the expansion of commercial radio services, operating under a reduced system of regulation, would lead inevitably to declining standards of programming. The commercial imperative to win large audiences and advertising revenues would become the priority, rather than quality journalism. In order for 'good broadcasting to flourish', it was claimed, 'it must operate in an environment protected from commercial or political pressures, from pressure to achieve quantitative rather than qualitative results. High quality radio tends to cost more' (Jenkins, 1989, p. 6). Despite the debate and more than 500 responses to the green paper, the proposals for radio contained in the subsequent 1988 white paper *Broadcasting in the '90s: Competition, Choice and Quality*, were unchanged in their essentials (Cmnd 517). *Broadcasting in the '90s* proposed that public-service radio should continue under the aegis of the BBC. The Corporation's services would be funded from the licence fee 'for some years to come' although BBC services would 'be subject to a much stronger stimulus of competition'. A new 'slim' Radio Authority was to be established which would license 'at least' three new national commercial services as well as hundreds of new local stations by the mid-1990s. Neither these, nor the existing independent radio stations, would be required to offer education, information or entertainment, although they 'may follow a public service pattern if they wish'. The white paper stressed consumer protection alongside the lighter regulatory touch. Both local and national stations would have to honour their 'promises of performance' to retain their licences. A competitive radio broadcasting market would be guaranteed by restrictions on ownership. No group would be able to control more than one national service and more than six local services. There would be a 20 per cent limit on radio interests in newspapers and vice versa (*Broadcasting in the '90s*, Cmnd 517, pp. 37–8).

The white paper recommendations found legislative expression in the Broadcasting Act 1990 which made provision for a new Radio Authority to allocate licences and regulate programming (Broadcasting Act 1990, Sec 83 (1)–(3) and 84) and three new national radio stations alongside a 'range and

diversity of local services' (Sec 85 (2) a–b). But there was no specific requirement in the Act for these new stations to broadcast news or current affairs
(Sec 85 (3) a). The allocation of licences, moreover, did not involve a 'quality threshold'; i.e., applicants did not need to convince the Radio Authority
of the quality of the programming to be provided. *Contra* the procedures for
granting licences for Channel 3 television (see chapter 9), national radio
licences would be awarded solely on the basis of the highest cash bid in a
'blind' auction; there was to be no 'exceptional circumstance' in which a bid
promising higher programming quality could be awarded the licence.

The Broadcasting Act 1990 declared that the BBC should continue as 'the
cornerstone of British broadcasting' (Home Office Press Release, 1
November 1990), but policy proposals to reform the Corporation's radio
services continued in the period prior to the BBC's charter renewal in 1996.
In the context of a government committed to privatising major industries
and securing 'value for money' in the public sector, many of the proposals
focused on 'rationalising' BBC services. In March 1991, a report published
by the Centre for Policy Studies (CPS) proposed that radios 1 and 2 should
be privatised. Both stations were at the margins of the BBC's public-service
remit and could readily be offered without prejudice to the output by a commercial provider. Privatising the services, moreover, would allow considerable savings; Radio 1 cost £28 million (9 per cent of the BBC radio budget
at 1991 levels) and Radio 2 £50 million (17 per cent) (Green, 1991, p. 22).
BBC local radio should also go. It had always been 'a poor relation within
the radio service', costing £282 per broadcast hour compared with £8,900
for Radio 4 (ibid.). BBC local radio stations, moreover, attracted small audiences, faced tough competition from ILR rivals and, in total, cost the
Corporation £46 million per annum or 16 per cent of total radio budget;
slightly less than Radio 2 or Radio 3 (ibid.). A second think-tank report, this
time by the Institute of Public Policy Research (IPPR), supported Green's
view that the BBC should 'lose its local radio stations' but also consigned
that 'recent oddity Radio 5' to the public-sector rubbish heap (Boulton,
1991, p. 11). The proposals gained political momentum on the
Conservative back benches, so that when the National Heritage Department
published the green paper *The Future of the BBC* in November 1992, it
raised a number of predictable as well as ominous speculations about BBC
radio services; 'there could be changes to the BBC's radio output' and 'some
further rationalisation may be necessary' (*The Future of the BBC*, 1992,
p. 20, para 4.9). Privatising radios 1 and 2 would reduce BBC services to
'three national radio channels, rather than five . . . another possibility would
be for the BBC to lose its local radio stations' (ibid., para. 4.10). In May
1993, the BBC document *Responding to the Green Paper* confirmed its
commitment to 'retain the current range of television and radio services
including local radio' (BBC, 1993a, p. 36). The proposal to privatise BBC
radio services was undermined by the findings of a study by the Henley
Centre which revealed that privatising Radio 1 would have 'a devastating

impact on commercial radio' and plunge Virgin 1215 and Atlantic 252 'substantially into the red' (Culf, 23 November 1993, p. 9). The July 1994 White Paper *The Future of the BBC: Serving The Nation, Competing World-Wide*, ended the speculation; the BBC's charter was to be renewed for 10 years beginning 1 January 1997 and there was to be no reduction in BBC national or local radio services (*The Future of the BBC*, Cmnd 2621, 1994, p. 18, paras 3.34–3.37). The white paper offered more general prescriptions of relevance to radio. The BBC was to continue as the main public-service broadcaster and licence-fee funding would continue until 2001 when, perhaps ominously, there would be a review of the licence system in the light of technological and other (non-specified) developments (ibid., p. 3, para. 1.17). Uniquely, the World Service would continue to be funded by foreign-office grant (see below, pp. 144–7) (ibid., p. 2, para, 1.9 and p. 19, paras. 3.38–3.42).

A major policy preoccupation for commercial services has been the question of the growing concentration of ownership and cross-media ownership. The white paper *Media Ownership: The Government's Proposals* addressed precisely this concern and proposed a considerable relaxation of existing regulations (*Media Ownership*, Cmnd 2872, May 1995). There were four specific proposals concerning radio. First, newspapers with less than 20 per cent of the national newspaper circulation market share (all major newspaper groups except News International and MGN), will be able to apply to the Radio Authority to control radio stations and vice versa, although only one national licence can be controlled and licences will not be granted to newspapers with more than 30 per cent circulation in the locality (ibid., p. 26, para. 6.28). Second, restrictions on television companies' ownership of radio stations will be abolished. Third, there was to be immediate secondary legislation to raise the limit on holding radio licences from 20 to 35 (ibid., pp. 27–8, para. 6.32). Finally, the government announced its longer-term intention to restrict any single media organisation to 10 per cent ownership of the total media market (ibid., p. 24, para. 6.16).

The Broadcasting Act 1996 gave legislative voice to these proposals with only minor modification; the long-term threshold for ownership of the total media market was raised to 15 per cent (The Broadcasting Act 1996 Schedule 2, p. 126). The Act signalled a major shake-up in the ownership of commercial radio. Local radio stations could now own two FM licences, triggering some stations to buy up their nearest competitors. The Act created a second precedent. Regional television companies and local newspapers could now buy radio stations outright rather than merely owning a part share of a station. The government's intention for the 1996 Act had been to relax regulatory controls on ownership but, viewed from a more critical perspective, the net effect when the Act's proposals came into force on 1 October 1996 was to unleash a rush of buying and selling and concentrate even further the ownership of the commercial radio sector.

The major purpose of the Broadcasting Act 1996 was to provide a framework for the establishment and expansion of digital broadcasting services in both public and commercial sectors – a framework previously outlined in *Digital Terrestrial Broadcasting: The Government's Proposals* (Cmnd 2949, HMSO, 1995). The Radio Authority has been invested with responsibility for regulating digital audio broadcasting (DAB), awarding licences and monitoring the new system (Broadcasting Act 1996, Pt II, Sec 42–4). There will be two national digital radio multiplexes (a bundle of digital channels) each capable of providing at least six radio services. One multiplex has been allocated to the BBC for its five national radio services which began digital broadcasting in September 1995. The other multiplex is devoted to the existing three commercial national stations (Classic FM, Virgin 1215 and Talk Radio) which are obliged to continue broadcasting their existing analogue service alongside the digital output, a process known as simulcasting. At least one multiplex has been assigned for local services with an additional multiplex available for extra local services reflecting demand. The criteria informing the Radio Authority's allocation of licences include the applicants' commitment to promote the development of digital terrestrial radio, their ability to provide a variety and plurality of programming and to provide services quickly and as widely as possible across the UK. Companies will be able to control one national multiplex and any number of local multiplex licences but will be restricted to owning one national DAB station and one DAB station, or under certain circumstances two, on each local multiplex.

Digital broadcasting will undoubtedly prompt a further expansion of radio services. But at the BBC there are no additional funds available for launching digital services; cuts in existing radio services and programme-making budgets are providing the launch capital. In the commercial sector, advertising revenues are growing but are failing to match the rate of growth of new stations; resources for programme making must be pared to the bone. The expansion of services with little, if any, additional funding, combined with the Radio Authority's lighter regulatory touch, suggests predictable consequences for programming quality. The managerial maxim of 'more for less' signals that the much-hyped digital broadcasting future may be bleaker than pundits imagine.

John Donne's bell and the death of Reith's BBC: Birt's radio policy

The BBC has been highly sensitive and responsive to these government initiatives in the period of charter renewal. John Birt's critics, typified by Dennis Potter in his brilliantly eloquent MacTaggart Lecture in 1993 (Potter, 1994, p. 47), argue that the BBC has been supine in the face of government pressures rather than stoutly defending its record of public-service broadcasting. The Corporation has been too ready to 'put its house in order' – on occasions even before being requested so to do. The BBC

> has already been driven on to the back foot by the ideology-driven malice of the ruling politicians and its response has been to take several more steps backwards, with hands thrown up, and to whimper an alleged defence of all that it has stood for in the very language and concepts of its opponents. This palpable ambivalence and doubt, where you pretend to be the commercial business that you cannot be, has led to the present near fatal crisis.
>
> (ibid.)

During the 1990s two BBC proposals for change have proved significant. First, the BBC intended to move towards what was termed 'bi-media' journalism. Journalists and news crews would gather and produce material for both television and radio services. A single specialist correspondent perhaps for legal affairs or even media would, in future, service television and a range of radio stations. Bi-media journalism promised considerable staff and financial savings and by 1990 had become 'a BBC buzzword' (Wallis and Baran, 1990, p. 69). For their part, critics suggested that bi-media working denies the uniqueness of radio journalism and the differences between radio and television cultures; worse, television tends to colonise and obliterate radio, leaving it with the leftovers of talents and resources: 'on the bi-media stage, radio will be the bit part player' (Karpf, 1996, p. 12). Radio, critics insist, is more than television without pictures. The policy of producer choice also dates from October 1991. The brainchild of John Birt, the scheme was intended to create a competitive internal market in the BBC by giving producers control of their own programme budgets and allowing them to go beyond the BBC for facilities for programme making when these were available more cheaply than in-house. Birt argued that producer choice would mean 'greater freedom for programme makers' and perhaps more significantly 'greater efficiencies' (*Guardian,* 30 October 1991). Critics suggested that producer choice would result in job cuts (5000 since 1990), a burgeoning of bureaucracy and a move towards the BBC becoming a publisher, rather than producer, broadcaster.

The most significant and recent policy changes at the BBC were announced on 7 June 1996 when Birt declared that he would remain director general until the year 2000 to oversee a radical restructuring of the Corporation. Critics immediately denounced the plan for downgrading domestic radio services, threatening the World Service, presaging widespread job cuts (the new bi-media site at White City will have room for only 60 per cent of current journalists) and triggering an expansion of bureaucracy (Tusa, 1996, p. 11, Karpf, 1996, p. 12 and Methven and Kelly, 1996, p. 2). John Tusa, Managing Director of the World Service from 1986 to 1992, claimed that while the policy statement was framed in 'management jargonocracy', its intentions were clear. 'Tolling like John Donne's bell,' he claimed, 'the words efficiency, resources, focus and the rest of the cliched lexicon of management analysis sound the death of Reith's BBC' (Tusa, 1996, p. 11).

The reforms propose four changes of consequence for radio. First, the BBC is to be structured into six key directorates: BBC Broadcast will commission and schedule all television and radio services; BBC Production will provide the 'world's largest broadcasting production powerhouse'; BBC News has responsibility for all news output; BBC Resources provides broadcasting resources for all BBC programmes; BBC Worldwide will be responsible for the marketing, sales and distribution of BBC output; and the Corporate Centre directorate will embrace personnel, corporate affairs, finance and information technology. Second, as noted above, responsibility for commissioning and scheduling all television and radio programmes is to be combined in a single directorate. This means that radio will no longer have an independent voice at Board of Management; it now has 'no one to fight for it in the BBC's inner sanctum' (Karpf, 1996, p. 12). Radio executives are conspicuous by their absence and many observers believe that radio will simply be swamped by television's agenda and demand for resources. Matthew Bannister, Controller of Radio 1, who has presided over the network during a controversial two-and-a-half-year period during which it has lost 5 million listeners, has been elevated to director of radio. Many observers believe Bannister is too junior and owes his promotion to his loyal support of Birt and his oversight of the *Extending Choice* document. Tusa, for example, believes that 'to elevate the Controller of Radio 1 to be the senior representative of BBC Radio in BBC management would have been laughed out of court at any time but the present. As a sign of where broadcasting priorities lie in radio, it is salutary' (Tusa, 1996, p. 11). The inclusion of television and radio under the single rubric of broadcasting in the new structure, moreover, will undoubtedly give additional impetus to moves towards bi-media journalism which many observers believe will eventually result in the demise of discrete radio departments. When the BBC anounced the structure of the production directorate in October 1996 only 2 of the 15 department heads worked in radio. Third, the World Service will retain responsibility for all foreign-language programming, but all programme making in English will be the responsibility of BBC Production and all World Service news and current affairs will come under BBC News rather than being made at Bush House. This proposal generated considerable public protest and a 'request' for BBC management to attend a meeting at the foreign office (see below, pp. 145). Fourth, the BBC plan intends to separate the commissioning and scheduling of programmes from their production. Critics object that programme making is an integrated and creative activity which 'consists not only of commissioning and producing but of such unmentioned and no doubt unmanageable and unquantifiable activities as having ideas' (ibid.).

Birt's policy proposals had less to do with broadcasting, of course, than self-confessed financial and organisational objectives; they were designed to deliver substantial savings (never cuts!) in programming costs, which must be reduced by 20 per cent over the next 10 years, to launch the BBC into the digital age. The proposals' consequences for radio are ominous. Jocelyn Hay, chair of the Voice of the Listener and Viewer, claimed to be 'extremely worried about the future of radio'. The proposals represent 'a significant diminution of the importance of radio' (cited in Culf, 1996a, p. 4). Such perceptions were undoubtedly influential in Director of Radio Liz Forgan's decision to resign four months previously, although Birt denied any connection. There also is a discernible irony here. A BBC producer argued that since the BBC is under increasing pressure to produce programmes cheaply, the resulting output does not warrant digital sound. 'We'll be making simpler, more basic programmes,' he claimed, 'which we could do perfectly well – and probably cheaper – on analogue, editing together with sticky tape' (cited in Karpf, 1996, p. 12).

From Ramadan Radio to the World Service: the current provision of radio services

After a slow start, radio services have enjoyed an explosive expansion over the decade since 1987. The establishment of the first ILR stations in 1973 meant that the BBC's radio monopoly had endured for more than half a century; it took almost another two decades before the first national commercial stations went on air in autumn 1992. But since the Broadcasting Act 1990, the burgeoning of commercial radio services has been prolific.

National radio

Expansion has also been evident in the public sector. Four of the BBC's national radio networks boast a pedigree which can be traced to the late 1960s and the policy document *Broadcasting in the '70s*. Radio 1 broadcasts pop music; Radio 2 also features popular music but in the 'easy listening' style with conversation and 'chat' for an older audience; Radio 3 broadcasts serious or 'classical' music, while Radio 4 carries news, current affairs, drama and some light entertainment, especially panel games. But in August 1990, these networks were joined by Radio 5, the BBC's first new national network for 23 years. In broadcasting terms Radio 5 enjoyed an eclectic, if not uncertain, identity. The station's programming combined sport from Radio 2 with schools programming from Radio 4 and initially shared output with other services: the Radio 3 lunchtime concert and programming from the World Service. Critics rounded on the station; with some justification, Radio 5 was denounced as 'a jerry-built shambles' (Dugdale, 1993, p. 13). Audiences were initially modest, but when the station eventually went off air, listening figures topped 4.5 million – a million more than Virgin 1215. But Radio 5 was doomed. In October 1993, John Birt announced a new 24-hour service which would combine sport with news – a programming intention which quickly earned the new station the designation 'Radio Spews'. The idea for the station derived from 'Scud FM', the cynical name for the BBC's continuous news broadcasts during the Gulf War (Hendy, 1994, p. 15).

Radio 5 Live began broadcasting on 28 March 1994. It had been a busy six months for controller Jenny Abramsky but the BBC needed to be on air well 'before the opposition, INR 3', the new commercial 'talk' station (Reynolds, 1994, p. 12). The network was the first at the BBC to be funded from two sources: the news directorate pays for the news and Network Radio finances the sport. The start-up budget was £30 million compared to £7.5 million for Virgin FM and £12 million for Classic FM (ibid.). The new station was seeking a new audience which would be younger and more 'male weighted'. Just how well Radio 5 Live has met 'the opposition' from Talk Radio UK is assessed below.

The three relatively new Independent National Radio (INR) stations are the progeny of the Broadcasting Act 1990, which closely defined their characteristic programming. INR 1 was to be 'wholly or mainly music' but 'not pop music', INR 2 could be popular music, while INR 3 was to devote programming to the 'broadcasting of spoken material' (The Broadcasting Act 1990, Sec 85 (2) (a) and (b). See also *Radio: Choices and Opportunities*, Cmnd 92, p. 23, para 4.16). But the birth of the new stations proved a troublesome delivery. By the 22 April 1991 deadline for applications to run the first of the three networks, no bids had arrived at the Radio Authority; the deadline was extended for one month (Henry, 22 April 1991). Potential bidders were deterred by the high set-up costs combined with anticipated low returns. The licence fee demanded by the Radio Authority (almost £1 million a year) coupled with transmission costs (£4 million) and the cash bid, meant that overall costs were prohibitive. But the climate of economic recession signalled that the successful bidder would be unable to charge the prices for advertising necessary to cover costs and provide a return (Henry, 22 April 1991, p. 3). A more encouraging three bids were received by the arrival of the second deadline in May 1991, but it seems as if from the outset, there was a good deal of scepticism about the viability of commercial radio nationally.

The successful bidder was Classic FM, which went on air in autumn 1992 and broadcast a 24-hour diet of classical music. The station was an immediate success with audiences and by early 1993 was reaching an average audience of 4.5 million listeners each week, which was well in excess of its early audience target of 2.8 million (Linton, 1993, p. 2). The INR 2 licence was awarded to Virgin 1215 which was launched on 30 April 1993. The station plays continuous 'up-market' pop music from the 1970s and 1980s and targeted 'CD buying' 35- to 45-year-olds as its core audience.

With a minimal staff of 42 compared to its major competitors Radio 1 and Capital Radio, which each employ 100 staff, Virgin 1215 wins an audience of 3.4 million compared to Radio 1's 11.2 million (data from Radio Joint Audience Research (RAJAR), cited in Culf, 18 May 1996). The licence for INR 3, which the Broadcasting Act 1990 stipulated must have a minimum 51 per cent speech content, was awarded to Talk Radio which bid £1.076 million above its nearest rival; five consortia bid for the licence. The station planned to broadcast virtually nothing other than phone-ins using 'shock jocks', a format borrowed unashamedly from the American experience. Emmis Broadcasting, part of the consortium, runs similar stations in Los Angeles, New York and Chicago. Talk Radio began broadcasting on Valentine's day 1995 but had already triggered 150 protest calls before going on air; it was to continue in much the same way throughout the station's first year (see below, pp. 152–5).

Local radio

In addition to its five national networks which broadcast throughout the UK, the BBC has independent network radio services in Scotland, Wales and Northern Ireland as well as 38 local radio stations in England. The reduced number of local stations since the late 1980s reflects a series of budget cuts which have forced some stations to close and others to merge. BBC local radio is a talk-based service focusing on local news and current affairs, information, community debate and local sport. The speech content of BBC local radio increased from 50 per cent in 1990 to 80 per cent in 1996 at a time when ILR stations have increasingly moved to a music format. In 1995 the BBC spent £67 million on local radio services which reached 7.5 million listeners every week – approximately 20 per cent of the adult population.

The most evident expansion in local or community services is in the commercial sector. At the end of 1992 there were 120 ILR stations but by mid-1996 this figure had grown to 176 with a further 28 stations delivered by cable and 14 by satellite; an additional 32 licences are about to be advertised (Radio Authority, 1996). There are also five regional ILR services broadcasting in the Severn Estuary (Galaxy Radio), the North West (JFM), the North East (Century Radio), the West Midlands (Heart FM) and Central Scotland (Scot FM). Additionally, in 1994 the Radio Authority awarded 262 28-day restricted service licences for local broadcasting to stations including Ramadan Radio and Radio Shankhill; applications for such restricted licences were up by 50 per cent on 1993 levels (Culf, 10 April 1995, p. 7).

The government's policy intention to encourage choice and diversity in programming seems more successfully achieved in local than national commercial services. Country 1035 offers country music, JFM 102.2 is devoted to jazz, blues and soul, London Greek Radio broadcasts music, news and information for Greek speaking listeners, while Supa AM provides Asian music and news. But underlying this nominal diversity there is a remarkable homogeneity of output. It is striking how many of these ILR stations (and the new regional licences) describe their programming as 'golden oldies', 'contemporary and classic hits' or 'easy listening'; there are few exceptions to this cheap and 'safe' broadcasting format. The market has not delivered the diversity that advocates of commercial broadcasting promised; on the contrary the operation of market forces seems to penalise any deviation from the populist mainstream.

Jazz FM, for example, began niche broadcasting jazz and related music to a specialist audience in March 1990, with start-up costs of £2.2 million. Within 16 months, 17 of the 45 staff were sacked as audiences fell to 520,000 rather than the anticipated 1 million. The managing director believed that Jazz FM had failed to identify its market. 'Too little was done according to what the market might want and too much was to do with what people here wanted internally.' To imagine that the metropolis might support a commercial radio station playing jazz was to commit the Reithian sin of 'elitism' (Mullin, 1991, p. 1). A takeover deal including the injection of a further £1 million has failed to turn around the station's fortunes. Despite playing more Sting and Sade than Charlie Parker, Jazz FM was reaching only 225,000 listeners weekly in mid-1996. Premier Radio, London's Christian radio service, has similarly been unable to survive market rigours. The station reduced staffing from 62 to 26 in order to break even on remarkably low monthly running costs of £100,000, but the modest weekly audience reach of 193,000 represents 2 per cent of the available audience in the M25 listening area. The London-based station Viva 963 AM, Britain's first radio station for women, went on air on 3 July 1995. The station sought self-consciously to offer a 'woman's perspective' with a different style of less politically laden news. Chairwoman Lynne Franks claimed Viva wished to attract 'intelligent career women who did not wish to be patronised with bland old-style knitting patterns and cooking recipes'. The station was determined to break out of the 'ghetto' of *Woman's Hour* (Franks cited in Culf, 5 May 1995, p. 8). The station spent £1 million on its pre-launch advertising campaign to attract ABC1 women, aged 25–44, to its diet of music and speech. Resident broadcasters are joined by guests such as Dilly Barlow and Eve Pollard who drives a political interview at the weekend. From the outset the station's budget was modest; staffing is likewise. Seven producers for the entire station is about half the number who work on *Woman's Hour*. But Viva never reached its target audience of 400,000 and by the last quarter of 1995 was attracting only 59,000 listeners a week (RAJAR data, 1996). By mid-1996, the station had been sold to Al Fayed's Liberty Publishing for £3 million. At weekends the audience for the station, now called Liberty, is so small it cannot be measured: less than 500 listeners. The recent experience of radio suggests that the market does not encourage, rather it detests, diversity. For a station with a distinctive voice, it is hard to be heard above the cacophony of 'classic gold' stations which currently overcrowd the airwaves.

News is undoubtedly the most expensive form of programming for both ILR and BBC local stations (Lewis and Booth, 1989, p. 103), but an IBA (Independent Broadcasting Authority) study in the early 1980s suggested that it was the major reason why local people listened to local radio services (Wright, 1980, p. 81). BBC stations display a greater commitment to local, national and even international news provision. The great majority of ILR stations are 'music only' stations with upwards of 80 per cent devoted to 'needle time' (Hetherington, 1989, p. 78). The 1987 green paper on radio, moreover, expressed concern about the 'clear impact' of economic considerations on ILR stations' ability to report local news (*Radio: Choices and Opportunities*, Cmnd 92, p. 12, para 2.7). But Hetherington's 1989 study concluded that the BBC not only provided more news, it provided better-quality news services. BBC local radio news services were judged to be less partisan in commentary, more detailed in coverage and staffed with greater numbers of journalists (Hetherington, 1989, pp. 80–1). Pennine Radio, for example, had only seven staff journalists at the time of Hetherington's study (ibid., p. 78). News on the ILR stations, moreover, was market driven. Mercia Sound's newsroom was, in Hetherington's view, the 'ILR's version of a popular tabloid newspaper, but without page three' (ibid., p. 151). The station's head of news is 'realistic' about his station's populist ambitions. 'News is pitched towards crime, human stories and events in the city of Coventry' (ibid., p. 151).

Given these shortages of staff journalists, BBC and ILR stations necessarily use other news sources, although these are limited. Press releases from local authorities and local business, copy from news agencies, the emergency services and reports from institutions like the law courts and Westminster routinely provide stories (London Radio Workshop, 1983, p. 52 and Gardner, 1986). Reliance on agency news – the Press Association, Reuters or Network News – is considerable. These agencies deliver a ready supply of news and used to provide subscribers with a teletype terminal which churned out a continuous stream of paper; the 'rip and read', however, has long since been replaced by a computer screen.

BBC local radio stations can call on the resources of BBC network news services including the General News Service (GNS). The GNS acts as an in-house news agency which distributes material to BBC local stations from its various specialist reporters on the City, Westminster or sports 'desks'. In the understaffed local newsrooms, where local journalists are under considerable pressure to produce regular bulletins across the newsday, the ready-made news stories from network sources are invaluable and typically provide between an quarter and a half of all news bulletins (London Radio Workshop, 1983, p. 70). In turn, the local stations feed news back to the five network stations (Barnard, 1989, p. 65). The ILR stations enjoy a similar service from Independent Radio News (IRN). Merged with ITN since

August 1992, IRN broadcasts live hourly bulletins of three minutes' duration between 6 a.m. and 6 p.m. which local stations can transmit; some stations choose not to mention that the news is from IRN (Hetherington, 1989, p. 151). Additionally, IRN pre-feeds audio and data at 20 minutes to the hour which allows local stations to mix their own locally generated news with the national news from London. The IRN Westminster desk provides daily and weekly round-ups of parliamentary news and similar services are available for financial news, sport and entertainment; there is also a special obituary service (IRN, 1996). On a typical day, stations will receive approximately 50 cuts of audio and 100 copy stories and, on most ILR stations, this IRN news supply constitutes the core of news provision. Judgements concerning the quality of local radio news vary considerably. Hetherington's 1989 study concluded fairly optimistically that local radio journalism was, despite some reservations, alive and kicking (Hetherington, 1989, p. 244); others remain sceptical (London Radio Workshop, 1983, p. 10). But one conclusion seems clear. Given local journalists' reliance on network news sources, listeners whether in Bournmouth, Barnsley or Berwick may well be hearing substantially the same news, whatever else is happening in their particular locale.

The World Service

The international dimension of Britain's radio services has, since 1926, found its voice through the BBC's World Service. Uniquely funded by an annual grant from the foreign office (£178 million in 1996/97), the BBC World Service enjoys an international reputation among listeners, politicians and broadcasters worldwide for the quality, authority and independence of its news programming. Unlike its American counterpart, Voice of America (VOA) or Radio Moscow or China's Radio International, the World Service has never been willing to become a propaganda organ of the Government (Hale, 1975, p. xv and Tusa, 1992, p. 15). An American textbook on broadcasting pays homage to the quality of World Service broadcasting: 'The BBC retains the highest credibility amongst external broadcasters. Throughout the world, listeners tune automatically to the BBC when in doubt about the authenticity of news sources. In terms of local disorder, it is not uncommon for foreign government officials to turn to the BBC for vital information about the state of affairs in their own country' (Head and Sterling, 1987, p. 30). The truth informing this accolade was confirmed by Mikhail Gorbachev, who tuned into the World Service during the Moscow *coup* of 1991, by Lech Walesa who listened during a period of imprisonment and by Terry Waite who was 'kept alive' spiritually and mentally by the variety of religious, cultural and news programming that the World Service broadcast 'with such excellence' (Tusa, 1992, pp. 16–23 and Engel, 20 June 1996, p. 2). World Service news is independent of government but does promote (albeit unconsciously) British values and consequently enacts what McNair describes as 'cultural diplomacy' or, in a different phrase, 'a goodwill creating function' (McNair, 1994, p. 118 and Wallis and Baran, 1990, pp. 126–7).

The World Service output is prolific. Every 24 hours the BBC World Service produces 200 news broadcasts transmitted in English and 36 foreign languages. In addition to the English service, there are the European Services (in Russian and various Eastern and Western European languages), the Latin American Service (Spanish and Portuguese) and the 'three As' – Arabic (nine hours daily), the African Service and the Asian Service, broadcasting to an area from Iran to Japan and Sri Lanka to Nepal (Wallis and Baran, 1990, p. 131): a total of 1036 hours direct programming each week to an audience of 140 million (Bellos, 1996, p. 9). The quantity and quality of World Service output bestows great authority on the service and consequently occupancy of the post of Head of External Services used to be considered 'a stepping stone to the Director Generalship itself' (Tusa, 1996, p. 11).

During the 1980s the World Service, notwithstanding its prestige, was subject to three threats (McNair, 1994, p. 118). First, the World Service appeared anachronistic at a time when Conservative politicians were enthusiastic about deregulation, sceptical about public service and, among some sections of the party's back bench, increasingly distrustful of the BBC political impartiality. Second, the collapse of the Soviet Union and the repressive regimes in Eastern Europe diminished the World Service's role as cultural diplomat. Finally, new satellite delivery systems were beginning to transmit transnational television news services (CNN) and undermining the future of World Service radio. The ability of the World Service to survive these various challenges certainly rested on its reputation for quality and its 'goodwill creating function', but perhaps more important in the days of Peacock was the service's cost effectiveness. In making a case for retention of the foreign office grant, the managing director claimed that the cost per listener per week was less than 2p; 'no other medium in the world can talk so fast, so credibly, so effectively, or anywhere near so cheaply' (Tusa, 1990, p. 66). The government was seemingly persuaded by these arguments and increased the World Service budget for the three-year period 1991 to 1993; since 1993, the story has been radically different.

John Birt's June 1996 proposals to restructure the BBC had significant consequences for the World Service (see above, pp. 138). Television and radio services were to be conjoined in a single directorate; radio was to lose its distinctive voice in senior BBC management. Worse, *World Service* news would no longer be produced by the distinctive news team at Bush House, but by the indigenous news and current affairs journalists in the BBC news directorate. In John Tusa's words, the World Service had been reduced to a 'subdivision of a division' (Tusa, 1996, p. 11). But this 'conclusive downgrading' of the World Service was simply the concluding logic of a three-year 'programme of marginalisation' by BBC management. Tusa believes the enemy has been the BBC rather than the government at home or any dictator abroad. Since 1993, the World Service had: been integrated into BBC Worldwide; been obliged to fight its battles with Whitehall and Westminster within the confines of BBC corporate interests; suffered the imposition of producer choice on a World Service management whose efficiency had been acknowledged by the National Audit Office; and lost many millions because of changes to BBC accounting procedures. Furthermore, the integrity of its transmission system had been undermined by the BBC's willingness to privatise its domestic and overseas transmitters (ibid.). But the threat to the World Service has not issued from within the BBC alone. In real terms (fixed 1991 prices) the funding of the World Service fell from £117.2 million in 1993 to £110.8 million in 1996/7; projections for 1997/8 are set at £104.9 million (Manning, 1996, p. 8). Financial pressures were immense (Kaye, 1996, p. 13). The foreign office had reneged on its triennial settlement for 1994–7 in the 1995 public expenditure round, resulting in an immediate £4.8 million shortfall in capital budget. Chair of BBC governors, Christopher Bland, cited the £10 million reduction in overall operating budget as a crucial factor in the proposals for the World Service which, he alleged, was 'under far greater financial pressure than any other part of the BBC' (Bland, cited in Culf, 16 July 1996, p. 3). In a letter to the *Guardian*, Bland was unashamedly frank about the motives behind the restructuring; it would allow 'the World Service to retain its unique qualities and character, while benefiting from economies of scale and investment in new technology' (*Guardian*, 24 July 1996, p. 14).

This requirement for the World Service to derive news provision from its domestic news services was damaging in at least two additional respects. While the overt rationale is cost cutting, the new arrangement will prove more expensive; World Service news is more efficient and produces programmes 28 per cent more cheaply than network news and with lower overheads (Manning, 1996, p. 8). But there is a more general and more significant concern. The World Service has been successful in articulating a genuinely global news agenda rather than simply offering a news service reflecting British concerns and interests – an achievement which has eluded the *Voice of America* (Wallis and Baran, 1990, p. 51). The news values informing the BBC's domestic news services are incompatible with the provision of a news service for the global citizen. The public response to Birt's June proposals was sufficiently indignant to suggest that listeners did not take the World Service for granted. In response to lively public debate, Christopher Bland was summoned to a meeting at the foreign office on 24 July 1996 which subsequently announced the establishment of a working group to reconsider the proposals for the World Service. A week later, the Foreign Affairs Committee criticised Birt's lack of consultation within the BBC and foreign office concerning the World Service changes and expressed its concern to 'ensure that the unique quality of the BBC World Service is not lost in a vast new superstructure within which its needs and priorities are overlooked or even disregarded' (Foreign Affairs Committee, 2nd Report, 1996). The BBC was advised that it should not consider any of its plans irrevocable. The foreign office possessed the ultimate sanction if it continued to disapprove of BBC policy; it could withdraw its funding for the service.

At the time of writing, it seems almost certain that Birt's proposals will go ahead. In 1992 Tusa placed a portentous observation on the record. 'Were the BBC to be undermined, were the World Service to become part of a weaker, more vulnerable broadcasting institution,' he claimed, 'then the values of the World Service which so many have relied on for 60 years, and so many others taken for granted, could be gravely threatened' (Tusa, 1992, p. 15).

The new Klondyke? Ownership, cross-media ownership and economic prospects in the commercial radio sector

Ownership of the commercial radio industry is characterised by three features. First, it is concentrated in a few large companies which dominate the market, although it is important to remember that even Capital Radio, the largest radio grouping, is modest by comparison with media players such as Pearson or News International (Williams, 1994, p. 43). Second, this pattern of ownership is becoming even further concentrated (and rapidly), driven by the economic necessities of the radio market and the deregulatory impulse of the Broadcasting Act 1996; by the year 2000, these trends may result in the entire commercial radio market being controlled by no more than three or four major groups. Takeovers have become a routine feature of life in the commercial radio sector. Finally, from the very beginnings of commercial radio in 1973, cross media ownership by both local newspapers and regional television companies has been a feature of the commercial radio market.

A small number of companies such as Capital Radio Plc, EMAP (East Midlands Associated Press) and GWR (Great Western Radio) dominate the ILR sector. Two indicators are used to assess concentration and form the basis for the statutory regulation of local radio ownership (Department of National Heritage, 1995, p. 26, para. 6.23). The first is the number of licences which a single radio grouping can own; the second is a points system devised by the Radio Authority which offers an approximate measure of audience size. The latter illustrates clearly the Radio Authority's 'very light touch' concerning this aspect of radio regulation. The system allocates all radio stations to one of five categories (A to D and National) reflecting audience size. Category D (1–400k listeners) scores 1 point, C (400k–1 million) scores 3 points, B (1–4.5 million) scores 8 points, A (4.5 million plus) scores 15 points and a national station scores 25 points; award of an AM rather than FM licence scores two thirds of the points for any category. No single company is allowed to own more than 35 stations or exceed more than 15 per cent of the available points (*The Broadcasting Act 1996* Sced 2, Sec 9-(1), p. 136). Consequently, Capital Radio, with its current total of 73 points, is at the limit. But this measure ignores so many relevant qualitative aspects of audiences, such as their class composition, age and earning power, that it becomes ineffective as a regulatory measure. Capital only has 15 per cent of the points system but the socio-economic and demographic profile of its audiences, combined with its dominance of the London radio market, deliver the company 30 per cent of the total industry turnover, a percentage much more likely to prompt a referral to the Monopolies Commission.

The extent to which this pattern of concentration of ownership is being consolidated can be established by comparing the contents of Table 7.1 with the ownership of stations revealed just over a year later in the *Radio Authority Pocket Guide* (Radio Authority, August 1996). GWR, for example, had expanded its stock of stations from 20 in May 1995 to 30 in August 1996, by acquiring Chiltern Radio. EMAP's purchase of Metro Radio in July 1995 for almost £100 million or 10 times the original flotation price, reveals the potential profits available in this media sector (Buckingham and Atkinson, 1995, p. 36). By August 1996, *Capital Radio* had reduced its licences to 10 but by retaining the lucrative London and Birmingham licences (Capital FM, AM Capital Gold, 96.4 FM BRMB and 1152 Xtra) with their substantial audiences, the company secured 15 per cent of points in the Radio Authority system. The reason behind this constant incorporation of smaller companies into larger groupings is to achieve economies of scale both through the more cost-effective deployment of staff and by attracting increased advertising revenues for the larger audience. The even-

Table 7.1 Major radio groupings defined by licences held and share of Radio Authority points, May 1995

Company	Share of total % points	Number of local licences
Capital Radio	9.9	15
GWR	9.8	20
EMAP Radio	9.5	9
Metro	6.9	12
Golden Rose	5.1	3
Virgin Radio	4.9	1
Scottish Radio Holdings	3.9	10
Classic FM	3.8	1
Reuters	3.8	2
Chiltern Radio	3.7	9
Chrysalis Group	3.5	2

Source: Department of National Heritage (1995), *Media Ownership: The Government's Proposals*, Annexe 2, Table 3, p. 35

tual consequence of this continuous process of takeover and concentration, however, is to parcel up the country into areas where different companies exercise a monopoly. In Scotland, 11 of the 21 licences are held by Scottish Radio Holdings, EMAP controls the majority of stations in the North East of England and Yorkshire, while Capital dominates the Midlands and London and the South East (*Radio Authority Pocket Book*, 1996 and Williams, 1994, p. 43). On 6 May 1997 London's Capital Radio paid £87 million for rival Virgin Radio. The new company, the largest private broadcaster in the UK, will challenge BBC Radio 1 for audiences.

Cross media ownership has been a feature of the commercial radio market from the outset. EMAP, currently the third largest owner of commercial radio stations, also owns 156 consumer and business magazines including *Q*, *Elle* and *Slimming Magazine* and 91 regional and local newspapers, although the company sold 65 of the latter to Johnston Press in June 1996 (see chapter 5). Local newspapers have always claimed an interest in their sister local radio stations. By 1976, 18 of the 19 ILR stations were partly owned by the press; by 1988 the figures had risen to 41 of 45 stations. By 1988, only four (Ayr, Red Rose, Tees and Wyvern) of the 44 ILR stations were independent of press ownership and in six stations (Aire, Orwell, Saxon, Hereward, Mercia and Piccadilly) the press stake was as high as 25–35 per cent (Seymour Ure, 1991, pp. 82–3).

Critics identify a clear link between this economic concentration and the lack of variety in commercial radio programming (Taylor, 1993, p. 12 and Williams, 1994, pp. 43–4). The vast majority of 'independent' local stations are part of larger media conglomerates which tend to adopt 'safe' scheduling strategies; there is little diversity. Most stations offer a mix of contemporary or 'classic' hits with inconsequential chat and traffic information; each invariably offers the same pledge 'Not to talk over your favourite records'. In truth there is virtually no 'talk' except the two minutes' news on the hour which is networked agency copy from IRN. But any 'localness' in most ILR stations' predictable output is lost as the station takes feed from other stations in the region owned by the same company; the search for audience, advertising revenues and economies of scale has transformed local radio into regional radio. The expansion of ILR stations in the last five years means an ever more extensive menu is available but the diet tends increasingly to taste the same.

These are certainly heady days for radio, with expansion in the number of stations, audiences and advertising revenues. The 19 ILR stations on air in 1976 grew to 99 by the end of 1988, 120 by 1992 and 176 in 1996. During 1997/8, 32 new licences will be available on VHF frequencies, while the arrival of digital broadcasting heralds the prospect of between 42 and 168 additional services. In 1994, commercial radio overtook the BBC in total audience share for the first time and, in the same year, advertising revenues grew by 20 per cent to £200 million; predictions estimate radio will enjoy 4.5 per cent of revenues by the year 2000, worth approximately £450 million (Buckingham, 1993, p. 13).

But there are also signals which suggest that the radio market may not have established any durable equilibrium and that the recent spurt of growth cannot be sustained. First, advertising revenues are increasing but the growth of new stations is outstripping them. Radio 'cannibalism', with new stations obliged to eat into one another's audiences and fight for the same advertisers, is commonplace. Second, the impetus behind the rapid expansion of stations seems to be provided more by 'those who fancy running a radio station than those who want to listen to it' (Buckingham and Atkinson, 1995, p. 36). New stations like Viva proved an almost immediate business disaster, failing to attract both audience and advertisers. Third, the fixed costs of radio are high and account for between 70 and 80 per cent of outgoings, which makes radio stations very vulnerable to any downturn in revenues. Fourth, the rapid expansion of radio has prompted shortages of skilled staff, competition to recruit them and rising salary costs; Capital's average staff cost rose by £2300 to £34,819 between 1993 and 1994 (ibid.). Finally, the eagerness with which some investors have tried stake their claim in the new radio Klondyke has resulted in overbidding for licences (an experience presaged in the 1991 bids for Channel 3 licences and repeated for Channel 5 bids in 1995). EMAP's 1995 purchase of Metro Radio for 10 times the 1989 price is one example; the willingness of Talk Radio UK to bid £3.8 million (£1 million more than its nearest rival) plus £350,000 a year additional costs, is another.

In combination, these factors suggest that the days of radio boom might be followed by a period of ignominious bust. Michael Green, acting managing director of BBC Network Radio, argued in May 1996 that 'any newcomers will need deep pockets to invest in talent and a programme proposition that stands out' (cited in Culf, 1 May 1996, p. 6). Deregulation has triggered an explosion of stations but it also brings harsher competition which will, in turn, reduce profits. The first victim in this chain of events will be programme quality; the decline is already too evident. The second will be the closure of the smaller, more vulnerable ILR stations.

The big turn on? Radio audiences

There has always been a fierce and, it is argued, healthy rivalry between the BBC and commercial services for the greater share of the radio audience. The proportion of the total radio audience won by the BBC has gradually declined as more and more ILR and then INR stations came on air. In 1994, for the first time, the independent radio sector leapfrogged ahead of the BBC in this endless ratings battle. Figures for the first quarter of 1996, however, re-established the BBC in pole position (see Table 7.2). A different indicator of audience size measures audience share; i.e., the percentage of total listening time accounted for by a particular radio station. The BBC achieved a 50.4 per cent audience share in the first quarter of 1996 compared to 47.2 per cent in

Table 7.2 Weekly audience reach* for BBC and commercial services, 1995/6

BBC	1995 4th quarter	1996 1st quarter
Radio 1	11.2	11.2
Radio 2	8.4	8.4
Radio 3	2.3	2.3
Radio 4	8.4	8.7
Radio 5 Live	4.8	5.2
BBC local/regional	9.5	9.5
Commercial radio		
Atlantic 252	4.5	3.8
Classic FM	4.6	4.9
Talk Radio UK	2.0	2.1
Virgin Radio AM	3.4	3.4
Local commercial	24.5	23.0

*Audience reach measures the number of listeners tuning in for at least five minutes per week with figures in millions
Source: RAJAR 1996

the last quarter of 1995. Audience reach, however, is the critical yardstick for a public service broadcaster because it 'measures how many licence fee payers are using our services' whereas audience share 'is largely determined by the number and nature of a station's competitors' (Forgan, 1995, p. 17).

A number of factors explain the reversal of BBC fortunes. First, the massive decline in listeners to Radio 1 seems finally to have bottomed out. In June 1993, Radio 1 enjoyed a weekly audience reach of 16.5 million but by the end of 1994 the figure had plummeted to 10.5 million, despite a £150,000 PR campaign organised by Lynne Franks, designed to revive the station's flagging fortunes (Boseley, 1994, p. 3). Audiences began to desert the station in the wake of resignations by star disc jockeys Dave Lee Travis, Simon Bates and Steve Wright; the revamping of the station by the new controller, Matthew Bannister, to include more news and talk seems to have exacerbated the decline (Harvey, 1994, p. 19). This large-scale desertion of listeners from Radio 1, moreover, provided ready audiences for the new commercial services. The arrival of Chris Evans to host Radio 1's breakfast show in April 1995 seemed to mark the revival in audience figures – assisted by a £2.5 million advertising campaign. Second, the 1996 figures include record audiences of 5.21 million for Radio 5 Live. Third, Table 7.2 records a decline in listeners to commercial stations. The most significant element in that decline is undoubtedly the loss of 1.5 million listeners to ILR stations across the quarter combined with the dip in audience for Atlantic 252. By contrast, Classic FM continues to build its audience, confirming substantially greater popularity than Radio 3, while Talk Radio also won an additional 100,000 listeners.

But there is little to celebrate at the BBC, despite edging ahead of its commercial rivals; the audience reach of each of its networks has declined considerably across the last three years. In the first quarter of 1993, audience reach for Radio 1 was 16.1 (+4.9 million on 1996 figures), for Radio 2 the figure was 9.8 million (+1.4), for Radio 3, 2.7 million (+0.4) and for Radio 4, 9.2 million. Even Radio 5, which was unceremoniously dumped to make way for Radio 5 Live, enjoyed a reach of 4 million listeners (−1.2) and just prior to going off air hit audiences of 4.8 million (RAJAR audience figures, 1993). The same period (1993–6) shows a marked increase of 30 per cent in audiences for commercial stations.

These uncertainties in audience trends were heightened when RAJAR's new methods for measuring radio audiences prompted a 'dramatic slump' in listening 'for nearly all stations' (Culf, 16 March 1996, p. 5). The established audience measurement method required a sample 50,000 listeners to complete pre-printed diaries indicating the times they were listening; the new system involved respondents compiling their own diaries by applying stickers to the stations to which they listened. The results were so eccentric they were scrapped.

The victor in this battle for the airwaves is uncertain even when the vagaries of audience research methods are discounted. But Liz Forgan, managing director of BBC Network Radio until her resignation in April 1996, forecasts a medium-term decline in the reach of BBC radio services: to below 50 per cent by the end of the 1990s, 40 per cent by 2005 and eventually 'settling' at about 30 per cent (Forgan, 1995, p. 17). The fall in audience will reflect 'two realities': the expansion of commercial stations and the BBC's commitment to public service broadcasting – in Forgan's words 'a programme strategy directed at delivering things the market will not offer, rather than at maximising ratings' (ibid). What is certain is that the radio audience, similar to the readership of newspapers, is largely static. 'All the activity in radio in the last two years has not added a single listener,' Forgan claims. 'Every incomer has built its audience by taking from an existing broadcaster' (ibid., p. 16). How long the existing body of listeners can provide the life blood for the explosion in radio stations, is a moot point.

Radio at the crossroads? Radio 5 Live versus Talk Radio

From the first suggestion in the Broadcasting Act 1990 that the new national commercial service INR 3 would be a station devoted to talk, the station was seen as a rival to Radio 4 and later Radio 5 Live (Reynolds, 1994, p. 12). The station's arrival was anticipated with an enthusiasm which Talk Radio's subsequent performance must long since have dissipated. 'For the first time ever,' a pundit announced with remarkable naivety, 'the BBC will face aggressive commercial competition in the territory where it gained its worldwide renown' (Walters, 1990, p. 28). To date, Talk Radio has provided little, if any, competition for the BBC news and sport service Radio 5

Live. In truth it is difficult to imagine two stations which are more distinctive in terms of their journalistic resources, the source and extent of their financial resources, their identified target audiences, the range and quality of programming they provide, and the divergent broadcasting philosophies which inform their scheduling; Radio 5 Live is a public service broadcaster, while Talk Radio is unashamedly market driven. A comparison of the early history and development of both stations offers useful insights into the current state and future direction of radio broadcasting in the UK.

Talk Radio UK was launched on 14 February 1995. The company bid £3.82 million for the licence and spent a further £8 million on launch costs. This is cheap radio. A launch staff of 50, supplemented by 10 freelances, offered an unimaginative diet of programming based around phone-ins hosted by celebrities such as Terry Christian, Jeremy Beadle, Anna Raeburn and Caesar the Geezer. This programming format is frequently and euphemistically described as 'interactive radio'. Managing director John Aumonier, borrowing Jenny Abramsky's analogy about the radio of the airwaves, claimed that if Radio 5 Live was the equivalent of a cross between the *Daily Mail* and the *Guardian*, Talk Radio would be more like the *Daily Mail* or *Today*. The station's hope of 4 million listeners a week rising to 5 million was unrealistic; it has never won more than 2.1 million. In terms of its profile, the target audience was in the '25–55 age range, a slight female bias and the C1/C2 socio-economic groups'. The director of programmes had a more ambitious and widely conceived constituency: 'we are seeking anyone aged 8 to 80, from stately homes to terraced houses, from single mums to company directors' (cited in Culf, 22 June 1995, p. 7). The new station triggered 86 complaints to the Radio Authority within its first 6 months on air, changed its programme director after 6 weeks, sacked its 'shock jocks' after 4 months, was fined £5000 for failing to keep tapes of broadcast output and was allegedly running up losses of £800,000 each month. Perhaps unsurprisingly, the launch was described as 'disastrous' and yet despite these calamities the station quickly attracted an audience of 2 million listeners; a year later, the station was holding fast at 2.1 million listeners.

Radio 5 Live, the innovative combination of sport and news, went on air on 28 March 1994 with a launch budget of £30.2 million. Unlike the 'disastrous' beginnings of Talk Radio UK, Radio 5 Live was that 'rare creature . . . a successful media launch' (Forgan cited in Culf, 1 August 1994, p. 2); the station's motto was 'first and live'. A lexicon of Birtian buzzwords, combined in suggestive antithesis, described the new station's 'mission': 'authoritative yet accessible' and 'friendly but accessible', 'extending Choice'. Radio 5 Live was to be 'fun', 'breezier' and more willing to take risks than Radio 4; it would also be 'rough and raw' (*Ariel*, 25 January 1994, p. 3). BBC research suggested existing networks were 'super serving' southern ABC1s, and Radio 5 Live was to seek a new audience which should be 'less metropolitan', aged 25–44 and more representative of social classes C and

D. A week before going on air, the BBC spent £1 million on a leaflet-based advertising campaign using marketing techniques to target precisely this audience profile (Reynolds, 1994, p. 12). But the BBC denied that the search for new audiences involved any journalistic move down market; the station was to be 'rooted in good journalism' (Loughran, 1994, p. 6). A senior policy executive at the BBC explained Radio 5 Live's mission: 'We are trying to create new programmes and new formats which are attractive to a wider range than simply the ABs and predominantly over 40s . . . but the market does not need another SkyNews from the BBC and we won't provide it . . . we will not dilute the integrity of our journalism' (interview 11 April 1994). The station's programming intentions were ambitious. Around the clock, there was to be news on the hour and half hour, sports headlines on the hour and a full sports summary on the half hour. Doubts about the compatibility of news and sports were soon resolved. From the outset, Abramsky conceived the new station as a newspaper and consequently sought to emulate the breadth and range of a print agenda. Radio 5 Live offers regular coverage of business, finance, health, education, the environment, Europe, Black and Asian issues, entertainment, fashion and science and technology (Hendy, 1994, pp. 15–16).

The station is journalistically well resourced. At launch, there were 160 journalists, 17 assistant editors, 8 editors and 12 dedicated Radio 5 Live allrounders located in the regions; the station can call on the expertise of the BBC's foreign and specialist correspondents (Loughran, 1994, p. 6 and Karpf, 29 March 1994, p. 24). A team of 60 journalists make 3000 hours of sports programming each year. The station is also financially well resourced, although the emphasis on live coverage, discussion programmes and sport offers Radio 5 Live opportunities to provide relatively cheap programming compared to other networks: £3100 for each broadcast hour compared to £9000 for Radio 4. Prior to launch Abramsky hoped for an audience of 3 million; in its first month the station attracted 4.7 million listeners but by 1996 this figure had grown to 5.2 million. On 30 April 1996, Radio 5 Live was named national radio station of the year at the Sony Radio Awards.

A comparison of the initial fortunes of Radio 5 Live and Talk Radio and the rivalry between them seems to symbolise a much more significant contest between the two philosophies and systems of broadcasting they embody: broadcasting informed on the one hand by the principles of public service; on the other, by the dictates of the market. The conclusion to be drawn from the early history of these two stations is clear. Even in 1996, a well-resourced service which places a premium on quality journalism will win greater audiences, as well as greater critical acclaim, than a commercial station, with fewer financial and journalistic resources, which heads unashamedly down market in the hope of winning an audience. The very early rejection of the 'shock jocks' reveals an admirable 'consumer resistance' to the more vulgarian aspects of American commercial radio. But

Radio 5 Live harks back to a public service past, while Talk Radio presages the market-driven broadcasting future – and a not too distant future. According to its own predictions, the BBC will retain only 30 per cent of radio market share by the year 2010; the pop and popular music output of radios 1 and 2 will account for more than half of that audience share. Commercial stations, with their formulaic programming, will dominate the airwaves; the reality is that they already do.

8

Blinkered visions

A history of British television

The Times's review of the opening night of commercial television displayed a curious mixture of fascination and annoyance with the advertisements that made their debut appearance on British television at exactly 12 minutes past 8 p.m. on 22 September 1955.

> It was not long before the first advertisement spot began to appear . . . in that curiously nasal synthetic tone that advertising has in the cinema. A pretty girl began to clean her teeth before us with Gibbs SR toothpaste; then in the manner of a panel game, 2 people at a table were asked what their favourite brand of drinking chocolate was, and they replied Cadbury's; a packet of margarine followed and so on, punctuating the different items during the rest of the evening. None appeared as particularly clever or memorable, though Dunlop managed a good shot of some tyres, National Benzole some agreeable shots of Devon, and Oxo introduced Mr Harry Corbett's Sooty to drop its cubes into a mug of hot water . . . Offensive would be too strong a word for these comic little interruptions of the entertainment, but one did feel nonetheless that a thick skin of resistance to them would be necessary before long.
>
> (*The Times*, 23 September 1955, p. 5)

Whether fascinated or annoyed, it is worth noting that the advertisements captured the journalist's attention more than the substance of the actual programming; three quarters of the review was devoted to appraising the content of these 'comic little interruptions'. There were other straws in the wind for programme content in the new commercial system of broadcasting with its in-built reliance on winning audiences and advertising revenues. *The Times* noted similarities between the first night of Independent Television Authority (ITA) broadcasting and some BBC programming, but the differences were undoubtedly more important; most notably, 'the ITA newsreel, which is introduced by Mr Christopher Chataway, hopes to spice its news items with the "reporting of idiosyncrasies"'. The review ended speculatively; 'what the actual quality is likely to be over the coming months of rivalry is still very much anyone's guess' (ibid.).

The idea that it might be possible to 'spice the news', rather than simply report it, was as novel to the world of broadcasting as commercial television itself; it would certainly have been anathema to John Reith and other pioneers of television broadcasting. Reith was also irreconcilably opposed to advertising, which he believed undermined the independence of broadcasting organisations. Reith was driven by a vision. Television, like its radio predecessor, should be guided by the principles of public-service broadcasting and attempt to 'educate and inform' rather than merely 'entertain'. Many journalists and broadcasters shared Reith's vision. Television, especially television news, was invested with an elevated, even moral, purpose. The new television technology offered potentially limitless opportunities for news journalism, but by itself the technology could achieve little; the essential ingredients were human imagination, creativity and commitment as well as journalistic integrity and skill. Television must be financed and organised in a way which encouraged such creativity; advertising and markets were destructive of these ambitions. The legendary American broadcaster Ed Murrow, who spoke publicly against the influence of the tobacco lobby in US broadcasting and who suffered witch hunting during the McCarthy period, captured television's reliance on human creativity in an eloquent phrase. 'This instrument,' he claimed, 'can teach, it can illuminate; yes, and it can even inspire. But it can only do so to the extent that humans are determined to use it to those ends. Otherwise, it is merely lights and wires in a box' (Murrow, cited in Kendrich, 1969, p. 30).

The argument presented in this chapter is that the recent history of television has revealed its growing estrangement from the public-service tradition. Television, in terms of its organisational structures, financial resources, editorial philosophy and programme contents, is increasingly driven by commercial considerations reflecting the operation of a competitive market. The development of new broadcasting technologies and delivery systems, radical changes in governments' media policies and shifting political and regulatory environments for broadcast media, have each contributed to the rapid and striking changes which have occurred since the mid-1980s. Reith's vision has increasingly been replaced by a mission; and the mission is shabby. It is a mission which prioritises winning audiences and making money above the commitment to quality programming.

The consequences of these organisational and structural changes for programming are predictable and evident. The investigative journalism of *World in Action* and *Panorama* has been replaced in the 1990s by tabloid populist programmes like *3D* and *The Big Story*. At the BBC, fears have been expressed about the quality of flagship news programmes as the news directorate struggles to make 30 per cent savings on its £190 million budget over the next five years; a saving which will require job cuts of 25 per cent.

Some distinguished broadcasters express grave concerns about the future of British news and current affairs journalism. Jon Snow, presenter of *Channel 4 News*, told a conference of the Voice of the Listener and Viewer that in the 'ruthlessly competitive world' of broadcasting, 'we now have to make money out of news'. In the late 1990s, as newszak increasingly replaces serious news journalism, television looks markedly less like an instrument which can teach, illuminate and inspire and much more like 'lights and wires in a box'.

This chapter catalogues and examines the development of this 'blinkered vision' by exploring the historical development of television across the last half century and examining the more recent and radical changes in the political context in which television operates. The following chapter analyses recent media policies, the expansion of television services and the changing patterns of ownership and audiences for television.

Television: a brief history

Glue, sealing wax and string: the early days of television

In June 1923 John Logie Baird placed a notice in the personal column of *The Times*: 'Seeing by Wireless – Inventor of apparatus wishes to hear from someone who will assist (not financially) in making working model' (*The Times*, 27 June 1923). In truth, the 32-year-old Scottish engineer was desperately short of cash to fund his experiments with television which he had been conducting in the unlikely surroundings of a small attic flat in Hastings. In 1925, two years before the British Broadcasting Corporation came into existence, Baird established his company, 'Television Limited', with a modest start-up capital of £500. Drawing on many earlier scientific discoveries, Baird's 'televisor' used a crude mechanical scanner to originate low-definition pictures of only 30 lines compared to the 405 lines of the broadcast system eventually adopted (Golding, 1974, p. 34). The bizarre appearance of Baird's prototype television displayed all the hallmarks of ingenuity combined with improvisation which might have characterised a device invented by Heath Robinson assisted by a troop of boy scouts; Asa Briggs describes the machine's improbable construction: 'An old tea chest formed a base to carry the motor which rotated a circular cardboard disc. The disc was cut out of an old hat box and a darning needle served as a spindle. An empty biscuit box housed the projection lamp. The necessary bull's eye lenses were bought from a bicycle shop at a cost of fourpence each (Briggs, 1965, pp. 519–20). The entire apparatus was 'held together with glue, sealing wax, and string' (ibid., p. 520). It is perhaps unsurprising that Baird initially found difficulty in finding financial backing for such a device.

But he began to achieve remarkable and exciting results; in 1924 he was able to transmit the first flickering images of a Maltese Cross two or three yards across his attic flat; in that unlikely setting, the principles of television technology enjoyed their first practical confirmation. In 1926, the Post Office granted Baird a licence to conduct experimental transmissions, eventually in cooperation with the BBC, which were remarkably successful. Still images were transmitted across the Atlantic, and in 1932 moving images of a Danish film star were broadcast from London to Copenhagen 600 miles away; in the following year there were 208 such experimental transmissions. But Baird's capacity to develop his system was plagued by his inability to generate the necessary and substantial funding, his refusal to replace the inefficient mechanical scanner with a superior electronic model and his 'paranoia' in dealing with sceptical and unduly cautious BBC engineers (Hood, 1983, pp. 58–9). Baird, moreover, had to confront a rival; and a well-resourced rival at that.

A competitor broadcast system was being developed by a consortium of the British company Electrical and Musical Industries (EMI), the powerful Radio Corporation of America (RCA) and the British Marconi Company. These three companies brought together a formidable mix of advanced research in electronics, experience in radio manufacture and substantial financial resources estimated at £180,000 a year – a remarkable sum in the early 1930s (ibid., p. 58). The system developed by EMI-Marconi used an electronic scanner to generate high-quality pictures of 405 lines, with 50 frames a second. Technologically, this broadcast system was very advanced compared to Baird's. It became clear that a choice had to be made between these two systems and in May 1934 Lord Selsdon was invited to chair a committee to 'consider the development of Television and to advise the Postmaster General on the relative merits of the several systems and on the conditions under which any public service of Television should be provided' (quoted in Smith, 1974, pp. 64–5). Selsdon's report made three significant recommendations. First, both the Baird and EMI-Marconi systems of television broadcasting should be developed further until one of the two systems unequivocally proved its superiority. Second, having considered the possibility 'of letting private enterprise nurture the infant service' the committee decided that 'it would be in the public interest' for television broadcasting to 'be entrusted to a single organisation'. Given 'the close relationship which must exist between sound and television broadcasting' the committee believed that 'the Authority which is responsible for the former – at present the British Broadcasting Corporation – should also be entrusted with the latter' (Selsdon, 1935, Cmnd 4793, para. 40); a view later confirmed by the Ullswater Committee (Sendall, 1982, p. 4). Finally, Selsdon rejected advertising and a special licence fee as viable or desirable sources of funding for the extensive development costs which television would inevitably incur. The committee recommended that the treasury and the BBC should share development costs from their respective shares of the licence fee (Selsdon,

1935, Cmnd 4739, para. 70). When the BBC began television broadcasting on 2 November 1936 the Baird and EMI systems were used side by side, which created inevitable problems. At a meeting in July 1936, a coin was tossed by Lord Selsdon to decide which of the two fiercely rival companies should conduct the opening transmissions; the Baird Television Company was lucky on the day but within months (February 1937) the Baird system was dropped because of the undoubted superiority of EMI technology. There was no place for glue, sealing wax and string in the rapidly developing, high-technology world of television broadcasting.

On 1 September 1939, two days before the outbreak of the second world war, the BBC closed its television service because of fears that the transmitter system might serve as a navigation aid to the enemy. But television had proved its popularity across a short period. The number of television sets had grown rapidly from 2000 in 1937 to 20–25,000 in 1939. Viewers in proximity of Alexandra Palace had already been 'able to watch Shakespeare, variety, the Derby and the return of the King and Queen from a visit to Canada' (Seymour Ure, 1991, p. 85). Stuart Hood offers a less generous appraisal of the early television output. Pre-war programming was targeted at small audiences in London and the prosperous south east of England, he claims, and was 'dominated by the concept of the West End show, of the revue and the kind of entertainment which was the middle class audience's idea of a night out' (Hood, 1983, p. 60). When television broadcasting was resumed in June 1946, Sir William Haley, the first post-war director general, articulated a view of television which was widespread; television 'was the natural extension of sound' (quoted in Briggs, 1979, p. 4). Television was not judged to be a radically different medium but simply 'an extension' of radio. Television was radio with pictures; Selsdon had confirmed as much. Consequently, from the outset, television was steeped in the traditions of Reith and the principles of public-service broadcasting (see chapter 6). The financial and organisational structures which the Sykes and Crawford committees respectively had established for radio broadcasting were grafted uncritically on to the new medium of television (Seymour Ure, 1991, p. 85 and Hood, 1983, p. 60). Television broadcasting was to be organised as a public-service monopoly funded by a licence fee which would be paid by everyone who owned a receiver. The board of governors would represent and protect the public interest and guarantee the independence of broadcasters by providing a buffer between broadcasters and any commercial or political interests which might seek to influence them. Television would broadcast to the entire country (geographically and culturally) and, most importantly, programming would be imbued with Reith's vision of elevating audiences by offering a range and quality of programming intended to 'educate, inform and entertain'.

Underlying and confounding these perceived similarities between radio and television broadcasting, however, were deeply rooted tensions which centred on the potential impact of television on the fortunes of radio. Early warnings were sounded. In 1946 Basil Nicholls, Haley's senior controller, argued 'it was important that the general enthusiasm for television should not be allowed to have an adverse effect on sound' (quoted in Briggs, 1979, p. 5). But few heeded such warnings and another BBC observer identified 'a tradition which came to be established of an automatic mutual hostility between Broadcasting House and BBC Television' (quoted in ibid.). For its part, television grew increasingly resentful of its radio ancestry and argued for its supremacy over sound broadcasting. Television's rapidly expansive claims on BBC resources were at the hub of this antagonism. Table 8.1 reveals the pace at which expenditure on television grew from less than one tenth of total expenditure in 1948 to more than one third in 1955. It is important to note that this growing allocation to television was achieved despite a growth of 53 per cent in radio expenditure across the same period. Television was also providing a greater proportion of BBC revenues as the income from combined sound and television licences increased substantially. Income from sound licences peaked at £11,819,000 in 1951 but by 1956 had fallen to £8,459,213. By contrast, the income from combined licences was approaching £6 million; separate radio licences eventually disappeared in 1971 (Seymour Ure, 1991, pp. 76–7 and Golding, 1974, p. 35).

The growth in licence income also signalled a substantial growth in the audience for television. The number of combined sound and vision licences grew from 14,560 in 1947 to 4,503,766 by 1955. The BBC seems to have been surprised by the pace of expansion and constantly underestimated the growth of television audiences in its planning. In March 1949, for example, the BBC anticipated 120,000 licences whereas the actual number of licences issued was 126,000. By 1952 the estimate of 800,000 was surpassed by the 1,449,260 licences issued while in 1955 the 'guesstimated' 2 million licences was less than half the 4,503,766 licences issued (Briggs, 1979, p. 241). This persistent underestimation of audience growth combined with lack of raw materials to create a shortfall in the production of television sets. At the end of 1947, only 34,000 sets were installed in 0.2 per cent of family house-

Table 8.1 Relative BBC expenditure on radio and television

Year	Radio £	Television £
1948	6,556,293	716,666
1949	7,073,883	906,685
1950	7,498,788	1,172,714
1951	7,860,883	1,718,578
1952	8,750,945	2,329,159
1953	8,682,815	3,401,042
1954	9,387,166	3,991,439
1955	10,018,779	5,043,908

Source: Briggs, 1979, p. 8

holds. But production was increased sharply and in 1955 the number of television sets (1,771,000) manufactured was greater than radio receivers (1,623,000) (ibid., p. 242). In 1948, Alastair Cooke observed that television sets in Britain would become as commonplace as in America where they were 'as humble as a hot dog' (quoted in ibid., p. 243). Audience access to television was also frustrated by the lack of signal reach which was initially restricted to a radius of 40 miles from Alexandra Palace. New transmitters in Sutton Coldfield (1949), Holme Moss (1951), Kirk O'Shotts (1952) and Wenvoe extended television services to 36 million and by 1956 to effectively the entire population (Seymour Ure, 1991, p. 86). In 1950, only 10 per cent of homes had television sets but by 1963 only 10 per cent were without a television (Golding, 1974, p. 35).

Television viewing expanded as more people acquired sets and as the number of hours of broadcasting increased. Television sets were widely, although unevenly, spread across all social classes. By the end of 1948, 37 per cent of televisions were in the highest Class I households (top 12 per cent), 34 per cent in Class II (20 per cent of the population) households and 29 per cent in Class III (69 per cent of the population) homes. This class skew to television ownership remained into the late 1950s when the cost of television sets began to fall. In 1949 the cost of a television ranged between £50 and £150 while the average weekly wage was just over £7; television rental was common practice. But demand for the new television services differed within as well as between social classes. Television was less popular among the better educated in Class II than the less well educated, although educational achievement was insignificant to television ownership in Class III (Briggs, 1979, p. 250).

Viewers were omnivorous in their appetites for the very limited diet of programming available in the early days of broadcasting – approximately 28.5 hours a week in 1946 (Seymour Ure, 1991, p. 186). A survey conducted in 1948 revealed that 92 per cent of viewers watched television on weekday evenings, 94 per cent on Saturday evenings and 93 per cent on Sunday evenings. Ninety-one per cent confirmed that they watched the entire output from 8.30 to 10.30 each evening. Thirty-one per cent of viewers allowed their children to stay up late on weekends and the new social practice of inviting neighbours in to watch television quickly became widespread (Briggs, 1979, p. 255). Even after commercial television began, there were 'closed periods' from 6 to 7 p.m. on weekdays, Sunday mornings and 6.15–7.30 on Sundays. The Sunday restrictions, quickly dubbed the 'God slot', were intended to prevent testing the faith of members of local congregations by seducing them into viewing rather than church attendance. The weekday breaks between 6 and 7 p.m. had a more prosaic purpose; the 'toddler truce' as it was known was supposed to allow mothers to detach their young children from the screen and get them to bed (Crozier, 1958, p. 92 and Sendall, 1982, p. 243). The toddler truce was lifted in 1957. Subsequently television has continued to expand its provision. The introduction of afternoon television in 1972 and breakfast television in 1985 meant that by 1990 television services were being provided around the clock on BBC and ITV.

Dog racing, bubonic plague and commercial television: breaking the BBC's monopoly

When television services were re-established after the war, there was considerable opposition to the continuing BBC monopoly in broadcasting and a growing support for the establishment of a commercial system of broadcasting. The Conservative government's proposal to introduce both measures in a White Paper in 1952 triggered a vigorous and widespread debate among politicians, the press and the general public. The intention to break the BBC's monopoly threatened one of the fundamental tenets of public-service broadcasting. John Reith, by then a member of the House of Lords, was predictably outraged. In a debate in the House in 1952, Reith made a memorable outburst. 'What grounds are there for jeopardising this heritage and tradition? . . . Why sell it down the river? . . . Somebody introduced dog racing into this country . . . And somebody introduced smallpox, bubonic plague and the Black Death. Somebody is minded now to introduce sponsored broadcasting into this country' (*Hansard*, House of Lords, 22 May 1952, col. 1297).

BEVERIDGE AND THE BBC MONOPOLY: NOT EVERYONE'S CUP OF TEA

The debate had begun in earnest in 1949 when the Labour government established the Beveridge Committee to examine and make recommendations on the future of broadcasting. The Committee was remarkably thorough in its investigations. It received 223 memoranda of evidence amounting to 1,640,000 words and eventually producing a lengthy and rather ponderous two-volume report of almost 1000 pages in January 1951. One newspaper expressed scepticism about the merits of the report in an enviable headline pun: 'This Is BBC's Beveridge But Not Our Cup Of Tea' (quoted in Briggs, 1979, p. 374). The Committee concluded in favour of retaining the BBC's broadcasting monopoly although it conceded that it prompted legitimate grounds for concern; the Committee considered, but eventually rejected, 'four distinct standpoints by people seeing in the present position dangers and evils of different kinds' (Beveridge, Report of the Broadcasting Committee, Cmnd 8116, 1951, para. 174). First, a group of critics from the right of the political spectrum expressed concern about the propaganda potential of the BBC monopoly and 'the danger of excessive power over men's thoughts concentrated in a single organisation' (para. 175). Second, Liberals and Fabians stressed 'the danger' arising from 'the excessive size and unwieldiness of the Corporation' (para. 176). Third, regional and cultural minorities objected to the metropolitan dominance in broadcasting and argued that Scotland and Wales with their 'distinctive cultures should have their own broadcasting systems' (para. 177). Finally, the writers, broadcasters and performers 'who look to broadcasting as a means of earning their living' expressed concerns that the existing monopoly left them without an alternative employer and nurtured self-censorship and undue caution in programme making and performance (para. 178).

Beveridge concluded that 'broadcasting should remain the prerogative of a single corporation' (para. 179) and also rejected by a majority of 7 out of 11 to continue the existing ban on television advertising and programme sponsorship on the ground that they would 'sooner or later endanger the traditions of public service, high standards and impartiality which have been built up in the past 25 years' (para. 376). But the Committee was genuinely divided in its findings and Selwyn Lloyd expressed his dissent from the overall conclusions by appending a minority report which was to prove highly influential in subsequent policy decisions (Briggs, 1979, p. 391). Lloyd declared himself 'of the opinion that independent competition will be healthy for broadcasting' and proposed a Commission for British Broadcasting which would licence a number of rival broadcasting companies 'to run national programmes on commercial lines, that is to say programmes the items in which would be produced or sponsored by those willing to buy time' (Beveridge, Report or the Broadcasting Committee, Cmnd 8116, Minority Report, para. 20).

The Labour government promptly accepted Beveridge's proposals but, equally promptly, lost the 1951 election to the Conservative government headed by Winston Churchill (Briggs, 1979, p. 406). His antipathy to the BBC, rooted in the Corporation's coverage of the general strike (see chapter 6) and his belief that the BBC was little more than a 'red conspiracy' (Hood, 1983, p. 63), signalled a shift in broadcasting policy. The new government rejected Beveridge's conclusions and proposed the end of the BBC monopoly. The government confirmed 'that in the expanding field of television provision should be made to permit some element of competition'. The government conceded the need to 'introduce safeguards against possible abuses' and proposed a 'controlling body . . . to regulate the conduct of the new stations' (Memorandum on the Report of the Broadcasting Committee, 1949, Cmnd 8550, 1951-2, paras. 7–9). The new policy generated tremendous controversy but divided politicians on lines more blurred than clear-cut party divisions. Within the Conservative party, for example, traditionalists like Lord Hailsham supported the BBC monopoly while newer MPs like John Profumo favoured the development of a commercial system of broadcasting. There was no clearer policy within the Labour party. Herbert Morrison threatened to abolish any commercial television system on the party's return to power, while a survey of Labour voters revealed their overwhelming preference for an additional commercially funded channel (Sendall, 1982, p. 37 and Hood, 1983, p. 65). The press was also divided although concerns about competition for its own advertising revenues largely disposed newspapers against commercial broadcasting. The *Manchester Guardian* and *The Times* opposed commercial television because they believed it would result in lowering the quality of programming (Crozier, 1958, p. 115).

The momentum behind commercial television was provided by the advertising lobby, television and other manufacturing groups, Conservative politicians opposed to monopoly and a backbench Conservative broadcasting group. The general public perception of the BBC as too remote and rather haughty as well as the wartime experience of Radio Luxembourg and the American Forces network with their lighter broadcasting style, combined to 'produce perhaps the most remarkable exhibition of political lobbying this country has ever seen'. It was 'a soufflé of high principles and politics and, one may add, of direct economic interest' (Wilson, 1961, p. 173). A central group in this campaign was the Popular Television Association (PTA), which organised mass letter-writing campaigns to newspapers expressing popular support for commercial television.

THE 1954 TELEVISION ACT: A LICENCE TO PRINT MONEY?

On 30 July 1954 the Television Act created the commercial system of television broadcasting and its regulatory body, the Independent Television Authority (ITA) (Sendall, 1982, p. 59). The BBC monopoly was replaced by what became known as the 'comfortable duopoly'. The ITA, rather like the BBC's board of governors, was to serve as a buffer or intermediary protecting programme makers from financial and political interests and pressures. The Act offered a peculiarly British and rather ingenious solution to the problem of isolating programme content from advertisers' influence by identifying distinctive sources of revenue for the ITA and the companies actually making the programmes. The ITA owned and operated the transmitters and received rental payments from the programme companies for their use. For their part, the companies earned their revenue by selling television time for advertising. The ability of advertisers to sponsor individual programmes, as they could in the American system, was specifically excluded (Seymour Ure, 1991, pp. 67–9). The Act required the ITA to police high programming standards. Programmes should be of a 'high general standard of quality', report news with 'due accuracy and impartiality' and exclude any material 'which offends against good taste or decency' (Television Act, 1954 Section 3 (I) (a)-(g)).

In the context of the heated debate which preceded the Act, its initial implementation represented something of a damp squib. When the ITA advertised the 14 regional franchises into which it had divided the country, there were only 25 applicants; far fewer than anticipated. It became clear, moreover, soon after ITV began broadcasting in September 1955, that four companies were dominating the network because of the sheer size and richness of their franchise areas combined with their financial, staffing and equipment resources; the 'big four' as they became known were Rediffusion, Associated Television (ATV), ABC Television and Granada. The 10 minor companies awarded franchises until 1964 included Anglia, Border, Channel, Grampian, Scottish, Southern, TWW, Tyne Tees, Ulster and Westward. On 4 May 1955, the ITA established ITN, under the joint ownership of the 14 companies, to provide a national news service for the new network (Sendall, 1982, p. 87 and Hood, 1983, p. 70). Local news was to be provided by the regional companies. Initially, some of the programme companies suffered considerable financial losses. This is perhaps unsurprising when, as Seymour Ure observes, ITV began broadcasting with only 3 per cent of households equipped to receive programming (Seymour Ure, 1991, p. 87). Even the big four were not immune to the initial financial uncertainties surrounding commercial television. Associated Television, for example, which held the potentially lucrative London franchise, lost almost £3 million, which was sufficient to prompt the major shareholder Associated Newspapers to withdraw. Cash-flow crises were commonplace in the early days. But those with sufficiently stiff resolve were quickly rewarded as losses turned into substantial profits. In 1958 Rediffusion's profits exceeded £4 million while in the following year ATV's profits topped £5 million. Even the smaller companies flourished as advertisers willingly paid the high rates they demanded to promote their goods in the context of the post-war consumer boom. Lord Thompson, chair of Scottish Television, announced, in a phrase which was to become a cliché, that a commercial television franchise was equivalent to 'a licence to print your own money'. On 10 March 1959 the Public Affairs Committee of the House of Commons subjected an ITA executive to extensive questioning about the excessive profits being earned by some of the regional companies (Sendall, 1982, p. 293).

The impact of commercial television on the BBC was considerable, with implications for its programming policies, its attitude towards audiences and, more directly, its staffing levels: commercial television offered production, performance and creative staffs an alternative source of employment. The impact on BBC news was striking.

> Newscasters . . . were encouraged to write informally and use colloquialisms. Their voices lacked the clerical blandness of many BBC announcers. They were permitted touches of humour and even of disrespect . . . Their stories were illustrated by film shot in a more realistic way with more impact and above all more sound. The impact on both the profession and the public was sensational.

> (Hood, 1967, p. 106)

The changes in programming style and content, combined with growing public concern about company profits, the need to evaluate ITV companies prior to refranchising in 1964 and the pressure from the BBC for a second channel, led the Conservative government to establish the Pilkington Committee in 1960.

PILKINGTON, QUALITY AND COMMERCIAL TELEVISION

Pilkington's report, published in 1962, was highly critical of ITV for the alleged triviality of much of its programming, its too frequent portrayals of violence, the low moral standards and adultery portrayed in drama and the lack of range and variety in programmes, especially at peak times. In brief, the ITA was castigated as an ineffective regulator because it had misunderstood its relationship with the programme contractors; 'it saw itself as advocate for them, it excused and defended them rather than controlled them' (Pilkington, 1962, Cmnd 1753, para. 572). There was a structural problem with commercial television:

> Independent television is intended to serve two purposes. First, it is to provide a service of television broadcasting . . . Secondly, and incidentally, independent television is to provide a service to advertisers. The two purposes of independent television do not coincide. Since the commercial product, the saleable product of the programme contractors, is not the programme but advertising time, the commercial rewards will derive from making that product as desirable as possible to those who want it, an aim largely incompatible with the purposes of broadcasting.

Pilkington offered a number of radical policy prescriptions. First, to prevent the ITV companies being influenced by the need to maximise audiences and win advertisers, the Committee recommended that the ITA should schedule programmes for the network and also assume responsibility for selling advertising time. The regional companies would have no direct relationship with advertisers and their role would be to produce programmes for sale to ITA. The government rejected this proposal, which has subsequently 'remained on the table' (Smith, 1974, p. 120). Second, Pilkington recommended that the BBC should establish a second programme service (BBC2, begun in 1964). Third, the technical standards of television broadcasting should be enhanced by a shift from 405 to 625 line transmission and broadcasting in colour. Finally, the ITA should take a number of steps to secure tighter control of advertising. The Television Act 1964 expanded the ITA's powers over programming schedules and also introduced a direct and progressive tax on the regional companies which became known as 'the levy'. The levy – a response to the exorbitant profits being made by the companies – was additional to the standard income-tax payments and the rentals which companies paid to the ITA. The first £1.5 million of advertising revenues were exempt but the next £6 million were taxed at 25 per cent, with any additional receipts taxed at 40 per cent (Hood, 1983, p. 76). Lord Thompson's remark about a 'licence to print money' must have caused him as much regret as Gerald Ratner's observation that his company only manufactured and sold 'crap'.

The reallocation of the franchises in 1967 revealed the continuing fragility of the new system and the vulnerability of programme quality in a commercial system. The franchise round was conducted by the ITA chaired by Lord Hill in considerable secrecy. Thirty groups representing television celebrities and varied newspaper, television and other media interests, bid for the now lucrative franchises. The new Yorkshire region, split from the previous Granada region, was expected to offer particularly rich rewards; 'a klondyke atmosphere surrounded the whole business of enfranchisement' (Smith, 1974, p. 131). But within a year of allocating franchises the system was thrown into crisis. Redundancies, strikes and a slower growth in advertising revenues than anticipated created difficulties for the new franchise holders. Programme standards fell sharply and below the quality promised in franchise bids. LWT (London Weekend Television) was rumoured to be near insolvency and was only saved by a refinancing deal organised by Rupert Murdoch. Some of the initial bids, which previously had been seen only by the ITA and the bidding companies, were leaked by the Free Communications Group and published in its journal *The Open Secret* in July 1969. The leak revealed that the claim by LWT's David Frost and Aiden Crawley that 'the quality of mass entertainment can be improved while retaining commercial viability', had yet to be proven (quoted in Smith, 1974, p. 132). The *Daily Telegraph* had earlier expressed scepticism about a paternalistic ITA's ability to regulate a competitive and commercially driven broadcasting network. 'With the best intentions in the world,' it announced, 'the ITA goes about its duty of trying to impose on programme contractors its own idea of what is best for the British to see. The contractors, on the other hand – with an eye and a half on the audience ratings – like to produce programmes which the British apparently enjoy seeing. Much of the resulting material is often tawdry and slapdash' (*Daily Telegraph*, 12 June 1967).

SERVING MINORITIES? BBC2 AND CHANNEL 4

While Pilkington had been severely critical of ITV, the report expressed unreserved praise for the BBC, which it described as 'the main instrument of broadcasting in the United Kingdom' (Hood, 1983, p. 74); it also recommended that the BBC should establish a second television channel. This channel's brief was to serve minority audience interests and produce programmes of high quality. Macmillan's Conservative government allocated the channel to the BBC in 1963 and broadcasting began in memorable fashion in 1964. A power failure on the opening night blacked out the studios. Viewers who switched on to see the improved picture quality of the new UHF/625 line pictures were presented with the bizarre image of Dennis Touey illuminated by the candelabra he was holding and apologising for this rather unpromising beginning for Pilkington's progeny. With hindsight, the power failure which blacked out screens seemed to presage the new channel's rather tentative early years. The programmes broadcast on the new UHF/625 lines frequency required viewers to fit a new aerial, the station's initial broadcast range was limited to London and the south east and, in its early years, programmes were broadcast for only four hours a night. The channel had been intended to serve minorities but, as one observer commented wryly, given these constraints, 'it could do little else' (Seymour Ure, 1991, p. 99).

The establishment of Channel 4, following a recommendation of the Annan Committee (1974–7) and the Broadcasting Act 1982, provided the fourth and 'balancing' element in television. The channel's brief was to encourage and support innovation by broadcasting a radically different kind of programming designed to appeal to minority interests which were not reflected in ITV or BBC programmes. ITV catered for the regions viewed as minorities within the nation, but Channel 4 would be a national service addressing the needs of cultural, ethnic and social minorities such as gay people, Asian and Afro Caribbean people, fans of Sumo wrestling, Italian football, gardening and Buddhism. These innovative programming intentions were to be resourced by similarly novel economic and financial arrangements. Channel 4 was owned by the Independent Broadcasting Authority (IBA – the ITA's successor); the other commercial programme companies were merely regulated by the IBA. Channel 4's income would derive from advertising, but only indirectly. The new channel was to be funded by the regional ITV companies on a subscription basis and, in return, the companies could sell advertising time on Channel 4 in their particular regions. These are some of the complex circumstances of the birth of the new channel. 'It was probably the only television channel in the world,' Harvey claimed, 'to combine a legislative requirement to experiment, to innovate and to complement the service offered by the existing commercial television channel, and all of this on an income guaranteed in advance by its parliamentary god-parents, under the direction of a Conservative government' (Harvey, 1994, p. 102). The new channel was essentially a publisher rather than producer broadcaster. Channel 4 would not make its own programmes but would commission them from independent producers, the regional ITV companies, ITN and overseas producers. The intention was that the novel funding arrangements would combine the provision of finances required to fund programming with the detachment from advertisers necessary to guarantee compliance with the channel's remit to provide minority programming – a perfect blend of public-service programming with private-sector finance. 'It is one of these funny British ways of doing things,' the second chief executive, Michael Grade, explained. 'We have the best of both worlds. We can accept advertising but we have a guaranteed revenue. Hopefully we can continue to be commercial, but make programmes which different groups enjoy watching, not which certain advertisers would like to be shown' (quoted in Wallis and Baran, 1990, p. 45).

From the mid-1980s, technological developments provided additional television services via the new delivery systems of satellite and cable.

Murdoch's Sky Television was launched on 5 February 1989 while its rival British Satellite Broadcasting went on air a year later; the two companies merged to form BSkyB on 2 November 1990. This technological impetus towards change in the broadcasting system was strengthened by the policies of the Thatcher government which favoured deregulation. The election of successive Conservative governments across the 1980s signalled a radically changed political context for television broadcasting in both the commercial and public sectors.

'Nothing to do with me': the changing political environment

On 29 January 1987, after a routinely scheduled meeting of the BBC board of governors, the director general Alastair Milne was sacked. Without any warning, Milne was summoned to the office of Marmaduke Hussey, who chaired the board of governors, and was told 'We want you to leave immediately' (Horrie and Clarke, 1994, p. 67 and Milne, 1988, p. 202). Less than five minutes after arriving for the meeting with Hussey, Milne had 'resigned', informed his personal assistant of his departure and left the building. Milne subsequently described these events as his 'execution'. Later that same day, the then prime minister, Margaret Thatcher, was asked to comment on Milne's departure amid growing press speculation that increasing government pressure on the BBC had been influential in the Director General's resignation. 'Nothing to do with me,' Thatcher declared, 'it's only a matter for the BBC. There has been no political pressure from me. I was informed about it just a very short time before it was announced' (*World in Action*, 29 February 1988). Thatcher's comments were more than a little disingenuous. Throughout the 1980s senior politicians within the Conservative government, including the prime minister herself, had mounted a sustained attack on the BBC, alleging that its news and current affairs programmes were biased and that the senior management of the BBC was unable to control wayward programme makers (Franklin, 1994, p. 76). The sacking of Milne was symptomatic of the changed, less congenial, political environment in which broadcasting, especially broadcasting at the BBC, was obliged to operate; the Conservative government seemed determined to bring the BBC to heel.

It was not unprecedented for relationships between politicians and broadcasters to become strained. The general strike (see chapter 6) and the Suez crisis had revealed the potential for schism between these two groups. Again, Harold Wilson was scathing in his comments about what he believed was the BBC's biased and hostile attitude towards him and tried to use the Corporation's reliance on the licence fee to secure more favourable coverage for himself and the Labour Party (ibid., p. 82). In democratic political systems a tension, which may lead to conflict, between politicians and the press which holds them accountable is not only inevitable but desirable. This was certainly the sentiment underlying the observation of Sidney Jacobson, editor of the *Daily Herald*, that 'relations between the government and the press are bad, getting worse and should under no circumstances be allowed to improve'. But the election of the Conservative government in 1979 signalled a discernible shift in the political climate which reflected the party's distinctive policy agenda but also the social composition and attitudes of its leadership. The party proposed a radical programme intended to disrupt the cosy post-war consensus which encouraged paternalistic elites and sustained an unduly interventionist state based on the notion of public service. The 'new' Conservatives were committed to 'rolling back' the state, giving capitalism its head and establishing free markets as the mechanism for allocating economic, social and welfare goods. Given this political agenda, it seemed obvious 'that the BBC, for many the very essence of the "Old Britain" Mrs Thatcher loathed', would be a target for the government's reforming zeal (Horrie and Clarke, 1994, p. xiii).

Four features of the new government and its policies seemed to set it on a collision course with the BBC. First, as McNair observes, the Thatcher government of the early 1980s was dominated by people who were politically and socially 'outsiders'. They were hostile to the traditional establishment which they believed rested on privilege rather than merit and individual achievement (McNair, 1994, p. 64). If the establishment had truly learned its politics on the playing fields of Eton, the political nous of the new right had been nurtured in the playground of the local comprehensive. The BBC, staffed by middle-class professionals educated at Oxbridge, seemed to exemplify the worst traits of the established cultural elite which Thatcher believed to be opposed to her revolution. Second, while the government was an enthusiastic advocate of the capitalist free market, the BBC seemed nothing less than an inefficient public bureaucracy which was financially unaccountable and protected from the rigours of the marketplace. It was funded by a public licence fee which Thatcher described as 'a poll tax backed by criminal sanctions' (Horrie and Clarke, 1994, p. xiv). Third, the Conservative government stressed the importance of individual choice and decision-making while the BBC, with its commitment to public-service broadcasting, was judged to be paternalistic. The BBC was out of touch with public (consumer) demand; it broadcast programmes which producers wished to make rather than those which viewers wished to see. Finally, emphasising an element of continuity between the old and new conservatives, the Thatcher government seemed to share, even cherish, Churchill's suspicion that the BBC was a 'red conspiracy' inherently opposed to conservative viewpoints and beliefs. These tensions between broadcasters and Conservative governments generated a succession of celebrated and very public conflicts across the 1980s. Government pressure on the BBC and its journalists was sustained and considerable (Barnett and Curry, 1994, chs. 2 and 3).

The first outbreak of skirmishing arose during the Falklands war in 1982 and revealed government sensitivities to media coverage. BBC broadcasters' insistence that in the interests of detachment and balance, British soldiers should be referred to as 'British' troops rather than 'our' troops or 'our boys' (a phrase popular with tabloid journalists), prompted angry objections from Conservative backbenchers in the House of Commons. Thatcher said she shared 'the deep concern . . . particularly about the contents of yesterday's *Panorama* programme . . . that the case for our country is not being put with sufficient vigour on certain – I do not say all – programmes' (House of Commons Debates, 11 May 1982). Peter Snow's observation on *Newsnight* that statements by all governments in circumstances of war were not always wholly truthful, was described by one Conservative backbencher as 'almost treasonable' (Milne, 1988, p. 89). Allegations of treason became allegations of bias in the following year when the BBC broadcast a *Panorama* programme entitled 'Maggie's Militant Tendency' which suggested that members of extreme right-wing political organisations were infiltrating the Conservative party; the headline in the following day's *Daily Mail* was 'Lies, Damn Lies And Panorama' (Horrie and Clarke, 1994, p. 56). The programme triggered considerable friction between the government and the BBC when two backbench MPs featured in the programme sued for libel. Milne was convinced that the programme was accurate in its conclusions but Hussey, chair of the BBC board of governors, agreed to withdraw from the legal proceedings and settle out of court. The damage to the BBC's reputation for fair, accurate and independent journalism was considerable.

In 1985 the *Real Lives* documentary and a *Panorama* programme about IRA operations at Carrickmore prompted further government criticism with Prime Minister Thatcher alleging that the BBC was providing terrorists in Northern Ireland with the 'oxygen of publicity'; she wanted the latter programme banned without having seen it. In 1986 in the run-up to the general election, Norman Tebbit, then chairman of the Conservative party, used the platform at the party's annual conference to accuse the BBC of 'speculation, error, propaganda' and anti-government bias in its reporting of the American bombing of Libya. Tebbit's claims proved unfounded (Masterman, 1987, p. 1) but their impact on morale at the BBC was substantial (Milne, 1988, p. 89).

Government criticisms were not wholly confined to the BBC. In 1988, Thames television's *This Week* team produced 'Death on the Rock', which examined the SAS shooting of three members of the IRA who were later discovered to be unarmed. The programme strongly challenged the official account of the incident. The government argued 'Death on the Rock' should not be broadcast because it would prejudice the subsequent inquest. Politicians' protests became so intense and sustained after the programme was televised, that Thames commissioned an inquiry whose findings were published as *The Windlesham–Rampton Report on 'Death on the Rock'*.

The report vindicated Thames and concluded that 'the programme makers were experienced, painstaking and persistent. They did not . . . offend against the due impartiality requirements of the IBA' (Windlesham and Rampton, 1989, p. 142). This conclusion, however, failed to convince politicians; the prime minster 'utterly rejected' the report (*Independent*, 27 January 1989, p. 1).

The government's attempts to influence broadcast news and current affairs grew more determined across the 1980s. Four interventions in the affairs of broadcasters are particularly memorable and significant. First, three days after Milne was sacked, the Special Branch raided Glasgow-based BBC Scotland and impounded papers and film relating to the *Secret Society* series in which investigative journalist Duncan Campbell alleged that government had deliberately misled parliament about the funding of a new spy satellite named Zircon. Assistant director general Alan Protheroe denounced the raid as a 'shabby, shameful and disgraceful state sponsored incursion into a journalistic establishment' (Protheroe, 1987, p. 4). Second, on 19 October 1988, the home secretary announced a ban on television and radio broadcasting of 'any words spoken' by the members of 11 political and paramilitary groups in Ireland (Miller, 1990, p. 34). Journalists were no longer to be trusted to report these issues guided by their own professionalism; censorship would prevent errors of judgement. Third, the revision of the Official Secrets Act in 1989 resulted in more restrictive controls on journalists, who were now prohibited from publishing certain broad categories of information. Presented by government as a liberalisation of the original Act of 1911, this new Act was described as an attempt to 'censor media, stop investigative journalism and establish stricter information controls than ever before in peacetime' (Ponting, 1988, p. 15). Finally, the government began to stack the higher echelons of the BBC with political sympathisers. A succession of appointments created a board of governors increasingly dissonant from programme makers but more willing to challenge the BBC's news and current affairs programmes. When Marmaduke Hussey, who had been chief executive of Times Newspapers during the 12 months strike closure at *The Times*, was appointed without any process of consultation to chair the board, *The Financial Times* believed that Hussey had been appointed to sort out the BBC; it headlined 'Can The Duke Bring The BBC To Heel?' (Milne, 1988, p. 188). Hussey's qualifications for the post were less than obvious. Neither Milne nor the board of governors had heard of him and Hussey himself, in a phrase reminiscent of Reith 60 years earlier, confessed that he knew 'very little about broadcasting and absolutely nothing about the BBC' (Horrie and Clarke, 1994, p. 52).

Margaret Thatcher's claim that the increasingly adversarial relationship between politicians and broadcasters throughout the 1980s was 'nothing to do with me' is difficult to sustain, given what is known about the history of period. The political climate for broadcasters was unprecedentedly severe with a Conservative government displaying a deep distrust and dislike of broadcasters – especially at the BBC. The government's belief that the organisational structures and finances of broadcasting required fundamental reform was nurtured in particularly inhospitable but fertile terrain.

|9|

Blinkered visions

Television policy and prospects

Since the mid-1980s, the organisational structures of television, as well as its financial resources, editorial philosophy and programme contents have, much like radio, become subject to commercial considerations arising from the highly competitive markets in which both media are obliged to operate. This chapter evaluates the extent to which governments' recent media policies, combined with the policy initiatives of broadcasters themselves, have revised every aspect of the finance and production of television broadcasting. It also surveys the expanding provision of commercial and public-sector television services, analyses the increasing concentration of ownership of British television and examines the changing audiences for the different television services.

Television: policy debates and disagreements

The decade which began with the publication of the Peacock report and ended with the Broadcasting Act 1996 has undoubtedly been the busiest for policy makers since the beginning of broadcasting. A flurry of activity has generated the Peacock Committee Report (1986), the white paper *Broadcasting in the '90s: Competition, Choice and Quality* and the Broadcasting Acts 1990 and 1996, which have transformed many aspects of the financial, organisational and regulatory landscape of television broadcasting. Change has not been limited to the commercial sector of broadcasting. The National Heritage Report *The Future of the BBC* supported retention of the licence fee (Cmnd 2098, p. 31), while the July 1994 white paper *The Future of the BBC: Serving The Nation, Competing World Wide* recommended the renewal of the BBC's charter for 10 years from January 1997, encouraged the BBC to expand its commercial activities to embrace the launch of new commercial cable satellite and terrestrial services at home and abroad, yet promised a review of the licence fee in

2001 – a policy promptly dubbed the 'space odyssey option'. For their part, broadcasters have contributed to this policy proliferation. John Birt, director general of the BBC, has, in the period prior to the renewal of the BBC's charter, devised and promoted a range of policy initiatives intended to reduce costs and improve efficiency, while sustaining the quality and range of programming appropriate to a public-service broadcaster. The BBC's policy statement *Responding to the Green Paper* offered a commitment to expand the commercial side of its operations through co-productions, programme sales, merchandising and the development of cable and satellite (BBC, 1993a, p. 49) and also promised to introduce an internal market via the system of 'producer choice' (ibid., pp. 40–2, and see below, pp. 185–7). Bookshelves in broadcasters' and policy makers' offices must be literally groaning under the weight of such a sustained and substantial output.

The commercial sector of television has perhaps experienced the greatest policy innovation, resulting in a revamped and increasingly competitive Channel 3, the new terrestrial Channel 5 and an extraordinary range of commercial channels delivered by cable and satellite and funded by a novel range of financial arrangements embracing advertising, subscription, sponsorship and 'pay to view'.

Competition, choice and quality? Policy for commercial television

In November 1988 the government published its white paper *Broadcasting in the 1990s: Competition, Choice and Quality*, which proposed radical changes to the commercial sector of television. The government wished to create 'a more competitive and open broadcasting market . . . without detriment to programme standards and quality'. Developments in broadcasting technology were generating a multi-channel broadcasting system and the government was convinced that consumers should be sovereign in this new broadcasting marketplace. The white paper placed 'the viewer and listener at the centre of broadcasting policy' and believed that 'the single biggest advantage' of its proposals was the intention to 'give the viewer and listener a greater choice and a greater say' (*Broadcasting in the '90s*, 1988, para. 1.2). Not everyone was persuaded. Critics argued that programme quality could not be sustained in a deregulated broadcasting system. The very subtitle of the white paper, *Competition, Choice and Quality*, made the government's priorities clear: quality was to come a poor third to competition and choice in the new broadcasting market. A member of Campaign for Quality Television described the white paper as 'a detailed epitaph for a television system which has been the envy of the world' (Prebble, 1988, p. 3).

THE BROADCASTING ACT 1990

The Broadcasting Act 1990 differed only marginally from the 1988 white paper despite 440 amendments tabled during its passage through parliament. One amendment, however, was highly significant and reflected the increasingly vocal concerns about the impact of the proposed changes on the range and quality of programming on Channel 3. In February 1990, the minister responsible for broadcasting announced that while Channel 3 franchises would in most cases be awarded to the highest bidder, 'in exceptional circumstances' a lower bidder might secure the licence. 'The primary exceptional circumstance in my judgement,' the minister conceded, 'is quality' (*Financial Times*, 5 February 1990). The white paper and the Broadcasting Act seemed content largely to ignore the BBC, announcing merely that it 'has a special role' and that it 'is still, and will remain for the foreseeable future, the cornerstone of British broadcasting' (*Competition, Choice and Quality*, 1988, para. 3.2). But changes to the commercial side of the broadcasting divide were substantive.

There were three significant proposals for reform. First, a new public body, the Independent Television Commission (ITC), would replace the Independent Broadcasting Authority (IBA) and the Cable Authority on 1 January 1990. The ITC's main responsibilities were to licence and regulate all commercially funded UK television services including Channel 3, Channel 4, the new Channel 5, teletext and the burgeoning commercial television services delivered by cable and satellite (*Broadcasting Act 1990*, Part 1, Chapter 1, Sects 1–2). The ITC's regulatory brief required the Commission to ensure that a wide range of television services, broadcasting high-quality programmes with an appeal across a broad spectrum of tastes and interests, were available throughout the UK. The Act also required the ITC to publish a code governing broadcasting standards and issue separate codes for advertising and sponsorship (ibid., Sects 6–8). Second, the Act proposed to allocate the licences to broadcast in the different Channel 3 regions by inviting companies to tender 'blind' and competitive bids in a franchise auction. Alan Peacock was allegedly amazed that Margaret Thatcher was so taken with the idea of auctioning franchises, which had never featured as more than a marginal proposal in his report (Davidson, 1992, p. 11). There were to be two stages to the auction process. First, applicants would submit programme proposals and business plans to the ITC, who would establish that each company's programming intentions were adequate to meet a 'quality threshold'. In the absence of 'exceptional circumstances' the licence would be awarded to the applicant who tendered the highest bid. The Act specifies in considerable detail the fairly rigorous requirements necessary to clear the quality threshold. These include the need to provide programmes which are diverse in range and appeal to a wide variety of tastes and the requirement to broadcast high-quality news and current affairs at specified peak viewing times

(*Broadcasting Act 1990*, Part 1, Chapter 2, Sects 16 and 31). The diet of programming must cater for all tastes: chip butties as well as coq au vin. Third, the Act empowered the ITC to issue a licence for a new terrestrial commercial service to be designated Channel 5 (*Broadcasting Act 1990*, Sects 28–30). The Act, however, specified nothing concerning the station's possible remit, preferring to devote the three sections which discuss Channel 5 to an analysis of the technical problems involved in transmission to an eventual maximum of 70 per cent of UK households. The government seemed unclear about its programming intentions for Channel 5 except that it should help to provide greater viewer choice. Little wonder that an article in the *Listener* described Channel 5 as a 'channel going spare' (Fiddick, 2 November 1989, p. 8).

Two other changes are noteworthy. First, the Act suggested that Channel 4 should retain its remit to broadcast innovative programming to minority audiences and nurture 'a distinctive character of its own' (*Broadcasting Act 1990*, Sect 25 (1)b), but proposed changes to the channel's revenue base. Since January 1993, Channel 4 has been required to sell its own advertising, with the ITC empowered to exact a levy from Channel 3 franchise holders to fund any revenue deficits (*Broadcasting Act*, Sects 26–7). The continuing success of Channel 4 in attracting audiences and revenues, however, has not only rendered this 'safety net' redundant but has also had the opposite and quite unanticipated effect of requiring Channel 4 to pay a proportion of its profits into subsidising Channel 3; Channel 4 paid £57.3 million in 1994 and £74 million in 1995 to be divided among the 16 Channel 3 companies, with the largest sums going to Granada, LWT (£15.9 million each), Central and Carlton (£21.9 million each). In February 1995, Channel 4 launched a campaign asking the government to review these funding arrangements saying that these monies should fund new programming ventures at Channel 4 rather than being distributed as profits to Channel 3 shareholders (Bragg, 1995, p. 17 and Grade, 1995, p. 17). The government was persuaded to revise the 'safety net' rules in the Broadcasting Act 1996; payments would be reduced by increment to zero by the year 1999. Second, the 1990 Act had implications for ITN. News programmes for Channel 3 and 5 services were to be provided by 'a nominated news provider' (*Broadcasting Act*, Sect. 31(2)). The Act required news bulletins to be transmitted live and simultaneously across the various Channel 3 companies. But Section 32 (9)b of the Act stipulated that Channel 3 companies collectively must hold 'less than 50 per cent of the shares' in the news provider. Prior to the Act, ITN was jointly owned by the 15 regional ITV companies; 51 per cent of shares would need to be sold. Worse, the Act did not specify that ITN should be 'a nominated news provider' or even that there might be only one such provider. The development of television news services at SkyNews has subsequently provided a potentially rival 'news provider'.

THE LEGACY OF PILKINGTON? COMPETITION VERSUS QUALITY

The Broadcasting Act and the White Paper which preceded it triggered an extensive and often acrimonious debate between advocates and opponents of the new market-driven broadcasting system. Those who have read the reports by Beveridge and Pilkington, with their forceful criticisms of commercial broadcasting, undoubtedly experience an overwhelming sense of *déjà vu*. In the late 1980s, critics argued that one inevitable consequence of introducing market forces into the broadcast system would be a reduction in the range of programmes. Critics were also highly sceptical about the suitability of the 'auction' as a mechanism for allocating broadcast licences; there were fears that it would encourage overbidding and divert funding away from programme budgets to the treasury. The requirement for Channel 4 to sell its own advertising, moreover, combined with increased competition for advertising revenues from Channel 5, Sky and other satellite and cable networks, would mean that Channel 3 companies would receive a relatively smaller share of a fairly stable advertising cake; the reality of sustained economic recession was a continued decline of advertising revenues during the early 1990s. Within the new market-driven system, moreover, there would be little if any incentive to make quality programmes. On the contrary, market forces would favour the broadcasting of low-budget populist programmes like game shows, soaps, repeats and old films, which would minimise programme costs but maximise audiences and advertising revenues. Why, the critics' argument ran, should broadcasters spend almost half a million pounds each broadcast hour to make high-quality drama programmes, when snooker attracts larger audiences? A market system cannot guarantee the quality, but only the popularity, of programming (Prebble, 1988, p. 3). The ITC, moreover, was to regulate with a 'lighter touch' than its IBA predecessor and consequently there would be inadequate 'quality controls' on programming. Some critics alleged the impact of a market system on political broadcasting would be especially harmful and prohibitive. In future there would be 'less political reporting and analysis on the two BBC channels and greater caution among the BBC's Producers and Editors . . . Programmes such as *Panorama*, *Newsnight* and *On The Record* will not be entirely neutered but they will risk hitting hard less often . . . Among the ITC companies almost certainly a diminution in the number of news and current affairs programmes' (Hetherington, 1989a, p. 11; see also Nossiter, 1986, pp. 33–8). With the benefit of hindsight, such a prognosis seems uncannily accurate.

When the ITC announced the results of the first auction on 16 October 1991, there were significant anomalies in the allocation of particular franchises as well problematic implications for British broadcasting in the longer term (Davidson, 1992). Four outcomes of the auction seemed to bear out the scepticism of its critics. First, the government's intention of increasing competition had evidently failed. Three franchises (Central Television,

Border Television and Scottish Television) were awarded uncontested: the companies retained their licences with minimal bids. Consequently, Central Television, which at the time enjoyed an annual turnover of more than £314 million, was able to retain its franchise for £2000; one of the most lucrative franchises in commercial television was effectively given away. Critics argued that the government should have specified a reserve price – perhaps £30 million for the larger franchises and £15 million for the smaller – if only to maximise treasury revenues (Fireman, 1991, p. 25). Subsequent auctions have followed a similar lacklustre pattern. The Radio Authority, for example, had not received a single bid by the closing date for tenders for the first independent national radio licence; the closing date was extended by one month (see chapter 7). The first round of bids for Channel 5 generated only a single applicant which the ITC rejected on the basis of an unsuitable business plan. This is hardly the fierce marketplace, characterised by the bullish language of competition, envisaged by the Broadcasting Act in 1990.

Second, the auction prompted overbidding. Anglia, Yorkshire and Tyne Tees each bid in excess of what the franchise could profitably sustain and committed annual payments to the treasury which constituted unrealistically high proportions of their anticipated advertising revenues. Critics suggested that once again staff cuts and declining-quality programmes would be the inevitable consequence. The overbidding reflected the fact that there seemed to be no consensual or 'objective' figure for the value to be placed on a particular franchise region. There were certainly substantial disparities in the bids which were offered within particular franchise areas. In the South East England region, Carlton TV's bid of £18,080,000 was barely one third of TVS's (Television South's) bid of £59,758,000; similarly, Channel TV bid £1000 while its unsuccessful rival bid £102,000. These disparities seem to be a consequence of the inherent financial uncertainties of the auction process which entails what one observer described as a 'SWAG analysis': a sophisticated wild-arsed guess (Fireman, 1991, p. 25). In 1990, applicants were obliged to calculate at 1993 (when the franchises would begin) the annual sum they would be prepared to pay in each year of the franchise, inflated as required after 1993. But the calculation involved factors which were wholly beyond their control. The obvious and most important consideration here was the amount of advertising that Channel 3 might attract across the 10-year period of the licence. Some companies undoubtedly miscalculated by overbidding, by failing to anticipate the recession's impact on advertising revenues, or by having to face competition from new broadcasters. As a consequence, some companies have not been able to sustain their initial franchise commitments to the ITC. In their efforts to become economically leaner, programme quality has again been the casualty. The breakfast station GMTV is an obvious example here.

Third, the outcome of the auction in 1991 created uncertainty about the criterion according to which franchises would be awarded. In the white paper the position had been uncontentious; franchises would be awarded to

the highest bidder. But the Broadcasting Act stated that 'in exceptional circumstances' the franchise could be awarded to a lower bidder promising
higher-quality programming. In 1991 only 5 of the 16 franchises were
awarded to the highest bidder; in 8 instances a lower bid was accepted, signalling an award on the basis of quality. Legally and procedurally, this is a
messy business. Three companies who were unsuccessful in the auction
despite having offered the highest bids – (two incumbents, TVS and TSW
(Television South West), and the company bidding for the Northern Ireland
franchise, TV-NI (Television Northern Ireland)) – sought judicial review of
the ITC decisions which were ultimately upheld. The managing director of
TSW claimed, 'We played by the rules but the goal posts were moved'
(*Guardian*, 2 November 1991). The auction process was no tidier when the
Channel 5 licence was re-advertised in May 1995. The four bids ranged
between £2 million and £36 million; the successful bidder was Channel 5
Broadcasting Limited which tendered a mere £22 million.

Finally, the results of the first auction enhanced the tendency towards
concentration of ownership and cross-ownership of companies. The inability of the Broadcasting Act 1990 to limit concentration of ownership was
illustrated dramatically by the merger of Sky and British Satellite
Broadcasting two days after the Act received royal assent. The Act prohibited companies such as Rupert Murdoch's News International from owning
more than 20 per cent of a domestic television service if they also owned
British newspapers; the merger, however, gave Murdoch a 50 per cent holding in BSkyB. Murdoch's ownership of Sky TV had not breached the legislation because it was an 'offshore' station based in Luxembourg and not
subject to ITC regulation. The new BSkyB station based in London clearly
breached the new law, but the government and ITC seemed powerless to
enforce it. BSkyB simply threatened to move its broadcasting base to
Luxembourg if the government refused permission to broadcast from
Britain. In such circumstances, the 750,000 viewers of the old British
Satellite Broadcasting would no longer be able to receive the service. The
Independent claimed that Rupert Murdoch 'was holding a pistol to the head
of the Government' (4 November 1990, p. 1). The successor Broadcasting
Act 1996 is even less likely to curtail this trend towards concentration of
ownership (see below, pp. 206–10).

CHANNEL 4: THE FATTED CALF?

Channel 4, as well as Channel 3, has recently been the focus of policy proposals. In June 1996, the government announced that the Downing Street
policy unit had been working on detailed proposals to privatise Channel 4.
The sale of the corporation would raise £1.5 billion for the treasury and
facilitate tax cuts; Chancellor Ken Clarke supported the proposal along
with the Department of National Heritage (Smither and Nowicka, 1996,
p. 9). The suggestion for privatising Channel 4 arose at a particularly

propitious moment, although it had long been a cherished ambition of Thatcherite backbenchers. The channel had recently been successful in reducing and eventually ending the system of 'safety net' payments to ITV which would leave an extra £90 million in Channel 4 coffers. The channel was also increasingly under attack for having allegedly reneged on its public-service remit by reducing the proportion of news, factual, arts and music and drama programming, while increasing its output of entertainment, US imports and repeats. David Elstein claimed that Channel 4 had 'fattened itself up' for the government (Culf and White, 1996, p. 1). Government sources suggested that the privatisation plan would be in the Conservative manifesto for the 1997 general election; the Labour party affirmed it had no plans to privatise the channel.

In a speech at the 1996 Edinburgh Festival, Michael Grade attacked the suggestion on two grounds. First, it was unnecessary since Channel 4 was neither inefficient nor did it require more capital – two classic justifications for privatisation. But Grade's main reason for opposing the change was that it would threaten the channel's special remit to broadcast innovative programmes for minority audiences in line with the best traditions of public-service broadcasting. Channel 4 was established as a public corporation designed to plough back profits into programme-making rather than distributing them to shareholders. The market was antipathetic to that remit. 'You can certainly have a privatised Channel 4,' Grade announced, 'or you can have Channel 4 with its full public-service remit. But you cannot have both' (Grade, 1996, p. 18). After privatisation Grade argued that Channel 4, like Channel 3, would become driven by 'the need to maximise the return to shareholders. In that situation, the remit, however explicitly defined, would represent the most you had to deliver to avoid regulatory sanction . . . this dynamic sucks money off the screen and out of British production. Thus the remit would effectively be a battleground not a shared objective' (ibid., p. 19). On 2 May 1997, Michael Jackson, previously BBC director of television and controller of BBC1, was appointed as Grade's successor as chief executive of Channel 4.

Auntie goes to market

During the 1980s the BBC was criticised by successive governments and the public for its alleged financial profligacy, its bureaucratic inefficiency and the partisanship and bias of its news and current affairs coverage. In the period prior to the renewal of its charter in 1996, the BBC needed to show that it was addressing these perceived shortcomings. Consequently, a number of government bodies and think-tanks, as well as the BBC itself, have formulated a whole raft of policies to generate change in three key areas: the BBC's licence fee and other revenue sources, its organisational structures and its programming philosophy especially in the areas of news and current affairs. Technological developments have generated a fourth policy objective: the need to plan for digital broadcasting.

CHIPS FOR FREE? FINANCING THE BBC?

The arrival of multi-channel television in Britain in the late 1980s required the BBC to confront a difficult question concerning its finances: 'when households enjoy ready access to a diverse range of free television channels, will viewers be willing to continue to pay a licence fee to fund BBC programmes?' Many observers believe the answer was 'no'. Ehrenburg and Mills expressed this conclusion differently: 'not many people would buy potatoes,' they claim, 'if chips were free' (Ehrenberg and Mills, 1993, p. 64). Government and broadcasters in the commercial sector argued that the BBC must find an alternative source of funding as its declining share of audience makes its claims to a licence-fee income increasingly illegitimate.

Damian Green's pamplet *A Better BBC*, published by the right-wing Centre for Policy Studies, concluded that a modified version of the licence fee should continue to provide the mainstay of the BBC's revenue (Green, 1991, p. 26). But the BBC should no longer remain the monopoly recipient of licence income. A new body, called the Public Service Broadcasting Authority (PSBA), invested with a 'specific brief to promote high quality television across the board', should distribute licence revenues between the BBC and other channels (ibid., p. 31). The BBC should retain its remit for quality broadcasting across a range of programmes, but would be expected to fulfil this brief with lesser funding. Green offers a three-pronged strategy for supplementing income. The BBC should cut costs by scrapping local radio and privatise radios 1 and 2 which lie at the margins of its public-service commitments (ibid., p. 41); it must become more efficient and cut waste; and it must find other sources of revenue – such as selling some of its stock of programmes, which form the largest video library in the world, to domestic and overseas buyers (ibid., pp. 36–37).

A second proposal by David Boulton, *The Third Age Of Broadcasting* published by the left-wing Institute for Public Policy Research (IPPR), argued in favour of abolishing the licence fee. Born in the first age of television monopoly, the rationale for the licence fee 'became shaky' in the second age of duopoly, but with 8 million satellite dishes predicted by the year 2000, 'its life has surely come to an end' (Boulton, 1991, p. 6). The licence fee is a regressive tax which costs £70–£80 million a year to collect, with evasion rife and likely to rise as the number of channels increases. Boulton rejects advertising and subscription and argues that the BBC should be funded by a grant from government which should make a direct charge on the taxpayer, much like the other public services of health and education. The revenue lost by abolition of the licence fee could be recouped by a tax on television and radio sets at the point of sale (ibid., p. 14).

The National Heritage report *The Future of The BBC*, published in

November 1992 and intended to trigger a debate, concluded somewhat reluctantly in favour of retaining the licence fee on the rather negative ground that, 'No-one has devised an obviously better system' (Cmnd 2098, 1992, p. 31). It certainly wasn't for lack of trying. The government itself had explored the various options of advertising, subscription and direct taxation and rejected each in turn. The government established the Committee on Financing the BBC (the Peacock Committee) in 1985 in the hope that it would recommend replacing the licence fee with advertising revenues. The government also believed that such a reform would promote competition in broadcasting, choice for viewers and efficiency among broadcasters. Advertising might also undermine the BBC's apparent insularity from outside criticism, break the monopoly of the ITV companies and lower the costs of advertising. But these ambitions came to grief when Peacock's conclusions rejected advertising as a suitable means to finance the BBC; a view later endorsed by the government's *Future of the BBC* (Cmnd 2098, pp. 33–4). Peacock acknowledged the degree of possible dissonance between 'the value to advertisers and the value to the audience of a particular programme'; indeed they 'may well differ markedly' (Peacock, 1986, p. 127). Two other considerations were influential. First, research studies showed that even limited advertising on the BBC would completely undermine the financial basis of the ITV companies. Second, advertising would compromise the quality and range of BBC programming which was among the best in the world, was highly respected by professional broadcasters in other countries and compared very favourably with programming in America, Italy and Australia which featured a high proportion of advertising at peak broadcast times (Hetherington, 1989a, pp. 3–4). The committee recommended an indexed licence fee to finance the BBC with a move towards a system of subscription by the late 1990s.

But a system of funding based on subscription is flawed for at least three reasons. First, as Ehrenberg and Mills illustrate, a subscription system might cost more to operate and incur greater collection costs (Green, 1991, p. 29). Second, subscription would involve encoding the television signal with the consequent need to convert sets and install set-top decoders. This might prove to be a long and costly procedure; Green estimates 20 years (ibid.). Blumler opposes subscription because it is incompatible with public-service broadcasting. He argues that a subscription service would disadvantage those kinds of programmes that people would be loath to pay for even though they regularly tap into them when available as part of a public broadcaster's general service – such as news and current affairs (Blumler, 1993, p. 36). Subscription, moreover, destroys the universality which is a central tenet of the public-service tradition.

Finally, there is the prospect of funding the BBC from general taxation. But income tax would have to be raised by a penny in the pound at standard rate to pay for BBC services; alternately, VAT would have to be raised by 0.5 per cent. A new tax on television equipment would put £300 on the cost of a new television (Cmnd 2098, p. 32). These new taxes would be politically difficult for any government to introduce. Funding by taxation, moreover, would increase broadcasters' dependence on government and make the BBC vulnerable to swings in the economy which would be 'prejudicial to the long term stability and planning which is needed for investment in both development and programmes' (Fisher, 1993, p. 71).

The government's reluctant conclusion in favour of the licence fee is perhaps more understandable when the problematic nature of the alternative sources of funding is considered. But the licence fee remains unpopular with the public. A MORI poll conducted after *The Future of the BBC* revealed that 60 per cent of respondents favoured replacing the licence fee with advertising; only 34 per cent were against (*Guardian*, 19 March 1993). Some commentators, however, deny any 'groundswell' of public opinion against the licence fee (Ehrenberg and Mills, 1993, p. 65); there was certainly a good deal more resentment in 1996 when viewers were asked to make a 'one-off' payment to view the Frank Bruno fight. On 6 July 1994, the government white paper *The Future of the BBC: Serving the Nation, Competing World Wide* confirmed that the licence fee would remain in place at least until 2001 when it would be reviewed in the light of new technology and the possibility of subscription funding; the linking of the fee to the retail price index (RPI) would be reviewed in 1996. Right on cue, John Birt used his MacTaggart lecture at the Edinburgh Film Festival on 23 August 1996 to make a public plea for a £5 to £6 increase in the cost of a colour licence from £89.50; at that time, the licence fee generated £1.8 billion annual revenue. The BBC had saved £500 million since 1991 through savings, staff cuts and increased efficiency and anticipated further savings of 15 per cent during the next three years, but the Corporation still confronted a shortfall of £300 million because of the costs of introducing digital television services (Brown, 1996, p. 17).

THE 'NEW ENGINE' OF THE BBC: PRODUCER CHOICE

The details of producer choice were announced in October 1991 and restated in the BBC's *Responding to the Green Paper* (BBC, 1993a, pp. 40–2). Designed by John Birt, the scheme was intended to create a competitive internal market in the BBC by giving producers control of their own programme budgets and allowing them to shop outside the Corporation for facilities for programme making. In part the scheme was prompted by the 1990 Broadcasting Act's injunction that the BBC should take 25 per cent of programmes from independent producers, but it was also clearly designed to refute allegations that the BBC was too large, overly bureaucratic and, most significantly, too costly.

The linking of the licence fee to the RPI in 1987 had reduced the BBC's revenue, creating a problem for programme-making budgets. Director General Michael Checkland established the Cobham Committee to see if a 15 per cent cut in programme-making costs could be achieved without sacrificing quality. The committee concluded that organisational changes designed to give producers greater choice in budgetary matters could deliver such savings; producer choice would become 'the new engine of the BBC' (Oliver, 1993, p. 118). Since April 1993, producers have been expected to buy the services they need – design, scenic services, costumes, studio space, graphics and post-production services – from whichever source is the most cost-effective. The BBC's in-house departments which had previously supplied these services now survive only if they can sell their services to programme makers. Birt believed that this simple organisational prescription might cure a range of broadcasting ills. He suggested that producer choice would deliver 'greater freedom for programme makers, more value on the screen, greater efficiencies, less bureaucracy and a devolution of power that will mean a more vigorous management culture in the BBC' (*Guardian*, 30 October 1991). But producer choice has been the subject of substantial criticism. Trade unions argue it has resulted in staff cuts. BECTU claim that 3500 of their members lost their jobs between 1991 and 1993, bringing job losses since Michael Checkland became director general in 1986 to 7000 or one quarter of the workforce at that date. New jobs are being created but not in programme making. BECTU complain that while 3500 technicians' jobs disappeared between 1991 and 1993, the Corporation advertised 368 non-programme-makers' jobs in the first three months of 1993. At BBC Manchester 113 programme-making jobs have been lost but 28 new posts created for non-programme makers (Muir, 1993, p. 4). Other critics argue that producer choice undermines the fundamental character of the BBC. If outside production resources are cheaper then eventually BBC departments will close. The inexorable logic of producer choice will be to move the BBC away from being a broadcasting organisation which makes programmes in the direction of becoming an organisation which simply commissions them – a concern which was greatly enhanced by John Birt's proposals in June 1996 for restructuring the BBC.

Finally, critics suggest that producer choice has prompted an explosion of bureaucratic inefficiency as producers set off to the new marketplace to discuss prices, haggle, strike deals and sign contracts with BBC service departments, before they can start making programmes. Producers complain that they have been forced to become 'small businessmen to run their business units' while resource departments in the BBC 'are spending thousands of pounds advertising their services to each other in glossy brochures and quoting prices on rate cards' (ibid.). A review by accountants Price Waterhouse in 1992 revealed that the Corporation spends £330 million (a quarter of the licence fee) on activities other than programme making. Birt has rebuffed these criticisms strongly. In his Fleming Memorial Lecture to the Royal Television Society in March 1993, he claimed the BBC's broadcasting skills as a 'national asset' and stressed that he did not intend 'to turn the BBC into a publisher-broadcaster'. Producer choice, moreover, did not nurture bureaucracy but would 'ensure that as much money as possible is channelled towards the most creative ends' (Birt, 1993).

BBC PROGRAMME POLICY AND THE HIMALAYAN OPTION

Whatever Birt's claims concerning the funding of programmes, it is clear that the emerging multi-channel environment has implications for programming at the BBC. In the current fiercely competitive broadcasting environment, the BBC can anticipate and has conceded a steady decline in audience share (BBC, 1992). The Corporation must decide where it wishes to locate itself and its programming in the new television market. Financial considerations are significant here. 'Aunty's Agony', concerning programming policy involves, at least in part, the need to decide whether 'the BBC can balance cost and quality' (Oliver, 1993, p. 13); expressed rather starkly, will competition for audiences prompt more Mr Blobby and less Late Review? But the BBC must confront a broader and more complex policy question: what is the appropriate role for a public-service broadcaster in the new circumstances of multi-channel television broadcasting? Should the BBC try to compete with the expansive new commercial services or try to define a distinctive programme identity?

The National Heritage Paper *The Future of the BBC* argued that the BBC could not continue to broadcast the existing wide range of programmes and suggested two possible ways of restricting output. First, the BBC could specialise in news and current affairs, arts and science programmes, religious broadcasting, programmes for minorities and 'programmes which are unlikely to be broadcast by other organisations. The BBC would broadcast few general entertainment programmes, but more programmes for minority audiences, so increasing the overall diversity and choice' (Department of National Heritage, 1992, Cmnd 2098, para. 4.5). Quickly dubbed the 'Himalayan Option', this strategy argued in favour of the BBC attempting to colonise the high ground of broadcasting; some observers were quick to point out that 'no proper role for public television can be found by asking it to do this' (Blumler, 1993, p. 30). Alternatively, the BBC could focus on programmes of particular interest to British audiences which reflect the 'British way of life, history and culture . . . and Britain's evolving place in Europe and the wider world' (Department of National Heritage, 1992, Cmnd 2098, para. 4.6).

The BBC recognised both options as the broadcast ghettos they potentially could become; the Corporation did not relish sharing the fate of inconsequence which is the lot of public-service television in the USA. Within two days, on 27 November 1992, the BBC rejected both options in *Extending Choice: The BBC's Role in the New Broadcasting Age*. The BBC strategy was to offer a slightly narrower range of high-quality and distinctive programmes which commercial broadcasters would not provide. But Birt explicitly rejected the 'Himalayan option', claiming that 'the BBC is not planning to become a cultural ghetto or to retreat into minority areas and intends to continue making programmes for everyone'. The BBC, moreover, 'is not interested in attracting large audiences for their own sake' (BBC, 1992, p. 8). In May 1993, the BBC confirmed this policy of providing a broad range of quality programming (BBC, 1993a, p. 36).

Distinguished media scholar Jay Blumler rejects the idea of defining the role of public service broadcaster in terms of the gaps left by commercial broadcasters – the public-service diet must consist of more than the scraps which fall from the banqueting table of commercial television. Instead, he suggests that 'we move the prescription up a notch in generality from programme specifics to important social functions that may go to the wall if television is dominated by profit seeking providers' (Blumler, 1993, p. 30). Blumler identifies four such 'communication tasks' for public television. First, television should provide 'communication' for citizenship to 'inform the national debate' as the BBC expresses it in *Extending Choice*. Second, there should be programmes for children which serve 'the curiosity and educative needs of growing youngsters', rather than cartoons with explicit toy-related product tie-ins which are indistinguishable from the advertisements between them. Third, a public broadcaster should comprise a 'national theatre of the airwaves' presenting the best of music, literature, art and science 'made available to the mass audience in an involving way'. Finally, the public broadcaster should reassert a sense of national identity amid the increasing availability of programming from overseas. Blumler argues that all programmes, including the most popular and entertaining programmes, should not only entertain but offer 'food for thought on those role conflicts and social problems that arise in characteristically British circumstances and terms'. In addition to these 'communication tasks' Blumler wants programme quality, diversity, innovation and 'the ability to surprise' (ibid., pp. 29–33). But Blumler concedes that such a programming strategy involves risks. Will viewers, he asks, become so accustomed to the proliferation of 'satellite snacks' that they lose their appetite for more 'substantial and varied meals' (ibid., p. 30). John Birt was convinced that the audience's appetite for serious programming, especially news and current affairs, remained as keen as ever, although the BBC was culpable for not presenting these programmes as well as it might have done. If the BBC was truly the 'cornerstone' of British broadcasting, it seemed unthinkable that, whatever other programming decisions were agreed, news and current affairs should not be reorganised and reinstated as central to the BBC's output; this was the principle tenet of 'Birtism'.

BIRTISM: ENDING THE 'BIAS AGAINST UNDERSTANDING'

The changes in the organisation of news services at the BBC which followed the appointment of Michael Checkland as director general in February 1987 and John Birt a month later, were undoubtedly a response to the substantial criticism of the Corporation's news and current affairs programmes, by the public, politicians, certain sections of the print media and even the BBC governors, which had been so evident throughout the 1980s (see above, pp. 170–4). Other factors contributed to these changes. New technology and the developing satellite and cable news services hardened the BBC's resolve to remain the brand leader in the expansive market for news services.

Birt was appointed to run the newly created Directorate of News and Current Affairs which brought all television and radio news journalists into a single organisational structure. Previously Birt had worked at LWT as producer of *Weekend World*, which was allegedly Mrs Thatcher's favourite current-affairs programme. Birt was deeply critical of BBC television news. In his speech to the Royal Television Society in April 1988, Birt voiced the first of many public criticisms of his colleagues working in BBC news. 'There are too many stitch-ups and stick-ups in our studios and in our films,' he claimed, 'too many contributors who vow never to return . . . The pursuit of accurate, impartial, fair and enquiring journalism of quality on television and elsewhere comes easiest to those who have open minds . . . it comes hardest to those imbued with a disdain for, and not just a healthy suspicion of, established centres of power' (Birt, 1988). He has continued to be publicly critical of BBC journalism. In a lecture at Trinity College Dublin in February 1995, Birt suggested that 'overwhelming and sneering' interviewers like John Humphreys were 'too tough' in their encounters with politicians (Brooks, 1995, p. 15).

Birt believed he possessed a cure for this malaise. The fine detail of his prescription had been elaborated a decade earlier in a series of articles written jointly with television presenter Peter Jay in *The Times* and reprinted in the newspaper on 23 March 1987 and in Jay's edited volume *The Crisis for Western Political Economy and Other Essays*. Their argument was that television news prompted a 'bias against understanding' in two ways. First, a high story count in short news bulletins prompted a rather staccato, 'bitty' feel to the news; journalists were failing to set stories within a broader news context. 'Present television news programmes,' Birt argued, 'cover a large number of stories – often more than twenty stories in less than half an hour. As a result the focus of any one story is extremely narrow' (*The Times*, 23 March 1987, p. 14). Birt and Jay argued that news should be analysed at different levels of depth to produce a connected series of stories across a certain news period. Birt elaborated the model by the example of the Birmingham pub bombing. A journalist's first job is to report the hard facts, the 'immediate circumstances' of the bombing: Where did the bomb explode? How many deaths occurred? In news reports later in the day, the journalist should 'widen coverage to set the explosion in the context of the bombing campaign and look at what security measures might be introduced'. Within a week, a more extensive item would address more general questions 'by putting the bombing campaign in the context of the Northern Ireland conflict' (Birt, 1987, p. 14). This approach to news would be in sharp contrast to the more typical 'hard news followed by the human suffering' approach (Wallis and Baran, 1990, p. 63) and would blur the traditional distinction between news and current affairs. The second factor generating a 'bias against understanding' was the professionalisation of news journalism. Journalists needed to be specialists with detailed knowledge of a particular field rather than 'jack of all trades' presenters whose skills were primarily those of experienced and seasoned broadcasters. The solution to the problem of the bias against understanding was to establish an integrated news and current affairs organisation which employed specialist journalists rather than generalised broadcasters.

As head of the News and Current Affairs Directorate, Birt was uniquely well placed to put this news 'philosophy' into organisational practice. Given the diagnosis, the prescription seemed evident. 'We should redesign television news programmes,' Birt announced, 'so that they devote much more time than they presently do to the main news stories of the day' (Birt, 1987, p. 14). News and current affairs programmes were revamped in line with the dictates of Birtism. The story count was reduced, offering increased and in-depth analysis of all news items. Current affairs programmes were structured according to a strict division of labour: *On the Record* dealt with domestic political concerns, *Assignment* explored foreign affairs while the *Money Programme* focused on economic issues. The seriousness of BBC news was consciously designed as a distinctive approach, striking a sharp contrast with the 'lighter', more human-interest news stories in the ITN provision for certain channels and bulletins. Birt believed this increased emphasis on news – and serious news – would be popular and win audiences; a view which receives prima facie endorsement in statistical comparisons of BBC and ITN audiences for news programmes between 1987 and 1991 (McNair, 1994, pp. 86–7). But such data are notoriously unreliable. Audiences for news programmes vary across the different seasons of the year and are markedly influenced by the popularity of the preceding and following programmes (Norris, 1996). News and current affairs programmes only occasionally win large audiences and 'a cynic might argue that a preponderance of specialists pedagogically spelling out the facts through in-depth analyses on the *9 O'Clock News* will make the BBC so boring that people will tune out' (Wallis and Baran, 1990, p. 69). Whatever the outcome for audiences, Birt's attempt to expand news provision when other news organisations are introducing 'News Bunnies' must surely be welcomed.

The designation 'boring', however, was among the least offensive accusations levelled against John Birt's innovatory style and approach to running the News and Current Affairs Directorate. Initially, the substantial criticism emanating from news journalists within the BBC was considered to represent little more than the inevitable grumblings of the old regime whose vested interests were being undermined by change; this was typically Birt's counterblast to his critics. Other critics suggested that Birtism was a child of its time. The new detailed, analytical style of news presentation seemed to take the heat out of news journalism and certainly generated far fewer occasions where politicians and broadcasters found themselves in conflict. This style of journalism suited the embattled governors, if not the journalists and programme makers, after many years of sustained bludgeoning by successive Conservative governments. Some observers had always believed that Birt had been 'moved in' to achieve precisely this aim: 'to tame the BBC in accordance with the pleasures of a strong government' (ibid., p. 62).

Some critics articulated more sinister concerns, suggesting that the management of the new directorate was centralising its control over news output. In a unitary structure like the BBC such control is easily exercised where the will exists. Shortly after Birt's arrival in 1987, BBC journalists expressed grave concerns about the wholly inappropriate intervention of management in editorial judgements concerning a *Panorama* programme about the kidnapping of Terry Waite. After the programme was completed, it was approved by directorate executives and sent to John Birt. He returned the programme with detailed written instructions about the ways he wished it to be re-edited at a cost of £10,000. The incident represented a worrying intrusion of management into editorial judgements. Another *Panorama* programme exploring facets of the Peter Wright spy case was halted by John Birt eight months into production because it 'had not been worked out in sufficient detail' (*World in Action*, 29 February 1988).

A number of journalists left the BBC because they were so concerned about the impact of Birtism and the new directorate on the quality of news provision. Robert Fox, a former BBC radio journalist awarded the MBE for his work during the Falklands war, left to join the *Daily Telegraph*. He denounced the increasing centralisation of BBC news in strong terms:

> Any journalistic operation has to rely on the skills of its front line reporters . . . If you have somebody sitting behind a desk at the top of the concrete battleship Broadcasting House, saying 'I'm terribly cleverer than you are. You really are rather silly and superficial boys because you have to rush around a lot and all this rushing around makes the blood rush to your head', then it is going to be a poor show – that poor show is already on the road. It is centrally controlled by one group of very high level managers . . . and the word that one hears over and over again, is Stalinism.

> (Robert Fox cited in *World in Action*, 29 February 1988)

Bringing the story of BBC news and current affairs more up to date, Birt's intervention in 1996 in a *Newsnight* programme about British Airways was reminiscent of his series of objections to *Panorama* programmes in the late 1980s. In September 1996 Birt axed a *Newsnight* report by distinguished freelance journalist Martyn Gregory which alleged a 'dirty tricks' campaign by British Airways against Virgin airlines; £100,000 had already been invested in making the report which was mid-production (Williams, 1996, p. 1). Birt, who is a friend of Robert Ayling, the chief executive of British Airways, faxed a report to Tony Hall, head of the News and Current Affairs Directorate, criticising the 'lack of rigour' in the programme's journalism. A senior BBC journalist claimed, 'This is the end of investigative journalism on *Newsnight*. It has driven investigative journalism into the sand' (Culf, 16 September 1996, p. 4).

CUTS AND BITES: THE DIGITAL TELEVISION REVOLUTION?

On 10 August 1995, then Heritage Secretary Virginia Bottomley launched the white paper *Digital Terrestrial Broadcasting* (Cmnd 2946), detailing the government's plans for digital television, with an appropriate soundbite: 'We stand on the verge of a revolution.' Apparently pleased with her metaphor of insurgency, she predicted 'a new era of television and radio' and warned, with a phrase reminiscent of Che Guevara, that 'We must seize the time' (quoted in Barnett, 1995, p. 16). Her agitprop remarks clearly impressed John Birt; within two months the BBC had published its own policy document, *Britain's Digital Opportunity* (BBC, 1995). A year later, the Broadcasting Act 1996 established the legislative framework for digital television (Pt 1 Sect 1–39).

Digital broadcasting is a highly complex and technical matter and this is reflected in the rather obtuse language of the Broadcasting Act. The system will work as follows. Initially, there will be six frequency channels or 'multiplexes' available for digital terrestrial television, each with a capacity to carry between three and six television channels plus additional services. The analogue television signal is converted to digital bites capable of compression and consequently a greatly increased amount of information can be transmitted along these multiplexes. The multiplex 'providers' will be powerful brokers who decide which television services to carry on their frequencies. The ITC will licence providers as well as the providers of programmes and other services on the multiplex. Existing broadcasters will be guaranteed capacity on a multiplex to allow them to provide new services while 'simulcasting' (i.e. broadcasting in analogue and digital mode) their existing channels. The BBC will have control of a complete multiplex, Channel 3 and Channel 4 will enjoy joint control of a multiplex which will also carry public service teletext, while Channel 5 will share a multiplex with S4C in Wales. On 31 October 1996, the ITC advertised the first bundle of four digital terrestrial licences. The ITC will award licences not on the basis of cash bids but on the strength of applicants' marketing and financial plans; the concern is to establish digital services as promptly as possible. Digital terrestrial television programming is expected in mid-1998 with approximately 18–25 new stations; digital satellite television will arrive earlier and offer up to 300 new stations (*Broadcasting Act 1996*, Sects 6–31).

The benefits for viewers include an improved sound and picture quality, cinema-style wide-screen viewing, an increase in the number of accessible channels and a range of other services. Using digital technology, a slim screen on the wall will serve as a television, radio, telephone and interactive computer. If digital television truly heralds a revolution, the unlikely beneficiaries of the dawning of this new age will be couch potatoes, who will be able to 'spud out' and shop, bank, speak to friends and watch television without leaving their living rooms. But the benefits for broadcasters seem less obvious. The capital investment in the new technology is substantial and even the costs of simulcasting, which have to be borne by the broadcasters, may be as high as £10 million each year (Brown, 1995, p. 11). In May 1996, launching an update of the BBC's vision of multi-channel digital broadcasting, John Birt claimed that a massive start-up capital investment of around £200 million would be necessary, requiring the BBC to cut a further 20 per cent from programme-making costs and administration; the privatising of the BBC transmission system will provide further resources for the digital enterprise. But even cuts of this magnitude would provide insufficient investment capital for the new digital services the BBC intends. The inevitable casualty will be programme quality.

Sceptics believe that financial considerations undermine the prospects for the much-advertised digital revolution, since there is unlikely to be sufficient funding for the additional channels, which will require programming budgets as well as start-up capital. There is a cross-party consensus that no public finance will be available to pump prime digital broadcasting beyond the existing commitment to the licence fee; but by the year 2005, the licence fee will account for no more than 20 per cent of revenues at the BBC (Pallister, 1996, p. 10). Advertising is not an option. More than a decade ago Peacock discovered that funding the BBC by advertising would prompt the collapse of some Channel 3 companies without an expansion of the overall advertising pool. Subsequently competition for revenues has become more fierce as Channel 3 has become obliged to compete with channels 4 and 5 and a host of satellite and cable channels for advertising income. This leaves subscription or pay per view as the only viable funding mechanisms for digital services. But programme making is very expensive and these options are unlikely to generate sufficient funding to allow programme making of the quality necessary to attract viewers. In 1995, for example, the total expenditure on programme making by the four terrestrial broadcasters was £2 billion or approximately £500 million each. The average cost for satellite and cable stations is less than £20 million. There is no reason to anticipate that viewers, as rational consumers, will pay for programmes on digital channels when they can already watch programmes of equivalent quality for free (Barnett, 1995, p. 16).

But there is another reason why some observers are sceptical about the prospects for terrestrial digital television; and it is crucial. Murdoch is placed to dominate the digital television market and exclude rivals (Porter, 1996a, p. 2). He will launch up to 200 digital satellite channels early in

1998 and to receive these channels viewers will need to buy a set-top decoder which will unscramble the digital signal. The decoder will cost approximately £500 but Murdoch is planning to subsidise costs to reduce the price to the consumer to nearer £200. There is no legal requirement for manufacturers to produce a set-top box which is capable of decoding both satellite and terrestrial signals and consequently whoever gets up and running first is likely to 'steal' the market – a lesson Murdoch learned in Sky's triumph over British Satellite Broadcasting with its 'squarial' technology. Murdoch's decoder will be on the market before any equivalent decoder can be agreed on by the terrestrial broadcasters. 'This is the crucial advantage he has seized,' Porter notes, 'for it is highly unlikely that the British market will accept two separate boxes for the satellite and terrestrial digital services.' In the 'race between the satellite and terrestrial delivery digital systems . . . Murdoch has a head start' (ibid.). Murdoch will become the gatekeeper of access to the new television technology. But the prospect for terrestrial broadcasters is even less promising than this. The BBC and Granada have signed up to be among the 150 services offered on Murdoch's satellite system – a strategy which threatens at least two dangers. First, BBC programming will be vulnerable to Murdoch's control. In much the same way that Murdoch ejected the BBC from his Star satellite service in Asia in March 1994, because BBC news items were offending the Chinese government, BBC programming will be subject to Murdoch's market-driven assessments of its suitability. Second, if the BBC and Granada use the BSkyB satellite, this reduces considerably any incentive which they may have to confront the substantial financial and other difficulties entailed in establishing their own independent terrestrial service, which would then be in competition with Murdoch. The Broadcasting Act 1996 offers no controls over Murdoch's operation of the gateway to ensure fair competition, but a European directive offers some prospect that the decoder would need to be adaptable to receive terrestrial services. A flurry of articles in the *Guardian*, *Independent* and the *Telegraph* (but not Murdoch's *Times*) on consecutive days in late October 1996 warned of the imminent prospect of Murdoch's potential to dominate the digital broadcasting market. The minister for trade and industry issued a statement expressing confidence that 'provisions are already in place . . . to ensure franchising of the key technology of the digital set-top box can take place on a fair, reasonable and non-discriminatory basis' (cited in Culf, 1996a, p. 10). While city media analysts believe that the 'establishment is discreetly waving Murdoch through', the Office of Fair Trading has been reassured by BSkyB 'that it would not act unfairly' (Porter, 1996a, p. 3). John Birt clearly remains unconvinced. In his MacTaggart Lecture, 'A Glorious Future', in August 1996, he saw a few blots on the horizon:

> If the digital age is to fulfil its true potential we need in the UK a unified regulatory framework to ensure open and non-discriminatory access to providers on fair financial terms . . . The first danger is the

dominance of the gateway into the home. No one person or group should be able to abuse control of the set-top box to inhibit competition.

(Birt, MacTaggart Lecture 23 August 1996 cited in *Guardian* 24 August 1996, p. 27)

Murdoch is also eager to gain a foothold in digital *terrestrial* broadcasting as well as digital *satellite* broadcasting and, to that end, has made what one observer described as 'the mother of all two way bets' (Horsman, 1997, p. 7). On 31 January 1997, the ITC announced it had received a bid for £300 million for a digital licence from British Digital Broadcasting (BDB), a consortium of BSkyB, Carlton and Granada. When the ITC evenually awarded the licence to BDB on 24 June 1997, it prohibited BSkyB from any shareholding in the company in order to weaken Murdoch's potential monopoly within the digital television market. Ironically, the exclusion of BSkyB could be advantageous to Murdoch in at least four ways. First, Carlton and Granada are rumoured to have agreed a compensation payment of £350 million to BSkyB in return for the company's withdrawal as a partner in BDB. Second, BDB will substantially extend BSkyB's market. BSkyB will provide all the premium channels in BDB's 15 channel package including Sky Sport, Sky Movies and the Movie Channel. These will generate high revenues which will now be exclusive to BSkyB. Third, Murdoch need no longer contribute the £300 million necessary for capital start up costs and, finally, Murdoch can use the digital terrestrial channel to publicise and promote his satellite digital channels. The *Guardian* believed that the advantages of this arrangement, imposed by the ITC, were so considerable for BSkyB that the paper's editorial (25 June 1997, p. 16) described the outcome of the franchise as a 'reluctant homage to Rupert Murdoch'. Too powerful to be an owner of BDB, Murdoch was already too powerful to be wholly excluded from the consortium since his control of films and sports programming is vital for the success of digital television broadcasting.

AUNTY GOES PRIVATE?

On 7 June 1996 John Birt announced his design for a major restructuring of the BBC. The plans had been drawn up furtively with little consultation at even senior management levels; the director of World Service radio was informed about plans to fuse part of the Service into the domestic news operation only hours before the press leaked the story (see chapter 6). The BBC would be restructured into six new directorates: BBC Broadcast which will commission and schedule television and radio programmes, BBC Production which will embrace all production facilities, BBC Resources to provide resources for all BBC programming and BBC News, BBC World Wide and BBC Corporate Centre. The proposals triggered controversy and suggestions from both broadcasters and media analysts that the restructuring presaged a more significant event: privatising via the back door. The separation of the commissioning from the production of programming and the separation of production from resources, both achieved in the June 1996 reforms, were crucial elements in Birt's longer-term plan to privatise parts of the BBC and convert the Corporation into a publisher broadcaster concerned only to commission excellent programmes rather than to produce them; the Channel 4 model or what the *Independent* described as a 'virtual corporation' (*Independent*, 31 August 1996, p. 5).

In an article in the *Independent* on 30 August 1996 Birt confirmed that he was considering a separate commercial status for BBC Resources. 'There is work in progress,' he announced, 'to see how Resources could be helped to trade more effectively in the external market, where it is already active, and to raise capital for future investment'. Birt denied any intention to privatise Resources, while BECTU, by contrast, identified his comment as 'a prelude to full privatisation of the BBC' (*Independent*, 31 August 1996, p. 1). Some observers believe that BBC Production will follow a similar path and become a commercial subsidiary making programmes for commercial broadcasters as well as for the BBC – a giant independent producer. The step from that status to full privatisation would represent no great leap for man although a considerable loss for mankind. Privatising the production and resources directorates would leave Birt with a publisher broadcaster BBC which could be financed by a reduced licence fee and income from the increasingly commercial activities to which Birt has dedicated BBC World Wide. Under Birt's stewardship, the BBC has become increasingly commercialised in its operations and philosophy. If Aunty decides she likes it at the market, she may never come home.

Getting a fuller picture: expanding television services since 1985

The character and stability of the British system of broadcasting, symbolised by the 'comfortable duopoly', remained virtually unchanged by the introduction of BBC2 in 1962 and Channel 4 in 1982. Since the mid-1980s, however, the rapid expansion in television services, prompted by the explosion of new channels as well as the extension of programming on existing channels, has extended and fundamentally reshaped British television broadcasting. This section examines the establishment of Channel 5, the rapid expansion in satellite and cable television services and the development of breakfast television services.

Even the 'traditional' broadcasters like the BBC have diversified their broadcasting operations. Since 1992, the Corporation has owned 20 per cent of the UK Gold channel (Pearson own 15 per cent, Cox Cable 38 per cent and Telecommunications Inc 27 per cent) which broadcasts repeats of many classic BBC series. The channel is delivered by satellite, funded by advertising and subscription and yet broadcasts programmes originally paid for by the licence fee. The BBC also broadcasts 24-hour news and current affairs on World Service Television (WSTV) since November 1991; the service is self-financing and profit making – not licence funded (BBC, 1996, p. 16). In 1995, the BBC, in conjunction with Pearson Plc, extended its commercial activities by launching two European satellite channels: BBC World (a news channel) and BBC Prime (an entertainment channel). All of these satellite channels are included in the BBC World Wide Directorate committed to providing commercially funded quality television. The notion of the BBC as a purely publicly funded broadcaster is anachronistic. The commercial sector has also witnessed change and an expansion of programming including a revamp of Channel 3, changes to Channel 4 and the establishment of a new commercial, terrestrial Channel 5.

GIVE ME 5

On 2 May 1995 the ITC received four bids for the new commercial, terrestrial Channel 5, from Channel 5 Broadcasting (£22,002,000), New Century Television Limited (£2,000,000), UK TV Developments Ltd (£36,261,158) and Virgin Television Ltd (£22,002,000). Almost 6 months later on 27 October 1995 the ITC awarded the licence to Channel 5 Broadcasting (C5B); in what by now was fast becoming standard procedure, Virgin Television which had submitted an identical bid and UK TV which bid £14 million more than C5B, launched a legal appeal against the ITC decision. For its part, the ITC must have been delighted to receive so many bids. When the licence was initially advertised in 1992, the ITC had received only a single bid by the closing date of 2 July; Channel 5 Holdings' tender was rejected because of its business plan and the future of Channel 5 seemed uncertain.

From the outset, sceptics have suggested that the formidable financial and technical difficulties which the licencee will be obliged to confront, have made the new channel an undesirable venture – a view seemingly endorsed by Rupert Murdoch's New Century bid of a mere £2 million. Channel 5 broadcasts will cause interference, requiring a vast army of 7000 trained technicians to visit at least 10 million homes to retune VCRs at an estimated cost of £51 million. This has been more problematic than the company envisaged when it began its retuning programme in August 1996. By mid-October only 1 million of the 13.5 million VCRs had been retuned and the company was obliged to ask the ITC for a postponement of the start date from January to March 1997. The company, moreover, needed to build more than 20 new transmitters at an additional cost of £30 million and persuade approximately 4 million viewers to buy and install new aerials to receive programming. Even after these modifications the new channel reaches only 75 per cent of the population and excludes some of the most lucrative areas for advertising. The financial disincentives seem equally persuasive. Conceived in the economically expansive 1980s, the new channel has been delivered in the considerably bleaker economic climate of the 1990s in which it must withstand enhanced competition for advertising revenues from Channel 4 and a host of satellite and cable services. The channel has also been obliged to mount an expensive advertising campaign to promote public recognition with brightly coloured billboard posters emerging in 1996 carrying the logo 'Give Me 5'. Pearson are planning to invest £110 million per annum on programming costs while advertising revenues are projected to deliver only £30 million in the first year rising to £165 by the year 2000.

Other difficulties lie ahead. There is little evidence of any sustained public demand for the new channel, whose destiny seems likely to be drowning at birth by the flood of digital channels which will come on stream within a year of Channel 5. From its inception in the Broadcasting Act 1990, moreover, the channel has never enjoyed a clear identity or programming remit. C5B appears to be no nearer in establishing such a remit. The contradictory gobbledegook contained within its licence application to the ITC is worthy of Big Brother in Orwell's *1984*. The channel will 'cater for a variety of tastes' but not be 'a replica of what other channels provide'. It will 'respond to public demand' without always following 'the wishes of the majority'. It will be the channel with 'a human face' and 'a user friendly schedule of programmes for everyone' (Channel 5 Broadcasting, 1995, p. 2). Peering behind the rhetoric of the 'human face', the programming strategy has a more predictable face. The licence won by Pearson and MAI will be able to exploit the vast libraries of Meridian, Anglia and Thames; C5B is planning to re-run those old classics, *Minder*, *The Sweeney*, *Dallas* and P.D. James murder mysteries. The new channel has eventually decided to describe its programming as 'modern mainstream'.

The news provision on C5B seems more promising: the provider ITN describes it as 'distinctive and with its own character' (Methven, 1996, p. 13). There is an emphasis on a European rather than an American news agenda and a promise to 'not simply bring news of London to the rest of Britain, but news from the whole of Britain to the rest of the nation' (Channel 5 Broadcasting, 1995, p. 6). The main news bulletin at 8.30 p.m. is supplemented by rolling bulletins on the hour, leaving the rest of the evening clear for the uninterrupted scheduling of films. Channel 5 news has generated 46 jobs at ITN based in Studio 2 at Grays Inn Road. The nightly news at 8.30 p.m., at Martin Lewis's suggestion, will 'present stories of triumph over adversity', stories which show 'people at work together and not always in conflict' (ibid., p. 4). This all sounds very jolly but such an approach to news seems at odds with most journalists' news values where conflict enjoys centre stage; this formula seems more likely to generate nothing more than fatuous newszak – news with a 'human face' that will upset no one. C5B's proposals for news coverage were rumoured to be influential in clinching the licence for the company. Given the paucity of C5B's news intentions, if Virgin's identical bid was truly rejected because of the quality of its planned news provision, it is possible only to speculate about the impoverished nature of Virgin TV's news programming plans. Eventually launched on 30 March 1997 by the Spice Girls' rendition of the 1960s hit song by Manfred Mann, '5-4-3-2-1', Channel 5 attracted better audiences than anticipated; but figures slumped immediately. Audiences peaked at 545,000 on Tuesday 1 April 1997 but halved to 254,000 by Friday 4 April: audiences for some programmes were down to 100,000. A spokesperson for Channel 5 claimed the new station did not 'expect people to change their viewing habits overnight'; but these are disappointing figures for the new terrestrial channel (Methven, 18 April 1997).

The satellite revolution and 'roller coaster journalism'

The greatest changes in the provision of television services in the UK have undoubtedly been triggered by the explosion of satellite and cable channels in the last five years. The first satellite channel was launched early in 1989, but by the end of 1995 the ITC had licensed 170 satellite and cable services (ITC, 1996, pp. 26–50). The broad range of programming available is evident in the names of the channels: from the Asian Music Channel to Adult Movies – from the Parliamentary Channel to the Cartoon Network. Much of the provision is targeted at minority audiences but satellite services also embrace the major entertainment channels such as Bravo, UK Gold and the Sky channels. Cable services offer a similar spectrum of programming serving ethnic (the Arabic Channel and the Afro-Caribbean Channel) and cultural (the Royal Opera House Channel and Performance) minorities.

The development of satellite television in Britain has been pioneered by Rupert Murdoch's Sky Television. Launched on 5 February 1989, Sky Television was Britain's first satellite service. The station's four channels – SkyNews, Sky Sports, Sky Movies and Sky 1 – matched the existing four terrestrials and doubled overnight viewers' access to television programming. More than a year later in April 1990, after a series of technical and financial delays, a rival company, British Satellite Broadcasting (BSB), came on air with a further five channels. Sky enjoyed a head start which proved to be crucial in its subsequent success, but BSB's commitment to the public-service tradition signalled higher-quality programmes delivered on a technically superior satellite system. The square receiver dishes ('squarials'), marketed initially as a distinctive feature of this high-tech system, quickly became the butt of many jokes with even supportive observers describing them as 'an object second only to the Sinclair C5 as an '80s absurdity' (Chippindale and Franks, 1991, p. xi); perhaps predictably, even on launch day, there was a shortage of the 'revolutionary' squarials. After eight months of fierce competition, including financially punitive advertising campaigns designed to give one company a market lead, the two broadcasters merged to form BSkyB on 2 November 1990 (Chippindale and Horrie, 1990, p. 291). The merger was effectively a rescue package and takeover by Sky which emerged as the dominant partner and whose populist programming policy prevailed. The merger breached the provisions of the new Broadcasting Act which had received royal assent only the previous day. The merger was also completed without any consultation with the regulatory body, the IBA; Chief Executive David Glencross was furious but powerless (ibid., p. 293).

The takeover exacerbated the severe financial pressures which satellite broadcasting was already exerting on Murdoch's wider media empire. In the last four months of 1989, the Sky operation out of London was losing £2 million a week (Wallis and Baran, 1990, p. 112). By August 1990, News International announced half-year losses of £266 million; the start-up costs for Sky were in excess of £121 million with an additional £95 million operating losses for the first few months. Sky Television was haemorrhaging cash from the financial reserves of News International, but the merger of the two companies required a further £200 million of refinancing capital. Buoyant sales of Murdoch's British newspaper titles provided this pump-priming capital for News International's expansion into satellite television; the process illustrated neatly how multinational corporations are able temporarily to underwrite losses in one sphere of operation with profits from other activities. Only conglomerate capital can provide the 'deep pockets' necessary to finance the substantial and sustained losses associated with the start-up costs of satellite broadcasting. As sales of Sky dishes began to grow, Murdoch encrypted the channels which viewers could once receive for free; by September 1992, viewers had to pay to view Sky Sports channel. By February 1993, Murdoch's satellite television operation was showing a modest profit of £7.5 million. On 1 September 1993, Murdoch relaunched his Sky network with a package of 15 channels plus three premier channels which viewers could receive for an annual subscription of £240. Murdoch, with characteristic flamboyance, described the launch as 'the most exciting development in satellite television's short history . . . we have spent nearly £1 billion on programming; we have changed news broadcasting; we have revolutionised football coverage; we have spent millions on original programming' (*Guardian*, 2 September 1993, p. 8). Ten million people living in 3.5 million households could now receive satellite television.

Murdoch's profits now began to soar. In the last half year of 1993, Murdoch's Sky Television reported profits of £84.8 million. In 1994, Sky Television increased the basic charges for subscribers by £3 a month which generated an additional £93 million in revenue (Buckingham, 1994, p. 3). By early 1995 Sky Television announced that the company's pre-tax profit was in excess of £5 million a week; it is not difficult to imagine how Lord Thompson might have described such a licence for satellite TV. It is worth noting that the combined profits of all the Channel 3 companies for the same period was £400 million. Audiences were also expanding with Sky claiming 4 million homes able to receive satellite services. The social composition of Sky's audience was also beginning to closely approximate the audience profile for ITV and Channel 4 services. In 1994, Sky audiences were 11 per cent AB compared to 13 per cent for ITV and 15 per cent for Channel 4, 24 per cent C1 (24 per cent ITV and 25 per cent Channel 4), 34 per cent C2 (27 per cent ITV and 26 per cent Channel 4) and 31 per cent DE compared to 36 per cent ITV and 34 per cent Channel 4 (*Guardian*, 5 February 1994, p. 10). Observers currently claim 18 per cent of households able to receive satellite and cable services but this figure is expected to rise to nearer 30 per cent by the turn of the century. Satellite broadcasting seems set fair to expand, especially with the arrival of digital services.

SKYNEWS: THE 'FLANNEL CHANNEL'

The launch of SkyNews on 5 February 1989 marked a significant development in British broadcasting. Since SkyNews was not (and is still not!) constrained by royal charter, broadcasting legislation or regulatory quangos, to be accurate, objective, serious minded or technically competent, some observers believed programming might compare poorly with ITN and BBC news services. From the outset, programming was certainly ambitious and produced with a miserly budget.

SkyNews broadcasts half-hour news bulletins on the hour for 24 hours. The remaining airtime is filled with American TV news, Australian fillers, bought-in documentaries plus, in prime time, the station's own current affairs programmes. At launch, this amounted to more than 14 hours of material per weekday, created by a total staff of 220 with an annual budget of £35 million for the whole service – an average of £4000 per hour. By contrast, ITN was producing four hours of broadcast news each day with a total staff of 930 and an annual income of £77 million. The different financial resources available to the two news organisations was striking. At any time, the Sky newsroom was staffed by 15–20 journalists, with each programming sequence of three hours being written and produced by a core of five people. 'Low cost, high adrenalin, roller coaster journalism' was one description of SkyNews output (Saynor, 1989, p. 29). More measured assessments exist. The research study concerning televising of the House of Commons concluded that SkyNews's reporting of the Commons 'must be judged a little disappointing compared to the performance of the network terrestrial stations' (First Report of the Select Committee 1989–90, p. 26). Saynor concedes that the effort to 'feed the monster of 24-hour news' can result in coverage which sounds perilously close to 'the flannel channel or the News from Nowhere station' (Saynor, 1989, p. 30).

From the beginning, SkyNews has tried to establish a distinctive news identity. A senior news editor explained that 'SkyNews will cover the kind of stories that the BBC would never touch'. For example, 'the story of a workaholic couple that wed on their lunch break and a valuable Shropshire cat that is for sale with its owner's home' (Wallis and Baran, 1990, p. 113). SkyNews has eventually gained a growing respectability for its programming and coverage of stories, especially fast-breaking news stories, although the channel has 'resisted the BBC's movement towards more specialist correspondents and unashamedly subordinated editorial decisions on coverage to financial constraints' (McNair, 1994, p. 106). In January 1994, it seemed as if McNair might have to reconsider his claim that 'the worst fears of "tabloid television" had not been realised' (ibid., p. 106), when Kelvin MacKenzie became managing director of SkyNews after he left the *Sun*. MacKenzie had no experience of working in television news but was on record as having denounced television journalists as a 'bunch of parasitical pansies'. Paradoxically, given these views, the rationale behind MacKenzie's appointment had been to 'raise the satellite station's image' (*Guardian*, 3 August 1994, p. 2). Michael Grade offered MacKenzie a dubious accolade by describing him as the only person capable of taking SkyNews down market; MacKenzie promptly illustrated the insightfulness of Grade's observation. The former *Sun* editor appointed columnist Richard Littlejohn to host a nightly chat show, secured an exclusive interview with Lady Bienvenida Buck, the mistress of the former chief of the defence staff, Sir Peter Harding, and devoted 30 minutes of prime-time breakfast news to the Harkness family revelations about former Tory minister Alan Clarke. A regulator at the ITC joked that he wouldn't be surprised if 'Kelvin didn't use Beavis and Butthead to anchor SkyNews'. Further such speculations were only forestalled by Murdoch's prompt sacking of MacKenzie in August 1994; the ex-editor seemed incapable of making the transition from tabloid newspapers to tabloid television. Eventually MacKenzie's creative muse was given its head when he joined Live TV. At MacKenzie's initiative, news reports are now accompanied by 'the news Bunny' – allegedly a journalist dressed in an appropriate costume – who signals his approval and disapproval of news reports by gesturing thumbs up or thumbs down. It is only possible to speculate about the sort of gesture which Mackenzie believes might be appropriate for the news bunny when the station is reporting tragic and dreadful news such as the incident at Dunblane.

Breakfast television: 'brash and whacky' news?

Breakfast television was introduced in Britain in 1985 as part of the general trend to extend programming across the day – and night! The BBC led the way with its three-hour early-morning programme. But from the outset, breakfast shows on each of the terrestrial channels have not been perceived as programme slots where a relentless focus on hard news stories would be appropriate. Justin Webb, who currently anchors BBC 1's *Breakfast News*, concedes that his mission is 'to inject irony, facetiousness and sarcasm where before there has too often been BBC-style pomposity and a gravitas that viewers can't swallow at that time of day . . . it's the least prestigious of the BBC's news programming' (cited in Sweeting, 1996, p. 11). On Channel 3, GMTV has tried to emulate its predecessor TV-AM's success by adopting a similar 'lighter touch' to news coverage than the BBC breakfast programme. In terms of the quality and depth of its news reports, Channel 4's *Big Breakfast* is quite simply inconsequential and infantile or, to adopt the 'marketing-speak' of television executives, the programme is 'brash, whacky, and kid-oriented' (Fiddick, 1993, p. 11). As the competition to win the breakfast audience has grown increasingly intense throughout the 1990s, the emphasis on serious news presentation has predictably declined.

The BBC breakfast show, more so than its rivals on Channels 3 and 4, is based on news and current affairs, although it increasingly includes regional news stories and 'gossipy human interest stories which can only be described as "soft"' (Sweeting, 1996, p. 11). The programme tries to offer a broad mix of national, regional and international stories with a hard and soft news emphasis. Justin Webb suggests the goal is to 'find a balance between doing a boat show in Bristol and the Israeli elections' and consequently there are days when the programme deserves the title 'Dog's Breakfast News'. The programme tries to steer a middle course between becoming 'the *Today* programme with pictures' and replicating 'GMTV's strangely nauseous version of *Hello* vision' (ibid.). There is no intention to ape the facile antics of the *Big Breakfast*, although the BBC programme does offer airtime to that now seemingly mandatory character on every news programme, the eccentric (whacky?) weatherman who, dressed in coloured wellies or shorts or balanced deftly on a floating map of the British Isles, seems engaged in the relentless quest to find a lively and interesting format for the rather tedious business of delivering the weather forecast.

TV-AM held the first commercial breakfast television licence. Its programming ambitions were detailed in its 1991 re-application to the ITC. TV-AM was 'a live, fast moving mixture of news information and entertainment in short self contained segments which viewers can dip in and dip out of . . . our "sofa style" is famous and we'll use it to give viewers important information with an approach which becomes a chat between friends' (TV-AM, 1991, pp. 4–6). The programme was eventually successful, capturing 70 per cent of the breakfast audience, but initially there had been difficulties. Audiences began to build substantially when, at the suggestion of executive Greg Dyke, the presenter Peter Jay was replaced by the puppet Roland Rat and eventually a collection of his rodent relatives! This was presumably one aspect of the station's 'warm and friendly style' also mentioned in the ITC bid. Roland and his chums proved to be a valuable asset as the growing audiences delivered increasing advertising revenues for TV-AM. In 1988, the company emerged victorious from its confrontation with the broadcasting union ACTT (Association of Cinematograph, Television and Allied Technicians) over the issue of 'who manages?' High revenues and reduced labour costs generated substantial profits for TV-AM and guaranteed a competitive round of tendering for the breakfast licence when it was re-advertised in 1991.

On 16 October 1991 when the ITC awarded the breakfast licence to Sunrise Television (later GMTV), Margaret Thatcher publicly announced her upset at the decision. TV-AM was allegedly her favourite channel, although its attractions were probably based less on the charms of Roland Rat, than the robust and uncompromising manner in which Chief Executive Bruce Gyngell had tackled what Mrs Thatcher considered to be trade union restrictive practices. Sunrise Television, owned by the Guardian and Manchester Evening News Group, LWT, Scottish Television and the Walt Disney Company (Sunrise Television, 1991, p. 2), made the largest bid for the licence: £34,610,000 compared to Daybreak TV's £33,261,000 and TV-AM's relatively modest £14,125,000 (Franklin, 1994, p. 67). Sunrise TV's bid (i.e. the proposed annual payment to the treasury) represented 40 per cent of the anticipated annual advertising revenues likely to accrue within the franchise area. This was by far the largest percentage of advertising income offered in annual payments by any Channel 3 company; only Tyne Tees (28 per cent) and Yorkshire TV (30 per cent), both believed to have overbid, came close to the Sunrise tender.

Within months of going on air in January 1993 GMTV was in serious financial difficulties which only in part reflected the initial overbidding. Between the time of winning the franchise in 1991 and of beginning to broadcast in January 1993, the world of breakfast television had turned upside down. GMTV had to confront a decline in advertising prompted by the recession combined with unexpected competition from Channel 4's new *Big Breakfast Show*; satellite breakfast programmes were also beginning to win audiences. By March 1993, GMTV's audience share was falling; GMTV had 38 per cent of the breakfast audience ahead of BBC1 (26 per cent), Channel 4 (24 per cent) and BSkyB (9 per cent); GMTV enjoyed only 55 per cent of the commercial audience and this with barely one in six homes receiving satellite (Fiddick, 1993, p. 11). The station was relaunched with new presenters and a new management team. Greg Dyke, who was installed as company chairman, claimed that a return to profitability by 1994 would be achieved by 'a slow increase in ratings and by reducing costs by £5 million a year' (*Guardian*, 12 April 1993, p. 12). But £5 million represented a sizeable 20 per cent cut in GMTV's operating budget for the year and in these circumstances programme quality, especially the quality and range of news provision, was once again the most likely casualty. Two months later, the ITC conceded to GMTV's request to reduce its news output and cut by one third the current affairs provision within the breakfast programme.

A year later in May 1994, when the ITC published its assessment of licencees' performance during the first operational year, GMTV was subject to considerable criticism and threatened with a fine up to £2 million if programming did not improve by September 1994. The ITC report claimed that news bulletins were 'too short to provide adequate coverage, depth or authority' while studio interviews were handled ineptly and proposals for regular investigative items, political digests and substantive current affairs interviews never materialised. GMTV's immediate response was to seek to emulate TV-AM, which had successfully deployed Roland Rat to rescue it from a disastrous launch. Since the GMTV launch had been even more troubled than its predecessors, only Barney – the educationally acclaimed 6ft. 4in. purple and green dinosaur which had proved very popular in America – would suffice to relaunch the show. As Dyke claimed with scant regard for the commitments made when applying for the breakfast licence, 'you have got to look at the business and cut your cloth accordingly' (Fiddick, 1993, p. 11).

Channel 4's serious breakfast diet of international political and business news, *Channel 4 Daily*, was scrapped in October 1992 and replaced by *Big Breakfast*, produced by independent company Planet 24 with news provided by ITN. Fronted by radio DJ and professional 'cheeky chappie' Chris Evans, Gaby Roslin and Paula Yates, the programme allegedly received 'positive critical reaction' (McNair, 1994, p. 100), although such an assessment is hard to sustain if the programme is judged by the quality of its news provision. In truth, the programme effectively eschews all news content, relying on short, snappy news bulletins, delivered on the hour and half hour but previewed 10 minutes earlier. Bulletins are punctuated by a musical chord at the end of each news story, creating a mood of frenetic pace. Each story is accompanied by a caption which attempts to capture the essence of the item in a punny or humorous phrase. The average length of news items, excluding sports stories, is approximately 13 seconds; some items are as brief as 8 seconds. Typically, 8 news items are reported in the bulletin which lasts 2 minutes 30 seconds. Employing a euphemism, ITN describes its news services as 'specifically designed to suit the *Big Breakfast* format as a fast moving, innovative programme' (ITN, 1996).

This was the news agenda presented on *Big Breakfast* on 14 November 1996.

Caption	News Story
The Duchess of Talk	Sarah Ferguson launches her biography with appearances on American chat-show programmes. 'Debt ridden Fergie denies Andrew is gay.'
Parents Plea	Parents of children killed at Dunblane to meet John Major.
International Rescue	UN aid to refugees in Zaire.
Nightmare Scenario	Near-collision by two aircraft at Heathrow.
Face the Music	MTV pop awards. Uncertain whether Oasis will attend even though nominated for 4 awards.

Fin End of the Wedge	Doctors 'scaling up' research on prospects of using fish in spare-part surgery.
Trouble at Lodge	Problems arising from police officers' membership of Masons.
Coventry Upset	Second division Gillingham beat Coventry.

The *Big Breakfast* does not follow breaking news stories although there is usually a single item change across the bulletins. The 7 a.m. story about Sylvester Stallone's daughter's heart operation (Baby Doing Well) was replaced at 7.30 by 'Fin End of the Wedge' and at 8.30 by 'One for the Ladies'. ITN News reader Peter Smith announced 'children's favourite the lady bird has turned out to be a sex crazed cannibal. A Cambridge scientist has revealed the females are highly promiscuous and the insects are able to mate each day for nine hours at a time and the insects will eat each other if nothing else is available' (*Big Breakfast*, 14 November 1996). This style of presentation perhaps explains why in 1993 the *Big Breakfast*, quite uniquely for a Channel 4 programme, was voted the *Sun* readers' favourite programme of the year. But the programme has proved popular from the outset and with more than merely *Sun* readers. Within weeks of going on air it had won an audience of 750,000 and after six months it had matched the BBC audience of 1.5 million and was threatening GMTV's audience of 1.9 million (Fiddick, 1993, p. 11).

Many observers agree, however, that while the news content of the *Big Breakfast* is risible – 'it hasn't dealt with the bitter social issues facing the unemployed in Liverpool and it never analyses the political situation in Chad' – the breakfast show is 'probably the most important programme Channel 4 has. To this station it's more vital than *Dispatches*, more crucial than *Channel 4 News*' (Armstrong, 1996, p. 13). The programme's significance resides not in its contribution to news coverage but its more prosaic contribution to Channel 4's advertising revenues. The *Big Breakfast* was responsible for generating 10 per cent of Channel 4's total £450 million income for 1995. There is also a cost bonus which makes the *Big Breakfast* the ultimate 'minimax' programme; at £20,000 per broadcast hour, the *Big Breakfast* is very cheap television.

In September 1996, the programme was revamped, after growing press criticism, although many of the essential programming elements remained intact. Ex-Gladiator Sharron Davies is the new programme anchor (her predecessor, Zoe Ball, has moved on to the children's programme *Live and Kicking*), while children's entertainer Keith Chegwin will remain on the programme team. The *Big Breakfast* is to have new programme segments, different music and different time schedules for the news. In the words of the producer, the *Big Breakfast* will 'look and feel very different but it will be recognisably the same show. We have tried to keep the successful elements but move everything on' (cited in ibid.). The *Big Breakfast*, it seems, will continue to serve up a daily diet of 'brash and whacky' nonsense interspersed with newszak.

Big is beautiful: concentration and cross-media ownership in the television market

The ownership of commercial television reflects the trends which are evident in press and radio; three are especially striking. First, there is a tendency towards increasing concentration of ownership, with fewer companies owning an ever greater share of the television market. Second, cross-media ownership is increasingly commonplace, with television companies being partly owned by media groups with newspaper or radio holdings. Both of these trends are increasing and, after the Broadcasting Act 1996, at a rate! Finally, the media industries operate in a global market with UK companies increasingly likely to be part of larger multinational media companies. The evidence to support such trends is readily available: as Seymour Ure observes, study of the growth of 'international media conglomeration risks piling example on example' (Seymour Ure, 1991, p. 117). But the risk is worth taking and the evidence deserves an airing. The significant and loudly canvassed concern about such patterns of ownership, which risks being drowned by the sheer flood of evidence, is that they diminish pluralism and choice, stifle diversity and empower owners to defend and advance their economic interests and political power; amid the deafening din of grinding axes, the debate concerning media accountability to the public can become lost (ibid. and Williams, 1994, p. 52).

Some of the Channel 3 companies awarded licences by the ITC to go on air in January 1993 were partly or wholly owned by other media or television interests. Meridian, for example, which won the franchise for the South and South East of England was owned by Lord Hollick's MAI Broadcasting Ltd (65 per cent), SelecTV (15 per cent) and Central Television (20 per cent). Carlton Television was owned by Carlton Communications (20 per cent), Italian independent television company and publisher RCS (5 per cent) and Daily Telegraph Newspapers (5 per cent), while Sunrise Television was owned by LWT, Scottish TV, Guardian and Manchester Evening News Group and Walt Disney. Associated Newspaper Holdings held the statutory maximum 20 per cent share in Westcountry Television while W.H. Smith and Pearson each held a 19.9 per cent share in Yorkshire Television. The new Channel 5 company is similarly owned by key players in the media market: Pearson (owner of the *Financial Times*), Thames Television Plc, Yorkshire/Tyne Tees Television (14 per cent) and until 1995 BSkyB (17 per cent), MAI Plc, CLT S.A. – a leading European television broadcaster – and Warburg Pincus, an American company with a varied portfolio of media investments including until 1994 a share in LWT.

Companies like Carlton owned considerable stakes in other media companies including other Channel 3 companies. In 1987, Chief Executive Michael Green bought a 20 per cent share in Central Television. Carlton also owns an 18 per cent share in ITN along with Granada, Reuters, Anglia and Scottish TV (ITC, 1995, p. 111). In November 1993, the ownership rules established by the Broadcasting Act 1990 were relaxed and Carlton promptly bid £758 million in a friendly takeover for Central Television. In November 1996 Carlton bought Westcountry Television for £85 million just ahead of Hollick's United News and Media. In November 1993, after a protracted tussle, Granada eventually won its takeover struggle with LWT and Meridian merged with Anglia; Tyne Tees had already joined forces with Yorkshire Television. In mid June 1997 the merger of Scottish Television with neighbouring Grampian and Granada's £652 million bid for Yorkshire/Tyne Tees Television marked new moves towards concentration in Channel 3. Two weeks later, Lord Hollick successfully bid £372 million for HTV. These shifts of ownership suggest the difficulties which new players experience in entering the UK television market; they also illustrate how the handful of large companies seem increasingly predatory on the smaller companies.

The evidence of cross media ownership is bountiful. Lord Hollick's United News and Media Group controls the Anglia, Meridian and HTV licences; MAI also owns a share of Channel 5 Broadcasting and, through its ownership of Anglia, controls a fifth stake in ITN. Additionally, since the merger between MAI and Stevens' United Newspaper group in the previous year, the company also owns the *Daily Express*, the *Sunday Express*, the *Star*, more than 100 regional newspapers, 15 regional magazines, more than 300 other magazines, newspapers overseas and an 11 per cent share in the Press Association (Williams, 1994, p. 33).

Rupert Murdoch's News Corporation undoubtedly offers the ideal type multinational media conglomeration which is bewildering in terms of both the size and the range of its operations around the globe. News Corporation owns and controls 16 television stations in America and Australia and 11 cable and satellite stations in five continents including the UK station BSkyB and the Asian station Star TV which alone enjoys an audience reach of more than 50 million. News Corporation also controls 10 film entertainment companies including the extensive Twentieth Century Fox and 50 newspaper groups including the Leader Newspaper Group in Victoria which produces more than 30 titles (the four UK titles and a range of other newspapers from the *New York Post* to the *Post Courier* in Papua New Guinea). Also included in the News Corporation portfolio are 29 magazines including the UK's *Times Higher Education* and *Times Literary Supplement*, 3 book publishers including HarperCollins, 21 printing companies and 21 other media-related companies such as Delphi Internet Services, Sky Radio and Festival Records (Cowe and Buckingham, 1996, p. 5).

In the mid-1990s, the operation of substantial multinational conglomerates such as News Corporation in an increasingly global media market prompted increased calls from within the British media industry for government to relax further the constraints on cross-media ownership. Industry lobby groups argued that it was vital for companies to merge into much larger business enterprises if they were to compete against conglomerates like News Corporation and Bertelsmann in the global media marketplace. The logic suggested that big was not only beautiful but essential for the survival of indigenous media industries. Consequently a major intention of the Broadcasting Act 1996 was to assess the extent to which changes in the regulation of media ownership were compatible with a government-devised public-interest test. The test requires the ITC to ensure that takeovers or new licences do not undermine diversity of information, have an adverse economic impact or restrict market forces (*Broadcasting Act 1996*, Sched 2, Part 4, paras. 9–13).

The government white paper *Media Ownership: The Government's Proposals* (Cmnd 2872), published in May 1995, set out a staged process for the future of media regulation and promised to bring forward legislation at the earliest opportunity to allow greater cross-media ownership between different media sectors. Schedule 2 of the Broadcasting Act 1996 gave effect to those proposals. The Act does not allow a free for all but it will result in considerable changes over a period. The 1996 Act also revised the definition of 'control' beyond the traditional idea of control where a person owns more than 50 per cent of the equity share capital in a company. The ITC may now determine that a person controls an enterprise if 'it is reasonable, having regard to the circumstances, to expect that he will be able, by whatever means and whether directly or indirectly, to achieve the result that the affairs of the body are conducted in accordance with his wishes' (*Broadcasting Act 1996* Sched 2, Part 1, para. 1 (3)). The Act abolishes numerical limits on the holding of television licences but establishes that no individual may hold licences for television services which jointly exceed 15 per cent of the total television audience – excluding BBC, Channel 4 and SC4 (*Broadcasting Act 1996*, Sched 2, Part 3, para. 2). These provisions allow British companies scope for merger while placing broad and general limits on media concentration. There is also a nationality-based disqualification which prohibits anyone who is not a resident of the UK or the European Economic Area from holding a licence for Channel 3, Channel 5, a domestic satellite service or a national or local analogue radio service (*Broadcasting Act 1996*, Sched 2, Part 2). The Act also facilitates convergence and encourages the emergence of larger British media groups owning both newspaper and television interests. The scope here is limited by the restrictions on national newspaper groups with a market share in excess of 20 per cent (measured by circulation over a six-month period), which are not allowed to control licences for a Channel 3, Channel 5 or a national or local radio service (*Broadcasting Act 1996*, Sched 2, Part 4, para. 4). These provisions obviously exclude Murdoch's News International and MGN from expanding into certain areas of British television because of their substantial newspaper holdings, but other newspaper groups are free to buy into television subject to a public-interest limitation. Local newspaper groups with more than 20 per cent of local market share may not control a licence to provide a regional Channel 3 service, but again smaller groups are unrestricted.

The 1996 Act relaxed the restrictions in the 1990 Broadcasting Act on the regulation of media ownership in a market already characterised by concentration and cross-media ownership. The general trend towards concentration of ownership in British television, like British newspapers and national and local radio, seems unlikely to be reversed or even halted by recent legislation. Three large companies – Granada, Carlton and United – dominate the Channel 3 television market. Each company has the previous maximum of two licences in its pocket but now has the prospect of owning more. Speculation surrounding the remaining small companies is intense, with only their strong share prices deterring predators – at least for the moment. It seems likely that in the short term, Channel 3 will become a single company.

Glued to the box? Audiences for television

Estimates of the amount of time which viewers devote to watching television vary considerably expressing, at least in part, the widely held perception that watching television is an activity which requires justification: 'I had nothing else to do'. Watching television is an essentially passive activity (Williams, 1974, p. 94), a fact which is captured by the disparaging description of viewers as 'couch potatoes'. But 'spudding out' (Ehrenreich, 1990) is very popular in Britain and during the course of the day the average person is likely to devote seven hours to watching television (Hart, 1991, pp. 26–7 and Seymour Ure, 1991, pp. 145–6).

The diet of television programming which viewers consume is extremely varied and reflects a number of social variables such as class, gender, age and even region of the country. Social class correlates with television viewing, with social classes A and B watching a weekly average of 17 hours 42 minutes while groups D and E watch a considerably greater average of 31 hours 44 minutes. Women (27 hours 28 minutes) watch considerably more television than men (22 hours 56 minutes) and there is a tendency for viewing to increase with age; 4–7-year-olds watch 17 hours 20 minutes of television each week while people over 65 average 37 hours 25 minutes (Franklin, 1994, p. 223). Estimates of children's viewing hours are especially prone to variation with one study suggesting children watch five hours television each night (*Daily Mirror*, 5 September 1994). Regional variation in viewing habits is also considerable. A study by Mintel International Group suggested that while 9 per cent of audiences in Yorkshire and the North East watch television for more than 11 hours a day, the equivalent figure for Wales and the South West is 2 per cent. The study also revealed that 25 per cent of viewers in the North East and North West watch more than seven hours television each day, the figures for Wales/South West (3 per cent) and the Midlands (5 per cent) being considerably lower (Mintel International, 1994). Research studies are unanimous, however, in signalling a general increase in television viewing across all groups reflecting both the expansion in television channels and the growth in broadcast hours.

Data revealing the growing number of television sets in each household and their distribution between different rooms tends to confirm that viewing hours are extending but also suggests that family viewing habits are changing, with children increasingly likely to view television alone in their bedrooms. Virtually all households (97 per cent) have a television set and the majority (64 per cent) have more than one set. In 28 per cent of households there are three or more sets – a figure which rises to 38 per cent of households with children and as high as 47 per cent of households with cable and satellite television services. Nearly all homes (97 per cent) have a television in the main living room while 38 per cent of homes have a set in the main bedroom, 37 per cent of households with children under 16 have televisions in the children's bedrooms and 12 per cent of households have sets in the kitchen (Winstone, 1996, p. 24). But if audiences have grown, the reasons for watching television remain the same: for entertainment, companionship, relaxation or simply to relieve boredom. People are also increasingly reliant on television for their information about world news. An ITC survey revealed that in 1995, 71 per cent of respondents cited television as their major source of world news compared to only 62 per cent in 1985 (ibid.).

The audiences which the various television services can hope to attract will inevitably change with the emergence of a multichannel broadcasting system. Until the arrival of Sky Television in 1989, the public and commercial sectors of television enjoyed approximately equal shares of the audience. In the National Heritage paper *The Future of the BBC*, the government estimated the figures for audience reach for BBC1 (92 per cent), BBC2 (80 per cent), ITV (92 per cent), Channel 4 (80 per cent) and satellite and cable (11 per cent) and also calculated audience share for BBC1 (34 per cent), BBC2 (10 per cent), ITV (42 per cent), Channel 4 (10 per cent) and satellite and cable (4 per cent) (Department of National Heritage, 1992, p. 7). The Department of National Heritage and John Birt both predicted that the BBC's share of television audiences would decline by 10 per cent at the turn of the century to stand at approximately one third of total television audience. By 1996, however, there was little evidence of decline in the BBC audience share although there was a noticeable increase in satellite audience share and a discernible decline in Channel 3 audience share. The BARB data for the BBC broadcasting research department gave BBC1 32 per cent audience share, BBC2 11.2 per cent, ITV 37.3 per cent, Channel 4 11 per cent and satellite and cable services 8.5 per cent. The continued expansion of audience share for satellite services seems inevitable with estimates suggesting a figure as high as 25 per cent of total audience by 2001; additionally,

50 per cent of households will be cabled by 2003. But satellite and cable services may recruit as heavily from existing viewers of Channel 3 as from the BBC. There are hopeful straws in the wind for the BBC. In a survey conducted in 1995, BBC television emerged as Britain's most popular medium. Some 80 per cent of respondents said they would be disappointed if the BBC was not available, compared to 76 per cent for Channel 3. Equivalent findings were available for national newspapers (64 per cent), Channel 4 (60 per cent), local newspapers (58 per cent) and satellite and cable television (28 per cent). The explosion of digital satellite channels predicted for 1998 will inevitably restructure viewers' preferences and, with an additional 250 channels available, it seems certain that the terrestrial channels will lose audience share. But if the BBC is able to establish a distinctive identity, its audience might prove more loyal than its terrestrial competitors' audiences, if only because the BBC audience is likely to have nowhere else to turn for certain types of programming.

PART IV

NEWSZAK:
REGULATING EXCESSES

|10|

Keeping it bright, light and trite

Regulating the tabloid press

At 6.38 p.m. on Monday 7 February 1994, the British national press began to receive reports about the death of Conservative MP Stephen Milligan. His semi-naked body had been discovered clothed in women's underwear. A plastic bag placed over his head and a ligature tightened around his neck, suggested an experiment in autoerotic asphyxiation which had gone tragically wrong. The following day, tabloid headlines announced: 'Tory MP Dies in Kinky Sex Game' (*Daily Star*); 'Tory MP Dies In Gay Sex Riddle' (*Mirror*).

Press coverage of the Milligan case highlighted many of the concerns, increasingly expressed by the public and politicians, about journalists' news-gathering and news-reporting practices. First, many reports of the MP's death were highly sensational. *Today*, for example, claimed that the secretary who found his body 'opened the door to his flat and walked into a scene like a porn horror movie' (*Today*, 8 February 1994, p. 2). Second, factual accuracy was eschewed in favour of journalistic speculation and misrepresentation. The *Mirror* suggested the MP 'choked to death possibly in a gay bondage sex game' (8 February 1994, p. 1). Third, the privacy of Milligan's family and friends, as well as of the dead man himself, was unduly invaded. Fourth, there was a row concerning the identity of the sources who initially leaked the story. Politicians alleged that police officers had accepted payments from journalists to leak information; a full police inquiry was promptly instigated. For their part, journalists identified the Conservative whips' office as the source of the story (Banks, 1994, p. 1). Fifth, BBC journalists complained that their news scripts had been censored and rewritten by senior news editors. BBC's *Nine O'Clock News* relegated the story to third position in its running order while ITN judged it to be the lead story of the day (Culf, 9 February 1994, p. 3). Finally, information about the MP's death was in the public domain before Milligan's family was informed; his parents learned of their son's death from a television news report.

Press reporting of Milligan's death was simply one notable case in a succession of cases in which the press invaded the privacy of individuals in a way which upset the delicate balance between the public's right to know and an individual's right to privacy. In his *Report of the Committee on Privacy and Related Matters* (Cmnd 1102, 1990) and the *Review of Press Self Regulation* (Cmnd 2135, 1993), Sir David Calcutt cited the sensational and invasive press reporting of the extra-marital affairs of Conservative minister David Mellor and Liberal Democrat leader Paddy Ashdown, as well as the break up of the royal marriages of the Prince and Princess of Wales and the Duke and Duchess of York, as evidence of the need for statutory press regulation.

Public disquiet about newspaper reporting has been a perennial feature of life in post-war Britain, prompting three royal commissions on the press (1947–49, 1961–62 and 1974–77), the Younger Committee on Privacy (1972) and most recently the Calcutt reports of 1990 and 1993. The by now familiar criticisms include, 'political bias, intrusion into privacy, inaccuracy, triviality and sensationalism . . . supplemented by fears about monopoly and the extent to which some newspapers have become the plaything of rich and powerful men' (Snoddy, 1992, p. 74). One senior journalist claimed 'the constant injunction from editors these days . . . is to keep every story BLT – to keep it bright, light and trite . . . it is part of a gravitational force of decline in journalism which has taken place in our lifetime.' Chequebook journalism, which involves buying the exclusive rights to publish interviews and stories, is a related phenomenon. This journalistic practice seems to place greater emphasis on scooping the opposition to a newsworthy story than the veracity of the published account. The disclosure that seven of the witnesses in the Rosemary West trial had received as much as £100,000 from media sources, prompted calls for legislation to outlaw the practice and prevent 'the criminal justice system turning into the entertainment business' (*Guardian*, 24 November 1995, p. 6). For their part, newspapers' response has been to 'ignore calls for reform – citing the intensity of competitive pressures and the fact that the public must approve of what newspapers do because it continues to buy them; play for time when the calls for reform cannot be ignored; and take action only when threatened with legislation by politicians who sound unusually determined' (ibid., p. 75).

A debate about the essential character of the press lies at the heart of concerns about the growth of newszak and the related issues of press freedom and press regulation. Two positions define the parameters of the debate. The first understands journalism to be a commercial activity which, like any other industry, must produce goods to be sold for profit in a marketplace. In this market, in accordance with the dictates of classical economic theory, 'consumers are sovereign' and the product must be manufactured to meet their requirements. Regulation, by the state or others, represents an imperfection which will debilitate the operation of the market mechanism. A free press means an unregulated or self-regulated press. Every restriction is undesirable. The alternative view considers journalism to be a public service in which market considerations are irrelevant. Worse, the market subverts journalism's essential function. A tension exists between the aspirations of journalism and the market context in which journalism must operate. Journalistic standards must be high and sustained by regulation if necessary. Some journalists favour 'a positive regulatory framework which imposes standards which would defy accountants, would defy the "commonsense" of always going for a big audience, but would encourage journalists to play their proper role in reporting, informing and keeping alive our body politic'. Lord McGregor, who chaired the Press Complaints Commission (PCC) until he was succeeded by Lord Wakeham on 22 November 1994, suggests that the debate can be reduced to a simple question: 'to what extent do you regard it as wrong in a democracy for people producing newspapers for a profit, or radio and television programmes for a profit, to supply goods which their purchasers wish to have?' (Interview). The clash of views between the two sides of this debate will resonate throughout the subsequent discussion of the new journalism and regulation.

This chapter explores newspapers' growing reliance on newszak by: discussing particular cases to clarify the nature of the new style of journalism; identifying briefly the factors which have prompted its growth; and, finally, detailing and assessing the effectiveness of the various statutory and voluntary controls designed to regulate journalism. Chapter 11 analyses changes in the range and character of media (both print and broadcast) reporting of parliamentary and political affairs, while chapter 12 considers the developing patterns of regulation for broadcast media.

Print and broadcast journalism are analysed separately for a number of reasons. First, much of the concern about newszak and the alleged invasion of privacy it occasions, has focused on newspapers rather than radio or television. What Dennis Potter described as the 'down market slide into the sewers' of tabloid journalism, is much more evident in our 'cynical, venal, genuinely prostituted and foreign owned press' than it is in television (Potter, 1993, pp. 22–3). Second, distinctive philosophies and traditions of regulation inform print and broadcast journalism, although increasingly they are obliged to constrain similar journalistic tendencies. Third, print and broadcast media face divergent futures and markets; published newspaper titles and circulations have suffered a sustained post-war decline, while radio and television services are burgeoning. Finally, print and broadcast media articulate different journalistic traditions. In broadcast journalism the hegemony of public-service ideals has fostered impartiality and neutrality in reporting while opinionated editorial and ideological pluralism have been considered the essential ingredients for a robust and healthy newspaper journalism. An important objection should be acknowledged at the outset. Not everyone who acknowledges changes in journalistic style concedes that they have been for the worse. On the contrary, Rupert Murdoch, in his 1989 MacTaggart lecture, challenged existing perceptions of 'quality broadcasting' as little more than 'the values of the narrow elite which controls British television and which has always thought that its tastes are synonymous with quality' (Murdoch, 1989, p. 5).

The ultimate tabloid story: From 'Di-Spy' to the Panorama interview

The Princess of Wales has become a tabloid phenomenon. She has been a central focus for tabloid journalism's attentions since her marriage in 1981. Press coverage of her early married life, the birth of her children, the subsequent break-up of her marriage and her increasingly acrimonious relationships with her husband and other members of the royal family has been quite remarkable for its sheer quantity as well as its invasive, personal and often prurient character. But in 1993, one incident of press reporting of the Princess of Wales proved outstanding for the public debate it prompted, as well as the insights it provided into the character of tabloid journalism and the problems confronting press self-regulation.

On 7 November, the *Sunday Mirror* published seven pages of pictures of the princess wearing a leotard and cycling shorts and using an exercise machine. The photographs had been taken using a 'peeping Tom' camera concealed in a panel above the princess's head. Bruce Taylor, the owner of the L.A. Fitness Club, had taken the photographs, sold them to Mirror Group Newspapers (MGN) for an estimated £125,000 and hoped to raise a sum in excess of £1 million from worldwide syndication. Lord McGregor was unable to persuade the *Mirror* editor and MGN Chief Executive David Montgomery that MGN should not publish further pictures in the *Daily Mirror* the next day. The *Mirror* had clearly breached Clause 4 of the PCC's voluntary code of conduct which states that 'intrusions and inquiries into an individual's private life without his or her consent, including the use of long lens photography to take pictures of people on private property without their consent, are not generally acceptable and publication can only be justified in the public interest' (PCC Report no. 23, p. 36). In a personal statement, McGregor (Culf, 8 November 1993, p. 3) called for advertisers to boycott Mirror newspapers; the *Mirror* responded by describing McGregor as 'an arch buffoon'. The publication of the pictures was judged by the majority of politicians, members of the public and many journalists and newspaper proprietors, to represent the nadir of journalism's ethical standards. The *Mirror*'s threefold defence that the pictures illustrated a potential security risk for the Princess of Wales, that the gym was a public place and that the photographs had merely been purchased rather than taken by its own photographers, did little to placate McGregor or the *Mirror*'s competitor newspapers (Young, 1993). The tabloid press, with its keen eye for the trite phrase, promptly dubbed the incident the 'Di-Spy' case.

On 9 November 1993, the then *Mirror* editor David Banks responded to sustained press and public criticism by announcing that Mirror Group Newspapers were leaving the PCC. The *Mirror* was challenging the PCC's authority and refusing to support the newspaper industry's agreed code of practice. Press self-regulation is credible only when it embraces all newspapers. The withdrawal of the *Mirror*, moreover, meant the revenue of the commission would be depleted by over £100,000 – a substantial proportion of its total revenues of £1.2 million. Eventually a peace settlement between David Montgomery and Lord McGregor was negotiated following interventions by Rupert Murdoch and Sir David English. MGN agreed to apologise to the Princess of Wales and make a donation to charity; MGN also apologised to Lord McGregor. A letter from the PCC to MGN withdrew the call for an advertising boycott and rival newspapers agreed to stop publishing hostile and critical stories about the *Daily Mirror*. On 10 November, MGN rejoined the PCC and agreed to accept commission rulings. The parties to the dispute had stepped back from the brink; self-regulation survived what seemed a near-fatal collision. A special two-hour meeting of the PCC discussed measures to enhance the credibility of self-regulation and prevent statutory intervention. The idea of a commissioner to deal with breaches of privacy was mooted and found favour. There was also support for the suggestion that the PCC code of practice should be written into editors' contracts of employment so that they could be sanctioned in the event of further breaches (Culf, 10 November 1993, p. 3). Both measures have subsequently been adopted.

The Di-Spy case is interesting for a number of reasons. First, the case reveals the potential for hostilities between newspapers in a highly competitive industry, where the ethical probity of publishing pictures, despite their extraordinarily high news value, is hotly contested. The *Mirror* suggested that competitor newspapers' objections might simply be dismissed as cant. Second, the case illustrated both the strength and fragility of self-regulation. McGregor conceded that 'we were within hours of the whole structure of self-regulation collapsing', but the incident also revealed 'the determination of all the industry, including MGN to make self-regulation work'. Interpretation of Murdoch and English's intervention as testament to the merit and viability of self-regulation may be legitimate, but it is also highly problematic. A system of regulation sustained and policed by the interventions of powerful individuals is potentially unstable, lacks any public accountability and seems to rest on arbitrary power rather than any legitimate authority. Third, the incident raises interesting and important questions about the extent to which advertisers should be able to influence newspapers' editorial content. Some journalists were evidently opposed to the call for an advertising boycott (Gliniecki, 1993, p. 3, Greenslade, 1993, p. 2). Finally, the case illustrates the tension between a newspaper's need to compete for readers and advertisers and its commitment to comply with the PCC code. A determined editor with an exclusive may not spike the story simply because it contravenes the code. Geoffrey Goodman observed that the 'concentration of media power in the hands of a few individuals who recognise no other discipline than the one of the market is becoming more and more problematic in the sense that it seems to fundamentally undermine the basis of journalistic ethics' (Goodman, 1994, p. 3).

PCC sanctions certainly proved ineffectual in deterring Piers Morgan, editor of *News of the World*, from publishing pictures of Countess Spencer outside a private clinic where she was receiving treatment for alcohol problems and bulimia: 'Di's Sister-in-Law in Booze and Bulima Clinic'. It required the full four-letter wrath of his proprietor, Rupert Murdoch, to remind the editor of the relevant sections of the PPC code of conduct which address issues of personal privacy (*Guardian*, 12 May 1995, p. 3).

Putting aside moral probity and compliance with professional standards and codes, the Di-Spy case also questions the potential market advantage which a newspaper might accrue from publication. Sales of the *Sunday Mirror* enjoyed a boost of 85–100,000 copies on 7 November when it published the photographs, but the following week sales dropped by 230,000. The *Daily Mirror* recorded a decline of 55,000 copies a day on its October average in the three weeks following publication of the pictures (Culf, 17 November 1993, p. 5).

On 4 May 1994, the Princess of Wales was again the focus for journalists' attentions. The *Sun* announced it had been offered photographs of 'Lady Di' wearing only a topless swimsuit and relaxing by a friend's swimming pool in Spain. The newspaper turned down the offer, claiming that the photographs were an unjustifiable breach of privacy. On 5 May, *Hello* magazine announced it had purchased exclusive rights to the pictures for an estimated £1 million but was not intending to publish them. Such protestations of journalistic probity were short-lived. A few months later when Major James Hewitt's ghosted 'bonkbuster' was published, in which he alleged a three-year relationship with Princess Diana, the tabloid press denounced him as a 'cad' and a 'rat', but at the same time provided extensive coverage to the story, feeding its readers' prurient interest. The *Sun* published pictures of the princess and six of Hewitt's previous lovers under the heading, 'The Galloping Major's String Of Fillies' (*Sun*, 3 October 1994, p. 3).

The Princess of Wales has, on occasion, courted the attentions of her many suitors in tabloid journalism. On 20 November 1995, the BBC's *Panorama Special* was devoted to an interview with the princess in which she spoke very openly about her relationship with James Hewitt, her marriage to Charles, his relationship with Camilla Parker Bowles, her increasingly acrimonious relationship with the royal family, the prospects for her divorce from Charles, the likelihood that she would succeed to the throne and Charles' suitability to be king. The interview triggered an explosion of newspaper coverage. Extensive press speculation in the week prior to the broadcast was matched by newspapers' analysis of the interview in the days following the *Panorama* programme. The day after the interview, which attracted an audience estimated at 21 million, the story featured as the front page lead in all national newspapers and headed the early news bulletins on radio and television. By 6 p.m., however, the return of a guilty verdict on Rosemary West and the agreement of a peace settlement in Bosnia, relegated the story in news agendas.

In the popular press coverage was extensive in quantity and tabloid in quality. The *Mirror* devoted its first seven editorial pages to the story – a total of 7560 cm² of coverage. The *Sun* (5400 cm²), *Star* (5400 cm²), *Express* (5400 cm²) and the *Mail* (5650 cm²) each gave the story an overwhelming news priority. The story also featured prominently in the broadsheet newspapers, with the *Guardian* allocating five full pages (9120 cm²) and an editorial to the interview. The *Telegraph* (7008 cm²) gave the story extensive coverage, while the *Independent* (2390 cm²) and the *Times* (2370 cm²) were less concerned to report the interview, perhaps reflecting the tensions which exist between print and television journalists. In the tabloids coverage focused on the intimate, personal and sexual aspects of the interview. The *Express* headline was typical: 'I Knew Charles Loved Camilla' (21 November 1995, p. 1). In the broadsheets the story was framed in terms of its constitutional relevance and its implications for the monarchy; *The Times* headline announced, 'I Will Not Go Quietly, Says The Princess' (21 November 1995, p. 1). Reporting in the *Sun* was characteristically tabloid. The front page announced a 'Royal Sensation', featured a half-page photograph of the princess and headlined in large print 'Diana; I Had An Affair With Hewitt'. On the inside pages extracts from the interview were attributed to 'Princess Di' – an informality intended to imply personal familiarity. Pages 2 and 4 featured a plethora of 'experts', including Deidre Sanders (the *Sun*'s agony aunt), Dr David Starkey ('Constitutional expert and Talk Radio UK host'), Max Clifford ('Stars' PR guru') and Gary Bushell (the *Sun*'s TV critic), who offered 'Di' a range of prescriptions under the questionable heading 'Expert Advice'. The *Guardian* used a similar tabloid presentation distinguished from the *Sun* only by the more intellectual character of its experts: Lord St John of Fawsley, Harold Brooks-Baker (the editor of *Burke's Peerage*) and Professor Cary Cooper (a psychologist). Returning to the *Sun*, the page 5 heading 'You The Jury' invited readers to register a telephone vote: 'Do you think Diana was right to go on *Panorama*? Did she betray the monarchy or was she justified in opening her heart?' The *Star* also invited readers to 'join the great Di-bate' on the 'Di-Hotline' (21 November 1995, p. 5). Such is the tabloid cache of 'Lady Di' that she managed to displace that other essential ingredient of the tabloid bill of fare, the 'Page 3 Lovely'. The photograph of topless 'Dishy Deborah Turpin' was relegated to page 7. Deborah, the *Sun* informed its readers, is 'learning to waltz, foxtrot and tango. Whoever she partners, they make a magnificent pair' (*Sun*, 21 November 1995, p. 7).

On this occasion it was the Princess who had initiated the contact with the media and, in the light of previous experience, she might have anticipated the style of coverage her interview would prompt in tabloid media. But whether complicitous or not, it must surely be judged more than a little disappointing when an important news interview with a senior member of the royal family is reported in a populist style, with a prurient obsession for sexual detail and a schoolboy's reliance on puns.

In July 1996, the royal drama seemed to be drawing to a close when the terms of the divorce of Charles and Diana were made public. But on 16 July, the day after the granting of a decree nisi, Lady Diana featured centrally in all the tabloids by announcing the withdrawal of her patronage from more than 100 charities she had previously sponsored. Diana's royal title of HRH had been removed as part of the divorce settlement and she felt she could no longer offer royal patronage to these charities. The *Mirror* stepped up its 'Great Diana HRH Debate' by publishing a photomontage of Diana curtseying to Princess Michael of Kent and asking readers whether they believed Diana should in future have to curtsey to 'lesser royals' (18 July 1996, p. 1). More was to come. On 8 October 1996 the *Sun*, under the headline 'Di-Spy Video Scandal: She's Filmed In Bra And Panties Romp With Hewitt', published five pages of still photographs allegedly showing Diana and her former lover James Hewitt 'cavorting' together: she riding on his back as he crawls on all fours. Later the same day, the video from which the stills were taken was denounced as a hoax using well-known theatrical lookalikes. *Sun* editor Stuart Higgins said he would be writing to Diana and James Hewitt to apologise. The following day, the *Mirror* ran a spoiler with a barely concealed relish at its competitor's gullibility in accepting and failing to check the veracity of the most recent 'Di-Spy' scandal. Lord Wakeham, chair of the PCC, wrote a letter to *The Times* in which he suggested that the recent spate of royal stories posed a threat to the successful regime of press self-regulation. 'Nobody would benefit from statutory regulation,' he claimed, which would result in the press 'being dragged into a quagmire of litigation' (cited in *Guardian*, 10 October 1996, p. 1). On 10th August 1997 the British media invaded Diana's privacy again when collectively they paid £700,000 for photographs of her allegedly kissing Dodi Fayed. The Lady Di story had returned with a vengeance; the story looks set to run and run.

Competing for that 25p: the aetiology of newszak

There is considerable agreement about the factors which have prompted the growth of newszak and tabloid journalism in newspapers; increased competition for readers and advertisers is the single most significant factor. A regional journalist detailed the changes impacting on editorial style and the shift to a more tabloid content.

We still do the investigations and all the things which we believe any self respecting newspaper should do, but we live in a competitive world, so in the last five years or so we have tweaked our content. We are competing for that 25p for the cover price and I think increasingly we are looking for the lighter story. Readers have become more inter-ested in soundbites or wordbites. I think if anything the major change is that we are catering for a public which has a grasshopper mentality and therefore you shorten the news items, you go for a lot of news items, you go for a big read and keep the story count as high as possi-ble in your publication in order to keep your audience's attention.

Competition is the prime mover in journalism's move down market. That 25p, that's the culprit!

A second factor is the increasingly concentrated ownership of British newspapers, which is uncontentious when five companies control 92 per cent of national weekly newspaper sales (chapter 5). In the local and regional press a similar pattern of monopoly ownership is evident with an increasing tendency for the same companies to own both national and local papers (Franklin and Murphy, 1994, pp. 12–17). The concern is that own-ership endows proprietors with editorial influence either directly or via their editors (Williams, 1994). An NUJ official claimed that 'if Murdoch falls out with an editor he sacks them. He's quite open about it.'

In the local press, particular forces operate to prompt changing journal-istic standards; the rapid rise and expansion of the local free press has been crucially influential (Franklin and Murphy, 1991, p. 85). Funded wholly by advertising revenues, free newspapers' concern is to provide readers for advertisers rather than to sell news to readers. Consequently, fewer journal-ists are required and advertising copy enjoys priority over editorial. An edi-tor claimed, 'the role of journalists on free newspapers is to fill the space between the advertisements. They try to give a scattering of coverage of the local scene and carry some local stories but their staffs are usually so small and 75 per cent of their total content has to be devoted to advertising'. Paid local weekly papers must compete in the same market, try to secure the same economies of staff and make similar compromises in editorial quality and range (Franklin, 1986, p. 26).

The introduction of individual contracts for journalists and the attempt to derecognise the journalists' trades union has subverted journalists' job security built on collective association and bargaining. In such circum-stances journalists are much less likely to be critical of editorial issues. Indeed, some trades unionists claim that editors 'are not having to think whether they are maintaining standards because fear is very common on certain papers now. Journalists who work for Murdoch, Montgomery or Rothermere, are working in fear whether on a national or a provincial.'

Finally, some regulators believe that politicians' failing reputation, prompted by such stories as the *Guardian* coverage of payments to ex-minister Neil Hamilton by political lobbyist Ian Greer (2 October 1996), means that politicians have more than previously come to be seen as a legit-imate target for press inquiries. A MORI poll, conducted in 1983 and again in 1993, which asked the public which of 15 professions they would trust to tell the truth, ranked politicians 13th and government ministers in the penultimate 14th position (Worcester, 1994, p. 36). Interestingly, the least trustworthy group, in 15th position, was journalists. In 1983, 19 per cent of respondents trusted journalists to tell the truth; by 1993 this figure had virtually halved to 10 per cent. Perhaps this lack of trust explains the public support for statutory regulation of the British press.

Regulating newszak

It is important to clarify two points at the outset of the debate concerning press regulation. First, newspapers are already subject to considerable regulation. William Waldegrave's 1992 white paper *Open Government* (Cmnd 2290) listed 251 statutory instruments restricting disclosure of information which limit media competence to report government activity (Stephenson, 1994, p. 8). Newspapers are also subject to 46 legislative restrictions including the various Official Secrets Acts 1911 to 1989 and the Prevention of Terrorism Act 1989 (see Stephenson, 1994 and Belsay and Chadwick, 1992, p. 5). Second, there is widespread public disapproval of some aspects of press behaviour, signalling possible support for reform. In 1992, a study by MORI asked whether 'the press generally behaves responsibly in Britain'; 51 per cent said 'no'. Approval varied between the different papers with 80 per cent citing the local press as 'behaving responsibly', but only 66 per cent approving broadsheets' behaviour and a mere 32 per cent supporting tabloids. Some 53 per cent of respondents believed that 'Tabloid newspapers were under too little control'. A significant 73 per cent of respondents felt it was unjustifiable for the press to do any of the following: publish photographs of members of the royal family on private property; record the voice of somebody on private property; place a surveillance or bugging device on private property; or enter private property (only 3 per cent thought this was acceptable). Almost identical figures were recorded for stories involving senior politicians (Worcester, 1994, pp. 30–2). A MORI poll commissioned in 1996 revealed that 85 per cent of Conservative and 90 per cent of Labour MPs want to see some form of privacy legislation introduced (*UK Press Gazette*, 26 February 1996, p. 2).

Journalists and editors routinely muster six arguments against statutory intervention. They believe: it is wrong in principle and constitutes censorship; it is impractical and unworkable; there are already too many statutory controls on press freedom; there is no evidence that it is necessary (complaints about privacy for example constitute a mere 15 per cent of total complaints received by the PCC); self-regulation is more flexible and allows a discourse, mediated by PCC, between readers and publishers; self-regulation offers the most effective sanction against potential offenders – namely peer review. A newspaper editor summarised his objection to statutory controls.

It's basically state interference and state censorship. We have too much law anyway. It is much better to have an intelligent code of practice drawn up by editors, policed by editors and lay people. When anything comes into question you are faced with the embarrassment of being judged by your peers. And editors do take notice of it. I know from my own experience of sitting on the PCC that there is a dialogue with publishers who have made it clear to their editors that they must follow these rules. Now that's surely a better way of operating than statutory controls which are impossible to operate.

A prominent regulator offered a principled objection to any system of regulation, including self-regulation. 'Freedom is the absence of constraint,' he claimed, and 'our [the PCC's] job is to maximise freedom.' Consequently, the 'principal role' of the PCC is conceived rather narrowly, negatively, but significantly, as 'to prevent direct governmental intervention in the press in the form of the sort of things which Calcutt wished'.

Other opponents express objections to particular mechanisms for regulation. One critic was unhappy with the proposal for a statutory press ombudsman because 'experience on the PCC reveals that a dozen heads are better than one' in deciding such matters. Opponents and advocates of statutory intervention share concerns about potential problems arising from a system of fines for breaches of regulatory codes. Fines intended to 'hit' the big publishers would need to 'be very big', but 'If the fines are small they are not really a sanction.' Draconian sanctions, moreover, create 'the danger that you will turn some journalists into martyrs' while standardised fines risk 'forcing newspapers out of business'. One regulator strongly disagrees with any regulatory framework intended to anticipate solutions to future difficulties. Life is not so simple. The press is

> so byzantine in its complexities that you can't run the whole thing as if it were a well regulated traffic system. I detest constitutions, manifestos or what Oakeshott used to call rationality in politics. We operate a code which is drafted in the spirit of self-regulation, is drafted by the industry. It is not written in tablets of stone, it is subject to revision and it's always under review. It will change, it will evolve, we will learn from experience.

Advocates of statutory regulation support a range of proposals from those which guarantee specific rights (for example to privacy or right of reply) to more general provisions such as the statutory Press Commission recommended by Calcutt (Calcutt, 1993, pp. 45–6). Three arguments are offered to justify statutory regulation. First, self-regulation is judged to have failed. The newspaper market is too competitive and the battle for readers too fierce to be regulated without the strong and effective sanction which only statutory regulation can guarantee. Second, the PCC, established and funded by the newspaper industry, is unable to achieve the independence necessary to police editorial standards effectively. A politician observed that 'self-regulation in any industry, whether the police or public sector, does not have a good track record'. The PCC is an especially poor regulator; it is 'frankly a weak and rather ineffectual body set up by the newspaper industry for their own needs'. Gerald Kaufmann, when chair of the National Heritage Select Committee, described the PCC as being rather 'like a eunuch trying to do the best in the circumstances' (cited in *Guardian*, 8 November 1996, p. 7). Third, statutory regulation is not necessarily antipathetic to press freedom. Clive Soley's private members bill proposed the creation of an Independent Press Authority (IPA) which would police journalistic standards but also have a major brief to encourage and support press freedom. A 'high profile body' like the IPA would, moreover, 'report annually to Parliament, perhaps via a select committee on issues concerning press freedom'.

Whoever is right, the last decade has witnessed a tidal wave of reforms, triggered by government, select committees, politicians, commissions and inquiries and the newspaper industry itself, to the existing system of press regulation. The great majority of reforms propose a more stringent regulatory regime. Reforms of press regulation can be dated from 1990 when the Press Council was abolished following a recommendation of the Calcutt Inquiry in July 1990. Established and funded by the Newspaper Society since 1953, the council came to be judged an increasingly inadequate brake on the plummeting standards of journalism in the aggressive, tabloid newspaper market of the 1970s and 1980s (Porter, 1984, p. 32 and Tunstall, 1983, p. 267). Calcutt's preference was for a statutory commission to regulate the press, but he recommended a two-year probationary period during which the newspaper industry should make a serious effort to improve self-regulation; the press was 'drinking in the last chance saloon'.

The Press Complaints Commission was established as the successor body on 1 January 1991; Lord MacGregor was appointed to chair the new commission. The PCC drafted a code of conduct with particular clauses specifically designed to address criticism of press conduct: newspapers should 'take care not to publish inaccurate, misleading or distorted information' (Clause 1); there should be a 'fair opportunity for reply to inaccuracies' (Clause 2); newspapers should 'distinguish clearly between comment, conjecture and fact' (Clause 3); press intrusions into 'an individual's private life without his or her consent, are not generally acceptable' (Clause 4 – PCC Code of Practice Report no. 29 March/April 1995, pp. 34–5).

Calcutt's second review of press behaviour, published on 14 January 1993, suggested that the PCC had 'not proved itself to be an effective regulator [despite] the sanction of the prospect of statutory intervention' (Calcutt, 1993, p. 63). Calcutt proposed three substantive reforms. First, a Statutory Press Complaints Tribunal should be established with powers to draw up a code of practice and impose substantial fines on newspapers that failed to comply with it (ibid., pp. 45–6). Second, three new criminal offences should outlaw: entering or remaining on private property without consent to acquire material for publication; using surveillance devices on private property to make a recording; and taking a photograph on private property without the owner's consent (ibid., p. 51). Finally, Calcutt recommended reconsideration of the idea of a new civil tort concerning infringement of privacy (ibid., p. 56). The Newspaper Society responded by arguing that the government should not become the author of a press code of practice; nor should government create criminal offences aimed solely at journalists (Newell, 1993, p. 15).

Two months after Calcutt, the Select Committee on National Heritage published its *Report on Privacy and Media Intrusion* (Cmnd 294-1) which recommended a new voluntary body to replace the PCC and a statutory press ombudsman, appointed by the lord chancellor, with powers to supervise press corrections, to fine newspapers and order the payment of compensation to complainants (Slattery, 1993, p. 2). Almost unnoticed behind the clamour which Calcutt was generating, Clive Soley MP was guiding his freedom and responsibility of the press bill through its second reading in the House on 29 January 1993. The bill proposed a statutory Independent Press Authority (IPA), appointed by the home secretary, with powers to order the publication of a free correction, in cases where factual inaccuracies were reported in a newspaper. Failure to obey an IPA order would lead to a high court order making the newspaper liable for contempt which could give rise to fines and/or imprisonment (Soley, 1992, pp. 2–3). But Soley was also 'worried about the loss of press freedom in Britain especially over the last twenty years or so' and consequently the Press Authority 'would report annually, perhaps via a Select Committee, to Parliament about issues concerning press freedom'. Soley's bill failed at third reading in April 1993.

Since 1993, politicians and the newspaper industry have offered a number of proposals to strengthen regulation. In May 1993, the PCC announced a series of reforms including the appointment of a majority of non-press members on the commission, changes to strengthen the code of practice and a help line to aid the public in making complaints (PCC Report no. 17, pp. 5–7). In July 1993, the lord chancellor, Lord Mackay, issued a consultation paper entitled *The Infringement of Privacy* proposing a new civil tort to protect privacy. The green paper suggests £10,000 as a maximum penalty for infringement. Later that same year, following the Di-Spy case, the Select Committee on National Heritage produced an addenda to its March report (HC 38) endorsing the new privacy tort. In January 1994, the PCC appointed Professor Robert Pinker to serve as privacy commissioner. Pinker envisaged a modest brief for the post, describing it as 'a change of procedure. I have the authority to take up any case, I take the initiative . . . like any other Commissioner I can ask for full documentation . . . I present my draft report to the full Commission which then reaches its view. So it's totally erroneous to describe me as an ombudsman. I'm not a lone ranger. I'm a member of the Commission, I do a job for the Commission.'

A government white paper, scheduled for publication in summer 1993, was repeatedly delayed. Many observers believed that the threat of statutory regulation was being used by the then secretary of state, Peter Brooke, to win concessions to strengthen voluntary regulation from the newspaper industry. Certainly that was the view of one senior press regulator; although he believed the strategy was flawed. 'I told the Secretary for National Heritage', he claimed, 'that the government needn't think that by holding back the white paper the industry will make concession after concession. I told him, you've got all you are going to get.'

In March 1994 the Association of British Editors (ABE), the Guild of British Editors (GBE) and the International Press Institute (IPI), undoubtedly frustrated by the government's inability to express a position, published 'an alternative white paper' entitled *Media Freedom and Regulation*. It concluded that it was unnecessary 'to create an entirely new civil wrong of infringement of privacy' which would 'risk seriously undermining legitimate public investigation by the media' (Stephenson, 1994, p. 19). In July 1995, the government finally published its views; in a document entitled *Privacy and Press Freedom* it concluded that statutory regulation was not desirable (Cmnd 2918, p. 16). In 1989, David Mellor had warned the press that it was drinking in the last chance saloon and in 1990, Calcutt's review of press self-regulation effectively called last orders. But by 1995, government attitudes were more conciliatory and Secretary of National Heritage Virginia Bottomley's offer of a reprieve from statutory regulation effectively announced a 'lock in'.

Two months previously, the government published a green paper detailing its proposals concerning cross-media ownership. Stephen Dorrell, then national heritage secretary, claimed the proposals contained in *Media Ownership: The Government's Proposals* were designed to reconcile the need for 'viable, expanding media businesses and proper safeguards for plurality of ownership and diversity of viewpoint' (quoted in Culf and Donovan, 1995, p. 1). Slightly modified, the proposals informed the subsequent Broadcasting Act 1996. Newspaper groups controlling less than 20 per cent of the national circulation market would be allowed to control an ITV or Channel 5 licence up to 15 per cent of the total television market defined by audience share; consequently, Murdoch's News Corporation (37 per cent) and MGN (26 per cent) would not. Regional newspaper groups wishing to own an ITV licence must be below 30 per cent of circulation in the relevant area. Future mergers between television and newspaper companies would be regulated by the ITC which would balance three public-interest criteria: promoting diversity, maintaining an economically viable industry and ensuring proper competition (*Media Ownership: The Government's Proposals*, 23 May 1995). Sir David English, chair of the British Media Industry Group which had been lobbying on behalf of Associated Newspapers, Pearson, the Guardian Media Group and the *Telegraph* was perhaps predictably content with the proposals. Murdoch declared himself 'angry'; the government had been 'seduced by the establishment once again into championing the average at the expense of the excellent' (Murdoch, 1995, p. 14). The Campaign for Press and Broadcasting Freedom shared Murdoch's view that the new rules might occasion a reduction in newspaper titles; the NUJ believed the proposals would 'sacrifice quality to the commercial interests of the big media companies' (Culf and Donovan, 1995, p. 1).

But in truth, few observers believe that this flurry of reforming activity, so evident over the last few years, has achieved much in terms of fundamental change. The Press Complaints Commission is barely discernible from its predecessor Press Council; the label on the bottle is different but the wine remains rather insipid and lacking in body. Most journalists, but fewer than ever politicians, are opposed to statutory regulation. The newspaper industry and the PCC, under the leadership of Lord Wakeham, seem convinced of the merits of voluntary regulations. In a speech at the British Press Awards in April 1995, Wakeham acclaimed the establishment of the PCC, by a historically diverse and fiercely competitive industry, as a 'logistical and political triumph'. Demands for a regulatory regime seemed incomprehensible. 'The PCC is undoubtedly the most effective self-regulatory system in existence,' Wakeham claimed, and yet 'demand for legislation continues' (Culf, *Guardian* 5 April 1995, p. 2).

Summary: newszak, regulation and press freedom

Press self-regulation has proved problematic and patchy in its effectiveness. The hub of the system since 1991 has been the Press Complaints Commission which, armed with a code of conduct drafted by editors and journalists, seeks to police standards of journalistic probity within the newspaper industry. Critics allege the PCC offers little more than a tokenistic Canute to the tidal wave of market forces which, increasingly throughout the 1980s and 1990s, has breached the dykes of voluntary regulation in an increasingly frenzied search for readers and advertisers. But the regime of self-regulation has recently been buttressed by the introduction of more severe sanctions, such as inclusion of the PCC code of conduct into editors' and journalists' contracts of employment. Since January 1994, a member of the commission has been allocated a particular brief to deal with incidents of alleged breach of privacy. But the PCC is already relatively under-resourced to fulfil its regulatory tasks, compared to the ITC. The 16-member PCC has a budget of £1.2 million and modest support staff; by contrast the 10 members of the ITC are supported by 190 full-time staff and resourced with an annual income in excess of £18.5 million (*ITC Annual Report 1992*, pp. 50–2).

The July 1995 white paper on privacy failed to propose a new statutory tort. There is undoubtedly some public support for such a measure, but the proposal attracts little support from the newspaper industry. Any workable system of regulation must enjoy the respect of journalists and their recognition of its legitimacy, otherwise it might only create journalistic martyrs willing to 'publish and be damned'. Statutory controls might also miss their target. It is a curious irony that proposals to outlaw the use of telephoto surveillance cameras and microphones – prompted by print journalists' activities – might have their profoundest effects on broadcast journalism's news-gathering activities.

But the overwhelming reason why statutory press regulation seems unlikely is that successive governments have been genuinely divided about the issue. In liberal democratic societies there is an almost intuitive reluctance to give politicians statutory involvement in press affairs. In Britain this undoubtedly reflects the state's infamous 'taxes on knowledge' designed to restrict press freedom and stifle public debate. This history has bestowed the legacy of a press which views every intervention by the state as a negative act necessitating hostility. Politicians are conscious of this, and although some MPs offer a generalised support for the idea of statutory press controls, their conviction crumbles when the detail of particular recommendations is unravelled. A senior regulator claimed that 'When they [MPs] were confronted by Calcutt and the idea of a statutory tribunal with a judge as chairman and the power to stop publication by injunction', many MPs who had previously supported statutory press controls 'rose up on their hind legs with alarm and I was rather cheered by thinking we still had some MPs who believe in ordinary freedom.' Some observers believe that successive governments' reluctance expresses nothing more than the vested political interest of the governing party. Clive Soley, for example, believed that the bill he introduced to secure a statutory right of reply was unsuccessful because the government was persuaded that if it 'became law the press couldn't run some of the stories they ran in the [1992] general election. The tax stories, for example, which reported lies about Labour.' One regulator believed that any government would be reluctant to introduce a statutory regime and 'offend the press in the run up to a general election'.

Some observers consider press regulation to be little more than 'fiddling around at the edges of the problem'. Economic sanctions are judged a necessary element in quality control. Even an 'anti-regulationist' like McGregor seemed to concede the case, albeit indirectly, by proposing an advertising boycott on the *Mirror*. The argument for reforming the structures of ownership of media organisations unfolds as follows. There seems to be considerable agreement that increasing market pressures and intensified competition for viewers, readers and in many cases advertisers, provides the central impetus behind changes in journalistic standards, the growth of 'infotainment' and the increasing prevalence of tabloid journalism. There is an important, contentious, but often unacknowledged, assumption here that 'going down market' will serve to increase rather than diminish audiences and readerships. But if this connection between market pressures and the editorial quality of journalism is conceded, then much existing regulatory activity which seeks to enforce codes of journalistic behaviour seems to miss its target. If declining standards are merely symptomatic of a more profound malaise, effective regulation must try to effect a cure on the root cause rather than the symptoms. Sustaining journalistic standards cannot be achieved by enforcing codes of good practice. Effective regulation requires the design and establishment of organisational structures, patterns of ownership and systems of finance for newspapers which encourage an emphasis on the reporting of significant issues of public consequence; logic requires similar arrangements for broadcasting.

But those who consider journalism to be an activity which, much like any other, best flourishes in a free market, believe such interventions more likely to subvert rather than enhance the achievement of excellence in any journalistic enterprise. Two divergent perceptions continue to inform the debate about the essential character of journalism. One considers journalism to be public service; the other understands journalism as a market activity; these perceptions have proved resistant to reconciliation. Consequently the desirability and effectiveness of regulation remains highly contested. In 1825 John Adams expressed scepticism about the possibility of resolving this problem in a letter to James Lloyd. 'If there is ever to be an amelioration of the condition of mankind,' he wrote, 'philosophers, theologians, legislators, politicians and moralists will find that regulation of the press is the most difficult, dangerous and important problem they have to resolve. Mankind cannot now be governed without it, nor at the present with it' (the Commission on the Freedom of the Press, USA, 1947). But some resolution of these tensions within journalism is urgently needed. Without a radical reassessment of the regulation of the British press, the new market-driven journalism of the 1990s will continue to offend individual privacy as well as standards of journalistic quality into the next millennium. Newszak will flourish without restraint.

11

From the gallery to the gutter

Changing newspaper reporting of parliament

The gallery tradition of reporting parliament is dead. The parliamentary pages of *The Times*, *Guardian*, *Financial Times* and *Telegraph* which routinely provided extensive coverage of proceedings have become a thing of the past, and few people seem to regret the loss. Simon Jenkins, ex-editor of *The Times*, confirmed in his evidence to the Nolan Committee that it had been his decision 'to stop parliamentary reporting. I couldn't find anyone who read it except MPs' (*House to House*, Channel 4, 17 January 1995). Other journalists disagree. One senior political commentator argued that the 'abandonment by the *Times* of its parliamentary page was the crucial change; it was the sheet anchor. It was highly symbolic . . . once the standard slides, it becomes a subconscious cue for everyone to follow suit.' The decline in coverage is uncontested, and is reflected in the jibe 'if you want to keep a secret make a speech about it in the House.'

A study by Jack Straw MP published in October 1993 revealed that the decline in coverage was not confined to *The Times* (Straw, 1993, p. 4). As if to underscore Straw's analysis, the *Financial Times* announced it was spiking its page of parliamentary reporting the day before his report was published. Other politicians, including House Speaker Betty Boothroyd and her predecessor Lord Weatherill (Weatherill, 1995, p. 13), have echoed Straw's objections. In March 1995, Peter Bottomley suggested that since so few journalists attended the House to report debates, their numbers in the press gallery should be monitored by the Serjeant at Arms. Simon Hoggart retaliated in his *Guardian* sketch (4 April 1995, p. 6). The debate on 3 April 1995 concerning the need to widen the M25 to 12 lanes had been attended, he noted, by only that same number of Labour backbenchers. The mere 13 MPs in the House for the committee stage of the finance bill, moreover, were completely outnumbered by the 16 journalists in the press gallery. Since MPs 'are not interested in the debates, why', Hoggart questions, 'should we imagine that our readers are?' (ibid.). Hoggart concedes 'there is a measure of ill feeling between journalists and MPs at the moment' (ibid.).

But this represents more than ritual hostilities. The roots of this antagonism lie deep; the consequences of journalists' neglect of parliament for public debate of parliamentary issues are more significant.

The previous chapter examined the increasing tendency of newspaper journalists – in spite of regulation – to follow and promote a tabloid news agenda. This chapter focuses specifically on the changing practices and standards of parliamentary journalism, for two reasons. First, the reporting of parliamentary and political life has been a central activity of journalism – and properly so. Parliament is the forum in which part of British democratic life is enacted. Initially, it was lawful to report only the decisions of parliament, not the debates through which it arrived at those decisions. Pioneers such as Samuel Johnson and other journalists fought hard to win access to the House. It seems odd that such a hard-won right should be surrendered voluntarily. Second, the decline in parliamentary reporting offers a particularly clear exemplar of the tendencies in journalism, especially the prominence of market above editorial considerations, which are changing its news-gathering activities, professional philosophies and ultimately the kinds of stories which constitute its published output.

More interested in Cantona than the match? Changes in newspaper reporting of parliament

This chapter addresses two questions. First, what are the major discernible changes in the style and content of parliamentary reporting which have occurred since the demise of a dedicated parliamentary page? Second, what are the perceptions of insiders such as political journalists about the character, causes and consequences of changes in newspapers' parliamentary coverage? Parliamentary reporting in *The Times*, *Guardian* and *Daily Mirror* between 1990 and 1994 was analysed to provide insights into the first question; interviews with senior political journalists working in print and broadcast media offer perspectives on the second. Evidence from both sources suggests that newspapers' parliamentary reports now fail to prescribe and explore a distinctive parliamentary agenda: discussions of parliament are subsumed under the broader terrain of 'politics' and coverage is structured by journalists' perceptions of what is newsworthy or what has news value. Less attention is given to serious contributions in the chamber than to gossip in Annie's Bar or the lobby. In the words of a distinguished political correspondent, 'everything is "lobbyised" these days . . . the separation between the gallery and the lobby, which is perhaps the really great demarcation dispute for this world, has completely broken down.' Consequently, the activities of government and prominent politicians enjoy a news prominence above reports detailing backbenchers' routine involvement in the proceedings of the House; there is a growing preference for stories reporting scandal or allegations of personal misconduct by individual MPs above analysis of important policy concerns such as education and health. Journalists offer a ready defence of such news priorities. 'Readers have become much more interested in what goes on behind the scenes than what is happening in the chamber,' claimed a senior political journalist. 'In that sense politics has become more like football. People are much more interested in reading about Cantona than the match.' Roy Hattersley offered a similar but more critical assessment in the 10th James Cameron memorial lecture, in which he bemoaned the increasing inclination to confuse 'politics and vaudeville' and for political journalists to trade in 'rumour, gossip and innuendo' (Hattersley, 1996, p. 2).

Jack Straw's study of newspaper reporting of parliamentary proceedings attributed the recent decline in coverage to the arrival of cameras in the Commons in 1989 combined with the retirement of senior political editors brought up in the gallery tradition (Straw, 1993). For their part, political journalists responded by suggesting that they were not downgrading parliamentary reporting but merely presenting politics in a different way (Riddell, 1995, p. 7). The neglect of parliament is recent. Barely a decade ago, Blumler summarised his review of the impact of sound broadcasting from parliament by claiming that, 'whatever complaints parliament might have with broadcasters, they should not complain about being ignored'. More than half the news items analysed by Blumler were 'solely or mainly parliamentary items, while three fifths included some mention of parliament . . . For British broadcasting,' he claimed, 'it can virtually be said that political news *is* parliamentary news' (Blumler, 1984, p. 258; emphasis in the original). Not so any more. One political correspondent described the change.

> Even when I started in parliamentary journalism about 22 years ago the *Times* had a very large room entirely staffed by people producing 'The Notice' – as it was called – which was at least an entire page every day of what was said in parliament. That was a huge operation; it wasn't much smaller than *Hansard*. We at the *Guardian* didn't sack, but we didn't replace, our last parliamentary reporter about a year and a half ago and the situation is the same everywhere.

A senior parliamentary correspondent, currently working in television broadcasting, confirms the changing fortunes of parliamentary coverage in newspapers across the last two decades:

> I started work in political reporting on the *Times* page in 1968. I was one of the 12 parliamentary reporters who used to do turns in the Commons taking shorthand notes; we did ten minutes for each question time and then twenty minutes for the debates. So I have seen during my career a complete reversal in reporting in the sense that you don't get that *Times* page record of what was said in parliament any more. You don't necessarily get anybody reporting a maiden speech, whereas we always used to report every maiden speech. There could

not be a more dramatic change in the sense that now all of the parliamentary reporting tends to be in sketch form. The only exception would be a very significant speech, a resignation speech or a budget. It would have to be an extremely prominent occasion before a speech would be reported verbatim which we used to do on the *Times* page. The *Guardian* of course, did have extensive parliamentary reporting, as did the *Telegraph* and the *Financial Times*. The *Times* did the most, but there were four papers which did a real 'Yesterday in Parliament' page.

The evidence to substantiate the decline in gallery reporting is more than anecdotal. Straw's study generated some dramatic findings. Coverage of parliamentary debates had reduced substantially from an average of between 400 and 800 lines in *The Times* and between 300 and 700 lines in the *Guardian* prior to 1988, to less than 100 lines in each paper by 1992. Straw reported no discernible long-term decline in parliamentary reports in the *Daily Mirror* although he conceded an initially lower baseline of coverage (Straw, 1993, p. 2).

The findings presented here derive from a study of all items of parliamentary coverage without regard to their location within the newspaper. The results confirm Straw's conclusion that journalists have come to consider parliamentary stories as being of little news significance. The 820 items of parliamentary coverage published in the *Guardian* (362 items or 13 per issue), *The Times* (346 items or 13 per issue) and the *Mirror* (112 items or 4 per issue), confirm the limited extent of reporting of parliamentary proceedings. But even this modest concern to report parliamentary affairs has not been sustained by some newspapers. *The Times* reduced its parliamentary coverage from 148 reports in 1990 to 111 in 1992, falling to 87 in 1994; a reduction of more than half across the four years. The *Guardian* has also reintroduced a parliamentary page (more accurately a 'half page') since April 1995 when the paper began to publish 'On the Record' – a selection of verbatim reports of parliamentary debates. But the *Mirror*, in line with Straw's findings, has increased its output of parliamentary stories, albeit from a very low baseline: 22 reports in 1990, 31 in 1992 and 57 in 1994.

When parliamentary stories are published they are typically given short shrift. Almost a tenth of newspapers' parliamentary reports analysed were less than 150 words, one quarter were less than 250 words and more than half (55 per cent) were less than 450 words in length. Such brevity may conform to the maxim of professional good practice which requires journalists to 'keep it simple, keep it straight', but surely fails to fulfil one of journalists' responsibilities in a democracy: namely to ensure their readers are informed about political affairs and thus enable them to make rational decisions, criticise governments and guarantee the accountability of governments. Some aspects of parliamentary proceedings are virtually ignored. The House of

Lords, for example, was mentioned in only 8 per cent of parliamentary reports across the five-year period.

But if the gallery tradition of reporting is all but lost, it is not wholly lamented. Some journalists believe 'it is unfortunate that we don't have gallery coverage'; another confirms that, 'one day I would like to see it brought back'. But the majority of journalists remain sceptical about the value and popularity of the previously extensive parliamentary reports with readers. 'When I was on the *Times*,' one journalist recalls, 'I fought to keep as much parliamentary coverage as we could, but certainly when surveys were conducted among our readers and when I finally lost the battles and a lot of the traditional gallery reporting was squeezed out, the surveys revealed it was only really MPs who were objecting because their names were not cropping up in reports any more . . . the general public seemed to be unconcerned about the change.' Editors are no longer persuaded by public-service arguments which suggest that the rationale for reporting parliament is not undermined by lack of reader demand – reporting of parliament is a central component in a parliamentary democracy and the latter is necessarily impoverished when the former diminishes. 'You can call it a decline in public service,' one journalist observed, 'but it is rather like taking off bus routes that nobody travels on.'

Other changes are evident in parliamentary reporting; at least four seem significant. First, the focus of parliamentary reports has shifted radically across the four years of the study. Items discussing personal scandal or allegations of misconduct by MPs now enjoy a greater prominence in parliamentary coverage than significant areas of government policy such as health, education and law and order. When the subject focuses of newspapers' parliamentary reports are rank ordered for frequency of appearance, 'scandal and misconduct' emerges as the third most popular from a list of 40 identified subject categories. Almost 1 in 10 of the 820 items of parliamentary coverage analysed focused on scandal and allegations of misconduct. This growing journalistic interest contrasts with the sharp decline in newspapers' coverage of education and local government which reduced fourfold and sixfold respectively across the period 1990 to 1994. Two significant points should be noted. The reporting of scandal constitutes an increasingly attractive focus for journalists' attentions across all types of newspapers. In 1990, scandal featured as the subject of only 8 reports from parliament; by 1992, it was 14; by 1994 it was 40. But this emphasis on scandal and misconduct is actually greater in some broadsheet papers than tabloids; it featured as the central ingredient in 40 *Guardian* stories (11 per cent of its parliamentary stories), 11 *Times* stories (3 per cent) and 11 *Mirror* stories (10 per cent).

A second trend is discernible: the growing journalistic preoccupation with the activities of government and senior politicians to the relative neglect of the back benches and the near wholesale exclusion of minority parties. One indicator of this trend is the prominence enjoyed by the Conservative party, which was governing during the period covered by the survey. The Conservatives enjoyed the 'lion's share' of coverage in almost three quarters (572) of published parliamentary stories, whereas the Labour party got an equivalent prominence in less than one fifth (138) of journalistic reports. Minority parties rarely achieve such news priority; parliamentary reporting is distinctly bi-partisan. The Labour and Conservative parties were the focus of journalistic attention on 710 of the 722 occasions (98 per cent) when a political party were prominent in coverage. By contrast, the Liberal Democrats were the prominent party on only nine (1 per cent) occasions. The six other parliamentary parties were relatively neglected; the same fate befell parties such as the Greens, who enjoyed no parliamentary representation but contributed to the broader political debate.

It is important to stress, of course, that these patterns do not necessarily reflect any press partisanship; any party might anticipate being the focus of attention when it is in government. Again, this reflects journalistic news values: the activities of government are inherently more attractive to journalists. Governments are the initiators of policy and events in the House; their statements and actions are authoritative and newsworthy. But while the *Guardian, The Times* and the *Mirror* each offer the Conservatives prominence in parliamentary reports, they do so to markedly different degrees. The *Guardian*, for example, offers prominence to the Conservatives above Labour in its parliamentary reports in the ratio of 3:1 (235 reports to 70). In *The Times,* however, the ratio is closer to 5:1 (246 to 51), while in the *Mirror* it is greater than 5:1 (91 to 17). It must be remembered that these figures do not express the direction of the coverage, favourable or unfavourable. Across all three newspapers, however, the ratio of reports in which the conservatives rather than Labour are prominent, has doubled from 2.5:1 (173 to 68) in 1990 to 5:1 (197 to 35) in 1994.

It is not only governments which journalists favour in their parliamentary reports. The extent of coverage received by different parliamentarians articulates parliamentary hierarchies. The higher up the parliamentary ladder that politicians manage to climb, the more substantial their public voice – at least as measured by the willingness of journalists to quote them. Back benchers in both the major parties speak with only a modest public voice. The opposition back benches were offered only 56 quotation opportunities which featured in 5 per cent of all parliamentary reports; equivalent figures for Conservative back benches were higher, at 114 quotations in 8 per cent of reports. But irrespective of party, journalists' preoccupation with senior politicians guarantees shadow spokespersons as much as government ministers greater opportunities to have their comments directly quoted in reports. Government ministers were quoted on 248 occasions in 26 per cent of parliamentary reports; the figures for shadow spokespeople were 166 in 18 per cent of reports. The prime minister enjoyed the maximum quotation opportunities: 77 quotations in 7 per cent of parliamentary reports. The leader of the opposition lagged slightly behind with 64 quotations in 6 per cent of reports. This focus of journalistic attention on senior parliamentary and political figures is perhaps even greater than the evidence here initially suggests. If particularly vociferous and currently newsworthy back benchers like Nicholas Budgeon and Bill Cash were excluded from calculatións, the skew in favour of the front bench would be considerably greater. Liberal Democrats, whatever their parliamentary rank, tend to fall victim to the evidently bi-partisan character of reporting. All Liberal Democrat politicians, including the leader, spokespeople for designated briefs and backbench MPs were offered quotation opportunities in only 3 per cent of parliamentary reports; the equivalent figure for the Conservative party was 41 per cent and for Labour 28 per cent.

The third new feature of parliamentary reporting is a growing trend for journalists to be highly critical in their appraisals of events in parliament. Across the study period, almost half (48 per cent) of journalists' reports were critical of politicians and parliamentarians, a quarter (22 per cent) were laudatory, with slightly more than a quarter (28 per cent) neither one or the other. But these figures conceal some significant points about journalists' attitudes to parliamentary affairs. First, both the *Guardian* and the *Mirror* display an increasingly critical slant: the number of critical reports in the *Guardian* increased from 54 in 1990 to 72 in 1994 and in the *Mirror* from 14 in 1990 to 48 in 1994; only *The Times* managed to reduce the critical stories from 40 in 1990 to 34 in 1994. Second, a related tendency is evident at *The Times*, where journalists seem increasingly reluctant to offer praise: laudatory comment characterised 45 reports in 1990 but only 19 in 1994. The *Guardian* and the *Mirror* displayed no significant decline in laudatory comment across the period: reduced from 21 to 18 in the *Guardian* and constant at six in the *Mirror*. Third, the ratio of critical to laudatory comment has increased significantly for reports published in the *Guardian* and the *Mirror*: from a ratio of 2.5:1 in 1990 to 4:1 in 1994 at the *Guardian*; from 2.5:1 to 8:1 at the *Mirror*. What is very striking is the extent of balance between critical and laudatory comment achieved across the study period in reports published by *The Times*: 104 critical reports compared to 102 laudatory ones. Fourth, the increasingly critical edge to the *Mirror*'s journalism across the period signals a lack of measured comment. This might be anticipated in a tabloid paper, but the critical to laudatory ratio of 8:1 reveals perhaps too little concern to provide a measured account for its readers. Fifth, to underscore the above point, there has been a reduction in the number of items in which the commentary was neither laudatory nor critical and of items in which commentary displayed both tendencies. The figures as a whole suggest that parliamentary coverage has become more polarised, less measured and less willing to be neutral in its appraisals of parliamentary affairs.

Finally, newspaper reports have offered parliamentarians few opportunities to articulate their views directly through quotations. Nearly half (47 per cent) of reports carried none, while a further 40 per cent contained only a very modest proportion of such materials (under 10 per cent of text length). Journalists are increasingly mediating between politicians and readers in their parliamentary reports. Three changes are apparent in the number and length of quotations across the period. First, the number without quotations has steadily declined from 132 (48 per cent) in 1990 to 110 (42 per cent) in 1994. Second, short quotations are increasingly likely to be reported: there has been an increase in those reports where they constitute under 10 per cent of the total text, from 89 (32 per cent) to 120 (46 per cent). Third, lengthier quotations seem less likely to be reported: the number of reports where quotations constitute 11–20% of the text have halved from 40 (15 per cent) to 22 (8 per cent); similar figures for reports where quotation materials constitute 21–30 per cent of the text show a reduction from 9 (3 per cent) to 6 (2 per cent). While politicians are more likely to be reported, therefore, their quotations are shorter. One interpretation here is that journalists are increasingly using politicians' soundbites. Predictably, quotations reflect seniority as noted above. Quotations by the prime minister and other ministers appeared on 325 occasions compared to 114 for the Conservative back benches, a ratio of almost 3:1 despite the greater numbers of back-benchers. Equivalent figures for Labour reveal 230 quotations by the leader of the opposition and shadow spokespersons compared with 56 for back-benchers, a ratio of more than 4:1.

But statistical profiles can fail to convey the substantive changes in journalistic style and parliamentary coverage which have occurred across the 1990s. Particular examples may prove more illustrative of recent trends in the range and quality of parliamentary coverage. It would be an easy matter, of course, simply to cite the copious coverage which both broadsheet and tabloid newspapers have devoted to the personal scandals involving MPs David Mellor, Tim Yeo, David Ashby, Graham Riddick and Neil Hamilton. But despite their relative frequency, such scandals remain exceptional. More routine coverage of parliamentary stories might better illustrate the personalised and narrow agenda which journalists now present in their reports.

On 17 January 1994, for example, the *Daily Mirror* devoted a double-page spread to parliamentary and political issues; it is unusual to find such extensive coverage in a tabloid newspaper. The headline across the two pages announced in large black letters, 'It's Civil War'. To the left of the headline a rosette graphic contained a picture of John Major's head and sported a logo claiming 'HE'S HISTORY'. Five political stories were reported. The main story was headlined 'The Blast Supper; Mystery Of Who Spilled No 10 Beans'and concerned a remark allegedly made by John Major at a dinner party for specially invited journalists, held in Downing Street, to mark the departure of Press Secretary Gus O'Donnell. Journalists from the *Sun* and *Mail*, who were not invited to the dinner, reported the remark in their newspapers the following day. There were potentially many issues for a political journalist to report, including the role of the lobby and news briefings, the increasingly collusive nature of relationships between the press and politicians and the question of why senior members of the press corps were dining at the PM's expense with the government's most senior press officer. The *Mirror*, however, was not interested in such matters – or at least was not concerned to report them. The first paragraph reveals the peg on which the journalist chose to hang the story and betrays much of the personalised and lightweight flavour of the piece.

> The mystery of the Downing Street dinner – or the big mouth at the feast – has turned into the decade's greatest political whodunnit. Did the Prime Minister really threaten to 'f—— crucify' Cabinet right wingers at a 'by special invitation dinner' for his departing press secretary? Or did a confidant over-embellish John Major's pre-dinner conversation hoping to prove his closeness to the PM?

The report continues by speculating that the informant might have been ITN lobby journalist Elinor Goodman but concedes 'it would take a detective with Inspector Clousseau's grasp of farce or the tortured logic of Inspector Morse to untangle the web of clues' (*Mirror*, 17 January 1994, p. 4). The parliamentary content and relevance of the story is slight. The second story, headlined 'Waller Admits It's My Baby', offered a brief (120 words), rather self-explanatory tale about 'Tory MP Gary Waller's' admission that 'he IS the father of a Commons secretary's love child'. The third story, headlined 'MP Defends £900,000 Council House Windfall', exposes 'Tory MP Teresa Gorman' for allegedly buying two houses from Westminster council for £55,000 and selling one for £445,000 while living in the other which is currently valued at £500,000; the whole story is reported in less than 100 words. The fourth story focuses on MP Peter Hain's request for a 'probe into house sales' in the London borough of Wandsworth (80 words), while the final story headlined 'PM On Trial' announced that John Major was to give evidence to the Scott inquiry during the coming week (150 words).

The front-page story of this issue of the *Mirror* confirms the paper's preference for personalised stories revealing alleged misconduct and scandal above discussions of policy debates. 'Major's New Skeleton; Charter Champ In £13 Millions Debts Probe' alleges that public relations 'boss' Angela Heylin, employed to 'rescue the Premier's ailing Citizen's Charter', had been unethical in her business affairs, prompting MPs to demand that 'she should be sacked' (*Mirror*, 17 January 1994, p. 1). Examination of other front pages reveals the newspaper's reluctance to address policy concerns. The *Mirror*'s front-page discussion of single-parent families, for example, featured two pictures of then Health Secretary Virginia Bottomley under the headline, 'I Was An Unwed Teenage Mum' (11 July 1992). More recently the *Mirror* reported the disruption of a military parade by the noise from a party thrown by Defence Secretary Michael Portillo, headlined 'Cops' Fury At Portillo's Yob Party' (*Mirror*, 7 June 1996, p. 5). An earlier story speculating on the sexual behaviour of some senior Conservative MPs reported political journalist David Seymour's belief that some Tory MPs keep their brains in their Y-Fronts; the headline was perhaps predictable: 'Y-Front Benchers' (*Mirror*, 3 June 1996). The list of examples to illustrate this recent trend in parliamentary journalism is as long as it is facile.

Even the general election fails to attract sustained and serious coverage. In 1992 election coverage in the tabloid newspapers was noticeable by its absence. The *Sun* and *Mirror* both led with the election story on only 9 of the 22 days of the campaign; the *Star* headlined election on only 4 days of the 4-week campaign (Franklin, 1994, p. 153). In 1997 coverage followed a similar pattern. On 18 March the *Sun* announced its 'historic decision' to offer support of the Labour party; 'The Sun Backs Blair; Give Change A Chance' its headline declared. The paper's belief that its previous support for the Conservatives had been influential was captured by Kelvin MacKenzie's boastful headline that 'It Was The Sun Wot Won It'. In 1997 the paper was similarly convinced of its significance to the electoral outcome and with stunning lack of originality declared, 'It's The Sun Wot Swung It' (*Sun*, 2 May, p. 2). The *Mirror*, which traditionally supports Labour and was rather churlish about the *Sun*'s newly found enthusiasm for the party, claimed with a similar lack of creative thinking, 'IT WAS TONY WOT WON IT . . . With A Little Help From His Loyal Friends . . . *Mirror* Readers' (*Mirror*, 2 May, p. 2). But the *Sun* was evidently delighted that the election was finally over allowing the paper to devote its editorial energies to the kind of stories it prefers. The paper's 'S-EXIT POLL', which featured 12 colour photographs of topless and scantily clothed young women, asked readers, 'Sick of the election? Reckon you've seen enough polls to last you a lifetime? Well think again, cos I've got some hustings to get you lusting! Today the campaign begins to elect the world's sexiest woman' (*Sun*, 2 May 1997, pp. 16–17). The *Star* (which added OOH, AHH, SWINGO-METAAH to its usual masthead) was also eager to connect election politics and sex. A photograph of Tony Blair captioned 'Things Can Tony Get Better – It's All Coming Up Red Roses', had to share the front page with a picture of topless model 'Gorgeous Gaynor Goodman' wearing suspenders and stockings, which was headed 'It's A New Dawn . . . Er, Actually It's Gaynor' (*Star*, 2 May 1997, p. 1). The extent of tabloid journalism's move down market can be measured by journalists' belief that this mix of soft pornography and newszak might pass for popular political humour and satire.

Journalists' perspectives on changing trends in parliamentary reporting

Political journalists hold quite divergent perceptions of the causes of recent changes. In interviews, they offered five possible explanations for the changes detailed above. These perspectives can be labelled: the journalist critics, the media pluralists, the MP publicity seekers, parliamentarians in decline, and the bored reader. Most journalists tend to subscribe predominantly to one of these accounts, although they may draw elements from a number in their efforts to explain the evident changes in parliamentary coverage.

The journalist critics

Some journalists believe the changes are part of a broader decline in journalistic standards prompted by deregulation and new technology; it is not unusual for Rupert Murdoch's name to be mentioned in this context. The decline in reporting from the chamber is self-evident,' claimed a senior political journalist,

> and it is explained by a gravitational force of decline in journalism which has taken place in our lifetime . . . which I place at the feet of that giant Rupert Murdoch and the standards he propagated so successfully . . . The *Times'* parliamentary page gradually got crushed. It was the last thing to get crushed and many other things got crushed on the way . . . there was actually one occasion when I wrote a story of 3–400 words, which was worth a story of 3–400 words, but they only used the Intro and it was completely meaningless – something like 'The PM fell under a bus last night' . . . so much has died in the pressure for good sexy news stories . . . But you can't defy gravity. That is why I used the phrase deliberately. It is a gravitational force of decline.

Others interpret the change in practice as a consequence of media deregulation. 'Deregulated media have led to enormous changes and a much more aggressive and competitive environment for journalism; less reporting from the gallery and more naked women broadly speaking . . . When Tory MPs complain about it to me, I say well you voted for deregulated media and you gave Rupert Murdoch what he has got, so you must bloody well live with it.' Deregulation is believed to have significant consequences for editorial content: 'There is a market-oriented, down-market agenda running,' the political correspondent of a broadsheet newspaper claimed, 'but it's not good enough to say that you are only giving the readers what they want, that's like the justification for hard core pornography. I'm not a libertarian in such matters.'

The pace of the decline has been accelerated by the advent of new technology which no longer requires journalists to be present in the chamber and reduces their contact with the House and its procedures. 'The whole process of news gathering and by extension of political reporting, has got much faster,' a journalist claimed, 'faxes, on-line newspaper offices, cable television and information highways mean that I can sit in my room and watch events on television rather than sit in the chamber.'

The media pluralists

Media pluralists argue that the decline in gallery reporting in newspapers is simply one consequence of the burgeoning of political reporting in other media (Riddell, 1995, p. 7). Complaints fail to understand how the nature of political debate has changed. Ministers and senior politicians used to make significant public statements in the House or in set-piece speeches, but now they prefer television. Broadcast media offer politicians a very desirable platform from which they can reach an audience measured in millions. Television has become an alternative forum to the chamber for the propagation of political ideas. A prominent sketch-writer observed, 'I have counted as many as seven camera crews on College Green at any one time and that implies seven MPs and there is likely to be less than seven MPs in the chamber at that time.' A different journalist was even more explicit: 'Every politician who goes across the Green to be interviewed is selling the chamber out.'

The number of broadcasting outlets has expanded considerably in recent years. Broadcasters have also allocated greater airtime to political programming. Sunday-morning broadcasting has become a political ghetto in which Frost, Dimbleby, Humphreys and Walden interrogate a succession of politicians eager to try to set the agenda of political discussion for the coming week. Consequently, Peter Riddell argues that 'ministers and shadows are popping up throughout the day from the favourite slot of 7.50 on the *Today* programme until 11.00 p.m. on *Newsnight*. There is a continuum of news and comment which does not stop on weekends but rather intensifies with the Sunday morning and lunchtime chat shows.'

The advent of cameras in the Commons in 1989 is a related phenomenon, but few journalists support Straw's contention that the televising of proceedings has been central to the decline in press interest. On the contrary, most believe that televising proceedings has opened up interest in the chamber. 'Much more important than the cameras in the chamber,' claimed one journalist, 'has been the existence of Millbank and the studios there; a major television facility five minutes away which instead of talking heads has something more interesting to watch.' All confirmed the significance of the Millbank complex of studios. 'Millbank is an extraordinary phenomenon. An entire media city. It has become the centre for political reporting, much more so than the House. If you want to find an MP, Millbank is the place to do it rather than the House. I have had some very interesting and informative conversations waiting for make up and there is no way round that.' Hoggart believes that 'the real political news is made not at the Commons but in the great broadcasting emporium at no 4 Millbank' (Hoggart, April 1995a, p. 6). Print journalists believe the succession of Sunday-morning talk shows are best described as 'cheap' television which is watched 'by no one except junkies and political correspondents'. It also offers, they believe, a 'perfect example of collaboration between the politicians and television'. Some are evidently resentful about politicians' preference for broadcast media.

Publicity-crazed MPs

Some journalists lay the blame for the reduction in gallery reporting from the House squarely with MPs themselves. MPs have become 'publicity crazed', trying to manipulate the media to promote their own agendas, favoured policies or personal careers. A senior BBC journalist claimed that some MPs 'undoubtedly value their appearances on television more than they value their appearances in the House'. There are, of course, a number of strategies for achieving publicity, but two were judged by journalists to be particularly significant.

First, MPs organise press conferences, usually in the morning, which can preempt events in the chamber. A distinguished parliamentary reporter blames the publicity strategies of individual MPs for the declining press attention to parliament.

> MPs have suddenly realised they have a captive audience in the Westminster press corps and they now arrange far more events in the morning. This means that every day there are three or four press conferences. From about six in the morning, the press gallery is staffed by reporters and it's only in about the last three to five years that the most enterprising MPs have realised that this can be exploited . . . and they time it so that it doesn't clash with the 11 a.m. Downing Street lobby briefing, so that by lunchtime most subs' desks and copy tasters have got enough political stuff to fill the papers and now often they will only use the highlights from the chamber. Politicians are themselves responsible for this decline in straight reporting of House of Commons debates.

The growing significance of standing and select committees, which also sit in the morning, means that industrious reporters may have gathered a good deal of political news by lunchtime. Add to this the changes to newspaper deadlines, which have moved forward, so that 'you're lucky if you can get a story in the first edition of the *Sun* after about one o'clock in the afternoon', and the simple organisational disincentives to reporting the later events in the House become clear.

Second, publicity-conscious MPs exploit soundbites. These terse 'ear-catching' phrases have become, in one journalist's phrase, 'the main medium of political exchange'. Soundbites are designed both to catch the attention of the political journalist and to capture the essence of a particular subject in a few words. They are a political shorthand which offer journalists headlines. They are mercilessly pursued by MPs with little regard for the consequences for the quality of political debate. For their part, journalists feel less compelled to report the sustained exchange of views in a parliamentary debate than the catchy soundbite. A sketch-writer offers an example of the impact on debate:

> Blair will have a Campbell soundbite to throw at the prime minister and as he starts the Tory hooligans and yobbos boo him and bray, but he will return to the soundbite time and time again to make sure that the TV companies have a good clear version that they can use. Five seconds or whatever which amounts to about fifteen words. If the debate is about the salaries of executives in what used to be the nationalised industries, the soundbite might be 'monopoly capitalists paying themselves monopoly money'.

Some MPs have increasingly come to prefer appearances in media to appearances in the House. The strategies they adopt to promote their particular interests are, some journalists believe, at the root of the decline in newspapers' parliamentary reporting.

Parliament in decline

None of the journalists interviewed believed that the changes in newspaper reporting of proceedings could be attributed solely or even predominantly to changes in the character of the House, its proceedings, or its members. All of them, however, mentioned such changes as a subsidiary explanation. Six particular changes were mentioned.

First, journalists claimed the House was no longer *the* centre of political interest but merely one among a number of political arenas; 'power has dribbled away from the chamber', a journalist claimed. Second, the quality of debate has diminished because the 'quality of MPs is much diluted'. Many journalists believed that broadly speaking, 'oratorical skills have disappeared. There is no one making speeches like they used to make speeches.' Third, events in the chamber have become rather predictable, in part reflecting the large inbuilt majorities enjoyed by governments thoughout the 1980s. So far as journalists are concerned, predictable stories are not newsworthy. The marginal majority enjoyed by the Major government, undermined by the 'whipless Euro-rebels' during 1995, created new possibilities for stories. A journalist on the *Telegraph* claimed that 'stories are basically about disagreements and rows and controversy. When a group like the Euro-rebels threaten to topple a government there is a story and they will get coverage, substantial coverage.' Modifying Lyndon Johnson's rather robust metaphor on how best to deal with critics, the journalist continued, 'it is always more interesting to have the views of those who are outside the tent pissing in than it is to report members of the Labour party whose job it is to piss in.' Fourth, journalists believe certain key features of parliamentary proceedings have been debased. The twice-weekly Prime Minister's

Questions have allegedly become a farce, with planted questions and predictable answers. In the words of one journalist, 'it has become a rabble of soundbites and shouting designed to capture the bulletins.' Tony Blair, responding at least in part to such criticisms, announced in May 1997 a reform to reduce PMQs to a single weekly session on Wednesdays.

Fifth, journalists argue that governments have become more adept at managing media. Less than 40 years ago, the 14-day rule prohibited broadcast discussion of any issue likely to be before parliament in the coming two weeks. Government statements were made in the House; they were exciting events. But this has changed. Government announcements are 'fine tuned much earlier now', with the announcement in the Commons much less of a surprise than previously; only resignation statements are unpredictable. 'So much of the government's business is stage-managed,' one journalist suggested, 'that the drama has been taken out of it.'

Sixth, the sheer expansion of government in some senses makes the House less newsworthy. What one journalist described as the 'overmighty power of the executive' means that the 'payroll vote', embracing ministers and personal parliamentary secrtaries, is 'up to about 130 by now. None of them talk except when they are paid to. You are left with old troopers, Ted Heath, Peter Shaw, Tony Benn and Enoch Powell.'

All journalists believed that politicians were held in a declining regard both by journalists and by the general public. In interview, many laughed when the question was posed. One cited an early sketch-writer on the *Guardian* who explained why he always refused drinks from politicians: 'I don't like to meet them,' he claimed, 'it might spoil the purity of my hatred.' Another commented that 'the letters we get from readers suggest they regard politicians as pretty unspeakable.'

Bored readers and viewers

In much the same way that each of the journalists interviewed cited changes in parliament and its procedures as a trigger for the declining number and changing character of newspaper reports from the House, the great majority spoke about what they variously described as a 'bored' or 'uninterested' readership. Adopting the discourse of the market, the widely expressed view was that the decline in published reports from the House was 'demand led'.

Some journalists explain the apparent lack of interest as a consequence of the 'sheer pace of life'. Few people (perhaps only politicians, journalists and academics) have the time to 'plough through long reports of Commons proceedings. Most people want a rapid digest, the essential news, selected and processed for them by others. That is part of the journalist's job.' Others explain readers' alleged lack of interest by reference to broader social and cultural changes, in part triggered by media themselves.

I think the public's taste has changed as a response to being led by Rupert Murdoch . . . because of television, because of changes in society. Speak to any teacher and they will tell you how much more difficult it is to get the attention of children and students. How do you compete for the attention of a student whose attention span is as long as a soap, or as long as a pop song or a video? I used to be a teacher . . . but teachers now tell me that there is nothing they can do short of taking their clothes off to get the attention of these children and similarly journalists find it difficult to attract the attention of readers unless they are taking their clothes off or other people's clothes off. But if we are then, in that atmosphere, to present them with a page of parliamentary debate – Christ!

While journalists explained the lack of reader interest in parliamentary reports in different ways, no one denied it. Some argued for a return to a fuller provision of gallery coverage on public-service grounds, but most conceded this to be unlikely given the competitive climate in which contemporary journalism is conducted. Journalists believe that many reports of parliament proceedings will be spiked for the foreseeable future.

Parliamentary journalism and systemic change

These five accounts by journalists may be identified as separate explanations for changes in the extent and character of parliamentary reporting. Alternatively, the five perspectives may be interpreted as being connected: they all illustrate broader changes in Britain's political communications system since the mid-1980s. If this is the case, there is another conclusion to be drawn. If changes in parliamentary reporting reflect deeper, more systemic changes, then the likelihood of reversing them is diminished. Systemic factors will be more resistant to reversal.

Changes to both the media-communications and political aspects of the political communications system seem clear; change has been endemic in British media since the mid-1980s. Policy proposals from the Peacock Report (1986) to the recent Broadcasting Act 1996 have triggered extensive changes within media structures, the economic organisation of media industries and the range and quality of their editorial output. The deregulation of radio and television has created a highly competitive environment for media industries prompting market-driven efficiencies including staff cuts, and the market imperative to generate low-cost popular programming. This has contributed to variable and declining standards of news and current-affairs journalism. Concerns about an alleged 'move down market' or the adoption of a 'tabloid agenda' have been expressed about programming at both ITN and the BBC. One journalist claimed that 'Competition means that the chase is on for the mass market and people tend to be going downmarket . . .

the managerial mood is that there isn't a demand for a really sharply written look back on the week with illustrations of what people said . . . programmes must be more "accessible", so there is a new phone-in called *On Line* where we get an MP in and people can fax or ring in on their video phones and ask MPs questions.' Edited highlights of debates from the floor of the House have been increasingly replaced by the more fashionable 'two-way' between the journalist in the studio and the journalist on College Green or outside Number 10. Increased competition in broadcast media in part reflects the proliferation of broadcast media outlets in recent years: the development of breakfast television, the launch of Channel 4, the provision of 24-hour television, developments in cable and satellite programming including BSkyB's 24-hour rolling news provision, BBC Radio 5 Live committed to 24-hour news programming, as well as the explosion of local BBC and ILR radio services.

Newspapers, at least to the same degree as broadcast media, must be aware of competition. The long-term post-war decline in titles and circulations has given rise to intense competition for readers and advertisers and has undoubtedly prompted sharp editorial judgements. As one journalist observed, 'At the moment there is great demand for advertising space in this paper and we are trying to maximise our profits and I suppose in terms of our political coverage we are giving the minimum of what a quality newspaper ought to be giving.' Another journalist commented, 'there is a terrible paranoia among broadsheet papers recently. Yes, it's worthy, but does it interest or excite and I think a view is taken that parliamentary coverage is not sufficiently interesting to justify doing it.'

These are radical changes to what was previously a very stable system of broadcast and print media which had evolved rather slowly across the greater part of the twentieth century. But there have been equivalent and to some extent complementary changes in the political system.

The 1990s has witnessed the 'packaging of politics' and a growing publicity awareness among politicians inside and outside parliament (Franklin, 1994). Media presentation of policies and politicians is seen as central to political, but especially electoral, success. Much of the campaigning strategy of governments, political parties, interest groups, politicians and parliamentarians is now devoted to media management designed to secure media coverage – but of the right kind! The phrase 'spin doctor' has entered the everyday vocabulary of politics. This change has coincided with, and seems to rely upon, a growing presidentialism in politics, a concern with personalities above policy and issue discussions; a belief that it is certain kinds of politicians, rather than policies, which attract voters, readers and viewers. Politics has decamped from smoke-filled rooms into air-conditioned studios. The television complex at Millbank (redesignated 'Mandelsonbank' by one journalist) was literally 'made' for this style of politics. The arrival of television in the Commons feeds the process; Prime Minister's Questions has been subverted by the soundbite culture of contemporary politics.

Parliament has also changed; the House is no longer the central political forum. MPs' competencies are judged to have declined; parliamentary events have become predictable and the business of the House is increasingly stage-managed by government. In December 1995, former speaker of the House, Lord Wetherill, lent his voice to the growing concerns expressed by senior politicians about the declining prestige and effectiveness of the Commons. 'Today the action has moved from the floor of the House to the select committees,' he claimed, 'so that apart from a few set-piece debates, the chamber is dead and, to a large extent, irrelevant' (*Guardian*, 19 December 1995, p. 9).

Public scepticism about politicians as individuals and as a group capable of effecting change seems rife. Newspaper sales routinely fall as they begin to report the general election; viewing figures for the extended television news bulletins during elections invariably collapse. There exists a growing public apathy concerning politics and in the increasingly competitive market in which journalism must be conducted, it seems unlikely that journalists will provide a news agenda the public appears not to want.

12

Pelvic news and proven winners

Regulating broadcast media

The decade since the mid-1980s has witnessed substantial changes to the financial, organisational and regulatory structures of British broadcasting. The various provisions of the Broadcasting Acts 1990 and 1996, reflecting the radical political environment of the 1980s which championed market forces and the deregulation of broadcast media, have generated a multi-channel system of broadcasting informed by new philosophies and funded by a diverse mix of finance embracing the licence fee, advertising revenues and subscription.

In the public sector, the National Heritage Report *The Future of the BBC* recommended retention of the licence fee (Cmnd 2098 p. 31), but the BBC in *Responding to the Green Paper* expressed a commitment to expanding the commercial side of its operations through co-productions, programme sales, merchandising and the development of cable and satellite (BBC, 1993a, p. 49) and introducing an internal market via the system of 'producer choice' (ibid., pp. 40–2). The July 1994 white paper *The Future of the BBC: Serving The Nation, Competing World Wide* recommended renewal of the BBC's charter from January 1997 but proposed a review of the licence fee in 2001. The white paper also encouraged the BBC to develop its commercial activites to embrace the launch of new commercial cable, satellite and terrestrial services at home and abroad. In January 1997, the BBC board of governors negotiated a joint-venture agreement with Flextech to establish up to eight pay-TV channels for broadcast on a subscription basis to 5 million British homes (Horsman, 1997, p. 15).

These changes have proved predictably contentious. Critics allege that their overall consequence has been to supplant a broadcasting system based on the tradition of public service with one which is more sensitive to market forces but less able to deliver the quality and range of programming which characterised its predecessor (Hetherington, 1989, Nossiter, 1986, Davidson, 1993, Franklin, 1994 and Williams, 1994). Advocates such as Michael Green, chief executive of Carlton Television, dismiss the charges, alleging that their opponents' vision has merely become clouded by 'the myth of a lost golden age of British television'. In his Fleming Memorial Lecture, Green argued that 'It does a disservice to the future to claim that the general programme quality of the past represents a high plateau of achievement from which we must inevitably slide downhill as competition bites and as new technology overturns the old certainties' (Fleming Memorial Lecture, 19 April 1994).

Senior figures in broadcasting, whose longevity in their posts provides an element of continuity across the two systems, have articulated some concerns about recent changes in programming. David Glencross, then chief executive at the ITC, in a speech to the Royal Television Society, for example, observed that while there is much to applaud in the current diet of programming on commercially funded television, 'there are some general programme issues which do arise' (Glencross, 1994). He shares the anxieties of American commentators that 'factual programming is on a downward path towards the triumph of infotainment over both information and entertainment'. This is what John Chancellor of NBC described in his 1993 Alastair Cooke lecture as 'pelvic news' based on the scheduling philosophy 'if it bleeds it leads' (ibid., p. 7). Glencross regrets the 'many more programmes recollecting and reconstructing crime, vicarious exposure of disasters or near disasters and exploitations of the sex lives of the famous and not so famous' (ibid., p. 8). Overall, he argues that the Channel 3 network requires 'a little more adventure and risk . . . An occasional evening dip in the ratings does not spell the end of life as we know it' (ibid.). He concedes that 'these kinds of programmes can be shown to deliver quite large audiences', but finds it 'a bit surprising that the BBC has followed suit or, in some cases, led the way with programmes like *How Do You Do That*, Michael Buerk's *Dial 999* and the series about East End gangsters'.

The black art of scheduling and pelvic news?

There is at least prima facie evidence to support Glencross's concerns about changes to ITV's factual programming. Thames Television's *This Week*, *First Tuesday* and *Viewpoint* have been 'dumped by competitive scheduling' to be replaced by *The Big Story* and *3D* which are both more populist and story-led rather than issue-led in their approach (Clarke, 1993, p. 6). Carlton Television's series *The Day I Nearly Died*, which reconstructed a series of tragic disasters including the death of football fans at Hillsborough, the Lockerbie plane crash and the Kings Cross Underground fire, seemed to exemplify Glencross's concerns (Pilkington, 1994, p. 6). In answer to allegations from charities working with victims that the programmes would 'turn tragedies into entertainment', the controller of factual programmes at Carlton claimed the series was 'in the best tradition of British documentary making' (ibid.). The change of style should perhaps not have proved so surprising. When Marcus Plantin was appointed network director for Channel 3 on 30 September 1992, he claimed he enjoyed 'the black art of scheduling'. In future decisions about programme scheduling, he committed himself to 'placing more emphasis on proven audience winners' (Henry, 1 October 1992, p. 3).

News at Ten: *'The mass of viewers are not interested in serious news'*

For many critics, ITN's *News At Ten* symbolises the growing supremacy of market pressures to attract audiences and advertisers over journalists' commitments to provide news and factual programming. In June 1993 the ITV Network Centre announced its intention to move ITN's *News At Ten,* which had occupied the 10 o'clock slot in the schedules for 26 years, to an earlier time to allow the uninterrupted showing of films and drama after the 9 p.m. adult viewing watershed. The Channel 3 network loses it ratings lead at 10 p.m. but, since two thirds of advertising revenues are earned between 6.30 and 10.30 p.m., sustaining prime-time audiences and advertisers is crucial. An extraordinary alliance of the prime minister, the leader of the opposition, the secretary of state for national heritage, as well as a cross-party group of MPs, opposed the move. The ITC insisted that since 8 of the 15 regional ITV companies had made a commitment to broadcasting news at 10 p.m. as a condition of their licences the commission was prepared to take legal action to hold them to that commitment.

The Network Centre formally withdrew the proposal but given Plantin's enthusiasm for the 'black art of scheduling', the feeling in ITV was 'no longer if *News at Ten* will be moved but when' (Clarke, 1993, p. 6). There have been a number of straws in the wind. In a speech to the Edinburgh Television festival, Plantin expressed his continued intention to change the timing of the evening news and rid the network of the 'corset of fixed points in the schedule' (Culf, 31 August 1993, p. 7). In November 1993 the ITV Network Centre hired lobbyists Ian Greer Associates in an effort to persuade backbench Conservative MPs of 'the commercial advantage to ITV of switching the news to 7 p.m.' (Culf, 12 November 1993, p. 2). In June 1995, Barry Cox, director of the ITV Association, felt it necessary, following criticism from advertisers about schedules and audiences in May, to announce that attempts to move *News at Ten* to an earlier or later slot were definitely 'not back on the agenda' (*Guardian*, 17 June 1995, p. 12). More recently, in a speech to the Broadcast Press Guild, Bruce Gyngell, head of Yorkshire Television, announced his belief that 'the mass of viewers' are not interested in 'serious news' and declared that 'to his dying day' he would 'use every effort in my power to have *News at Ten* moved' (Kelly, 27 November 1995, p. 14). The determination to end *News at Ten's* 'disruption' of the evening schedules is clearly still on the agenda of significant players.

World in Action, ITV's oldest and perhaps most prestigious current affairs programme, offers a second example of the pressure which competition for ratings between BBC and ITV can apply to well-established and highly regarded current affairs programming; on 7 April 1994 *World in Action* was dropped from the schedules for two months. Replaced by a bumper edition of the soap opera *Coronation Street* and a James Bond film, the Network believed *World in Action* could not deliver sufficiently large audiences in competition against the BBC's additional episode of its popular soap *East Enders*; *World in Action*'s average audiences are 8.1 million. David Plowright, the creator of *World in Action* who was sacked from Granada Television in February 1992 following a dispute about programming policy, claimed it was 'a severe blow for serious current affairs journalism' and a 'further manifestation of the consequences of deregulation that encourages TV executives to treat viewers as consumers rather than citizens requiring a public service' (quoted in *UK Press Gazette*, 10 January 1994, p. 10).

There is other evidence to suggest a lesser importance for news and current affairs programming in the commercial sector of broadcasting. On 4 May 1994, for example, the ITC relaxed the quota of news and current affairs specified in the licence of breakfast television company GMTV. Under the new terms of its licence, GMTV's commitment to current affairs programming was reduced from a minimum 3 hours 47 minutes each week to 2 hours 30 minutes. The company denied that the 'easing' of its licence terms would 'signal a move downmarket' (Culf, 5 May 1994, p. 10).

Similar trends are evident in regional television and prompt equivalent concerns. Yorkshire Television, for example, has moved a new 'high quality current affairs programme, *Edit Five*, which specialises in heavyweight investigative journalism' out of prime time to a 10.40 slot. The daily news programme *Calendar* continues to devote the first half of its programme to 'hard news reporting' but has adopted a 'lighter more tabloid approach' to the second half. It is now a 'news magazine programme rather than a 100 per cent news programme' and there is some concern about 'the very inconsequential nature of some of the items which are appearing in what after all is the main news magazine programme of the day'.

News at Ten: *going down market?*

Changes to news and current affairs programming extend beyond rescheduling, with some observers increasingly concerned about programmes moving down market and adopting a tabloid agenda because of pressures to attract audiences and advertisers. The starting point for this shift in journalistic style has sometimes been identified as November 1992, when, having celebrated 25 years of broadcasting, the format of *News at Ten* was extensively 'revamped'. The new hi-tech graphics which opened the programme and the replacement of two presenters with a single newscaster was considered to be 'a sign that ITN is gearing itself up for the new more competitive world' (Henry, 4 July 1992, p. 3). But the presentation of news too often seems to obscure the clarity of the story. Apocalyptic theme tunes, remarkable graphics and virtual reality backdrops, which seem more appropriate to entertainment than news programmes, have become commonplace. Veteran ITN reporter Desmond Hamill offers consolation to 'poor old Trevor McDonald sitting in the Starship Enterprise setting, as if he is about to blast off into outer space, calling up his reporters on these "Big Brother is watching you" screens' (quoted in *J'Accuse the News*, Channel 4, 1 November 1994). ITN rejects the charge that it is going 'downmarket' but David Mannion, then head of ITV programmes, conceded that there would be 'more emphasis on the "human side". News must be interesting and it must be accessible.' Citing a report on the collapse of the economy in the former Soviet Union which featured a woman selling her child to make ends meet, Mannion suggested that 'the idea' was 'to make the big issues relate to people's lives in a way that sometimes statistics don't' (Mannion in *Guardian*, 4 July 1992, p. 3).

A study comparing the content of ITN News at 5.40 p.m., BBC1 News at 6.00 p.m., SkyNews at 5.00 p.m. and Radio 4 News at 6.00 p.m., concluded that increased competition and market pressures were significant factors shaping programme contents and that 'ITN and Sky operate to a tabloid agenda while BBC TV and radio operate to a more serious one' (Gabor and Barnett, 1993, p. 8). Six findings informed this conclusion. First, BBC news is more likely to eschew a narrow domestic agenda in favour of foreign news. Stations allocated significantly different percentages of broadcast time to foreign news: BBC1 22 per cent, ITN 11 per cent, Sky 9 per cent and Radio 4 20 per cent (ibid., p. 9). Second, ITN reported a greater number of stories about sport, television and show business: ITN 27 per cent, Sky 23 per cent, BBC1 15 per cent, Radio 4 11 per cent (ibid., p. 9). Third, BBC television and radio news were more likely to report industry and business news: BBC1 11 per cent, Radio 4 8 per cent, ITN 5 per cent and Sky 0 per cent (ibid.). Fourth, while all news organisations allocated considerable time to reports about Northern Ireland, there were significant differences in the percentage of time devoted to reports about *violence* rather than the *politics* of Northern Ireland. The 13 per cent of airtime devoted to Northern Ireland by Radio 4, for example, divided into 10 per cent politics and 3 per cent violence; for BBC television the division was 10 per cent and 5 per cent. For ITN, however, the 16 per cent airtime allocated to Northern Ireland split equally between politics and violence, as did the 27 per cent of Sky's airtime (ibid.). Fifth, the format as well as the content of news was assessed. The average length of BBC1 items was 2 minutes 8 seconds; for ITN 1 minute 30 seconds (ibid.). Research on television news in eight countries conducted by Heinderyckx, confirmed the BBC's preference for lengthy reports (Heinderyckx, 1993, p. 430). Distinguished journalist John Simpson believes the length of news items is a significant indicator of an organisation's journalistic integrity. 'Depend on it,' he claimed in the Huw Weldon Lecture in 1994, 'a news organisation whose reports get consistently shorter than say two minutes is going down market – it's an infallible sign.' On this judgement, 'downmarket' would provide an adequate assessment of ITN's news provision for Channel 4's *Big Breakfast* where the average length of news stories is 13 seconds with some as brief as 8 seconds (see chapter 9). Finally, ITN displayed a greater enthusiasm for including live material and 'two-ways' between the newscaster and reporter, designed to give pace and immediacy to reports. Only 1 per cent of BBC1 airtime was devoted to live reports compared to 19 per cent for ITN and 32 per cent for Sky (Gabor and Barnett, 1993, p. 9).

A more recent study which compared a sample of *News at Ten* programmes broadcast prior to the Broadcasting Act 1990 with an equivalent sample broadcast in 1995, confirmed much of Barnett and Gabor's analysis (Pilling, 1995). Findings revealed: a substantial decline in international news from 43 per cent of content in 1990 to 15 per cent in 1995 (ibid., p. 13); an increase in entertainment and sports news from 8.5 per cent to 17 per cent (ibid.); a reduction in average story length from 2 minutes 10 seconds to 1 minute 45 seconds (ibid., p. 14); and a proliferation of live 'two-way' interviews. Other aspects of ITN's changing programme philosophy included the cultivation of star journalists (Michael Brunson) and presenters (Trevor McDonald), the near-obsessive use of video graphics and a general emphasis on the packaging of news (ibid., p. 26). Ex-ITN foreign correspondent Desmond Hamill claims that if, like ITN, 'you are obsessed with ratings, you've got to give a much weightier balance to entertainment rather than information. Now if that's the way it's going to be, fine, then I wish those editors and the people who run TV would spare us this sanctimonious nonsense about nothing changing . . . It does' (Hamill, *J'Accuse the News*, Channel 4, 1 November 1994).

A senior executive at ITN echoes Mannion's view that the language of 'upmarket', 'downmarket' and 'infotainment' can be misleading and inappropriate. He believes news stories can be divided into two distinctive categories. In the first category belong those stories which 'are of such overriding importance that, while they might not have any direct affect on the viewer, they need to be reported anyway'. He cites events in Bosnia and Rwanda as examples of such stories. 'But there is a second level of stories' which interest 'British viewers and affect their daily lives'; issues such as 'what's going on in Britain's schools? and what's going on Britain's roads?' These stories are not 'infotainment or tabloid stories, I think they are just good interesting news stories but they don't have some of the more traditional entry points of the news stories' (Interview).

The distinction between the two categories of stories rests upon a revised perception of the role of the reporter which reflects a lesser emphasis on public-service commitments and a greater stress on the need to provide stories which interest viewers – a market consideration. ITN is not a broad-caster but a provider of programmes which must meet the requirements of broadcasters.

> There is a massive difference between ITN and the BBC. BBC news is part of the BBC. ITN news is on a contract. We are an independent supplier to ITV. All programmes on ITV are made by suppliers on a contract to the Network Centre which specifies the nature of the pro-grammes it wants. So all I am, to denigrate myself, is the guy who gives the customers what they want. I am not taking a higher, purer judge-ment which my counterpart at the BBC is – this is what the British peo-ple deserve or should have. I am saying this is what the customer is paying me £50 million pounds a year to make and I'm pretty unapolo-getic about that.

Consequently it is 'the broadcasters who have decided where they want to position themselves in the market. ITV wants to position itself in one place, *Channel 4 News* wants a different place. ITV has decided they want to do more stories which are of relevance to the British viewer.' But ratings are the crucial determinants; the audience is sovereign.

> I'm much more analytical now in terms of ratings. I mean I have rat-ings information coming out of my ears overnight. I know on a minute by minute basis what time people turn off and on during the previous night's news. I'm having that developed into a schematic analysis for the production team to see, so we are more and more focused on the maximisation of the audience ratings.

The news editor in the reformed British broadcasting system is consigned to the role of an 'ambassador' attempting to reconcile the potentially conflict-ing demands of the broadcaster for stories which will interest audiences and the regulator's requirement for high journalistic standards: 'I understand what ITV want and I understand what the regulator wants and I'm trying to pitch the programmes in a way that meets both aspirations. If ITV ask for something which I believe the regulator will not accept, I will tell them that.'

In regional newsrooms changing news values, prompted by the same requirement to attract audiences, seem to display a similar trend towards journalistically less 'hard' stories. A comparative study of regional news output by the BBC and Meridien Television revealed the latter's much greater reliance on crime stories and a marked emphasis on sport as well as the more frequent use of items based on two-way exchanges between jour-nalists (Campbell, 1994, p. 21). The emergence of particular news formats such as two-ways may have an economic root. News is expensive and con-sequently local programmes may be 'filled out' with other material. In America this has been occurring for a good while and Altheide believes that it is economic pressures which generate ' "happy talk" formats, involving anchormen bantering back and forth in order to entertain viewers. This strategy often includes clowning with weather reporters and generally having a good time' (Altheide, 1974, p. 15): chirpy, cheeerful and cheap.

The BBC: between purity and pragmatism

The BBC, which derives its revenues largely from public subscription to a licence fee, is perhaps less sensitive but not wholly immune to market concerns. Editors and journalists in the BBC believe that it continues to enjoy a reputation as the world's premier news and current affairs service. A senior executive at the BBC announced confidently that 'even people who are not regular BBC watchers and listeners feel that when there's a big occasion, when it really matters to them to know the truth, they press the button for the BBC. We lose that reputation at our peril.' He added determinedly, 'We won't lose it.'

But while the BBC is eager to insist on the integrity of its journalistic standards, there is a discernible willingness to concede the impact of an increasingly competitive broadcasting environment on programming. Employing Blumler's terminology, BBC broadcasters are straddling the horns of a dilemma between 'purity' and 'pragmatism' (Blumler, 1993, p. 404). The argument, much like that of the executive at ITN cited above (see p. 255), eschews the discourse of 'going down market', preferring to invest the programming goal with the objective of seeking new and wider audiences. A senior editorial policy advisor claimed,

> We have to compete for audiences but I don't think that the people who count in the BBC wish it to move in a tabloid direction as regards its agenda. But even within our News and Current Affairs Directorate, which prides itself in setting the highest ethical and editorial standards for journalism in this country, there is a recognition that while not in any way watering down those standards, one can attract new audiences and broader audiences using techniques which are tabloid, production techniques which are popular but without diluting the editorial agenda.

He illustrates his distinction between 'production techniques' and the 'agenda' by reference to an innovative weekly current affairs programme entitled *Here and Now*. The programme explores issues

> which are important to people, good and interesting stories, but it does them in a way which is very accessible, by scripting them in a way which is very conversational and informal and using production techniques, camera styles, graphics which are fast moving and which a very wide range of our audience can identify with. In other words it isn't boring, but that doesn't mean that it is tabloid in the sense of sensational, trivial, prurient or insignificant.

Radio 5 Live is one of the more recent manifestations of this new 'compromise ' between 'creating new programme formats which are attractive to wider audiences than ABs predominantly over 40' while not 'diluting our journalistic integrity'.

Others offer a less convoluted rationale for the changing character of news and current affairs presentation on BBC television. Steve Hewlett, editor of *Panorama*, acknowledges the importance of audience ratings and the need to make the programme 'popular and accessible'. 'It's about basic storytelling,' he concedes, 'we live in "zapland" where the remote control is far too easy to reach and so it is absolutely incumbent upon us to make *Panorama* into something people want to watch' (quoted in *Press Gazette*, 27 September 1996, p. 17).

Minimax programming: James Bond versus *World in Action*

The factors responsible for producing changes in broadcast news and current affairs journalism are varied and often overlapping. They embrace: the impact of the Broadcasting Acts 1990 and 1996 on resource availability and programming philosophy; the expansive role for market forces and greatly enhanced competitiveness of the British broadcasting system; the increasing concentration of ownership in media generally and television in particular; the reduction in journalistic staffs; the particular problems confronting ITN; and the changing culture of the BBC.

The Broadcasting Acts 1990 and 1996 have contributed to changing programming priorities and standards in three ways. First, the Acts have created a broadcasting system which requires broadcasters to be more sensitive to market forces and place a premium on popular rather than quality programming. The Acts encourage a 'minimax' programming philosophy where the broadcasting of low-budget populist programmes like game shows, soaps and repeats, minimises programme costs but maximises audiences and advertisers. News and current affairs is consequently doubly damned: expensive to produce and relatively unpopular with viewers. McManus argues that when 'the business goal of maximising profit dominates' it is likely that 'rational organisations will offer the least expensive mix of contents that garners the largest audiences that advertisers will pay to reach' (McManus, 1992, p. 799). Journalistic and economic ambitions are not necessarily hostile and some events deemed newsworthy by journalistic norms might remain so measured by purely financial considerations; examples could include 'the crash of an airplane or a fatal fire in a tenement. But given the actual news market and the particular nature of news as a commodity, the logic of maximising often conflicts with the logic of maximising public understanding' (ibid., p. 800). In brief, why schedule *World in Action* in prime time when reshowing a James Bond film will double the audience?

Second, the 1990 Act has made less money available for programme making at network and regional levels by introducing a system of blind auction for the licences to broadcast which has diverted money from programme makers' budgets into treasury coffers. In 1993, for example, Channel 3's tender payments to the treasury amounted to £360 million approximately a quarter of the network's advertising and sponsorship revenues for the year and a sum that represents more than Channel 4's total revenues in the first year of selling its own advertising. As Glencross observed, 'the cost of an entire national television channel is being handed to the Treasury in addition to the normal corporation tax paid by Channnel 3 companies' (Glencross, 1994, p. 2). Resource considerations are also influential in programming decisions at the regional level. Bids for the regional broadcast licences varied substantially. Central Television, for example, which enjoys an annual turnover in excess of £314 million, secured its licence for the minimum bid of £2000. Yorkshire, Anglia and Tyne Tees television were each judged to have bid in excess of what the franchise could profitably sustain in their anxiety to secure the licence. Consequently, the various regional companies have highly variable budgets available for regional programme making. Granada Television (which bid £9 million or 6 per cent of advertising revenues for its licence) is able to commit £25,000 to each half-hour regional programme, whereas at Yorkshire Television (which bid £38 million or 30 per cent of advertising revenues) 'the average budget for a half-hour programme is about £11,000 which is a very substantial reduction in real terms in the last few years and means that a number of areas for legitimate programme making are automatically ruled out because they'd just be too expensive to make'. In these circumstances, companies try to make good the shortfall via sponsorship and co-productions. But co-productions can prove problematic since regulators are eager to ensure licensees meet their commitments to regional rather than cross-regional programming.

Third, the Broadcasting Act 1990 granted Channel 3 companies greater control of their own schedules. Prior to the Act the IBA had to approve advance programme schedules; its successor the ITC regulates with a lighter touch. When the ITV Network Centre rescheduled *World in Action*, the ITC quite properly observed that it 'had no jurisdiction in the area . . . we can't prevent ITV acting competitively as a result of commercial pressure' (Marks, 1994, p. 10).

The increasingly competitive character of British broadcasting is also reflected in changing journalistic styles and standards. Since 1993, Channel 4 has been financially independent of Channel 3 and a competitor for its advertising revenues. The arrival of Channel 5, the establishment of the three INR stations, the proliferation of more than 180 satellite and cable television services and the imminent arrival of digital television have substantially intensified competition for viewers, listeners and advertisers (ITC, 1996, p. 25). Walter Cronkite, veteran anchor of CBS news, claims that in America competition has been corrosive of programme quality. 'As

American TV networks have fought in recent years to hang on to a viable share of a shrinking pie,' Cronkite claims, 'the trend towards trivialising and infotainment has been exacerbated' (Cronkite, 1997, p. 2).

The BBC is not immune to pressures of competition. The belief that licence-fee revenues place the BBC beyond commercial pressures has always been a myth. A senior BBC executive conceded that the BBC has 'always had to compete although sometimes we've been a little slow in recognising that'. But competition is necessarily keener when the BBC is 'faced with very substantial inroads into its audiences by viewers of satellite and cable'. Consequently, 'it is important that we maintain significant audience share and very significant audience reach' while the BBC is reliant on its 'licence fee, which is dependent ultimately on the will of the people to pay it, and hence the willingness of governments to continue it . . . While the opposition proliferates by definition both are going to be under threat and suffer . . . We can't allow the BBC to become a sort of PBS station à la United States.' At the BBC, the response to competition has been to seek out 'new audiences and broader audiences'. The establishment of BBC's Radio 5 Live, in April 1994, offers an obvious example. Its purpose was 'to attract to the BBC a range of people who are not getting any of their sport or journalism from the BBC at the moment . . . we want to grab a wider range of people so that they will stay with us in the future, particularly young people who will then grow up with us.' The BBC never goes 'down market' but perennially searches out 'broader audiences'.

But although greatly intensified, competition up to the late 1990s has not been as fierce as broadcasters might have anticipated. In the 1993 allocation, three companies (Border, Scottish and Central) won their franchises uncontested and Channel 5, following considerable financial and technical difficulties, did not come on stream until April 1997, although Channel 3 company business plans were drafted on the assumption of a January 1994 start date. The expansion of satellite provision was initially tardier than anticipated and has relied overwhelmingly on subscription revenues rather than advertising or sponsorship. The breakthrough in cable provision seems imminent rather than achieved.

The relaxation of the rules of ownership for Channel 3 companies in early 1994 triggered a spate of takeovers and mergers (Carlton/Central, Meridien/Anglia, and Granada/LWT), which some observers suggest has effected a regrouping of the larger ITV companies. These observers are pessemistic about the consequences for programmes and content and especially the regional identity of Channel 3 services. They argue that the smaller Channel 3 companies are 'isolated and under threat on the margins. Substantial changes in the nature of ITV programmes, a departure from any commitment to public-service television and the end of regional programming will be the result' (Williams, 1994, p. 41). Regulators place less significance on the impact of ownership on programme content. 'No matter who actually owns the licence,' one regulator observed, 'the programme conditions in that licence remain the same.' Within a few years there will 'probably be no more than two or three ITV companies . . . but they will still be running 15 regional licences as separate entities'. The peculiarities of British audiences must be taken into account. Some regulators do not believe 'regional viewing will diminish because viewers like it . . . regional programmes regularly attract audience shares of 40 per cent or more.'

Substantial reductions in journalistic staffs across recent years have also contributed to changing journalistic standards. By November 1990, in anticipation of their bids for the franchise auction, Central Television and Thames Television had reduced their workforces by 467 and 300 respectively. The job cuts meant that Central had reduced its staff from 2000 to just under 1000 in three years. Similar job losses occurred at other ITV companies and at ITN. BECTU claim that 3500 of their members lost their jobs between 1991 and 1993, bringing the total job losses under Michael Checkland's director generalship to 7000, or one quarter of the workforce – a trend continued and heightened under John Birt. A BBC executive argued that such reductions were 'traumatic', but insisted that they have not 'resulted in the BBC offering less than a first class service of journalism'. The Broadcasting Act's requirement that 25 per cent of programming must emanate from the independent sector means that considerable numbers of jobs could be lost without conseqence for programming. Efficiencies deriving from new working practices such as multi-skilling and bi-media journalism allegedly offer further opportunities for staff savings without impact on journalistic standards. Some managers argue that while reductions in sound and lighting crews may occasionally give rise to pictures of diminished technical quality, the increased mobility of the smaller crews has provided shots we 'wouldn't have had let alone quibble about the sound or lighting'. But such assessments are contentious. A BECTU official argued that the reduction in the number of staff journalists has created a greater reliance on agency copy. In the commercial sector, where economic pressures are particularly intense, 'we've seen the end of the days when they had a correspondent in virtually any city you cared to think of. You've only to look at the foreign desk of GMTV to realise that if it wasn't for the agency tapes, you'd never hear about the rest of the world.' Scarce resources, he claims, are inimical to investigative journalism, which requires a news organisation to commit a skilled and experienced journalist and camera crew, perhaps for many months, with no guarantee that they 'will dig up anything worth showing in your main news bulletin . . . But if you are just filling a bulletin with infotainment you can assign a rookie journalist who just completed the postgrad course at the London College of Printing and send them off and they will come back with a 45 seconds package about a fashion show.'

The situation at the BBC is highly complex. There have certainly been substantial job cuts but some areas of news and current affairs have been buttressed in accordance with the dictates of Birtism with its mission to eradicate any 'bias against understanding'. In July 1993, for example, the BBC announced 170 new jobs in regional journalism and a year later Radio 5 Live created more than a hundred new jobs for journalists. There is none the less, as a senior journalist claimed, 'the feeling that the BBC doesn't do the news as well as it used to despite the fact that they have poured almost unlimited resources into news and current affairs'. A BECTU official identified the difficulty as a 'problem of culture; the edict approach to news gathering and transmission which dissects and dessicates news stories to the point where they are boring. The whole style of newsgathering at the Beeb has become a laboratory exercise which has less and less contact with the real world. Journalists seem to be embroiled in conferences about scripts, policy and the mood of the programme. There seems to be an immense amount of bureaucracy for a journalist to wade through.' This view has been very publicly endorsed by senior broadcasters such as Mark Tully and Martin Bell (*Press Gazette*, 27 September 1996). Brenda Maddox agrees, suggesting that Birt has delivered the opposite of the 'leaner, more creative BBC' which he promised. 'Instead,' she claims, the BBC is a 'top heavy new bureaucracy with layers of accountants and analysts, committee papers and paper mountains which yield second rate programmes and demoralised staff' (Maddox, 14 July 1993, p. 7).

ITN has had to confront particular difficulties as a news organisation. At the end of 1991, the company had overspent by £9.8 million as a consequence of financial mismanagement, the recession and the company's inability to rent out accommodation in its new headquarters. The Broadcasting Act exacerbated these difficulties by its requirement that ITN move into profit and that a majority stake in ITN should transfer from the 15 ITV companies to outside investors. Substantial job cuts were inevitable and senior journalists began to suggest that ITN was no longer a viable and serious international news organisation (*Guardian*, 29 July 1991). In April 1993 a consortium headed by Carlton Communications bought a controlling share in ITN; David Gordon was appointed chief executive. A year later, in a speech to the Royal Television Society, Gordon announced the that ITN's troubles were over; it had been 'in the eye of the storm' but it was 'in remarkably good shape' (Gordon, 12 April 1994). ITN has restructured its editorial management and deployed new technology alongside revised working practices, to ensure that 'standards of journalism are high' (ibid., p. 5) while making a profit of £5.6 million in 1993 (ibid., p. 7). Cost-effective but high-quality; the circle was apparently squared. But Stewart Purvis replaced Gordon on 28 March 1995 following a major row between the latter and Michael Green, the head of Carlton Communications. Purvis immediately confirmed that *News at Ten* would not be moved from its 10 p.m. slot. A month later, Purvis announced that *Channel 4 News* would be revamped in the run-up to its contract renewal with Channel 4. Projected changes included 'a more comprehensive headlines and weather service' plus a new set designed to 'give a warmer look'; the relevance of the latter to the production of quality broadcast news is perhaps less than obvious (*Guardian*, 28 April 1995, p. 8). In October 1996, in his lecture 'Making a Business out of a Crisis' to the Royal Television Society, Purvis announced further reductions of income without any loss in quality.. There would be no journalist redundancies in 1996 despite ITN's reduced future income from ITV news services: a reduction of £5 million on the total of £57 million in 1997 with a further £17 million in 1988. The cash shortfall would be made good by efficiencies in working practices and overheads, the arrival of Channel 5 and the growth of ITN's non-ITV business. 'Even under the fiercest pressure,' Purvis claimed, there is no question of 'doing anything that compromises the quality of the programmes' (Purvis cited in Methven, 31 January 1996, p. 4). It is hard to imagine that such persistent and substantial cuts in budget can be sustained without injury to the quality of programing.

Maintaining journalistic quality: regulating broadcast media

Attitudes towards regulating media in Britain are characterised by a discernible schizophrenia. Paradoxically, while the prevailing assumption has been that regulation of newspapers would constitute an unwarranted intrusion into press freedom, the desirability of statutory regulation of radio and television broadcasting is typically considered axiomatic. Regulation of both print and broadcast media, however, involves the need to establish an institutional mechanism which secures journalists' freedom and independence while at the same time securing high standards of journalism and guaranteeing journalists' accountability to the wider community. In the UK, the regulatory mechanism has assumed the form of an appointed committee to serve as an intermediary between broadcasters and politicians. In the public sector this intermediary is the BBC board of governors; in the comercial sector of broadcasting it is the ITC.

Governing the Beeb

The quality and journalistic standards of BBC programming are protected by the BBC board of governors, the twelve members of which, who are appointed by the home secretary, defend the independence of the BBC from outside pressures whether commercial or political. But they also serve as 'trustees to the public to ensure that the BBC's programme services maintain standards of excellence, offer value for money and reflect the needs of the audience' (*Future of the BBC*, 2nd report, 1993, vol. 1 p. xvii). The day-to-day running of the BBC and the production and broadcasting of programmes are the immediate responsibility of a board of managers. The board of governors oversees the managers, ensures programming conforms to charter specification and represents the public interest (*The Future of the BBC* Cmnd 2098, 1992, p. 38).

But a number of other factors embracing broadcasters' professional commitments, their statutory obligations, as well as their need to comply with codes of professional practice, sustain and police journalistic output. The tradition of public-service broadcasting for example has always stressed the need for high-quality programming informed by the Reithian mission to 'educate, inform and entertain'. Legal constraints such as the various Representation of the People Acts, demand balance and impartiality in election coverage, while the annex to the BBC's licence and agreement obliges the BBC to accept a duty 'to ensure that programmes maintain a high general standard in all respects (and in particular in respect of content and quality), and to provide a properly balanced service which displays a wide range of subject matter' (quoted in *Producers' Guidelines*, 1993, pp. 20–1).

In November 1993, the BBC published an updated edition of *Producers' Guidelines* which was distributed to 15,000 editorial staff. In his Introduction to the *Guidelines*, Director General John Birt claimed 'they represent the most comprehensive and coherent code of ethics in broadcasting' and embody 'the editorial and ethical principles which drive the BBC'. The 46 sections of the 276-page guide deal with a range of issues for journalists including accuracy, impartiality, privacy, broadcasting and terrrorism, violence in television programmes, taste and decency, game shows and people shows and matters of law. The *Guidelines* insist, for example, that BBC programmes should not 'offend against good taste or decency or . . . be offensive to public feeling' (*Producers' Guidelines*, p. 86). The guide also sets out 'stringent rules' concerning the protrayal of violence, especially where violence is directed against women and children (ibid., p. 79).

The *Guidelines* offer detailed advice as well as mandatory instruction concerning privacy: 'it is essential we operate within a framework which respects people's right to privacy, treats them fairly, yet allows us to investigate and establish matters which it is in the public interest to know about' (ibid., p. 34). 'Doorstepping' is explicitly forbidden without the prior permission of the controller of editorial policy. A BBC senior editor claimed the guidelines guaranteed that the BBC will only use the 'doorstep' as 'a means of last resort to get answers to important questions when other attempts have failed to get answers. We absolutely won't use it as a dramatic device or a means of boosting audiences . . . programmes on other networks do use doorstepping in this way, but the BBC won't while I'm in this job.'

The BBC also believes that 'media scrums' which intrude on people who suddenly find themselves at the centre of media interest are undesirable. It may on occasion 'be proper' to withdraw from such unethical behaviour even if this means not accessing 'material which other organisations gather and publish' (*Producers' Guidelines*, p. 40). A BBC policy advisor offered an example. 'When Lord Caithness suffered the tragic loss of Lady Caithness who killed herself allegedly because she had learned of his having an affair, most of the media surrounded his home . . . My colleagues in News and Current Affairs took the view that in the days imediately following the tragedy, we would not be part of that media scrum and if he'd come out and said something which was newsworthy well we wouldn't have had it.' The BBC fosters 'an ambition to set the agenda for ethics and journalism even more clearly than we do now'. The publication of the *Producers' Guidelines* represents a central element in that broader campaign.

All in the best possible taste? The lighter touch and quality thresholds

The ITC, which regulates commercially funded television services, including satellite and cable services, which originate in the UK, is intended to operate with a 'lighter touch' than its predecessor the IBA. One element in that lighter touch is that the ITC has not inherited the IBA's prerogative of approving programme schedules. In broad terms the ITC has complied with its brief but circumstances have sometimes obliged it to exercise a more heavy-handed style of regulation; the refusal to allow ITV to reschedule *News at Ten* illustrates a more resolute style.

The ITC can only issue licences to broadcast on conditions closely specified by the Broadcasting Act 1990. Bidders for the licences to broadcast must leap what has come to be known as the 'quality threshold' (*The Broadcasting Act 1990*, ch. 2, part 1, sec. 16 (2) (a–h)). Broadcasters' projected programme intentions must include: news programmes and current affairs programmes 'which are of high quality and deal with national and international matters' (2a); regional programmes (2c); programmes produced within the broadcast region (2d); religious and children's programmes (2e); programmes catering for a wide variety of interests and tastes (2f); a 'proper proportion' of programmes originating in Europe (2g); and 25 per cent of programmes originating in the independent production sector (2h). Quality control is therefore 'built in' to the system of commercial broadcasting. The Broadcasting Act 1990 also requires the commission to draw up and enforce a code governing due impartiality in programme services (Section 6.1 (a)–6.8), as well as a more general programme code (Section 7.1–7.4) giving guidance relating to programme content. Similar to the BBC's *Producer Guidelines*, the 46 pages of the code, divided into 11 sections, set out a number of rules and requirements for programme makers concerning offence to good taste and decency (S1), the portrayal of violence in programmes (S1.6), privacy and gathering of information (S2), impartiality (S3) and presentation of religious matters (S9) (*The ITC Programme Code*, January 1993).

The ITC may be triggered to consider breaches of its programme code by receipt of a complaint; during 1994 it received 3065 complaints. But, if the ITC in the course of its routine monitoring of programmes decides the code has been breached, it may act without a complaint and impose a formal warning, require an on-screen apology, impose a financial penalty or shorten or, in very extreme cases, revoke a company's licence; ultimately the ITC can pull the plug. Peer criticism, however, even above financial penalties, is judged the most effective of this range of possible sanctions. A regulator claimed that 'programme makers are proud of their programmes and any licencee who is hauled over the coals . . . will be desperately embarassed. The whole industry will know they have been judged inadequate and I think that any licencee will make a great attempt to improve the position if that were the case.'

The ITC also undertakes an annual assessment of programming, on all 15 Channel 3 licences plus Channel 4 and Teletext; the first review was completed in June 1994. A regulator from the ITC expressed the overall objective of the assessment with admirable clarity: to look at 'what was promised on the licence application' and compare that with 'what's appeared on the screen'. There were three components to the assessment. First, to establish whether the companies provided programmes across the nine programming strands embracing regional, educational and arts programmes. Second, to check the 'minutages are about right' and that sufficient programmes in each category have been broadcast. Finally, to assess the quality of programming. Appraisals of programme quality necessarily reflect subjective considerations, but the ITC has attempted to 'reconcile a number of factors including . . . resources in terms of budget but also in terms of talented experienced programme makers with flair'. According to Peter Fiddick, this initial review of Channel 3 licences 'exuded liberal public service values both in its praise and well publicised criticism' (*Guardian*, 30 May 1994, pp. 16–17). An example of the 'well publicised criticism' was contained on the front page of the same newspaper three days earlier. The headline of Andrew Culf's page one story claimed '"Stale" ITV Told To Improve'. Like many headlines it had little to do with the story. Culf explained that 13 of the 16 licencees were given ITC approval for their record, with Granada's programme output described as 'strong', Anglia's 'impressive' and Yorkshire's 'successful'.

The review offered four summary findings. First, most companies were given a clean bill of health. Second, GMTV received a formal warning about its unsatisfactory programming and was told that it could face a fine of up to £2 million if performance did not improve dramatically. Third, Carlton was told that a significant improvement would be expected in its performance across 1994. Most of its network programmes were unimpressive and the company had delivered only about one quarter of the 500 hours of network programmes it had promised in its licence application. Finally, the ITC claimed the schedules from the ITV network centre had been cautious and unadventurous with too great a reliance on predictable game shows and light-entertainment formats. Drama concentrated on police and crime stories – what David Glencross called 'flashing blue light television' – to the exclusion of virtually everything else. The ITC rejected the suggestion that news and current affairs programming had gone down market, but criticised the lateness of the slots given to arts programmes such as *The South.Bank Show*. The companies judged much of the criticism to be unfair and countered with three arguments. First, the review period covered 1993 but was not published until mid-1994; programme commitments had already been made until the end of the year. If any company had not anticipated ITC criticism, it was already too late for them to remedy the problem in the current year. Second, GMTV claimed that the ITC criticism was badly timed. The company was just beginning to win credible audiences after a very problematic start-up period (see chapter 9). ITC criticism reported a state of affairs which no longer existed and offered little encouragement for improvement. But it was the final response from the network which was the most telling and pointed to the tensions in the ITC position. Channel 3 claimed, with some justification, that viewers constitute the ultimate judges of programmes; on that count Channel 3 had scored very highly indeed. At the time of the review, ITV's total share of the audience was 43 per cent; a very comfortable lead over its main rival, BBC1.

These data pose a pertinent question. Is Channel 3 intended to broadcast popular programmes based on market considerations? If this is a legitimate objective for Channel 3, to be drawn from the Broadcasting Act 1990, then audience size is the ultimate benchmark for programming. But, as Fiddick observed, the ITC persists in bringing public-service commitments to its regulatory task. It seeks to guarantee not merely the provision of popular programmes but the provision of what it considers to be quality programmes. The difficulties involved in reconciling these requirements is evident.

The second ITC Review, published on 11 April 1995, noted critically that ITV's 'undoubted popularity with viewers appeared to inhibit new scheduling and commissioning initiatives . . . especially in the most commercially significant areas of the schedule – drama, entertainment and comedy' (ITC, 1995, p. 3). ITV was also criticised for marginalising religious programmes (p. 7), moving some regional programmes out of peak time (p. 3) and displaying an overreliance on imported American cartoons in children's programming (p. 6). More significantly, the ITC alleged an 'apparent lack of nerve' for interrupting *World in Action's* run for six weeks when BBC1 launched an extra edition of *Eastenders* (p. 5); the Commission also expressed concern about the rather abrupt shift to adult programming after the 9 p.m. watershed (p. 3). The third review (1996) again cautioned against the evident supremacy of commercial over public-service considerations. The ITC identified 'a noticeable shift in the overall balance of the schedule towards more entertainment led programmes . . . with less documentary and arts output; and the less obviously popular programming such as education, religion and arts was often in the margin of the schedules . . .

We think the balance has shifted and is approaching or is at the limits of where it should be' (ITC, 1996a).

In 1995, the ITC issued a formal warning to Channel 4 for breaching its licence following a series of items of questionable taste featured on the late-night youth programme, *The Word*. The commission identified three items in the programme's 'Revenger' strand which, they alleged, 'took them over the edge of acceptable standards of taste and decency': in the first, an actor playing the role of an elderly man emptied the contents of a colostomy bag over a 'victim'; the second featured Santa Claus vomiting over a member of the audience; the third presented the enviably gifted and appropriately titled 'Mr Powertool' pulling a woman in a chair across the studio floor by a rope attached to his penis (Culf, 8 June 1995, p. 6). Michael Grade objected that the commission's criticisms derived from its members being too distanced by age and background from the average viewer; it clearly never occurred to Mr Grade that some 'average viewers' might be offended by his description of this puerile drivel as 'their taste'. The only ground for a defence of such items can be a broadly expressed commitment to freedom of speech; not a public-service commitment to quality and range of programming.

Paradoxically, the regulation of broadcast media content has proliferated alongside the economic deregulation of media during the 1980s. Two new regulatory bodies, with a brief that spanned the public and commercial sectors, received statutory recognition in the Broadcasting Act 1990. The Broadcasting Complaints Commission (BCC) was established in 1981, to consider and adjudicate complaints received from individuals who believe they have been treated unjustly or suffered an unwarranted infringement of their privacy in a broadcast programme (*Broadcasting Act 1990*: sect. 143(1)). The Broadcasting Standards Council (BSC) was chaired by William Rees-Mogg from its inception in May 1988 until he was replaced by Lady Howe in June 1993. The Broadcasting Act offered the BSC the brief to construct a code of conduct for broadcasters offering guidance concerning television portrayals of violence, of sex and of 'matters of taste and decency generally' (*Broadcasting Act 1990*: sect. 157 (1)). Many broadcasters were sceptical about the need for the BSC and the usefulness of its code of conduct, arguing that the system of regulation for broadcasting had become unduly complex. One broadcaster stated that he 'would be glad to see the back of this host of "neighbourhood watch style" commissions and quangos who poke their fingers into the media'.

Given this proliferation of regulatory watchdogs, it is perhaps unsurprising that on occasion contradictory judgements have led to a regulatory muddle in which dog has shown a willingness to bite dog! ITC assessments of the market demand to see Mr Powertool, for example, were not shared by the BSC, who felt his athletic performance was unlikely to 'result in widespread offence' (Culf, 8 June 1995, p. 3). The July 1994 white paper, *The Future of the BBC: Serving the Nation, Competing World Wide*, suggested a new body to replace the BSC and the BCC which would monitor output and offer advice. There was widespread support among broadcasters and some regulators for the white paper proposals to tidy up the system; 'there's certainly a good case for wrapping up the Broadcasting Complaints Commission and the Broadcasting Standards Council' one regulator argued. The National Heritage Select Committee report suggested that the public was confused by the 'present tangled skein' of complaints bodies which should be replaced by a new single body dealing with complaints concerning BBC, ITV, Channel 4, satellite, cable and all radio services (*The Future of the BBC*, 2nd report, December 1993).

The Broadcasting Act 1996 gave life to a new body, the Broadcasting Standards Commission (BSC), although the commission did not officially come into existence until April 1997. Stephen Whittle, managing director of the BSC, constructed a new code on fairness and privacy for broadcasters to establish a level playing field of standards and ensure that independent producers and other contributors did not have to meet different standards for different channels. If the new code is breached the consequences will be the same: 'punishment by embarrassment'. The BSC insists on a broadcast apology (Methven, 1996, p. 5). On 22 January 1997, the *Guardian* front-page story reported on Labour's new media policy to merge the ITC, Oftel and the BBC board of governors into a single 'super regulator' known as the Office of Communications or Ofcom. The party leadership promptly equivocated about the proposal, suggesting it was a longer-term objective (*Guardian*, 22 January 1997, p. 1).

There are still further mechanisms for regulating broadcasting. The public is able to present its views to broadcasters via a number of mechanisms. The ITC has 10 viewer consultative councils which feed back to the commission about programme quality, while in 1993 the BBC announced its intention to poll 2 million viewers (10 per cent of licence holders) in a rolling referendum about the Corporation's performance (*Guardian*, 28 May 1993, p. 9). Interest groups such as Voice of the Listener and Viewer and the National Viewers and Listeners Association offer broadcasters constant feedback about programming. The expanding global market for television programming will increasingly make national regulation redundant, but the government seems determined to regulate certain aspects of the free market in broadcasting which it has created. On 14 November 1995, Virginia Bottomley, secretary of state for national heritage, banned the Sweden-based hard-core pornography channel XXXTV from Britain by making the supply of the decoder equipment necessary to receive the channel a criminal offence. She did not want 'television to deliver a pornographic diet of degradation . . . Protecting children outweighs any consideration of pornographers and profitability' (Culf, 15 November 1995, p. 7). This phrase captures neatly the unhappy mix of economic libertarianism and moral authoritarianism which were the hallmarks of Thatcherism.

Summary and assessment

The regulation of broadcast media has proliferated during the 1980s with a complex range of regulatory bodies exercising overlapping regulatory briefs; albeit in some cases with a lighter touch. But some observers believe that the fundamental purposes of regulation should be revised to achieve different goals. Regulation should not be negative, seeking to proscribe certain programmes on the grounds of taste, or their explicit portrayals of violence or sexual behaviour. It should become more positive and offer prescriptive formulas about the range and quality of programming. Commercial broadcasters 'would then have an answer to shareholders who ask "Why is the news still at ten?" The answer would be because that is what journalistic standards and regulatory requirements both demand.'

The Broadcasting Acts of 1990 and 1996 and the competitive era they established for British broadcasting are considered to be culpable for many of the current changes to broadcast journalism. There have been calls for reform. Distinguished television journalist David Plowright, ousted as chairman of Granada Television in February 1992 because of his advocacy of editorial above financial priorities, called for change when commercial pressure prompted the rescheduling of *World in Action* in April 1994. 'Parliament,' he claimed, 'should make amends for the absurd Broadcasting Act of 1990 as a matter of some urgency' (Marks, 1994, p. 10).

The system of auction franchise has been the focus of particular concerns and recommendations for reform. On 16 October 1991, when the ITC announced the results of the first auction, the process was described as 'botched beyond belief' (*Independent*, 18 October 1991). Critics argued that the auction generated such anomolies that it was unthinkable the system might be used to allocate the franchise for the new terrestrial station, Channel 5; the unthinkable happened, with similarly contested outcomes. The ITC awarded the franchise to Channel 5 Broadcasting on 27 October 1995 despite having received a bid from UKTV which was £14 million higher; the rejection of Virgin TV's bid became the subject of judicial review. A common criticism of the auction process and consequently a suggestion for reform, has been that there is no system of reserve price. Critics allege government should have demanded £30 million for the 'Big 5' franchises, £15 million for the smaller franchises and perhaps £2 million for the smallest. The establishment of a reserve would: maximise treasury revenues; prevent companies such as Central Television from securing lucrative franchises for virtually nothing (£2K); and eradicate the lack of consensus about the value of particular franchises – in the South East region Carlton TV bid £18 million while TVS bid £59.7 million.

But perhaps the auction system should simply be abolished. Prior to 1990 regional broadcasters paid a retrospective annual levy, based on a percentage of aggregate revenues, after the deduction of programming costs. The system displayed a built-in premium on allocating resources to programme making. Alternatively, it should be possible to establish a more 'objective' valuation for franchises than currently exists, by calculating average revenues across the 10-year period of the previous licence and projecting them forward with a linkage for inflation. Companies would need to offer this agreed price and allocation could rest squarely on projected programme quality rather than 'the highest bid'. The system of auction would be replaced by a system of renting.

Even more radical reforms have been proposed to restore journalistic quality. In chapter 10, for example, it was argued that sustaining journalistic standards could not be achieved merely by enforcing codes of good practice. Effective regulation requires putting in place organisational structures, patterns of ownership and systems of finance for newspaper production which encourage an emphasis on journalistic quality. Similar requirements are a precondition for sustaining range and quality of programming, especially news and current affairs programming, on broadcast media. Without these conditions in place, the anarchic 'logic' of the competitive market will continue to substitute newszak for news journalism.

Appendix

Legislation restricting the media

Administration of Justice Act 1960
Adoption Act 1976
Air Force Act 1955
Aliens Restriction (Amendment) Act 1919
Army Act 1955
Broadcasting Act 1990
Children Act 1989
Children and Young Persons Acts 1933, 1963 and 1969
Civil Service Reform Act 1978
Contempt of Court Act 1981
Copyright, Designs and Patents Act 1988
Criminal Justice Acts 1925, 1987 and 1988
Customs Consolidation Act 1876
Data Protection Act 1984
Defamation Act 1952
Domestic and Appellate Proceedings (Restriction of Publicity) Act 1968
Family Law Act 1986
Financial Services Act 1986
Forgery and Counterfeiting Act 1981
Incitement to Disaffection Act 1934
Indecent Displays (Control) Act 1981
Interception of Communications Act 1985
Judicial Proceedings (Regulation of Reports) Act 1926
Magistrates Courts Act 1980
Magistrates Courts (NI) Order 1981
Matrimonial Causes Act 1973
Naval Discipline Act 1957
Northern Ireland (Emergency Powers) Act 1975
Obscene Publications Act 1959
Official Secrets Acts 1911 to 1989

Police Act 1964
Police and Criminal Evidence Act 1984
Prevention of Corruption Act 1906
Prevention of Terrorism (Temporary Provisions) Act 1989
Public Order Act 1986
Race Relations Act 1976
Rehabilitation of Offenders Act 1974
Representation of the People Act 1983
Sexual Offences Act 1956
Sexual Offences (Amendment) Acts 1976 and 1992
Telecommunications Act 1984
Theft Act 1968
Trade Union Reform and Employment Rights Act 1993
Tribunals of Enquiry (Evidence) Act 1921
Unsolicited Goods and Services Act 1971
Wireless Telegraphy Act 1949

Source: Stephenson, H. *Media Freedom and Media Regulation.*

References and further reading

Advertising Association (1994) *Advertising Association Annual Report* Advertising Association, London

Ainley, B. (1994) *Blacks and Asians in The British Media: An Investigation of Discrimination* London School of Economics, London

Ainley, B. (1995) *Blacks and Asians in the British Media: A Study of Discrimination* PhD thesis, University of London

Altheide, D. (1974) *Creating Reality: How TV News Distorts Events* Sage, London

Althusser, L. (1971) *Lenin and Philosophy and Other Essays* New Left Books, London

Altick, R.D. (1957) *The English Common Reader* University of Chicago Press, Chicago

Annan, Lord (1977) *Committee on the Future of Broadcasting* Cmnd 6753, HMSO, London

Andrews, A. (1859) *The History of British Journalism* Vol. 1 Haskell House Publishers, New York

Armstrong, S. (1996) 'Breakfast Bites back' *Guardian* 19 August, p. 13

Armstrong, S. (1996a) 'How Max Made A Name For Himself' *Guardian* 13 May, pp. 10–11

Aspinall, A. (1973) *Politics and the Press 1780–1850* Harvester Press, Brighton

Asquith, A. (1978) 'The Structure, Ownership and Control of the Press 1855–1914' in Boyce, G., Curran, J. and Wingate, P. (eds) *Newspaper History: from the 17th Century to the Present Day* Constable, London, pp. 98–117

Association of Free Newspapers (1990) *A–Z of Britain's Free Newspapers and Magazines* Association of Free Newspapers, Gloucester

Audit Commission (1995) *Talk Back: Local Authority Communication With Citizens* HMSO, London

Audit Commission (1993) *Have We Got News For You* HMSO, London

Bainbridge, C. and Stockdill, R. (1993) *The News of the World Story* Harper Collins, London

Baistow, T. (1985) *Fourth Rate Estate* Comedia, London

Banks, D. (1994) 'Put Up Or Shut Up!' *UK Press Gazette* 14 February, p. 1

Barnard, S. (1989) *On the Radio: Music Radio in Britain* Open University Press, Milton Keynes

Barnes, S. (1987) 'Advertising: Frees Lead On' *AFN News* June/July, p. 6

Barnett, S. (ed.) (1993) *Funding the BBC's Future* British Film Institute, London

Barnett, S. (1994) 'Information Diffusion in our Democracy: Policy and Practice in Television News' in *Public Policy Review* vol. 2, no. 2, pp. 5–9

Barnett, S. (1995) 'Yawn Of A New Age' *Guardian*, pp. 16–17

Barnett, S. and Curry, A. (1994) *The Battle for the BBC* Aurum Press, London

BBC (1996) *Broadcasting at its Best* BBC, London

BBC (1995) *Britain's Digital Opportunity: BBC's Response to the Government's Proposals For Digital Terrestrial Broadcasting* BBC, London

BBC (1993a) *Responding to the Green Paper* BBC, London

BBC (1993b) *Equality* no. 6, June, London

BBC (1993c) *Producers' Guidelines* BBC Publications, London

BBC (1992) *Extending Choice: The BBC's Role in the New Broadcasting System* BBC, London

BBC (1992a) *Equality* no. 1, June, London

BBC (1969) *Broadcasting in the Seventies* BBC, London

Bellos, A. (1996) 'London Calling And The World Keeps Listening' *Guardian* 18 July, p. 9

Belsay, A. and Chadwick, R. (1992) *Ethical Issues in Journalism and the Media* Routledge, London

Benjamin, I. (1995) *The Black Press in Britain* Trentham Books, Stoke

Bertrand, C.J. (1990) 'Dissent and Media Accountability: The Case for Press Councils' *Intermedia* vol. 18, no. 6, pp. 10–14

Beveridge (1951) *Report of the Broadcasting Committee* Cmnd 8116, HMSO, London

Bevins, A. (1990) 'The Crippling of the Scribes' *British Journalism Review* vol. 1, no. 2, pp. 13–18

Birt, J. (1993) 'The BBC', the Royal Television Society Fleming Memorial Lecture, BBC, London

Birt, J. (1988) 'Decent Media', Keynote Address to the Royal Television Society, April

Birt, J. (1987) 'Bias: Where TV is Guilty' *The Times* 23 March, p. 14

Black, J. (1991) *The English Press in the Eighteenth Century* Croom Helm, London

Black, J. (1987) *The English Press in the Eighteenth Century* Gregg Revivals, Aldershot

Black, P. (1972) *The Biggest Aspidistra in the World* BBC, London

Blumler, J.G. (1993) 'Public Service Broadcasting in Multi-Channel Conditions: Function and Funding' in Barnett, S. (ed.) *Funding the BBC's Future* London, British Film Institute, pp. 26–42

Blumler, J.G. (1993) 'Meshing Money with Mission: Purity versus Pragmatism in Public Broadcasting' *European Journal of Communication* vol. 8, no. 4, pp. 403–25

Blumler, J.G. (ed.) (1992) *Television and the Public Interest: Vulnerable values in West European Broadcasting* Sage and the Broadcasting Standards Council, London

Blumler, J.G. (1984) 'The Sound of Parliament' *Parliamentary Affairs*, no. 3, summer, pp. 250–67

Blyth, J. (1996) 'Journalist Death Toll Falls But More Than Ever In Jail' *Press Gazette* 29 March, p. 9

Boseley, S. (1994) 'BBC Calls In Absolutely Fabulous PR Firm To Rescue Radio 1' *Guardian* 10 August, p. 3

Boseley, S. and Culf, A. (1996) 'Forgan Exit Stuns BBC' *Guardian* 20 February, p. 1

Boulton, D. (1991) *The Third Age of Broadcasting* Institute for Public Policy Research, Social Policy Paper 3, London

Boyce, G. (1978) 'The Fourth Estate: The Re-appraisal of a Concept' in Boyce, G., Curran, J. and Wingate, P. (eds) *Newspaper History: from the 17th Century to the Present Day* Constable, London, pp. 19–41

Boyce, G., Curran, J. and Wingate, P. (eds) (1978) *Newspaper History: from the 17th Century to the Present Day*, Constable, London

Boyd-Barrett, O. (1970) 'Journalism, Recruitment and Training: Problems in Professionalisation' in Tunstall, J. (ed.) *Media Sociology* Constable, London, pp. 181–202

Boyd, A. (1993) *Broadcast Journalism: Techniques of Radio and Television News* Focal Press, Oxford

Bragg, M. (1995) 'Pennies From Brookside' *Guardian* 13 December, p. 17

Briggs, A. (1995) *The History of Broadcasting in the United Kingdom: Competition 1955–1974* Oxford University Press, Oxford

Briggs, A. (1979) *The History of Broadcasting in the United Kingdom*, vol. 4 *Sound and Vision* Oxford University Press, Oxford and London

Briggs, A. (1970) *The History of Broadcasting in the United Kingdom*, vol. 3 *The War Of Words* Oxford University Press, Oxford and London

Briggs, A. (1965) *The History of Broadcasting in the United Kingdom*, vol. 2 *The Golden Age of Wireless* Oxford University Press, Oxford and London

Briggs, A. (1961) *The History of Broadcasting in the United Kingdom*, vol. 1 *The Birth of Broadcasting* Oxford University Press, Oxford and London

The Broadcasting Act 1990 (1990) HMSO, London

Broadcasting Committee (1962) *Broadcasting Committee Report* (Pilkington) Cmnd 1753, HMSO London

Broadcasting Committee (1949) *Broadcasting Committee Report* (Beveridge) Cmnd 8116, HMSO, London

Broadcasting Committee (1936) *Broadcasting Committee Report* (Ullswater) Cmnd 5091, HMSO, London

Broadcasting Committee (1926) *Broadcasting Committee Report* (Crawford) Cmnd 2599, HMSO, London

Broadcasting Committee (1923) *Broadcasting Committee Report* (Sykes) Cmnd 1951, HMSO, London

Broadcasting Complaints Commission (1992) *Broadcasting Complaints Commission Annual Report 1991–92* BCC, London

Broadcasting in the 1990s: Competition, Choice, Quality (1988) HMSO, London

Broadcasting Research Unit (1985) *The Public Service Idea in British Broadcasting: Main Principles* Broadcasting Research Unit, London

Bromley, M. (1994) *Teach Yourself Journalism* Hodder and Stoughton, London

Brooks, R. (1995) 'Birt Out To Tame His Monster' *Guardian* 17 May, p. 15

Brown, M. (1996) 'All The D-G's Men' *Guardian* 22 July, pp. 18–19

Brown, M. (1996a) 'Bunny I Shrunk The News' *Guardian* 4 March, p. 11

Brown, M. (1995) 'Digital TV = Debate, Despair And Dilemma' *Guardian* 11 September, p. 11

Buckingham, L. (1995a) 'New Rules Open Way To Counter Murdoch' *Guardian* 12 May, p. 9

Buckingham, L. (1995) 'Reed Sells UK Newspapers For £205m' *Guardian* 23 November, p. 20

Buckingham, L. (1994) 'BSkyB To Increase Subscription Rates' *Guardian* 27 August, p. 3

Buckingham, L. (1993) 'Higher Volume Helps Boost Sunday Business' *Guardian* 24 December, p. 13

Buckingham, L. and Atkinson, D. (1995) 'Radio Proves Costly Turn On' *Guardian* 29 July, p. 36

Burn, G. (1995) *Fullalove* Secker and Warburg, London

Busfield, S. (1994) 'ITN Shake-Up To Put Effort Into Journalism' *UK Press Gazette* 3 January, p. 1

Calcutt, D. (1993) *Review of Press Self Regulation* Cmnd 2135, HMSO, London

Calcutt, D. (1990) *Report of the Committee on Privacy and Related Matters* Cmnd 1102, HMSO, London

Campbell, V. (1994) 'A Comparative Study of Regional News on BBC and Meridien Television', unpub. MA thesis, University of Keele

Carter, M. (1971) *An Introduction to Mass Communications* Macmillan Student Editions, London

Channel 5 Broadcasting (1995) *Application to the Independent Television Commission for the Channel 5 Licence*

Charon, J.M. (1993) *Cartes de Presse, Enquete sur les Journalistes* Stock, Paris

Chippindale, P. and Franks, S. (1991) *Dished: The Rise and Fall of British Satellite Broadcasting* Simon and Schuster, London

Chippindale, P. and Horrie, C. (1990) *Stick It Up Your Punter: The Rise and Fall of the Sun* Heinemann, London

Christian, H. (1977) *The Development of Trade Unionism and Professionalism among British Journalists* PhD thesis, University of London

Clarke, S. (1993) 'Fact On The Run' *Telegraph* 1 November, p. 6

Cohen, P. and Gardener, C. (1982) *It Ain't Half Racist Mum* Comedia/Minority Press Group, London

Cole, J. (1996) 'All Part Of The Service' *Guardian* 4 March, p. 13

Coleridge, N. (1994) *Paper Tigers: The Latest, Greatest Newspaper Tycoons and How They Won the World* Mandarin, London

Cowe, R. (1995) 'BSkyB Profit Surges To £5 Million A Week' *Guardian* 8 February, p. 13

Cowe, R. (1994) 'Newspaper Price War Hits Publishing Shares' *Guardian* 24 June, p. 2

Cowe, R. and Buckingham, L. (1996) 'How The Murdoch Global Tax Maze Leads To A Fortune In Savings' *Guardian* 16 July, p. 5

Cox, H. and Morgan, D. (1973) *City Politics and the Press* Cambridge University Press, Cambridge

Cranfield, G.A. (1978) *The Press and Society: from Caxton to Northcliffe* Longman, London and New York

Cranfield, G.A. (1962) *The Development of the Provincial Newspaper 1700–1760* Clarendon Press, Oxford

Crisell, A. (1986) *Understanding Radio* Methuen, London

Critcher, C., Parker, M. and Soudhi, R. (1975) *Race in the Provincial Press: A Case Study of Five West Midlands Newspapers* Centre for Contemporary Cultural Studies, Birmingham

Cronkite, W. (1997) 'More Bad News' *Guardian* 27 January, p. 2

Crozier, M. (1958) *Broadcasting: Sound and Vision* Oxford University Press, London and New York

Cudlipp, H. (1980) *The Prerogative of the Harlot: Press Barons and Power* The Bodley Head, London

Culf, A. (1997) 'BBC Faces Upheaval In Labour Plan' *Guardian* 22 January, p. 1

Culf, A. (1996) 'BBC Axes Attack On British Airways' *Guardian* 16 September, p. 4

Culf, A. (1996) 'Birt Pleads For Bigger Licence Fee' *Guardian* 24 August, p. 2

Culf, A. (1996) 'No Concessions In World Service Row' *Guardian* 16 July, p. 3

Culf, A. (1996a) 'Birt To Oversee New BBC Shake Up' *Guardian* 8 June, p. 4

Culf, A. (1996b) 'BBC Tops Radio Ratings' *Guardian* 18 May, p. 10

Culf, A. (1996) 'Tough Going As Stations Fail to Find Listeners' *Guardian* 1 May, p. 6

Culf, A. (1996) '"Fiasco" Claim Over Radio Survey Slump' *Guardian* 16 March, p. 5

Culf, A. (1995) 'Bottomley Bans Porn TV Channel' *Guardian* 15 November p. 7

Culf, A. (1995) 'Talk Radio Gets Rid of Shock Jocks' *Guardian* 22 June, p. 7

Culf, A. (1995) 'Mr Powertool Drags Channel 4 Into Big Trouble' *Guardian* 8 June, p. 7

Culf, A. (1995) 'Blueprint To Sweep Away Complex Media Rules' *Guardian* 24 May, p. 4

Culf, A. (1995) 'Women's Radio Men-Friendly' *Guardian* 5 May, p. 8

Culf, A. (1995) 'Talk Radio Told Off For Obscenity' *Guardian* 2 May, p. 6

Culf, A. (1995) 'Wave of Restricted Radio Hits Peak' *Guardian* 10 April, p. 7

Culf, A. (1995) 'Newspapers Facing Fight To Avoid Privacy Legislation' *Guardian* 5 April, p. 2

Culf, A. (1995) 'Watchdog Gets An Earful From Talk Radio's Audience' *Guardian* 15 February, p. 7

Culf, A. (1994) 'Radio 5 Live Gives BBC "A Rare Success"' *Guardian* 1 August, p. 2

Culf, A. (1994) 'Spreading The Word' *Guardian* 23 May, pp. 16–17

Culf, A (1994) 'Rigid News Quota Eased For Leading Breakfast TV Station' *Guardian* 5 May, p. 10

Culf, A. (1994) 'Journalists Accuse BBC Of Censorship' *Guardian* 9 February, p. 3

Culf, A. (1994) 'Privacy Adjudicator To Watch Over Press' *Guardian* 10 January, p. 1

Culf, A. (1993) 'Radio 1 Sale Would Wipe Out Rivals' *Guardian* 23 November, p. 9

Culf, A. (1993) 'Crack In Mirror Sales' *Guardian* 17 November, p. 5

Culf, A (1993) 'News At Seven Lobby To Target MPs' *Guardian* 12 November, p. 2

Culf, A. (1993) 'Mirror Newspapers Rejoin Press Complaints Body' *Guardian* 11 November, p. 1

Culf, A. (1993) 'Rivals Press Mirror To Rejoin Commission' *Guardian* 10 November, p. 3

Culf, A. (1993) 'Press Counts The Cost Of Outrage By Mirror' *Guardian* 8 November, p. 3

Culf, A. (1993) 'Royal "Peeping Tom" Revives Press Curb Calls' *Guardian* 8 November, p. 1

Culf, A. (1993) 'ITV Retaliates On News At Ten Block' *Guardian* 31 August. p. 7

Culf, A. and Donovan, P. (1995) 'Media Shake-up Leaves Angry Murdoch Isolated' *Guardian* 24 May, p. 1

Culf, A., Weale, S. and Bates, S. (1993) 'Princess To Sue Mirror Group As Press Complaints Body Totters' *Guardian* 9 November, p. 1

Culf, A. and White, M. (1996) 'Fight Over Tory Plan To Sell Off Channel 4' *Guardian* 27 August, p. 1

Curran, J. (1990) 'Culturalist Perspectives of News Organisations: A Reappraisal and a Case Study' in Ferguson, M. (ed.) *Public Communications: The New Imperatives* Sage, London, pp. 114–34

Curran, J. (1989) 'The New Revisionism in Mass Communications Research: A Reappraisal' in *European Journal of Communications*, vol. 5, pp. 135–64

Curran, J. and Seaton, J. (1988) *Power Without Responsibility: The Press and Broadcasting in Britain* 3rd edn, Routledge, London

Davidson, A. (1992; 1993) *Under the Hammer: Greed and Glory Inside the Television Business* Mandarin Books, London

Deacon, D. (1996) 'The Voluntary Sector in a Changing Communication Environment' in *European Journal of Communication*, vol. 11, no. 2, June, pp. 173–201

Deacon, D. and Golding, P. (1994) *Taxation and Representation: The Media, Political Communication and the Poll Tax* John Libbey, London

Dearlove, J. and Saunders, P. (1984; 1991) *An Introduction to British Politics* Oxford, Polity Press

Delano, A. and Hennington, J. (1995) *The News Breed: British Journalists in the 1990s* The London Institute, London

Delano, A. and Hennington, J. (1995) 'Hacks: Read All About 'Em' *Guardian* 16 October, pp. 14–15

Department of National Heritage (1995) *Media Ownership: The Government's Proposals* Cmnd 2872, HMSO, London

Department of National Heritage (1994) *The Future of the BBC: Serving the Nation, Competing World-Wide* Cm 2621, HMSO, London

Department of National Heritage (1992) *The Future of the BBC* Cmnd 2098, HMSO, London

Dixon, D. (1986) 'Children and the Press 1866–1914' in Harris, M. and Lee, A. (eds) *The Press In English Society from the Seventeenth to Nineteenth Centuries* Acton Society Trust, London

Donegan, L. (1995) 'Union Busting Mould Breaker Never Found A Secure Niche' *Guardian* 17 November, p. 2

Donegan, L. (1993) 'Motley Crew At PCC Accused Of Condemning Tabloid Out Of Hand' *Guardian* 9 November, p. 4

Donovan, P. and Atkinson, D. (1994) 'Satellite Profits Pay Cost of Newspaper War' *Guardian* 3 August, p. 2

Dougary, J. (1994) *The Executive Tart and Other Myths* Virago, London

Dugdale, J. (1995) 'The Big League' *Guardian* 28 August, pp. 12–13

Dugdale, J. (1995a) 'Seeing And Believing' *Guardian* 4 September, pp. 12–13

Dugdale, J. (1993) 'Breaking Up Is Hard To Do' *Guardian*, p. 13

Dyke, G. (1994) 'And Now The Bad News' extracts from the MacTaggart Lecture 1994 in *Guardian* 27 August, p. 27

Ehrenberg, A. and Mills, P. (1993) 'What Is The BBC Worth To Viewers?'

in Barnett, S. (ed.) *Funding the BBC's Future* London, British Film Institute, pp. 51–68

Ehrenreich, B. (1990) 'Spudding Out' in *The Worst Years of our Lives: Irreverent Notes from a Decade of Greed*, Pantheon, New York, pp. 15–18

Engel, M. (1996) 'Waves Of Protest' *Guardian* 20 June, pp. 2–3

Engel, M. (1996a) 'Papering Over The Cracks' *Guardian* 3 October, pp. 2–3

Engel, M. (1996b) *Tickle the Public* Victor Gollancz, London

Evans, H. (1984) *Good Times, Bad Times* Coronet, London

Fallows, J. (1996) *Breaking the News: How the Media Undermine American Democracy* Pantheon Books, New York

Fiddick, P. (1993) 'Breakfast Battle Hots Up' *Guardian* 12 April, p. 11

Fiddick, P. (1989) 'Channel 5 Going Spare' *The Listener* 2 November, pp. 8–9

Fireman, B. (1991) 'Snags and Swags' *Guardian* 20 May, p. 25

Fisher, M. (1993) 'Paying The Piper' in Barnett, S. (ed.) *Funding the BBC's Future* British Film Institute, London, pp. 68–75

Fletcher, I. (1988) 'The Future is Free' *AFN News* April/May 1988, pp. 8–10

Forgan, L. (1995) 'Why Less Is Still More' *Guardian* 6 November, pp. 16–17

Forgan, L. (1994) 'Nobody Told Me to Run Off and Do Embroidery, Ever' in Dougary, G. (ed.) *The Executive Tart and Other Myths* Virago, London, pp. 65–73

Forgan, L. (1991) 'The Big, The Bad, The Glory' *Guardian* 26 August, p. 21

Fountain, N. (1988) *Underground: The London Alternative Press 1966–74* Comedia, London

Frank, J. (1961) *The Beginnings of the English Newspaper 1620–1660* Harvard University Press, Cambridge, Mass.

Franklin, B. (1996) 'Why The Sun Does Not Shine On Mr Major' *Parliamentary Brief* March, pp. 18–21

Franklin, B. (1995) *Parliament on the Spike: Changing Journalistic Traditions in the Reporting of Parliament* Final report to the Nuffield Foundation of a study analysing national press coverage of parliamentary proceedings 1990–4

Franklin, B. (1994) *Packaging Politics: Political Communications in Britain's Media Democracy* Edward Arnold, London

Franklin, B. (1991) 'Watchdog or Lapdog? Local Press Reporting of the West Yorkshire Metropolitian County Council' in *Local Government Studies* Jan./Feb. pp. 20–41

Franklin, B. (1989) 'Local Parties, Local Media and the Constituency Campaign' in Crewe, I. and Harrop, M. (eds) *Political Communications: The General Election Campaign of 1987* Cambridge University Press, Cambridge

Franklin, B. (1986) 'Public Relations, the Local Press and the Coverage of Local Government' *Local Government Studies* July/August pp. 25–34

Franklin, B. and Murphy, D. (1994) 'The Local Rag in Tatters: The Decline of Britain's Local Press', paper presented to the conference 'The End of Fleet Street' City University London, 5 February

Franklin, B. and Murphy, D. (1991) *What News? The Market, Politics and the Local Press* Routledge, London

Frayn, M. (1995) *The Tin Men* Penguin, London

French, P. and Rossell, D. (1991) *The Press: Observed and Projected* National Film Theatre Dossier no. 6, London

Gabor, I. (1995) *Driving the News or Spinning Out of Control: Politicians, the Media and the Battle for the News Agenda*, inaugural lecture delivered at Goldsmith's College, 30 November

Gabor, I. and Barnett, S. (1993) 'Changing Patterns In Broadcast News', unpublished paper presented to the annual conference of the Voice of the Listener and Viewer, November

Gall, G. (1996) 'New Technology, Industrial Relations and the Regional Press' unpub. PhD thesis, The Business School, UMIST

Gall, G. (1993) 'Journalism for Changing Times: the Impact of New Technology and Industrial Relations on the Editorial Content of the Regional Press', paper presented to the annual conferrence of the Political Studies Association, University of Leicester, 21 April

Galtung, J. and Ruge, M. (1973) 'The Structure of Foreign News' in Cohen, S. and Young, J. (eds) *The Manufacture of News: Deviance, Social Problems and the Mass Media*, Constable, London, pp. 62–73

Gandy, O. (1982) *Beyond Agenda Setting: Information Subsidies and Public Policy*, Ablex Publishing, New Jersey

Gardner, C. (1986) 'How They Buy The Bulletins' *Guardian* 17 September

Glasgow University Media Group (1980) *More Bad News* Routledge and Kegan Paul, London

Glasgow University Media Group (1976) *Bad News* Routledge and Kegan Paul, London

Glencross, D. (1994) 'Superhighways and Supermarkets', a speech to the Royal Television Society, 8 March

Gliniecki, A. (1993) 'Call To Boycott Papers Ignored' *Independent* 9 November, p. 2

Glover, D. (1984) *The Sociology of the Mass Media* Causeway Press, Ormskirk

Glover, S. (1995) 'The Free Man Of Wapping' *Evening Standard* 10 May, p. 59

Golding, P. (1994) 'Telling Stories: Sociology, Journalism and the Informed Citizen' *European Journal of Communication* vol. 9, no. 4, pp. 461–85

Golding, P. (1974) *The Mass Media* Longman, London

Golding, P. and Middleton, S. (1982) *Images of Welfare: Press and Public Attitudes to Poverty* Blackwell, Oxford

Golding, P. and Murdock, G. (1973) 'For a Political Economy of Mass Media' in Miliband, R. and Saville, J. (eds) *Socialist Register* pp. 205–34

Golding, P. and Murdock, G. (1978) 'Theories of Communication and Theories of Society', Communication Research, July, pp. 339–56

Goodhart, D. and Wintour, P. (1986) *Eddie Shah and the Newspaper Revolution* Coronet Books, London

Goodman, G. (1994a) 'Another Outing for the New Journalism' *British Journalism Review*, vol. 5, no. 2 pp. 3–6

Goodman, G. (1994) 'The Power to Say: No' *British Journalism Review*, vol. 5, no. 4 pp. 1–4

Goodman, G. (1993) 'Too Much To Read' *British Journalism Review*, vol. 4, no. 1, pp. 3–5

Gordon, D. (1994) 'ITN in the Digital Age' unpub. speech to the Royal Television Society, 12 April

Gordon, P. and Rosenberg, D. (1989) *Daily Racism: The Press and Black People in Britain* Runnymede Trust, London

Grade, M. (1996) 'Standing Foursquare' *Guardian* 2 September, pp. 18–19

Grade, M. (1995) 'Give Us Our Money Back' *Guardian* 13 December, p. 17

Green, D. (1991) *A Better BBC: Public Service Broadcasting in the '90s* Centre for Policy Studies, London

Green, M. (1994) Fleming Memorial Lecture, 19 April

Greenslade, R. (1996) 'It's Out, But Is It The Biz?' *Guardian* 22 April, p. 13

Greenslade, R. (1995) 'The Battle Rages On' *Guardian* 3 July, p. 17

Greenslade, R. (1993) 'McGregor and the Lady Diana Pictures' *UK Press Gazette* 6 November, p. 2

Greenslade, R. (1992) 'The Unpopular Press' *Guardian* 19 October, pp. 16–17

Grisham, J. (1992) *The Pelican Brief* Century, London

Guild of Editors (1995) *Survey of Editorial Training Needs* Guild of Editors, London

Gunter, B. and Winstone, P. (1993) *Television: The Public's View 1992* John Libbey, London

Hale, J. (1975) *Radio Power* Paul Elek, London

Hall, S. (1967) 'The World of the Gossip Column' in Hoggart, R. (ed.) *Your Sunday Paper* University of London Press, London, pp. 68–81

Hall, S., Critcher, C., Jefferson, T., Clarke, J. and Roberts, B. (1978) *Policing the Crisis*, Macmillan, London

Hamill, D. (1991) 'After The Break, The Crisis At ITN' *Guardian* 29 July, p. 23

Harcup, T. (1996) 'Racism Warning For Black Journalists' *Press Gazette* 18 October, p. 13

Harcup, T. (1994) *A Northern Star: Leeds' Other Paper and the Alternative Press 1974–1994* Campaign for Press and Broadcasting Freedom, Pontefract

Harris, G. and Spark, D. (1993) *Practical Newspaper Reporting* Focal Press, Oxford

Harris, M. (1978) 'The Structure, Ownership and Control of the Press 1620–1780' in Boyce, G., Curran, J. and Wingate, P. (eds) *Newspaper History: from the 17th Century to the Present Day*, Constable, London, pp. 82–98

Harris, R. (1990) *Good and Faithful Servant* Faber, London

Harrison, M. (1992) 'Politics on The Air' in Butler, D. and Kavanagh, D. (eds) *The British General Election of 1992* Macmillan, London, pp. 155–80

Harrison, M. (1985) *Whose Bias?* Policy Journals, Berkshire

Harrold, A. (1992) 'Delay To Radio News Station' *Guardian* 16 September, p. 1

Hart, J. (1991) *Understanding the Media* Routledge, London

Hartmann, P. and Husband, C. (1974) *Racism and the Media* Davies Poynter, London

Harvey, C. (1994) 'Spotty Youth Station' *Guardian* 8 August, p. 19

Harvey, S. (1994) 'Channel 4 Television: From Annan To Grade' in Hood, S. (ed.) *Behind the Scenes: the Structure of British Television in the Nineties* Lawrence and Wishart, London

Hattersley, R. (1996) 'Hattersley Attacks Media "Trivialising"' *Press Gazette* 26 April, p. 2

Head, A. (1995) 'Alive and Well in the Provinces' *British Journalism Review* 6(2), pp. 66–71

Head, S. and Sterling, C. (1987) *Broadcasting in America* Houghton Mifflin, Boston

Heinderyckx, F. (1993) 'Television News Programmes in Western Europe: A Comparative Study' *European Journal of Communication* vol. 8, no. 4, December, pp. 425–51

Hemels, J. (1995) 'Democratization and Control of the Media: The Issues and the Debate in the Netherlands', paper presented to the conference 'The Press and Europe' held at City University London, 4 February

Hendy, D. (1994) '. . . But Is It Too Fast For Its Own Good?' *British Journalism Review*, vol. 5, no. 2, pp. 15–17

Henry, G. (1994) 'World In Action Is Sidelined By Soap' *Guardian* 7 April, p. 1

Henry, G. (1992) 'ITV Names Man To Head Advert-Led Strategy' *Guardian* 1 October, p. 3

Henry, G. (1992) 'News At Ten Prepares For Its Hour Of Reckoning' *Guardian* 4 July, p. 3

Henry, G. (1991) 'Three Bids For National Radio' *Guardian* 23 May, p. 1

Henry, G. (1991) 'Caught In the Middle Of A Radio Muddle' *Guardian* 22 April, p. 3

Henry, G. (1991) 'ITN Languishing In The Financial Glasshouse' *Guardian* 28 March

Herbert, H. (1976) *The Techniques of Radio Journalism* A.&C. Black, London

Herman, E.S. and Chomsky, N. (1988) *Manufacturing Consent: The Political Economy of the Mass Media*, Pantheon, New York

Hetherington, A. (1989) *News in the Regions* Macmillan, London

Hetherington, A. (1989a) 'The White Paper: Thatcher, Peacock and Who Remembers Reith?' unpub. paper presented to a conference on the future of broadcasting, York, 24–5 February

Hetherington, A. (1985) *News, Newspapers and Television*, Macmillan, London

Hetherington, A. (1981) *Guardian Years* Chatto and Windus, London

Hewlett, S. (1996) 'The Popularizing Of Panorama' *Press Gazette* 27 September, p. 17

Hind, J. and Mosco, S. (1985) *Rebel Radio* Pluto, London

Hoggart, S. (1995a) 'Rehabilitated Major Remains Dimwit At Heart' *Guardian* 26 April, p. 6

Hoggart, S. (1995b) 'Zero Hour Looms On Westminster Road To Nowhere' *Guardian* 4 April, p. 6

Hollingsworth, M. (1986; 1989) *The Press and Political Dissent* Pluto Press, London

Home Office (1988) *Broadcasting in the '90s: Competition, Choice and Quality* Cmnd 517, HMSO, London

Home Office (1987) *Radio: Choice and Opportunities* Cmnd 92, HMSO, London

Hood, S. (1983) *On Television* Pluto, London

Hood, S. (1972) *The Mass Media* Macmillan, London

Hood, S. (1967) *A Survey of Television* Heinemann, London

Horrie, C. and Clarke, S. (1994) *Fuzzy Monsters: Fear and Loathing at the BBC* Heinemann, London

Horsman, M. (1997a) 'Digits In The Pie' *Guardian* 10 February, p. 7

Horsman, M. (1997) 'BBC Plan To Launch Several Pay-TV Channels' *Independent* 28 January, p. 15

Horsman, M. (1996) 'BBC: Birt's Break-Up Corporation' *Independent* 31 August, p. 5

Horsman, M. (1996) 'Birt's Shake Up Hits A Wall Of Protest' *Independent* 31 August, p. 1

Horstmann, R. (1993) *Writing for Radio* 2nd edn, A.&C. Black, London

Horstmann, R. (1991) *Writing for Radio* A.&.C Black, London

Hoyland, P. (1990) 'Central TV Slashes Another 467 Jobs Ahead of Battle To Keep Franchise' *Guardian* 27 November, p. 16

Hunter, F. (1982) *Grub Street and Academia: The Relationship between Journalism and Education 1880–1940 with Special Reference to the London University Diploma for Journalism 1919–1939* PhD thesis, Centre for Arts and Related Studies, City University London

Ingham, B. (1991) *Kill the Messenger* Harper Collins, London

Ingham, B. (1990) *Government and Media: Co-existence and Tension*, lecture delivered at Trinity and All Saints College, Leeds, 22 November

IRN (1996) *The IRN Service* Independent Radio News, London

ITC (1996) *Factfile 1996* ITC, London

ITC (1996a) *1995 Performance Review* 26 April, ITC, London

ITC (1995) *ITC Annual Reports and Accounts 1995* ITC, London

ITC (1994) *ITC Code of Programme Sponsorship* ITC, London

ITC (1994) *The ITC Programme Code* ITC, London

ITC (1994) *Programme Complaints and Interventions Report Oct.–Dec. 1993* ITC, London

ITC (1993) *The ITC Code of Advertising Standards and Practice* ITC, London

ITN (1996) *Independent Television News* ITN, London

Jenkins, S. (1989) 'In Defence Of Quality' *The Listener* 6 July, pp. 4–6

Johnson, A. (1996) 'Electronic Newspaper Research Launched' *UK Press Gazette* 29 May, p. 9

Johnson, M. (1985) 'ILR Twelve Years On' *Airwaves*, summer, pp. 10–11

Jones, C.J. (1980) 'Media Councils in the Western Hemisphere' in Bruun, L. (ed.) *Professional Codes in Journalism* International Association of Journalists, Prague

Junqua, D. (1993) 'Formation au Journalisme et Deontologie' *Apres-Demain*, no. 353–4, April–May

Karpf, A. (1996) 'Sound Off, Vision On' *Guardian* 12 June, p. 12

Karpf, A. (1994) 'Familiar Air Despite Promise Of "Raw and Rough" Coverage' *Guardian* 29 March, p. 24

Karpf, A. (1987) 'Radio Times – Private Women and Public Men' in Dickey, J. and Stratford, T. (eds) *Out of Focus: Writings on Women and the Media* Women's Press, London, pp. 169–76

Kaye, M. (1996) 'How Birt Is Decimating The World Service' *Press Gazette* 5 July, p. 13

Kaye, M. (1995) 'Waves Of Protest' *UK Press Gazette* 27 November, p. 28

Keeble, R. (1994) *The Newspapers Handbook* Routledge, London

Kelly, T. (1996) 'Snow And Naughtie Warn Of Dangers Of Drive For Ratings' *Press Gazette* 20 September, p. 5

Kelly, T. (1995) 'Gyngell Calls For A Major Shakeup Of News On ITV' *Press Gazette* 27 November, p. 14

Kelly, T. (1990) 'ITN Job Fears Remain After £6.5 Million Lifeline' *UK Press Gazette* 22 October, p. 11

Kendrich, A. (1969) *Prime Time: The Life of Edward R. Murrow* Knopf, New York

Kettle, M. (1996) 'Birt Faces World Service Shutdown' *Guardian* 18 July, p. 1

Koss, S. (1984) *The Rise and Fall of the Political Press in Britain*, University of North Carolina Press, London and Chapel Hill

Kuhn, R. (1995) *The Media in France* Routledge, London

Landry, C., Morely, D., Southwood, R. and Wright, P. (1985) *What a Way to Run a Railroad: An Analysis of Radical Failure* Comedia, London

Leapman, M. (1993) 'BBC Code Curbs Doorstepping' *Independent* 17 November, p. 3

Leapman, M. (1993) 'They Published And We're All Damned' *Independent* 10 November, p. 1

Lee, A. (1978) 'The Structure, Ownership and Control of the Press, 1855–1914' in Boyce, G., Curran, J. and Wingate, P. (eds) *Newspaper Histolry from the Seventeenth Century to the Present Day* Constable, London, pp. 117–29

Lee, A. (1976) *The Origins of the Popular Press in England 1855–1914* Croom Helm, London

Lewis, C. (1989) 'Lessons In Shah's Folly' *UK Press Gazette* 30 January, p. 17

Lewis, P. and Booth, J. (1989) *The Invisible Medium: Public, Commercial and Community Radio* Macmillan, Basingstoke

Liberty and CPBF (1994) *Censored: Freedom of Expression and Human Rights* Liberty and the Campaign for Press and Broadcasting Freedom, London

Linton, M. (1995) *Was It The Sun Wot Won It* Fourth Estate, London

Linton, M. (1993) 'Classic FM Secures Victory Over Pop With 4.49 Million Listeners' *Guardian* 4 May, p. 2

London Radio Workshop (1983) *Nothing Local About It: London's Local Radio* Comedia, London

Lord Chancellor's Department (1993) *Infringement of Privacy* HMSO, London

Loughran, C. (1994) 'Countdown To The New Network' *Ariel* 25 January, pp. 6–8

MacArthur, B. (1993) 'After The Goldrush' *Press Gazette* 20 December, p. 25

MacArthur, B. (1992b) 'The British Keep Reading Despite The Box' *British Journalism Review*, vol. 3, no. 4, pp. 65–6

MacArthur, B. (1992a) 'Perhaps It Was The Sun Wot Won It For John Major' *Sunday Times* 12 April

MacArthur, B. (1991) 'Gloom, Doom But No Boom' *Press Gazette* 17 June, pp. 6–8

MacArthur, B. (1988) *Eddie Shah, Today and the Newspaper Revolution* David and Charles, London

Mackey, S. (1994) *Controversy in Town Hall Public Relations*, unpub. PhD Faculty of Arts, Deakin University, Australia

Maddox, B. (1993) 'Big Brother's Reign Of Terror At The BBC' *Daily Telegraph* 14 July, p. 7

Mancini, P. (1993) 'Between Trust and Suspicion: How Political Journalists Solve the Dilemma' *European Journal of Communications*, vol. 8 no. 1, March, pp. 33–53

Manning, L. (1996) 'Foreign Office Spending Cuts A Threat To Independence' *Guardian* 19 July, p. 8

Marcuse, H. (1969) 'Repressive Tolerance' in Wolff, R.P., Moore Jar, B. and Marcuse, H. (eds) *A Critique of Pure Tolerance* Cape, London

Marks, N. (1995) 'Don't Drink Or Smoke – What Do You Do?' *UK Press Gazette* 23 October, p. 15

Marks, N. (1994) 'Current Affairs Veterans Slam Absurd 1990 Act' *UK Press Gazette* 10 January, p. 10

Marx, K. [1887] (1970) *Capital* vol. 1, Lawrence and Wishart, London

Marx, K. (1973) *Grundrisse* translation and foreword by M. Nicolaus, Penguin, Middlesex

Marx, K. [1894] (1972) *Capital* vol. 3, Lawrence and Wishart, London

Marx, K. and Engels, F. [1845] (1965) *The German Ideology* Lawrence and Wishart, London

Masterman, L. (1987) *Television and the Bombing of Libya* UK Media Press, London

May, T. and Clouston, E. (1995) 'Scotland's National Paper Up For Sale' *Guardian* 11 July, p. 3

McGregor, O.R. (1977) *Royal Commission on the Press: Final Report* Cmnd 6810, HMSO, London

McIntyre, I. (1993) *The Expense of Glory: A Life of John Reith* Harper Collins, London and New York

McManus, J. (1994) *Market Driven Journalism* Sage, London and New York

McManus, J. (1992) 'What Kind of Commodity is News?' *Communications Research* vol. 19, no. 6, pp. 780–812

McNair, B. (1994) *News and Journalism in the UK: A Text Book* Routledge, London

McQuail, D. (1994) *Mass Communication Theory* 4th edn, Sage, London

Meggy, G. (1923) *Journalism: A Correspondence Course* The Premier School of Journalism, London

Melvern, L. (1988) *The End of the Street* Methuen, London

Methven, N. (1997) '5 News Audience Peaks At Half A Million Viewers' *Press Gazette* 18 April, p. 2

Methven, N. (1997) 'ITV Targets Youth Ahead Of C5' *Press Gazette* 31 January, p. 4

Methven, N. (1996) 'BSC Starts Work On Code' *Press Gazette* 10 May, p. 5

Methven, N. (1996) 'ITN Wins Praise From ITC But Staff May Still Strike' *Press Gazette* 8 January, p. 6

Methven, N. and Kelly, T. (1996) 'Mixed Reaction To BBC Changes' *Press Gazette* 14 June, p. 2

Miliband, R. (1970) *The State in Capitalist Society* Weidenfeld and Nicolson, London

Millar, S. (1996) 'Internet Revolution Creating Underclass' *Guardian* 22 October, p. 10

Miller, D. (1990) 'The History Behind A Mistake' *British Journalism Review* vol. 1, no. 2, pp. 34–44

Milne, A. (1988) *DG: The Memoirs of a British Broadcaster* Hodder and Stoughton, London

Mintel International (1994) *Television, Leisure, Intelligence* Mintel International Group, London

Morgan, J. (1996) 'Marr Hits At "Waddling, Transvestite, Giggling" Broadsheet Rivals' *Press Gazette* 18 October, p. 14

Morgan, J. (1995) 'New Moves At Scotsman After Barclays Buys Titles' *UK Press Gazette* 13 November, p. 7

Morgan, J. (1993) 'English Smoothes Hackles Raised In Mirror PCC Row' *UK Press Gazette* 15 November, p. 3

Morley, D. and Whitaker, B. (1986) *The Press, Radio and Television: An Introduction to the Media* Comedia, London

Muir, H. (1993) 'How Birt Is Tying BBC In Red Tape' *Telegraph* 4 May, p. 4

Mullin, J. (1995) 'Easy Come, Easier Go For Would Be Barons' *Guardian* 28 December 1995, p. 3

Mullin, J. (1991) ' "Elitist" Jazz FM Gets A Retune' *Guardian* 12 July, p. 1

Murdock, G. (1980) 'Class, Power and the Press: The Problems of Conceptualisation and Evidence' in Christian, H. (ed.) *Sociological Review* special monograph

Murdock, G. and Golding, P. (1978) 'The Structure, Ownership and Control of the Press, 1914–76' in Boyce, G., Curran, J. and Wingate, P. (eds) *Newspaper History: from the 17th Century to the Present Day* Constable, London, pp. 130–51

Murdock, G. (1982) 'Large Corporations and the Control of the Communication Industries' in Curran, J. Gurevitch, M. and Woollacott, J. (eds) *Mass Communications and Society* Methuen, London, pp. 118–50

Murdoch, R. (1995) 'Cross? You Bet' *Guardian* 29 May, pp. 14–15

Murdoch, R. (1989) *Freedom in Broadcasting* the MacTaggart Lecture delivered at the Edinburgh Film Festival, 25 August

Murphy, D. (1988) 'The Alternative Local Press' unpub. paper presented to the annual conference of the Political Studies Association, Plymouth, 12–14 April

Murphy, D. (1974) *The Silent Watchdog*, Constable, London

National Heritage Select Committee Report (1993) *Privacy and Media Intrusion* Cmnd 294–1, HMSO, London

National Union of Journalists (1994) *NUJ Membership Survey 1994* conducted by the Trades Union Studies Unit, Ruskin College Oxford, available from NUJ, London

Neil, A. (1996) *Full Disclosure* Macmillan, London

Nevett, T. (1986) 'Advertising and Editorial Integrity In The Nineteenth Century' in Harris, M. and Lee, A. (eds) *The Press in English Society from the Seventeenth to Nineteenth Centuries* Acton Society Trust, London

Newell, D. (1993) 'Medicine We Can't Swallow' *UK Press Gazette* 18 January, p. 15

Newton, K. (1996) *The Mass Media and Modern Government* research paper, Wissenschaftszentrum für Sozialforschung, Berlin

Newton, K. and Artingstall, S. (1992) 'Government and Private censorship in Nine Western Nations in the 1970s and 1980s' unpub. paper, University of Essex Department of Government

Noon, M. (1994) 'From Apathy to Alacrity: Managers and New Technology in Provincial Newspapers' *Journal of Management Studies*, vol. 31, no. 3, pp. 19–32

Norris, P. (1996) 'Tuning In and Tuning Out: The Attentive Public in British Election Campaigns' paper delivered to the Elections, Public Opinions and Parties annual conference, Sheffield University, 13–15 September

Nossiter, T. (1986) 'British Television: A Mixed Economy' in *Research on the Range and Quality of Broadcasting Services* West Yorkshire Media in Politics Goup, HMSO, London

Oakley, C. (1995) 'The Root Cause' *UK Press Gazette* 27 November, p. 24

Oliver, M. (1993) 'BBC Spending: Adapting to a New World Order' in Barnett, S. *Funding The BBC's Future*, British Film Institute, London, pp. 108–21

Pallister, D. (1996) 'BBC Digital Launch Due In 18 Months' in *Guardian* 10 May, p. 10

Pardoe, J. (1989) 'The Alliance Campaign' in Crewe, I. and Harrop, M. (eds) *Political Communications: The General Election of 1987* Cambridge University Press, Cambridge, pp. 55–61

Paulu, B. (1981) *Television and Radio in the UK* Macmillan, London

Peacock, A. (1986) *Committee on Financing the BBC* Cmnd 9824, HMSO, London

Peak, S. and Fisher, P. (1996) *The Media Guide 1996* Fourth Estate, London

Peak, S. and Fisher, P. (1995) *The Media Guide* Fourth Estate, London

Periodicals Training Council (1996) *Editorial Employment* Periodicals Training Council Research Report no. 32 January, London

Pilkington, Sir Henry (1962) *Report of the Committee on Broadcasting* Cmnd 1753, HMSO, London

Pilkington, E. (1994) 'TV Series on Disasters May Worsen Anxiety of Survivors' *Guardian* 9 April p. 6

Pilling, R. (1995) 'Changing News Values in ITN Bulletins for ITV' unpub. MA thesis, University of Keele, Dept. of Politics

Pollard, E. (1995) 'Crest Of A Wave' *Guardian* 12 June, p. 16

Ponting, C. (1988) 'A Fundamentally New Approach To Controlling Information' *UK Press Gazette* 31 October, p. 15

Porter, H. (1996a) 'The Keeper Of The Global Gate' *Guardian* 29 October, pp. 2–4

Porter, H. (1996b) 'Lay Off Fergie' *Guardian* 2 October, p. 4

Porter, H. (1984) *Lies, Damned Lies and Some Exclusives* Hodder and Stoughton, London

Porter, J. (1987) 'Distribution of Frees in Europe Nears 200 Millions' *AFN News* June/July p. 6

Potter, D. (1994) 'The 1993 MacTaggart Lecture' in Bragg, M. (ed.) *Seeing the Blossom* Faber and Faber, London

Potter, D. (1993) 'A Malediction on Murdoch – and his Imitations' *British Journalism Review*, vol. 4, no. 2, pp. 21–6

Pound, R. and Harmsworth, G. (1959) *Northcliffe* Cassell, London

Prebble, S. (1988) 'ITV Fears Loss Of Quality' *Broadcast* 31 March, p. 17

Press Complaints Commission (1994) 'Code of Conduct' in *Press Complaints Commission Report no. 23* January/February pp. 36–9

Protheroe, A. (1987) 'The Use and Abuse of the Official Secrets Act' *The Listener* 12 February, pp. 4–5

Randall, D. (1996) *The Universal Journalist* Pluto, London and Chicago

Reith, J. (1925) *Personality and Career* George Newnes, London

Report of the Committee on Financing the BBC (Peacock) (1986) Cmnd 9824, HMSO, London

Reynolds, G. (1994) 'Radio Five Live: Fast and Fizzy' *British Journalism Review*, vol. 5, no. 2, pp. 10–14

Richards, J. (1991) 'The Journalist in British Films' in French, P. and Russell, D. (eds) *The Press: Observed and Projected* NFT Dossier No. 6, London, pp. 23–33

Riddell, E. (1990) 'Shocks In The Airwaves' *Guardian* 18 June, p. 28

Riddell, P. (1995) 'The Press Is Not Ignoring Parliament' *The House Magazine* 20 February, p. 7

Rock, P. (1973) 'News As Eternal Recurrence' in Cohen, S. and Young, J. (eds) *The Manufacture of News* Constable, London, pp. 73–80

Runnymede Trust (1995) 'Out Of Touch In Towers' *The Runnymede Bulletin* March, p. 8

Sampson, A. (1996) 'The Crisis at the Heart of our Media' *British Journalism Review* vol. 7, no. 3, pp. 42–56

Sands, P. (1996) 'A Training Task Facing Editors' *UK Press Gazette* 8 January, p. 16

Saynor, J. (1989) 'Sky Witness News' *The Listener* 20 July, pp. 28–30

Scannell, P. and Cardiff, D. (1991) *A Social History of British Broadcasting* vol. 1, Blackwell, Oxford

Scannell, P. and Cardiff, D. (1982) 'Serving the Nation: Public Service Broadcasting Before the War' in Waites, B. Bennett, T. and Martin, G. (eds) *Popular Culture, Past and Present* Croom Helm, London

Schlesinger, P. (1990) 'Rethinking the Sociology of Journalism: Source Strategies and the Limits of Media-Centrism' in Ferguson, M. (ed.) *Public Communication: The New Imperatives* Sage, London, pp. 61–84

Schlesinger, P. (1978) *Putting Reality Together* Constable, London

Schlesinger, P. and Tumber, H. (1994) *Reporting Crime: The Media Politics of Criminal Justice* Oxford University Press, Oxford

Scott, J. (1991) *Who Rules Britain?* Polity Press, Oxford

Searle, C. (1989) *Your Daily Dose: Racism and the Sun* Campaign For Press and Broadcasting Freedom, London

Sebba, A. (1994) *Battling for the News: The rise of the Woman Reporter* Sceptre Books, London

Seddon, M. (1996) 'Spot the Difference' *Fabian Review* vol. 108, no. 4 pp. 8–9

Selsdon, Lord (1935) *Television Committee Report* Cmnd 4793, HMSO, London

Sendall, B. (1982) *Independent Television in Britain* vol. 1 *Origin and Foundation 1946–62* Macmillan, London

Seymour Ure, C. (1991) *The British Press and Broadcasting Since 1945* Basil Blackwell, Oxford

Seymour Ure, C. (1987) 'Leaders' in Pimlott, B. and Seaton, J. (eds) *The Media in British Politics* Avebury, Aldershot

Sharpe, H. (1996) 'EMAP Sell-off Sparked by Heathrow Meeting' *Press Gazette* 7 June, p. 1

Slattery, J. (1996) 'Harold Evans Tells Editors To Stop News Mutating Into Trivia' *Press Gazette* 1 November, p. 10

Slattery, J. (1993) 'Statutory Control For Press?' *UK Press Gazette* 29 March, p. 2

Slattery, J. (1987) 'We Thought We Had Turned The Corner' *UK Press Gazette* 6 July, pp. 4–5

Smallman, A. (1996) 'Telling The Editorial From The Adverts' *Press Gazette* 10 May, p. 11

Smallman, A. and Morgan, J. (1996) 'Dump Truck Designer Brown Bails Out *Sunday Business*' *Press Gazette* 13 September, p. 1

Smith, A. (1974) *British Broadcasting* David and Charles, Newton Abbot

Smith, A. (1979) *The Newspaper: An International History* Thames and Hudson, London

Smithers, R. (1996) 'Anti-Woman Bias Of Fleet Street Under Fire' *Guardian* 3 July, p. 7

Smither, R. and Nowicka, H. (1996) 'Channel 4 To Resist Sell-Off Plan' *Guardian* 17 June, p. 9

Snoddy, R. (1992) *The Good, the Bad and the Unacceptable* Faber, London

Snoddy, R. (1988) 'Last Of The Old Breed Of Fleet Street Barons' *Financial Times* 6 June, p. 8

Snoddy, R. (1987) 'In The Post-Revolutionary Climate' *Financial Times* 27 June, p. 7

Snow, J. (1997) 'More Bad News' *Guardian* 27 January, p. 3

Soley, C. (1992) *Freedom and Responsibility of the Press* Private Member's Bill, HMSO

Soley, C. (1992) 'A New Privacy Bill' *Free Press* July/August, pp. 2–3

Sonninen, P. and Laitila, T. (1995) 'Press Councils In Europe' paper delivered to the WAPC conference, Helsinki, 1 June, p. 29

Sparks, C. (1993) 'Goodbye Hildy Johnson: The Vanishing "serious" press' in Sparks, C. and Dahlgren, P. *Communication and Citizenship: Journalism and the Public Sphere* Routledge, London, pp. 58–75

Spillius, A. (1996) 'Friend Or Foe?' *Guardian* 13 May, p. 10

Stephenson, H. (1994) *Media Freedom and Media Regulation* the Association of British Editors, the Guild of Editors and the International Press Institute, London

Straw, J. (1993) *The Decline in Press Reporting of Parliament* unpub. paper available from the author at the House of Commons, October

Street Porter, J. (1995) *Talent Versus Television* 20th James MacTaggart Lecture at Edinburgh International Festival, *Guardian* 26 August

Strick, H. (1957) *British Newspaper Journalism 1900–1956* PhD thesis, University of London

Sunrise Television (1991) *An Application for the National Channel 3 Breakfast-Time Licence*, May, Sunrise Television Ltd, London

Sweeting, A. (1996) 'World Wide Webb' *Guardian* 20 August, p. 11

Taylor, G. (1993) *Changing Faces: A History of the Guardian 1956–88* Fourth Estate, London

Taylor, L. (1993) 'Mandarins With No Bite' *Guardian* 26 April, p. 12

The Television Act 1954 HMSO, London

Texier, C. (1995) 'An Overview of the Current Debate on Press Regulation in France' paper presented to the conference 'The Press and Europe' City University, London, 4 February

Troyna, B. (1981) *Public Awareness and the Media: A Study of Reporting on Race* Commission for Racial Equality, London

Tuchman, G. (1972) 'Objectivity As Strategic Ritual: An Examination of Newsmen's Notions of Objectivity' *American Journal of Sociology* vol. 77, pp. 660–79

Tunstall, J. (1996) *Newspaper Power* Oxford University Press, Oxford

Tunstall, J. (1995) 'From Gentlemen To Journos' *British Journalism Review*, vol. 6, no. 3, pp. 54–9

Tunstall, J. (1983) *The Media in Britain* Constable, London

Tunstall, J. (1971) *Journalists at Work* Constable, London

Turow, J. (1989) 'Public Relations and Newswork: A Neglected Relationship' *American Behavioral Science* 33(2), pp. 206–12

Tusa, J. (1996) 'A Mission To Destroy' *Guardian* 10 June, p. 11

Tusa, J. (1992) *A World in Your Ear* Broadside Books Ltd, London

Tusa, J. (1990) *Conversations with the World* BBC Books, London

TV-AM (1991) *Application for the National Channel 3 Breakfast-Time Licence: A Summary* TV-AM, London

Van den Bergh, P. (1995a) 'What's My Lineage' *UK Press Gazette* 23 October, p. 18

Van den Bergh, P. (1995b) 'Scribes For Hire' *UK Press Gazette* 27 November, p. 40

Van Dijk, T. (1991) *Racism and the Press* Routledge, London

Veljanovski, C. (1989) *Freedom in Broadcasting* Institute of Economic Affairs, London

Wainwright, M. (1994) 'Star Of North Falls After 30 Years Of Shoestring Scoops' *Guardian* 21 January, p. 9

Wallis, R. and Baran, S. (1990) *The Known World of Broadcast News* Routledge, London

Walters, C. (1990) 'Move Over Brian Redhead, It's Ben Elton' *Guardian* 18 June, p. 28

Warren, L. (1923) *Journalism From A–Z* Herbert Joseph Ltd, London

Waugh, E. (1964) *Scoop* Penguin, London

Weatherill, B. (1995) 'House Of Shards' *Guardian* 29 December, p. 3

Weiner, J.H. (1969) *The War of the Unstamped: The Movement to Repeal the British Newspaper Tax, 1830–1836* Cornell University Press, Ithaca, NY and London

Whale, J. (1977) *The Politics of the Media* Fontana, London

Wilby, P. and Conroy, A. (1994) *The Radio Handbook* Routledge, London

Williams, A. (1996) *The Media: The Hierarchy of Information, the Reliance on Official Sources and the State* unpub. MA thesis, University of Sheffield

Williams, F. (1957) *Dangerous Estate: The Anatomy of Newspapers*, Longmans, Green and Co., London

Williams, F. (1956) 'The Editor and the Proprietor' in *New Statesman and Nation* 11 August, pp. 20–1

Williams, G. (1997) 'The Perils Of Working For A 3 Billion Media Empire' *Press Gazette* 24 January, p. 13

Williams, G. (1996) 'The BBC And British Airways' *Free Press* September/October, no. 94, pp. 1–3

Williams, G. (1994) *Britain's Media: How They are Related* Campaign for Press and Broadcasting Freedom, London

Williams, J.B. (1908) *A History of English Journalism* Longmans, Green and Co., London

Williams, R. (1974) *Television, Technology and Cultural Form* Fontana, Glasgow

Williams, R. (1965) *The Long Revolution* Penguin, London

Willis, P. (1986) 'How Today Literally Became A Live Wire' *UK Press Gazette* 31 March, p. 7

Wilson, H. (1961) *Pressure Group: The Campaign for Commercial TV* Methuen, London

Windlesham, Lord and Rampton, R. (1989) *The Windlesham–Rampton Report on 'Death on the Rock'* Faber and Faber, London

Winstone, P. (1996) 'One Is Not Enough' *Spectrum*, ITC no. 23, autumn, p. 24

Winstone, P. (1996a) 'Revealing Sources' *Spectrum*, ITC no. 20, winter, p. 24

Women in Journalism (1995) *Women in Journalism Launch Pack* Women in Journalism, London

Worcester, R. (1994) 'Demographics and Values: What the British Public Read and What They Think About Their Newspapers' paper presented to the conference 'The End of Fleet Street' City University, London, 5 February

Wright, A. (1980) *Local Radio and Local Democracy* Independent Broadcasting Authority, London

Young, H. (1993) 'Privacy Curbs Would Only Be The Half Of It' *Guardian* 11 November, p. 24

Index